SAT® Subject Test:

SPANISH

2008–2009 EDITION

OTHER KAPLAN BOOKS FOR COLLEGE-BOUND STUDENTS

AP Biology
AP Calculus AB/BC
AP Chemistry
AP English Language & Composition
AP English Literature & Composition
AP Environmental Science
AP European History
AP Human Geography
AP Macroeconomics/Microeconomics
AP Physics B & C
AP Psychology
AP Statistics
AP U.S. Government & Politics
AP U.S. History
AP U.S. History in a Box
AP World History
SAT Comprehensive Program
SAT Premier Program
12 Practice Tests for the SAT
SAT 2400
SAT Critical Reading Workbook
SAT Math Workbook
SAT Writing Workbook
SAT Vocabulary Flashcards Flip-O-Matic
Extreme SAT Vocabulary Flashcards Flip-O-Matic
Spotlight SAT: 25 Lessons Illuminate the Most Frequently Tested Topics
SAT in a Box, Second Edition
SAT Strategies for Super Busy Students
The Ring of McAllister: An SAT Score-Raising Mystery
Featuring 1,046 Must-Know SAT Vocabulary Words
Frankenstein: A Kaplan SAT Score-Raising Classic
The Tales of Edgar Allan Poe: A Kaplan SAT Score-Raising Classic
Dr. Jekyll and Mr. Hyde: A Kaplan SAT Score-Raising Classic
The Scarlet Letter: A Kaplan SAT Score-Raising Classic
The War of the Worlds: A Kaplan SAT Score-Raising Classic
Wuthering Heights: A Kaplan SAT Score-Raising Classic
Domina El SAT: Preparate para Tomar el Examen para Ingresar a la Universidad
SAT Subject Test: Biology E/M
SAT Subject Test: Chemistry
SAT Subject Test: Literature
SAT Subject Test: Mathematics Level 1
SAT Subject Test: Mathematics Level 2
SAT Subject Test: Physics
SAT Subject Test: U.S. History
SAT Subject Test: World History

SAT® Subject Test:

SPANISH

2008–2009 EDITION

Alice Gericke Springer

New York

This publication is designed to provide accurate and authoritative information in regard to the subject matter covered. It is sold with the understanding that the publisher is not engaged in rendering legal, accounting, or other professional service. If legal advice or other expert assistance is required, the services of a competent professional should be sought.

Vice President and Publisher: Maureen McMahon
Editorial Director: Jennifer Farthing
Development Editor: Monica P. Lugo
Production Editor: Karina Cueto
Production Designer: Ivelisse Robles-Marrero
Typesetter: ITC
Cover Designer: Carly Schnur

© 2008 Grace Freedson's Publishing Network

Published by Kaplan Publishing, a division of Kaplan, Inc.
1 Liberty Plaza, 24th Floor
New York, NY 10006

Printed in the United States of America

March 2008
10 9 8 7 6 5 4 3 2 1

ISBN-13: 978-1-4195-5187-1

Kaplan Publishing books are available at special quantity discounts to use for sales promotions, employee premiums, or educational purposes. Please email our Special Sales Department to order or for more information at kaplanpublishing@kaplan.com, or write to Kaplan Publishing, 1 Liberty Plaza, 24th Floor, New York, NY 10006.

Table of Contents

ABOUT THE AUTHOR

Alice Gericke Springer, Ph.D., did her graduate work at Vanderbilt University in Nashville, Tennessee. For over 20 years she has taught Spanish at Montgomery Bell Academy, where she is currently head of the foreign language department. She has taught Advanced Placement Spanish Language and Spanish Literature for over 20 years and served for six years as a faculty consultant for the Educational Testing Service. She also worked as a consultant for the College Board, giving workshops and teaching summer institutes in AP Spanish in Kentucky, Tennessee, Virginia, Alabama, Georgia, and Florida. In addition, she has given workshops at regional foreign language conferences, and is a member of the Tennessee Foreign Language Teachers' Association, SCOLT, AATSP, and ACTFL. Dr. Springer has studied and traveled extensively in Mexico, Spain, and Central and South America and frequently takes students on work and language study trips to Central America and Spain.

The author gratefully acknowledges the help she has received from her husband John, for technical support; Pamela Gómez, for reading text; Grace Freedson and Donnie Roth, for their encouragement and helpful suggestions; and Mrs. Adrienne Parker, for her photographs. She is also deeply indebted to Fernando Soldevilla for his critical reading of the Spanish in the text, and to Ruth Baygell for her patience and conscientious editing.

AVAILABLE ONLINE

FOR ANY TEST CHANGES OR LATE-BREAKING DEVELOPMENTS

kaptest.com/publishing

The material in this book is up-to-date at the time of publication. However, the College Board and Educational Testing Service (ETS) may have instituted changes in the test after this book was published. Be sure to carefully read the materials you receive when you register for the test. If there are any important late-breaking developments—or any changes or corrections to the Kaplan test preparation materials in this book—we will post that information online at **kaptest.com/publishing**.

FEEDBACK AND COMMENTS

kaplansurveys.com/books

We'd love to hear your comments and suggestions about this book. We invite you to fill out our online survey form at **kaplansurveys.com/books**. Your feedback is extremely helpful as we continue to develop high-quality resources to meet your needs.

STRATEGIES IF YOU ARE A HERITAGE SPEAKER

For Spanish-speaking students—heritage speakers—taking the SAT Subject Test in Spanish, it may be useful to approach the test preparation a little differently than many English-speaking students. For the most part, you will find that the SAT Spanish Test is no problem. Let's look at some of the advantages and problems you may encounter.

YOU DO HAVE AN ADVANTAGE

In some ways, you will have a distinct advantage if you are accustomed to hearing Spanish spoken and can understand most of what you hear. You do not necessarily have to know how to speak it fluently. If you have extensive exposure to Spanish outside of a classroom, you should probably take the exam *with* the listening comprehension portion. The test with the listening comprehension component is given once a year in the fall.

Your advantage is that you do not need to do the decoding—encoding process that many English speakers do when they're first learning Spanish. It takes years to build confidence in understanding vocabulary as structures in another language, no matter how good the program of study is in an English-speaking context.

VOCABULARY AND GRAMMAR MULTIPLE-CHOICE QUESTIONS

Here are some ways you will find your previous experience with Spanish helpful:

1. You will be able to process what you hear faster, and you will have a sense of what sounds correct. Sometimes you may make a decision on an answer based on what sounds "right" to you. You'll probably be more able to distinguish between words that sound alike but are very different in meaning.

   When you come to a question on the test that you're not sure how to answer, run through the answer choices, saying them to yourself in your mind. You will be able to decide on an answer based on what sounds correct, instead of simply on what looks right. For example,

   > Si el servicio del café es bueno, vale dejar _____ en la mesa para el camarero.
   >   A) un piropo   B) un propuesto   C) una propina   D) una promesa

   If you have heard the whole word *propina* many times in the context of what happens in a café, you will know the correct answer. Be careful not to focus only on the first syllable of a word. These types of questions are on the test to see if you are paying attention and reading carefully.

2. You will not be thrown off guard by false cognates, words that sound alike in Spanish and English. For example, you probably are very aware that some words do not mean the same thing in Spanish that they mean in English. *Embarrazada* means "pregnant," and should not be used when the correct word would be *avergonzada,* meaning "embarrassed." There are many words like these. You can probably think of many humorous mix-ups with false cognates. Another common example is the following:

    Se usa ____ y agua para limpiar las manos sucias.
    A) jamón   B) jabón   C) sopa   D) sopapilla

    Sopa looks to an English speaking person as though it should mean "soap," when it really means "soup."

3. You may have familiarity with a larger vocabulary than someone who only studied Spanish for two or three years. The test does not ask you to write anything, so you need only to recognize words that you may have heard before.

    On this test, you'll find Spanish taken from everyday situations, and a few from literature. Mostly, however, it is what an educated Spanish-speaking person would use. As you know, there are lots of ways to communicate an idea or describe something. If only one word or structure would work, computers would do translations more quickly than a person.

    Spanish is a very rich language in its vocabulary. Instead of simply saying that a young child is bad, there is a wealth of other adjectives to use. The child could be *trarvieso, precoz,* or even *mezquino.* Instead of saying that a person is *simpática* you would probably recognize other words, such as *genial, cortés,* or *compasiva,* depending on the more specific characteristic each of the words implies.

4. You probably have heard a Spanish-speaking person take a noun and make a verb out of it. You can make the transition quickly from the meaning in one part of speech to another. For example, when describing how a road winds around, you would recognize *serpentear.*

SOME THINGS TO BE CAREFUL ABOUT

The words that are used on the test may not be the ones most commonly heard in your country of origin.

1. There are differences between Spain and the Americas. Words, of course, but also customs.

    You need to make allowances for those differences. An obvious example would be *una tortilla,* that in Mexico refers to a kind of flat bread made from corn or wheat flour. In Spain, it is something like an omelette, with eggs, potatoes, and perhaps other things added.

2. Even in the Americas, each country has its own vocabulary. The vocabulary used on the SAT Spanish Test is a very basic one, recognized in all countries. A word used in Puerto Rico for a local bus could be one thing, a *guagua,* but in Guatemala, it would be a *camioneta.* On the SAT Spanish Test, you would most likely see the word *autobús.*

3. Words that Spanish speakers have taken from English and made into Spanish words probably will not appear on the exam. *Grocería*, for a *tienda de omcestibles* or *supermercado*, or *parquear* for *estacionamiento*. English words that refer to technology, such as email or surfing or Internet, do not have ready translations. In Spain there are specific Spanish words for words like "click here," but you will be able to recognize these without much trouble.

READING COMPREHENSION

Sometimes the reading comprehension can be a problem for heritage speakers, not because you cannot understand what the selection says, but because you do not understand the questions. It helps to remember that on these kinds of tests, you are expected to *infer* meaning—understand things that are implied, but not stated in the body of the passage.

Below are some suggestions for understanding reading passages:

1. Scan the selection first to get a general idea about what it is about.

2. Read the questions.

3. Reread the passage, looking for the material you need to find to answer the questions.

4. Pay attention to questions about "How" and "Why" in particular. These kinds of questions require you to interpret the words and actions in the passage.

5. Often it helps to visualize the scene, or the conversation. Sometimes the context reveals clues to meaning.

6. Make sure that you don't just pick an answer that lifts words from the text.

7. Imagine that you are a character in the passage and how you would act or react.

8. Pay special attention to pronouns. They tell you *who does what to whom*.

9. These passages are short. Try to imagine the action that would occur before and after what you read in the selection.

10. Practice with readings on your own. Select a wide variety of sources: magazines, newspapers, websites, recipes, instruction manuals for things you buy, pamphlets from different places like parks, advertisements, and short stories from magazines or literature.

MOST IMPORTANT

Relax and work efficiently—but not too quickly.

Part One

The Basics

Chapter 1: **About the SAT Subject Tests**

- Frequently Asked Questions
- SAT Subject Test Mastery

You are serious about going to the college of your choice. You would not have opened this book otherwise. You have made a wise choice, because this book can help you by preparing you to make the highest score you can on the SAT Spanish or Spanish with Listening Subject Test. But before you begin to prepare, you may need some general information.

FREQUENTLY ASKED QUESTIONS

Before you begin, let's look at what the SAT Subject Tests are all about so you'll understand how doing well on them will help you on your college application. The information here is accurate at the time of publication, but it's a good idea to check the test information on the College Board website at www.collegeboard.com.

What Are the SAT Subject Tests?

Known until 1994 as the College Board Achievement Tests, the SAT Subject Tests focus on specific subjects, such as chemistry, biology, American history, Spanish, and French. In all there are over 20 tests, each one-hour long.

How Do the SAT Subject Tests Differ from the SAT?

The SAT is primarily a test of your verbal and math skills. While you do need to know some vocabulary and some formulas, it is designed mostly to measure how well you read and think rather than how much you remember. SAT Subject Tests are very different: They measure what you know about specific disciplines. Sure, critical reading and thinking skills are included, but their main purpose is to determine exactly what you know about history, chemistry, the Spanish language, and so on.

As for the SAT Subject Test: Spanish, there are actually two tests: the Spanish Test, and the Spanish with Listening Test, which has an added listening component. You decide which one you want to take. But before you decide, check to see what the college you want to attend requires.

How Do Colleges and Universities Use the SAT Subject Tests?

Many people will tell you that the SATs measure only your ability to perform on standardized tests, that they measure neither your reading and thinking skills nor your level of knowledge. Maybe they're right. But these people don't work for colleges or universities. Those schools that require SATs think they're an important indicator of your ability to succeed academically. As a result, they use your scores to help them make admissions decisions and/or placement decisions in the subject.

> With a high score on your SAT Subject Test: Spanish you might be exempt from beginning level college Spanish courses. Take the test as soon as you are ready: You don't need to wait until your senior year.

Like the SAT, the SAT Subject Tests provide schools with a national standard measure of academic performance, which they use to compare applicants from different high schools and different educational backgrounds. As you know, there are great differences in the level of difficulty of Spanish programs given throughout the country, and the information from the SAT Subject Test: Spanish helps schools decide whether you're ready to handle their curriculum.

SAT Subject Test scores may also be used to decide what course of study is appropriate for you once you've been admitted. A low score on the Spanish Test, for example, can mean that you need to begin at the beginning with your study of Spanish. Conversely, a high score might mean you'll be exempt from the introductory Spanish courses.

Which Subject Tests Should I Take?

The simple answer is: those that you'll do well on. High scores, after all, can only help your chances for admission to college. You can take up to three subject tests on any given test day, but you do not have to take three tests on the same day. Unfortunately, many schools require that you take a particular test, such as Math. Some schools, however, give you some choice in the matter, especially if they want you to take a total of three Subject Tests. So before you register to take any test, check with the schools you're interested in to find out exactly which tests they require. Don't rely on high school guidance counselors or admissions handbooks for this information; they might not have the most up-to-date information.

Also, you do not have to wait until your last year of high school to take the SAT Subject Tests. You should take a subject test as soon as you have completed the highest level course in that discipline. You will do much better taking the Spanish test right away, instead of after a year of not studying the subject.

When Are the SAT Subject Tests Administered?

Most of the Subject Tests are administered six times a year: in October, November, December, January, May, and June. A few are offered less frequently, such as the Spanish with Listening Test. Due to admissions deadlines, many schools insist that you take the test no later that December or January of your senior year in high school. You may even have to take them sooner if you're interested in applying for early admission to a school. Those schools that use scores only for placement decisions may allow you to take them as late as May or June of your senior year.

The SAT Subject Test: Spanish is commonly used for placement purposes. Keep in mind that you can take the Spanish Test in your junior year if you are not going to study Spanish in your senior year.

How Do I Register for the SAT Subject Tests?

The College Board administers the SAT Subject Tests, so you must sign up for the tests with them. The easiest way to register is online. Visit the College Board's website at www.collegeboard.com and click on "SAT Subject Tests" for registration information. If you register online, you immediately get to choose your test date and test center and you have 24-hour access to print your admission ticket. You'll need access to a credit card to complete online registration.

If you would prefer to register by mail, you must obtain a copy of the *SAT Registration Booklet*. This publication contains all of the necessary information, including current test dates and fees. It can be obtained at any high school guidance office or directly from the College Board.

If you have previously registered for an SAT or SAT Subject Test, you can reregister by telephone. If you choose this option, you should still read the College Board publications carefully before you make any decisions.

How Are the SAT Subject Tests Scored?

The SAT Subject Tests are scored on a 200–800 scale. In the case of the Spanish with Listening Test, the sections are weighted differently from the Spanish Test because there is an additional listening component, but the final score is still given on the 200–800 scale.

What's a "Good" Score?

That is a tricky question. The obvious answer is: the score that the colleges of your choice demand. Keep in mind, though, that SAT Subject Tests scores are just one piece of information that schools will use to evaluate you. The decision to accept or reject your application will be based on many criteria, including your high school transcript, your SAT score, your recommendations, your personal statement, your interview (where applicable), your extracurricular activities, and the like. So, failure to achieve the necessary score doesn't automatically mean that your chances of getting in have been damaged. If you want a numerical benchmark, a score of 600 is considered very solid. (Years ago, you could withhold a score you were unhappy with, but that is no longer the case.)

What Should I Bring to the Test Center?

It's a good idea to get your test materials together the day before the tests. You'll need an admission ticket; a form of identification (check the the College Board website to find out what is permissible); a few sharpened No. 2 pencils; and a good eraser. Also, make sure that you have good directions to the test center. (We even recommend that you do a dry run getting to the site prior to test day—it can save you the anxiety of getting lost!)

> The night before the test, pack:
> - Your admission ticket
> - Identification
> - A few No. 2 pencils
> - A good eraser

SAT SUBJECT TEST MASTERY

Now that you know a little about the SAT Subject Tests, it's time to let you in on a few basic test-taking strategies that can improve your scoring performance.

Use the Test Structure to Your Advantage

The SAT Subject Tests are different from the tests you're used to taking. On your high school tests, you probably go through the questions in order from beginning to end. You probably spend more time on hard questions than on easy ones, since hard questions are generally worth more points. And you often show your work since your teachers tell you that how you approach questions is as important as getting the right answer.

Well, none of that applies to the SAT Subject Tests. Here, it is to your benefit to move around within the test. Hard questions are worth the same number of points as easy ones, and it doesn't matter how you answer the questions or what work you did to get there—only your answers count.

The SAT Subject Tests are highly predictable. Because the format and directions of the subject tests remain unchanged from test to test, you can learn them in advance. On test day, the various question types, the format, and the instructions shouldn't be new to you.

Many SAT Subject Test questions are arranged by order of difficulty. The questions often get harder as you work through different parts of the test. This pattern can work to your advantage. As you work, be aware of where you are in the test. You can easily pace yourself.

When working on the initial questions, don't be afraid to trust your first impulse—the obvious answer is likely to be correct. As you get to the end of a test section, though, you'll need to be a little more suspicious. Now the answers probably won't come as quickly and easily—if they do, look again because the seemingly obvious answers may be wrong. Watch out for answers that just "look right." They may be distracters—wrong answer choices deliberately meant to entice you.

You don't need to answer the questions in order. You're allowed to skip around as you'd like. Don't dwell on any one question, even a hard one, until you have tried every question at least once.

When you run into questions that look tough, circle them in your test booklet and skip them. Go back to them later if you've got time. On a second look, troublesome questions can turn out to be remarkably simple.

If you've started to answer a question but get confused, quit and go on to the next question. Persistence may pay off in high school, but it usually hurts your SAT Subject Test score. Don't spend so much time answering one hard question that you use up several minutes of valuable time. That'll cost you points, especially if you don't even get the hard question right.

The SAT Subject Tests have a "guessing penalty" that can work in your favor. The College Board likes to talk about the "guessing penalty" on the SAT Subject Tests. That's a misnomer. It's really a wrong answer penalty. If you guess wrong, you get penalized. If you guess right, you're in great shape.

The fact is, if you can eliminate one or more answer choices as definitely wrong, you'll turn the odds in your favor and actually come out ahead by guessing. The fractional points you lose are meant to offset the points you might get "accidentally" by guessing the correct answer.

The SAT Subject Test answer grid has no heart. It sounds simple, but it's extremely important: Don't make mistakes filling out your answer grid. When time is short, it's easy to get confused going back and forth between the test booklet and the answer sheet grid. If you know the answers, but misgrid, you won't get the points. Here's how to avoid mistakes.

Circle the questions you skip. Put a big circle in your test booklet around any question numbers that you skip. When you go back, they'll be easy to locate. And, if you accidentally skip a box on the grid, you can check your grid against your booklet to see where you went wrong.

Circle the answers you select. Circling your answers in the test booklet makes it easier to check your grid against your test booklet.

Grid five or more answers at once. Don't transfer your answers to the grid after every question. Transfer them after every five questions. (Remember, you've circled the answers in your test booklet.) That way, you won't keep breaking your concentration. You'll save time and gain accuracy.

> First impulses are okay at the beginning of the test, but be suspicious of them toward the end. There may be traps.

> Make sure you fill in the oval that corresponds to the question. A machine scans your answer sheet, and it does not look to see where you went wrong.

A Strategic Approach to SAT Subject Test Questions

Apart from knowing the format of the tests, you've got to have a system for attacking the questions. You wouldn't try to find someplace in an unfamiliar city without a map, and you shouldn't approach the SAT Subject Tests without a plan. What follows is the best method for approaching SAT Subject Test questions systematically.

Think about the questions before you look at the answers. The test makers love to put distracters among the answer choices. If you jump right into the answer choices without thinking first about what you're looking for, you're more likely to fall for one of these traps. When you know the grammar well you'll recognize the right answer and can save time otherwise spent trying to justify one or another answer choice.

Guess—when you can eliminate at least one answer choice. You already know that the "guessing penalty" can work in your favor. Don't simply skip questions that you can't answer. Spend some time with them in order to see whether you can eliminate any answer choices. If you can, it pays for you to guess.

Pace yourself. The SAT Subject Tests give you a lot of questions in a short period of time. You can't afford to spend too much time on any single question. Keep moving. If you run into a hard question, circle it, skip it, and come back to it later if you have time.

You don't have to spend the same amount of time on every question. Ideally, you should be able to work through the more basic questions at a brisk clip, and use a little more time on the harder questions. One caution: Don't rush through basic questions just to save time for the harder ones. The basic questions are points in your pocket, and you're better off not getting to some harder questions if it means losing easy points because of careless mistakes. Remember, you don't get extra credit for answering hard questions.

> Don't worry if you have to leave some questions blank. You can still get a high score with a few unanswered questions.

Locate quick points if you're running out of time. Some questions can be done more quickly than others because they require less work or because choices can be eliminated more easily. If you start to run out of time, locate and answer any of the quick points that remain.

When you take the SAT Subject Tests, you have one clear objective in mind: to score as many points as you can. It's that simple.

Chapter 2: **Getting Ready for the SAT Subject Test: Spanish**

- The Spanish Test
- The Spanish with Listening Test
- Question Types
- Test-Taking Strategies
- Managing Stress

The first thing you should know about the Spanish Test is that there are two different subject tests: the Spanish Test and the Spanish with Listening Test. The Spanish with Listening Test is given less frequently, offered only in November and at certain centers.

You do not need to take both tests. Both tests evaluate your knowledge of the basic rules of Spanish grammar and vocabulary. (Don't worry, you won't have to explain the rules, though you will have to apply them. Nor will you have to speak Spanish for the test.) On the Spanish with Listening Test, however, you will have to understand spoken Spanish.

THE SPANISH TEST

The Spanish Test examines your ability to understand only written Spanish. In other words, it tests your knowledge of vocabulary, structure, and your ability to understand what you read. The Spanish language on this test does not correspond to what is taught in any particular textbook, but it does reflect the language used throughout the Spanish speaking world.

The Spanish test is one hour long, and contains 85 multiple-choice questions in three parts: Parts A, B, and C. Parts A, B, and C are each weighted as one third of your score. Part A is a fill-in-the-blank section testing vocabulary and structure. Part B consists of longer selections with fill-in-the-blank questions testing vocabulary and structure. Part C is reading comprehension, with questions based on your ability to interpret what you read.

Part A: On the first part of the test you will find fill-in-the-blank sentences. For each sentence given, you will need to find the correct word, *modismo*, or structural selection. When the question deals with vocabulary, there will be four answer choices; though each choice will be a correct part of speech or have a correct structure, only one choice will make sense in the sentence.

Part B: In this section, you will have to fill in the blanks contained in various paragraphs. The questions focus on vocabulary or structure. You'll need to be able to understand the longer context with these selections. In other words, you must look for clues in the passage to help you answer the questions.

Part C: The reading comprehension section tests you on the sort of Spanish you would find in printed material, such as prose fiction, nonfiction, magazine articles, advertisements, and pamphlets. The questions test the main ideas, themes, supporting ideas, details, and attitudes communicated in the language of the selection. In order to do well you need to interpret language, and at times infer meanings indicated by word selection, syntax, and the style of writing as well as the type of printed material.

THE SPANISH WITH LISTENING TEST

The Spanish with Listening Test is offered only once a year in certain test centers. In addition to all of the contents of the Spanish Test described above, this test has a listening component. In a variety of ways it tests your ability to understand spoken Spanish, so be prepared to understand accents from different parts of the Spanish-speaking world. The material you will hear will come in the form of conversations, radio or television promotions, or narratives.

> For the Spanish with Listening Test, you must bring a CD player with earphones to the test center. You may not share a CD player with another test taker. CD players with recording or duplicating capabilities cannot be used on test day. Bring fresh batteries.

For this test, you must bring your own CD player with earphones. One will not be provided for you at the test center. CD players with recording or duplicating capabilities cannot be used on test day. Make sure the CD player is in good working order and has fresh batteries before test day. You don't want to begin the test only to have your CD player malfunction.

Section I: Listening will take approximately 20 minutes. You will receive a CD to use in your player. In all, there are about 35 questions on Section I. This section accounts for about 40 percent of the Spanish with Listening Test.

Part A: In this part you will see a series of about 10 photographs. For each photograph you will hear four choices; you must choose the one that best describes the picture or expresses what might be said by someone in the photograph. You will hear the choices spoken only once, so listen carefully. Only the photograph will be printed in your test booklet; there are no captions.

Part B: There are about 10 short conversations. After each one you will hear four possible statements or exclamations that could complete or continue the conversation.

Of these, you must select the most appropriate one. Neither the conversations nor the answer choices are printed in your test booklet, so you'll have to listen carefully.

Part C: First you will hear a series of about a dozen conversations, short narratives, or items you would hear on the radio, television, or public announcements. Then you will see questions and answer choices in your test booklet. These will not be spoken. You will have 12 seconds to answer each question.

Section II: Reading covers vocabulary, structures, and reading comprehension. The format and content in this section are exactly the same as in the Spanish Test, except that it consists of about 50 questions and accounts for about 60 percent of your score.

Part A: This part tests vocabulary and structures. The sentences are presented with a blank in each one. You will have four choices from which to select the most appropriate answer to complete the meaning of each sentence. This part is exactly like its corresponding part on the Spanish test.

Part B: In this part you will find longer selections with blanks to fill in from four choices that correspond to the blanks. This part is exactly like the corresponding one on the Spanish Test.

Part C: Reading comprehension is the last part of the test. There will be several selections with questions about the information contained in the passage.

Which Test Should I Take?

If you have had a lot of experience listening to and understanding spoken Spanish, you should feel comfortable taking the Spanish with Listening Test. If you are most comfortable reading Spanish, you'll probably want to take the Spanish Test. You can be confident of good results on the test if you have done well in an intensive two-year high school program, or in three or more years of study in which you have learned a lot of vocabulary, syntax, and grammar. If you are a heritage student, meaning a student whose parents or grandparents speak Spanish, though you may not have grown up speaking Spanish yourself, you may understand enough to do well on the Spanish with Listening Test.

Choose the test that will result in the highest score for you. For colleges and universities, there is no practical distinction between the two tests. In other words, there are no special requirements or preference given in admission to schools based on one test or the other.

SCORING

For the Spanish Test, each section is worth one-third of the final score. For the Spanish Test with Listening Test, the listening section is worth about 40 percent, and the reading section about 60 percent. Generally, if you can answer about 50 percent of the questions correctly on either test, you can score between 500 and 600.

> If you correctly answer half the questions, you will probably score above 500.

Since all your answers are marked on a form that can be scanned, the answer sheets are machine scored. For each correct answer, you will earn one point. However, for every three questions that are incorrect, you will lose one point.

Questions left blank or marked with more than one answer are not counted. However, if you leave too many questions blank, you will have fewer correct answers, and the lower your final score will be. If you change a mark on your answer sheet, be careful to erase completely your first choice so that the scanner will read your revised choice correctly.

Using a computer, your raw score is processed and converted to a scaled score ranging from 200–800 points. If you take the Spanish with Listening Test, you will also receive subscores for reading and for listening.

QUESTION TYPES

The Spanish Test contains three types of multiple-choice question: sentence completion; paragraph completion; and reading comprehension. The Spanish with Listening Test contains an additional three question types: picture prompt; rejoinder (completion or continuation); and listening comprehension. These last three question types are based on material you hear from a CD.

On your answer sheet there will be five columns in which to mark your answer. That's because the SAT Subject Test answer sheet is a standard sheet for all the subject tests, not just Spanish. Some subject tests contain five answer choices, though this is not the case with Spanish. Do not let the extra column confuse you. Mark your answer only in the spaces corresponding to A, B, C, or D. Do not make any marks in column E.

1. Sentence Completion Questions

This type of question presents a sentence containing a blank. You must choose from four possible answer choices to complete the sentence. These questions deal with issues of vocabulary and structure.

Directions: Select the most appropriate choice to complete the meaning of the sentence and mark in the corresponding oval on your answer sheet.

1. Para gozar de buena salud y mantenerse en forma, se aconseja _____ bien y hacer ejercicio a diario.

    (A)   alejarse
    (B)   alimentarse
    (C)   desarrollar
    (D)   proponer

All of the answer choices are infinitives, so this question must deal with vocabulary. If all of the choices are the appropriate part of speech, or the same tense and mood of the conjugated verb form needed for the sentence, you know to think about vocabulary.

The verbs *gozar* and *mantenerse* indicate a process of doing something. If you do not know *gozar*, you could guess that *mantenerse* means "to maintain" because it is a cognate (a word that sounds alike in English and Spanish). *Mantenerse en forma* when translated literally does not make much sense, but you could get the idea of maintaining form. You may recognize *ejercicio*, and relate exercise to maintaining form, or staying in shape. Perhaps you remember *salud* means "health." But you can get the idea about keeping healthy as the idea of the sentence.

If you understand the idea of the sentence, you will see that, although (A) begins with the same letters "al" contained in the correct answer (B), it makes no sense. *Alejarse* means "to move away." You may be looking for a word like *comer* as the answer: If you know that the alimentary canal goes from your mouth to your stomach, you know that *alimentarse* is the best answer. (C) *desarrollar* means "to develop." While you do want to develop good habits or develop muscles by doing exercises daily, the word would need an object in order to fit here. (D) *proponer* means "to propose." One can propose doing exercises, but again, with the adverb, *bien*, after the blank, it doesn't really fit.

2. Una medida del _____ en la vida es la felicidad y cariño que se siente en un hogar propio.

    (A) éxito
    (B) sentimiento
    (C) campo
    (D) suceso

Since all of these choices are nouns, the question again deals with vocabulary. You could mistake *éxito* for exit, but this is a false cognate, a word that does not mean the same thing as the English word it sounds like. *Éxito* means success, so it's a perfect fit to complete the sentence. If you did not know the word *medida*, you could still associate *éxito* with *felicidad*, *cariño*, and *hogar*, words meaning "happiness," "affection," and "home."

But what if you did not know what *éxito* meant? *Sentimiento* means "feeling" or "sentiment," so it is related to *felicidad* and *cariño* as well as the verb *se siente*. But this choice does not relate the idea of *medida*, meaning "measure," and *vida*, meaning "life." Even without knowing *medida*, you know it has something to do with quantifying or qualifying life because of the linking verb *es*, as well as the adjective *propio* coming after the noun *hogar*. Something in life, happiness and love that one feels in one's own home is the idea of the sentence. *Campo*, choice (C), means a lot of things, mostly related to "country" or "field," but sometimes it's used in a figurative way, like a *campo abierto*, a "clear coast" or "having no obstacles." That figurative meaning could be related to happiness and love, too, but does not relate to a measure of success in life. Choice (D) *suceso*, is another false cognate. It means "event," so it does not make any sense in the sentence, either.

In this example you can see that there is no substitute for knowing the meaning of the word *éxito*, but you can eliminate some choices. You could eliminate (B) and (C) because they do not fit the idea of the whole sentence. You could then guess between (A) and (D). Be wary of such an obvious cognate as *suceso*; it would be too easy for this kind of test. (A) is the answer.

3. Si necesitas un lápiz para hacer el examen, _____ prestaré uno.

    (A)   te
    (B)   la
    (C)   tú
    (D)   se le

First, scan the sentence. Then look at the choices: You'll notice that they're all pronouns: This must be a grammar question. When you first scanned the sentence, you should have noticed that the subject of the verb is second person singular, *tú*. That means you need to use a second person singular pronoun. Right away, (D) is out, since it uses a third person form.

In the last clause of the sentence, you see that the ending on the verb is first person singular, future tense and *uno*, which refers to *lápiz*. You don't even need to know what *lápiz* means; whatever it means, the clause says "I will loan you one." Since *uno* is the object of the verb, you don't need a direct object pronoun. And since *lápiz* is masculine, indicated by *un* and *uno*, (B), a feminine direct object pronoun, is out. That leaves (A) and (C), both second person singular. (C), *tú*, is a subject pronoun, but it would be highly unusual to use a subject pronoun in front of a verb that has a first person ending. (A) could be a direct object, indirect object, or reflexive pronoun, though you do not need to specify. (A) is correct.

4. Cuando llegué a la ciudad de madrugada, no encontré a _____ caminando al trabajo por las calles.

    (A)   alguien
    (B)   alguno
    (C)   nadie
    (D)   ningún

All of these answer choices are indefinite adjectives or pronouns. Be careful not to simply translate into Spanish the word you would use in English. (A) means "someone," "anybody," or "somebody," which would make sense in English. But in Spanish you need a negative indefinite pronoun, because *no* comes in front of the verb. (B) is an adjective, which could be used except that there is no noun to go with it. It is also not negative. (D) is wrong because the phrase *caminando al trabajo por las calles* indicates that the speaker is talking about people. *Ningún*, on the other hand, is a negative indefinite adjective. It has to refer to a noun, and there isn't any noun it refers to. It also helps to know that *madrugada* means "early morning." (C) is the correct answer because it is a negative indefinite pronoun.

2. Paragraph Completion Questions

This part of the test consists of a paragraph with blanks. There are four possible answer choices for each blank. Remember to scan the whole paragraph first, looking for details that will help you make the best selection. These questions deal with vocabulary and structure.

> Look for clues to the answer in the context of a word or phrase. Notice the gender of nouns, adjectives, pronouns, verb tenses, and mood.

Directions: For each paragraph below, there are numbered blanks indicating that a word or phrase has been omitted. For each numbered blank, choose the completion that is most appropriate given the context of the passage. Fill in the corresponding oval on the answer sheet.

Un día hubo un incendio: un almacén, ayudado (5) el viento, se quemó en dos minutos, El dueño descubrió el fuego y lo declaró a gritos. Estaba aburrido del almacén y (6) venderlo, sin encontrar comprador. Su compatriota declaró que aceptaría cualquier regalo que no (7) un almacén. El dueño, desesperado, quería marcharse, (8) , no quería abandonarlo y un día cuando el viento empezó a soplar, no (9) más y decidió quemarlo.

El almacén no tenía seguro, y se sospechó que estuviese demente: un almacenero, que quema su (10) sin tenerlo asegu-rado, no puede (11) sino picado de vinagre, y en realidad (12) estaba, de remate.

5.   (A) por
     (B) para
     (C) sin
     (D) en

6.   (A) quiere
     (B) querra
     (C) quiso
     (D) querría

7.   (A) era
     (B) fue
     (C) fuera
     (D) había sido

8. (A) a lo mejor
    (B) por lo tanto
    (C) por si acaso
    (D) sin embargo

9. (A) apoyó
    (B) ignoró
    (C) ayudó
    (D) soportó

10. (A) casa
    (B) tienda
    (C) puesto
    (D) negocio

11. (A) estar
    (B) ser
    (C) haber
    (D) tener

12. (A) la
    (B) se
    (C) le
    (D) lo

For question 5, (A) is correct, because the preposition *por* indicates the agent that does an action. Although the true passive voice structure uses *ser* and a past participle, it is implied in the paragraph that the fire is helped by the wind. No other choice completes the meaning of the implied passive structure in this passage.

For question 6, the correct answer is (C). The conditional and future of *querer* do not make sense, and the next part of the sentence makes it clear that the preterite is correct. Remember that in the preterite the verb *querer* means "to try to," which is most appropriate to complete the meaning of the passage.

For question 7, (C) is the answer. The subjunctive mood is used because it occurs in an adjective clause that refers to *cualquier*. The context is that the colleague would accept any gift that was not a store. The gift that the proprietor of the store wants to make to the colleague is the store. The gift becomes a nonexistent gift because the colleague will not accept it. If the antecedent—the noun that the adjective clause modifies—is nonexistent, then you need to use the subjunctive. You need to use the imperfect subjunctive because the whole passage is told in the past tense. No other choice makes sense grammatically in this context.

Question 8 is a vocabulary question. *A lo mejor* means "perhaps" or "maybe." *Por lo tanto* means "therefore," or "for that reason." *Por si acaso* means "in case." *Sin embargo* means "nevertheless." In the context of the passage the best choice is (D) because it introduces the next logical step in the story. The proprietor wanted to leave the building behind. So when the opportunity presented itself (in the form of the wind that would make short work of the building), he would set it on fire. *Sin embargo* is the only choice that makes the logical transition.

All of the words in question 9 are in the same third person preterite form, so you know that this is a vocabulary question. You need a word that describes the proprietor's attitude. The verbal tenses and the vocabulary preceding this blank show that he is a desperate man, and the verbal tense of the verb *librar* is the conditional. The word you want would mean "he could not stand (or tolerate)" the situation any longer. *Apoyar* means "to support." *Ignorar* means "to not know" or "to not be aware" of something. *Ayudar* means "to help." *Soportar* means "to tolerate." If you did not know the other words, you might link *support* with *tolerate*, making (D) a good guess. And in fact, (D) is the answer. Think of synonyms for words in English that you are looking for, and frequently you can find cognates.

To answer question 10, note that the pronoun at the end of *tener* is masculine singular, as is the adjective *asegurado*. That means (A) and (B) are wrong, because they're feminine singular. (C) *puesto* is masculine singular, though it means a "stall," and the passage refers to an *almacén*, which is bigger than a stall. *Negocio* means "business," (D), which is the correct answer.

Question 11 deals with various verbs that can mean *to be* in Spanish. The correct answer is (A) *estar*, because the verb describes the emotional and mental state of being of the proprietor of the store. He is crazy in the sense that he is acting crazy to have burned a store that was not insured. *Ser* would indicate that he was a crazy man, not just that he behaved in such a manner.

You should also notice that in the phrase after *sino*, the verb *estaba* is used. *Hacer* and *tener* can mean "to be" but only in specific *modismos* that do not make sense in this context.

For question 12, the answer is (D). The pronoun *lo* refers to the whole idea of the proprietor acting crazy. (A) is a direct object pronoun that is the correct gender and number to refer to *realidad*, but it makes no sense in the context of the passage. The reflexive pronoun *se*, choice (B), does not make sense with *estar*, nor does choice (C), an indirect object pronoun.

3. Reading Comprehension Questions

Directions: Read each of the following selections. After each selection there is a number of questions or incomplete statements. Choose the best answer for the sentence completion and mark the corresponding oval on your answer sheet.

Y así fue, una noche vi que entraba en casa con un envoltorio chato y rectangular, que metía furtivamente en su cuarto. En seguida supe que era el retrato de Rosaura. Puse sobre aviso a mis hijas, y en un momento en que nadie nos oía le pregunté a Camilo:

—¿Le trajo?

—Sí —susurró, mirando miedosamente en derredor. —Después de cenar. En su habitación. Cuando los otros se hayan acostado.

Tal como lo convinimos, una vez que los huéspedes se fueron a dormir, yo y mis hijas, como cuatro contrabandistas, nos metimos en la habitación de Camilo.

—¡A ver, a ver!—dijimos. Pero él se puso un dedo en los labios, reclamando silencio. —¿Qué pasa?

—¿No hay peligro?

—¿Peligro de qué?

—De que alguien venga.

—Pero no, todos duermen. Y si alguien viene, ¿qué hay?

—No, no quiero, no quiero. Ustedes saben cómo son.

—Está bien. Le digo que duermen.

—¿Réquel también?

—Réquel se fue al cine y no volverá hasta pasada la medianoche.

—¿Y Coretti?

—Ronca como un cerdo.

—¿Y la señorita Eufrasia?

Protestamos a coro, aunque en voz baja:

—¡Por Dios, Don Canegato! Duermen todos. ¡Apúrese! ¡Queremos ver el cuadro!

Tomó el envoltorio, lo depositó amorosamente sobre la cama y empezó a desenvolverlo. Y el rostro de Rosaura apareció ante nosotras.

13. ¿Quiénes hablan en este pasaje?

   (A)   un grupo de mujeres

   (B)   un hombre y una mujer

   (C)   dos mujeres

   (D)   un hombre y un grupo de mujeres

14. ¿De qué hablan las personas?

   (A)   un plan de robar un retrato

   (B)   un hombre misterioso

   (C)   un acontecimiento misterioso

   (D)   una persona peligrosa en la casa

15. ¿Cuándo ocurre la acción?

    (A)   por la mañana

    (B)   por la tarde

    (C)   de noche

    (D)   al amanecer

16. Esta escena tiene lugar en

    (A)   una casa privada.

    (B)   un hotel.

    (C)   una pensión.

    (D)   una cárcel.

17. ¿Cuál es la actitud de la persona que narra la historia?

    (A)   Tiene miedo de encontrar a un intruso.

    (B)   Teme que alguien las descubra.

    (C)   Se alegra de que todos duerman bien.

    (D)   Queda satisfecha de haber adivinado la verdad.

The clue to question 13 is in a pronoun at the very end of the selection, *nosotras*, which indicates a group of women. There is a man, indicated by the pronoun *él* and the title don Canegato, so it is a mixed group of a man and a woman and her daughters. Though some of the conversation is between the mother and her daughters, notice the pronoun *él* in the line "*él se puso un dedo en los labios*," which makes (D) the only correct choice.

For question 14, the answer is (C). Though the topic is a picture of Rosaura, the picture itself is not the main focus of the passage. The main focus is the action of a man who brings a wrapped package into the house and does not reveal its contents until confronted. The man is not mysterious, though the word *furtivamente* would seem to indicate that he has something to hide. He seems quite willing to show what he has at the end, and the word *amorosamente* reveals that he is quite comfortable showing the women something he treasures.

For question 15, all of the references to people sleeping, indicated by the words *duermen* and *ronca*, leave only (C) or (D) as possible choices. The lines "Cuando los otros se hayan acostado" and "una vez que los huéspedes se fueron a dormir" indicate that it is bedtime at night, not toward the dawn. The correct answer is (C).

For question 16, the future is used in the main clause of the sentence in line 20, indicating probability. While there's no specific mention of where the action takes place, there is one strong clue in the passage: *huéspedes*, which means "guests." This word would indicate a lodging place of some kind, making (B) and (C) the only possible choices. Since the lodging place is run by a woman and her daughters, it would suggest a home that takes in boarders. (C) is the most logical answer. A *pensión* is a "boarding house."

In question 17, the words *furtivamente, susurró, miedosamente, contrabandistas,* and *protestamos* indicate dark, negative emotions. The narrator, who is the mother, states "En seguida supe que era el retrato de Rosaura" at the beginning of the passage. The use of the preterite of *saber* means that she knew at that moment, from her intuition, that the package was a picture of Rosaura. She did not know for certain, however (D) is the best answer. The other choices pick up on the idea of fear of discovery at a secretive meeting, and the fact that everybody else is gone or sleeping, but only (D) summarizes the attitude of the narrator. The exclamation "¡Queremos ver el cuadro!" indicates that she is pleased with herself.

Now let's look at a Reading Comprehension question with an advertisement.

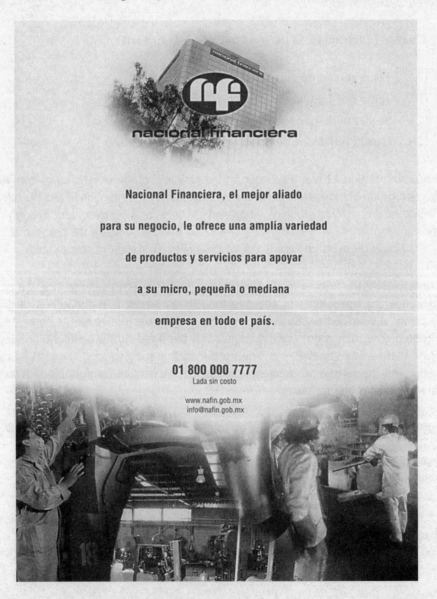

18. ¿A quién está dirigido este anuncio?

    (A)   a un programador de computadoras

    (B)   a un comerciante en busca de fondos

    (C)   a un turista de vacaciones en México

    (D)   a un banquero promocionando su banco

19. ¿Qué se ofrece en el anuncio?

    (A)   menos impuestos gubernamentales

    (B)   préstamos para empezar un negocio

    (C)   un servicio para ahorrar dinero

    (D)   consejos y asistencia bancaria

> In reading ads, look at how nouns are related to get the general idea. Identify who would be most interested in reading the ad, and who would most likely place the ad, as well as what the ad promotes.

For question 18, the service offered is assistance in starting up a business, so the answer is (B). This is indicated by *negocio* and *su ...empresa*. Although the ad is for a financial institution, a banker (D), would not be interested in using the services offered. And a tourist (C), would have no need for a large variety of products and services.

As for question 19, you might find the vocabulary a challenge, but perhaps you recognize some words related to financial matters. The ad is offering more than money, though. The bank wants to be a business partner, indicated by the words "el mejor aliado para su negocio." These words offer products and services that correspond to *consejos y asistencia*. The answer is (D).

Ahora, los habitantes de la Tierra se saben capaces de destruirse por mediación de la energía nuclear o de suicidarse por dejación del cuidado a la naturaleza. Pero también, por primera vez en la historia, han constatado que pueden llegar a recrearse mediante la ingeniería genética. Nunca antes pareció el hombre más dueño de su destino, de su vida y de su muerte, y el siglo a inaugurar parecería configurarse como el punto crítico en que la humanidad está obligada a repensarse como organización y como especie. Los actuales horizontes de la ciencia, de la informática, de la biología molecular o de la física cuántica son de tal potencia, mientras las situaciones de pobreza en dos terceras partes del mundo son tan clamorosas, que el siglo XXI habría de edificarse con la mayor conciencia de la calidad. El siglo que alumbra, el primero en que todo el planeta se constata interdependiente y vivo como una sola comunidad, habrá de ser el tiempo en que prevalezca la razón de la solidaridad y los fines de imperativo humano.

20. ¿Qué intenta hacer el autor en este párrafo?

    (A) Criticar el pasado
    (B) Anticipar el futuro
    (C) Describir la ciencia
    (D) Alabar la inteligencia humana

21. Según el párrafo, ¿a qué ha llegado el ser humano actual?

    (A) A presentar un peligro al mundo
    (B) Ha alcanzado grandes logros.
    (C) A aparentar una autodestrucción.
    (D) A demostrar una ignorancia de la realidad

22. Según el autor, este momento en la historia es importante porque

    (A) cada ser humano puede realizar sus sueños materiales.
    (B) hay muchos problemas, como la pobreza, que se necesitan solucionar.
    (C) la ciencia puede resolver todos los problemas del mundo.
    (D) el ser humano necesita tomar una decisión de qué y cómo quiere ser.

23. Según la lectura, en el futuro el mundo tiene la posibilidad de ser

    (A) una colección de comunidades aisladas.
    (B) una utopía sin límites.
    (C) más pobre que nunca.
    (D) más unida por la necesidad de cooperar.

This passage deals with a vision of the future. It begins with a rather dark view, but it turns to the possibilities for change, particularly with respect to helping those in need. According to the author, the human race is at a turning point: it has to decide how to apply the scientific and medical advances that have been made. In other words, the new century is an opportunity and a challenge.

For question 20, the words *por primera vez en la historia* at the start of the passage indicate the author is looking to the future. He later returns to the future with "el siglo XXI habrá de edificarse con la mayor conciencia de la calidad." This would indicate that (B) is the answer. (A) can be eliminated, because although he mentions the mistakes of the past, he does so in order to emphasize the opportunities brought by the new century. And while the author mentions science, he does so to show how it can be used, not how it can be described, so (C) is out. As for (D), the greatness of human intelligence has yet to be proven, so that is wrong as well. The answer is indeed (B).

The best answer for question 21 is (B). While the reading suggests that people have arrived at a point where they might self-destruct, there is no indication that the author thinks such a disaster will come to pass, so (A) is wrong. "Se saben capaces" indicates an awareness of the problem. "Los actuales horizontes de la ciencia" and all the rest are the tools. And at the end of the passage, "habrá de ser el tiempo en que prevalezca la razón de la solidaridad" indicates an awareness of the situation, so (C) and (D) are out.

The last sentence in the passage is the key to question 22: It is rephrased in the answer, (D). When you take the test, try to rephrase complicated sentences in your own words without translating the whole passage. Pick out words you know and see how they are related thematically. Then you will have the general topic without translating.

For question 23, the answer is (D). The words *todo el planeta se constata interdependiente y vivo como una sola comunidad* tell you that the world can learn to live together. Do not be fooled by answers that have words lifted from the text, as in choice (A).

4. Picture Prompt Questions (Listening Test Only)

For each question in this part you will see a numbered photograph in your test booklet. As you study the picture, you will hear on tape four choices of something that could be said about the picture, or something that someone in the picture might be saying. You will have 7 seconds each for 10 questions. Let's look at a sample:

Directions: In this part of the test you will see some photographs. As you look at each picture, you will listen to a set of four answer choices. Select the answer choice that best describes what you see in the picture or what someone in the scene might say. Mark the corresponding oval on your answer sheet. You will hear each set of choices only once.

On the CD you will hear:

24. (Man)   (A) Espero que perdamos el partido.
              (B) Será estupendo si marco un gol.
              (C) Ese jugador no me agrada.
              (D) No toques la pelota, Juan.

(7 seconds of silence)

The best answer is choice (B). The other choices all refer to the game, but do not relate to the object of the game, which is to score a goal. It is unlikely that anyone would say the other three options, so choice (B) is the most logical answer to this question. You mark the corresponding oval on your answer sheet.

5. Rejoinder Questions (Listening Test Only)

For these questions you will hear a short conversation, followed by four possible ways to complete or continue the conversation. The responses are called *rejoinders*. You will *not see* the conversations or the questions printed in your test booklet; you will see only instructions to mark your answer sheet at the appropriate time. There are about 10 conversations; you will have 7 seconds each to make your selection. Listen carefully to the instructions of the speaker. Let's look at a sample.

Directions: In this part of the test you will hear several short conversations or parts of conversations. Then you will hear four selections that could continue or complete the conversation. Select the answer that most logically continues or completes the conversation and mark your answer on your answer sheet.

You will hear:

25. (Boy)   El fin de semana pasado conocí a tres muchachas españolas.

Then you will hear:

(Girl)   (A) Fue un fin de semana aburrido.
           (B) ¿De veras? ¿Quién te las presentó?
           (C) Hace tiempo que las vi.
           (D) ¿Quieres salir conmigo este fin de semana?

(7 seconds of silence)

The correct answer is (B). Remember that the preterite of *conocer* means "to meet." The girl is interested in where the boy met the three girls. The other answer choices discuss a boring weekend, an invitation to go out, and a comment about how long it has been since she has seen the Spanish girls. None of these naturally follows in this conversation.

You will hear:

26.   (Boy)   ¡Huy! Ese examen estuvo dificilísimo. Nunca voy
                    a sacar buenas notas con este tipo de pruebas.

      (Girl)   Sí, siempre tengo miedo de los exámenes de esta clase.

Then you will hear:

      (Boy)
                    (A) Este profesor exige mucho.
                    (B) Sí, el profesor es muy bueno.
                    (C) Ni yo, tampoco.
                    (D) Me gustan sus exámenes.

(7 seconds of silence)

The best response is (A) because the boy is agreeing with the girl's comment. The other responses refer to the teacher, the exams, or a nonsense statement. (A) explains why the exams are so difficult for the students.

6. Listening Comprehension Questions (Listening Test Only)

These questions contain longer conversations or selections. You will find the questions and choices printed in your test booklet; they will not be spoken on the CD. For each conversation you will see one or more questions. You will have 12 seconds to answer each question.

Directions: You will now hear a series of selections. For each selection you will see printed in your test booklet one or more questions with four possible answers. Fill in the your selection on your answer sheet.

You will not hear the questions on the CD. After listening to the selection, read the question or questions. You will have 12 seconds to answer each question.

You will hear:

27.   (Narrator)   Escuchen esta conversación en el aeropuerto de
                     Barajas en Madrid.
      (Woman)   Buenos días. ¿En qué puedo servirle?
      (Man)   Buenos días. Tengo reservaciones para el vuelo a
                     Buenos Aires a las diez. Pero veo que no saldrá
                     hasta las dos.

(Woman)	Pues, sí, ese vuelo tiene procedencia de Londrés y va atrasado a causa del tiempo.
(Man)	Es un problema para mí. Tengo una reunión muy importante de mi compañía en Buenos Aires.
(Woman)	Lo sentimos mucho. Pero ya se sabe que en esta época hay demora de vez en cuando a causa del tiempo.
(Man)	Bueno. No hay remedio. Quizás haya otro vuelo que pueda conseguir.
(Woman)	Vamos a ver. Creo que será posible.

(12 seconds of silence)

28. ¿Qué problema tiene el hombre?

(A)   La agente no le habla con cortesía.

(B)   Hace mal tiempo de donde viene el avión.

(C)   Su compañía va a despedirlo.

(D)   No puede conseguir otro vuelo.

(12 seconds of silence)

29. ¿Cuánto tiempo tendrá el hombre que esperar?

(A)   dos horas

(B)   tres horas

(C)   cuatro horas

(D)   diez horas

(12 seconds of silence)

30. ¿Cómo reacciona el hombre al problema?

(A)   Se desespera.

(B)   Se enfada.

(C)   Se queja.

(D)   Se resigna.

For question 28, the answer is (B). The problem is that the plane is delayed from London because of the weather. If you missed the meaning of the word *tiempo*, you could have picked up on *a causa*. You also need to pay attention to the preposition *de* in the answer. (A) can be eliminated because the agent is courteous to the man. And (C) is out because the company is not going to fire the man (*despedir*, when it is not reflexive, means "to fire"). And at the end of the conversation, the agent states there may be another flight for the man to take, so (D) is clearly wrong.

For question 29, the answer is (C). You need to pay attention to details like the hours that the agent and the man discuss. The flight is supposed to leave at 10:00, but has been delayed until 2:00. Jot down numbers as you listen, especially items of time.

For question 30, the answer is (D). The line "No hay remedio," and his optimism about finding another flight show resignation about the situation. He is not desperate or angry, nor does he complain, so (A), (B), and (C) are wrong.

TEST-TAKING STRATEGIES

There is no substitute for knowing a lot of vocabulary, for having a solid foundation in grammatical structures and syntax, and for having strong reading comprehension skills. But there are also some strategies you can use to maximize what you know.

1. If you can eliminate one or two answer choices to a question, then you're probably safe to make an educated guess. Haphazard guessing is not a good idea.

2. With fill-in-the-blank questions, predict the correct word, modismo, or structure that would complete the meaning of the sentence. Don't waste time translating every word in the question.

3. Use what you may know from other languages like French or Portuguese to guess the meaning of some words. Spanish is a Romance language, meaning that most vocabulary comes from Latin. Many words in English come from Latin, so look for cognates.

4. With the longer fill-in-the-blank passages, scan the whole passage before answering the question so you do not miss important clues. Sometimes the ending of an adjective will give you a clue to the gender of a noun, or a person in the paragraph. This would be significant in answering a pronoun question, for example.

5. If you recognize an obvious correct answer to a question, don't waste time going through all the other answer choices.

6. On the reading comprehension questions, scan the passage quickly, then read the questions so you have an idea about the kind of information you'll need to find.

7. To find the main idea or theme of the passage, look at what all the nouns or all the verbs have in common in the context of the passage. To find information about supporting details, look at adjectives and adverbs.

8. If there are two answer choices that appear to be closely related, or if two choices say completely opposite things, there is a strong possibility that one of them is the correct answer. On the other hand, if two choices appear to say the same thing in different words, there is a strong possibility that both answers are incorrect.

9. On the photograph prompt questions, do not try to translate as you listen. Inevitably you will miss the words that come next, and they may contain essential information.

10. For the listening questions, visualize the conversation or description and then jot down some key words in your test booklet. Make a note of possible answers and ignore choices that make no sense in the context of the situation.

And, if you have time between selections, scan the choices before the passage is played. You cannot stop or pause your CD, but you may finish answering some questions before the next passage begins.

MANAGING STRESS

The countdown has begun. Your date with the test is looming on the horizon. Anxiety is on the rise. The butterflies in your stomach have gone ballistic. Your thinking is getting cloudy. Maybe you think you won't be ready. Maybe you already know your stuff, but you're going into panic mode anyway. Don't freak! It's possible to tame that anxiety and stress—before and during the test.

Remember, a little stress is good. Anxiety is a motivation to study. The adrenaline that gets pumped into your bloodstream when you're stressed helps you stay alert and think more clearly. But if you feel that the tension is so great that it's preventing you from using your study time effectively, here are some things you can do to get it under control.

Take Control

Lack of control is a prime cause of stress. Research shows that if you don't have a sense of control over what's happening in your life, you can easily end up feeling helpless and hopeless. Try to identify the sources of the stress you feel. Which ones of these can you do something about? Can you find ways to reduce the stress you're feeling about any of these sources?

Focus on Your Strengths

Make a list of areas of strength you have that will help you do well on the test. We all have strengths, and recognizing your own is like having reserves of solid gold at Fort Knox. You'll be able to draw on your reserves as you need them, helping you solve difficult questions, maintain confidence, and keep test stress and anxiety at a distance. And every time you recognize a new area of strength, solve a challenging problem, or score well on a practice test, you'll increase your reserves.

Imagine Yourself Succeeding

Close your eyes and imagine yourself in a relaxing situation. Breathe easily and naturally. Now, think of a real-life situation in which you scored well on a test or did well on an assignment. Focus on this success. Now turn your thoughts to the Spanish Test, and keep your thoughts and feelings in line with that successful experience. Don't make comparisons between them; just imagine yourself taking the upcoming test with the same feelings of confidence and relaxed control.

Set Realistic Goals

Facing your problem areas gives you some distinct advantages. What do you want to accomplish in the time remaining? Make a list of realistic goals. You can't help feeling more confident when you know you're actively improving your chances of earning a higher test score.

Exercise Your Frustrations Away

Whether it's jogging, biking, pushups, or a pickup basketball game, physical exercise will stimulate your mind and body, and improve your ability to think and concentrate. A surprising number of students fall out of the habit of regular exercise, ironically because they're spending so much time prepping for exams. A little physical exertion will help to keep your mind and body in sync and sleep better at night.

Avoid Drugs

Using drugs (prescription or recreational) specifically to prepare for and take a big test is definitely self-defeating. (And if they're illegal drugs, you may end up with a bigger problem than the Spanish Test on your hands.) Mild stimulants, such as coffee or cola can sometimes help as you study, since they keep you alert. On the down side, too much of these can also lead to agitation, restlessness, and insomnia. It all depends on your tolerance for caffeine.

Eat Well

Good nutrition will help you focus and think clearly. Eat plenty of fruits and vegetables, low-fat protein such as fish, skinless poultry, beans, and legumes, and whole grains such as brown rice, whole wheat bread, and pastas. Don't eat a lot of sugar and high-fat snacks, or salty foods.

Work at Your Own Pace

Don't be thrown if other tests takers seem to be working more furiously than you. Continue to spend your time patiently thinking through your answers; it is going to lead to better results. Don't mistake other people's sheer activity as signs of progress or higher scores.

Keep Breathing

Conscious attention to breathing is an excellent way to manage stress while you're taking the test. Most of the people who get into trouble during tests take shallow breaths: They breathe using only their upper chests and shoulder muscles, and may even hold their breath for long periods of time. Conversely, those test takers who breathe deeply in a slow, relaxed manner are likely to be in better control during the session.

Stretch

If you find yourself getting spaced out or burned out as you're taking the test, stop for a brief moment and stretch. Even though you'll be pausing on the test for a moment, it's a moment well spent. Stretching will help to refresh you and refocus your thoughts.

HOW TO TAKE THE DIAGNOSTIC TEST

This test is a Diagnostic; that is, a test that helps you to identify the areas in which you need work. Once you have gone through all the questions, you should check your answers and see how many you got wrong and how many you got right. Try to identify the areas in which you need work. Maybe verb conjugation trips you up. Maybe pronouns are the problem area. Whatever the case, the results of the Diagnostic should be used to help you maximize your study.

Before you begin the exam, find a quiet room where you can work uninterrupted for one hour. Make sure you have several No. 2 pencils with erasers, as well as a watch. Use the answer grid provided to record your answers.

Time yourself. (Set your watch on the table in front of you, so it's easy to see.) Spend no more than one hour on the questions. And once you begin the exam, don't stop until you've reached the one-hour time limit.

An answer key follows the test, so you can score yourself and see how you performed. Once you are able to see the areas in which you are strong, you'll be able to focus on those areas in which you need help. This is the first step in preparing for the SAT Spanish exam.

Good luck!

Answer Grid
Diagnostic Test

1. Ⓐ Ⓑ Ⓒ Ⓓ
2. Ⓐ Ⓑ Ⓒ Ⓓ
3. Ⓐ Ⓑ Ⓒ Ⓓ
4. Ⓐ Ⓑ Ⓒ Ⓓ
5. Ⓐ Ⓑ Ⓒ Ⓓ
6. Ⓐ Ⓑ Ⓒ Ⓓ
7. Ⓐ Ⓑ Ⓒ Ⓓ
8. Ⓐ Ⓑ Ⓒ Ⓓ
9. Ⓐ Ⓑ Ⓒ Ⓓ
10. Ⓐ Ⓑ Ⓒ Ⓓ
11. Ⓐ Ⓑ Ⓒ Ⓓ
12. Ⓐ Ⓑ Ⓒ Ⓓ
13. Ⓐ Ⓑ Ⓒ Ⓓ
14. Ⓐ Ⓑ Ⓒ Ⓓ
15. Ⓐ Ⓑ Ⓒ Ⓓ
16. Ⓐ Ⓑ Ⓒ Ⓓ
17. Ⓐ Ⓑ Ⓒ Ⓓ
18. Ⓐ Ⓑ Ⓒ Ⓓ
19. Ⓐ Ⓑ Ⓒ Ⓓ
20. Ⓐ Ⓑ Ⓒ Ⓓ
21. Ⓐ Ⓑ Ⓒ Ⓓ
22. Ⓐ Ⓑ Ⓒ Ⓓ
23. Ⓐ Ⓑ Ⓒ Ⓓ
24. Ⓐ Ⓑ Ⓒ Ⓓ
25. Ⓐ Ⓑ Ⓒ Ⓓ
26. Ⓐ Ⓑ Ⓒ Ⓓ
27. Ⓐ Ⓑ Ⓒ Ⓓ
28. Ⓐ Ⓑ Ⓒ Ⓓ
29. Ⓐ Ⓑ Ⓒ Ⓓ

30. Ⓐ Ⓑ Ⓒ Ⓓ
31. Ⓐ Ⓑ Ⓒ Ⓓ
32. Ⓐ Ⓑ Ⓒ Ⓓ
33. Ⓐ Ⓑ Ⓒ Ⓓ
34. Ⓐ Ⓑ Ⓒ Ⓓ
35. Ⓐ Ⓑ Ⓒ Ⓓ
36. Ⓐ Ⓑ Ⓒ Ⓓ
37. Ⓐ Ⓑ Ⓒ Ⓓ
38. Ⓐ Ⓑ Ⓒ Ⓓ
39. Ⓐ Ⓑ Ⓒ Ⓓ
40. Ⓐ Ⓑ Ⓒ Ⓓ
41. Ⓐ Ⓑ Ⓒ Ⓓ
42. Ⓐ Ⓑ Ⓒ Ⓓ
43. Ⓐ Ⓑ Ⓒ Ⓓ
44. Ⓐ Ⓑ Ⓒ Ⓓ
45. Ⓐ Ⓑ Ⓒ Ⓓ
46. Ⓐ Ⓑ Ⓒ Ⓓ
47. Ⓐ Ⓑ Ⓒ Ⓓ
48. Ⓐ Ⓑ Ⓒ Ⓓ
49. Ⓐ Ⓑ Ⓒ Ⓓ
50. Ⓐ Ⓑ Ⓒ Ⓓ
51. Ⓐ Ⓑ Ⓒ Ⓓ
52. Ⓐ Ⓑ Ⓒ Ⓓ
53. Ⓐ Ⓑ Ⓒ Ⓓ
54. Ⓐ Ⓑ Ⓒ Ⓓ
55. Ⓐ Ⓑ Ⓒ Ⓓ
56. Ⓐ Ⓑ Ⓒ Ⓓ
57. Ⓐ Ⓑ Ⓒ Ⓓ
58. Ⓐ Ⓑ Ⓒ Ⓓ

59. Ⓐ Ⓑ Ⓒ Ⓓ
60. Ⓐ Ⓑ Ⓒ Ⓓ
61. Ⓐ Ⓑ Ⓒ Ⓓ
62. Ⓐ Ⓑ Ⓒ Ⓓ
63. Ⓐ Ⓑ Ⓒ Ⓓ
64. Ⓐ Ⓑ Ⓒ Ⓓ
65. Ⓐ Ⓑ Ⓒ Ⓓ
66. Ⓐ Ⓑ Ⓒ Ⓓ
67. Ⓐ Ⓑ Ⓒ Ⓓ
68. Ⓐ Ⓑ Ⓒ Ⓓ
69. Ⓐ Ⓑ Ⓒ Ⓓ
70. Ⓐ Ⓑ Ⓒ Ⓓ
71. Ⓐ Ⓑ Ⓒ Ⓓ
72. Ⓐ Ⓑ Ⓒ Ⓓ
73. Ⓐ Ⓑ Ⓒ Ⓓ
74. Ⓐ Ⓑ Ⓒ Ⓓ
75. Ⓐ Ⓑ Ⓒ Ⓓ
76. Ⓐ Ⓑ Ⓒ Ⓓ
77. Ⓐ Ⓑ Ⓒ Ⓓ
78. Ⓐ Ⓑ Ⓒ Ⓓ
79. Ⓐ Ⓑ Ⓒ Ⓓ
80. Ⓐ Ⓑ Ⓒ Ⓓ
81. Ⓐ Ⓑ Ⓒ Ⓓ
82. Ⓐ Ⓑ Ⓒ Ⓓ
83. Ⓐ Ⓑ Ⓒ Ⓓ
84. Ⓐ Ⓑ Ⓒ Ⓓ
85. Ⓐ Ⓑ Ⓒ Ⓓ

Diagnostic Test

Part A

Directions: Select the most appropriate choice to complete the meaning of the sentence and mark the corresponding oval on your answer sheet.

1. Antes de salir, tengo que ___ la tarea para mañana.

   (A) hablar
   (B) soñar
   (C) proponer
   (D) acabar

2. Los muchachos volvieron a casa antes de que la lluvia los ___ anoche.

   (A) mojara
   (B) viniera
   (C) cayera
   (D) secara

3. Antes de comer es buena idea lavarse las manos con agua caliente y ___.

   (A) sopa
   (B) crema
   (C) comida
   (D) jabón

4. Enrique no vino a la fiesta, ___ varios amigos lo llamaron para invitarlo.

   (A) todavía
   (B) aunque
   (C) sino
   (D) sin que

5. Regresamos a casa sin que ___ de nosotros ganara un premio en el carnaval.

   (A) nadie
   (B) ninguno
   (C) algún
   (D) ningún

6. El tió Juan estaba muy ___ esa noche; no dijo nada en toda la noche.

   (A) alegre
   (B) callado
   (C) perezoso
   (D) mimado

7. Cuando me gradúe de esta escuela, voy a ___ a la universidad.

   (A) limpiar
   (B) atender
   (C) asistir
   (D) acontecer

8. El ___ de fútbol saldrá para participar en el campeonato estatal mañana.

   (A) gimnasio
   (B) campo
   (C) deporte
   (D) equipo

GO ON TO THE NEXT PAGE

9. ¡Qué suerte! Anunciaron esta noche que un amigo ___ ganó la lotería.

   (A) suyo
   (B) cuyo
   (C) el mío
   (D) el que

10. Para tener ___ en la vida, se necesita trabajar un poco y tener buena suerte.

    (A) suceso
    (B) pérdidas
    (C) cuidado
    (D) éxito

11. Señora, son las ocho y los invitados están ___ para cenar.

    (A) llevando
    (B) llamando
    (C) llegando
    (D) invitando

12. No ___ dormir ni un momento anoche a causa de la tormenta.

    (A) puedo
    (B) pude
    (C) podrá
    (D) pueda

13. Con todas las luces ___ se veía claramente quién andaba por la calle.

    (A) encendidas
    (B) apagadas
    (C) despiertas
    (D) paradas

14. Raúl, si no comprendes la materia, debes ___ preguntas en clase.

    (A) olvidar
    (B) hacer
    (C) pedir
    (D) hablar

15. Señora, le recomiendo ___ con una taza de café para concluir su cena.

    (A) desierto
    (B) pastel
    (C) pasto
    (D) pastilla

16. Nos molesta tener que ___ hasta que todos los otros estén listos.

    (A) espera
    (B) esperará
    (C) esperaría
    (D) esperar

17. Siempre se siente muy orgulloso al ___ un proyecto difícil.

    (A) robar
    (B) caber
    (C) realizar
    (D) llorar

18. No quiero ver esa película, ___ la vi la semana pasada.

    (A) pero
    (B) ahora
    (C) ya
    (D) sino

19. Magdalena, sé buena con tu ___ ; no nos visita a menudo.

    (A) prima
    (B) primera
    (C) primaria
    (D) primer

20. Vi que el ___ en la pared era una copia de una pintura famosa.

    (A) cuarto
    (B) cuatro
    (C) cuadro
    (D) cuaderno

GO ON TO THE NEXT PAGE

21. El que dice que ese curso es fácil no sabe ___ exigente que es el profesor.

    (A) el
    (B) la
    (C) le
    (D) lo

22. Cuando terminó la clase, ___ todos se levantaron y salieron.

    (A) en seguida
    (B) no obstante
    (C) al contrario
    (D) sin embargo

23. Gregorio subió las escaleras ___ porque estaba cansado

    (A) actualmente
    (B) claramente
    (C) lentamente
    (D) sabiamente

24. La calle era muy ___ y casi no podían pasar dos coches al mismo tiempo.

    (A) amplia
    (B) ajena
    (C) estrecha
    (D) gruesa

25. Miguel, ¿puedes prestarme una corbata? Se me olvidó llevar una ___ esta mañana.

    (A) con él
    (B) conmigo
    (C) contigo
    (D) con Vd.

26. Fabián se despidió de su amigo sin ___ ni una palabra.

    (A) dice
    (B) dijo
    (C) diciendo
    (D) decir

27. Cuando ___ la verdad del asunto anoche, se la contamos a los otros en seguida.

    (A) supimos
    (B) sabíamos
    (C) supiéramos
    (D) hubiéramos sabido

28. Nadie me dijo nada, ___ quiero saber lo que dice la gente.

    (A) ni
    (B) que
    (C) más
    (D) o

29. Los ___ habitantes de la ciudad la hacen la más grande del hemisferio.

    (A) miles
    (B) ciento de
    (C) millones de
    (D) cientos

30. Ramón y Julia, apúrense. Nos ___ sólo media hora para la próxima clase.

    (A) queda
    (B) quedan
    (C) quedamos
    (D) queden

31. Mi amiga tomó mi libro, pero me lo ___ mañana.

    (A) redoblará
    (B) tocará
    (C) devolverá
    (D) girará

32. Cuando vayas al supermercado, ___ el favor de comprar leche.

    (A) hágame
    (B) me hace
    (C) te haces
    (D) hazme

GO ON TO THE NEXT PAGE

Part B

Directions: For each paragraph below, there are numbered blanks indicating that words or phrases have been omitted. For each numbered blank, choose the completion that is most appropriate given the context of the entire passage. Fill in the corresponding oval on the answer sheet.

Note: Em dashes at the beginning of a line represent the quotation marks in Spanish.

Alguna vez, el abuelo nos (33) en el pequeño carrito a su casa de campo en (34) del pueblo, y, (35) el camino era bonito por la (36) antigua, entre árboles altos, las tardes (37) en aquella casa no nos atraían. Las hermanas de Bernardino vestían a la moda antigua—habíamos visto mujeres (38) como ellas en el álbum de fotografías del abuelo—y (39) con el pelo puesto en lo alto de la cabeza. Nos parecía extraño que un niño de nuestra edad (40) hermanas que parecían tías, por lo menos.

33. (A) llevaba
    (B) llevara
    (C) ha llevado
    (D) hubiera llevado

34. (A) las calles
    (B) las afueras
    (C) el centro
    (D) la plaza

35. (A) según
    (B) actualmente
    (C) hacia
    (D) aunque

36. (A) cartera
    (B) carta
    (C) carretera
    (D) carpeta

37. (A) delgadas
    (B) estrechas
    (C) anchas
    (D) tranquilas

38. (A) vestido
    (B) vestida
    (C) vestidos
    (D) vestidas

39. (A) se quejaban
    (B) se peinaban
    (C) se afeitaban
    (D) se dormían

40. (A) tenía
    (B) tuviera
    (C) había tenido
    (D) habría tenido

GO ON TO THE NEXT PAGE

En dos años de (41) por las tierras de Andalucía él ya se conocía de memoria todas las ciudades de la región. Estaba (42) en explicar esta vez a la chica por qué un simple pastor sabe leer: (43) hasta los dieciséis años en un seminario. Sus padres querían que él (44) cura, motivo de (45) para una simple familia campesina que trabajaba (46) para comida y agua. (47) latín, español y teología. Pero (48) niño soñaba con conocer el mundo. Cierta tarde, al visitar a su familia, había tomado (49) y había dicho a su padre que no quería ser cura. Que quería viajar.

41. (A) cruceros
    (B) recorridos
    (C) principios
    (D) tiempo

42. (A) piensa
    (B) pensar
    (C) pensada
    (D) pensando

43. (A) estando
    (B) está
    (C) haya estado
    (D) había estado

44. (A) era
    (B) sería
    (C) sea
    (D) fuera

45. (A) venganza
    (B) cortesía
    (C) orgullo
    (D) desarrollo

46. (A) por casualidad
    (B) apenas
    (C) a propósito
    (D) hacia

47. (A) Estudia
    (B) Estudió
    (C) Haya estudiado
    (D) Hubiera estudiado

48. (A) según
    (B) casi
    (C) hasta
    (D) desde

49. (A) pena
    (B) coraje
    (C) temor
    (D) envidia

GO ON TO THE NEXT PAGE

Una vez estaba esperando un taxi en una avenida central de México, a pleno día, cuando vi acercarse a __(50)__ que no pensé detener, porque había una persona __(51)__ junto al conductor. __(52)__, cuando estuvo más cerca comprendí que era una ilusión óptica: el taxi __(53)__ libre. Minutos después le conté al conductor __(54)__ había visto, y él me dijo con una naturalidad absoluta que no era ni mucho menos una alucinación mía. —__(55)__ ocurre lo mismo, sobre todo de noche—, me dijo.—A veces paso horas enteras dando __(56)__ por la ciudad sin que nadie me __(57)__, porque siempre ven una persona en el __(58)__ de al lado—.

50. (A) él
    (B) uno
    (C) una
    (D) ella

51. (A) se sienta
    (B) sentarse
    (C) sentado
    (D) sentada

52. (A) Sin embargo
    (B) A lo mejor
    (C) Casi
    (D) Sin que

53. (A) tenía
    (B) era
    (C) estaba
    (D) hacía

54. (A) el que
    (B) lo que
    (C) la que
    (D) el cual

55. (A) Siempre
    (B) Cuando
    (C) Mientras
    (D) Durante

56. (A) visitas
    (B) vistas
    (C) vueltas
    (D) vuelos

57. (A) detiene
    (B) detuvo
    (C) detenga
    (D) detuviera

58. (A) tejido
    (B) suelo
    (C) coche
    (D) asiento

GO ON TO THE NEXT PAGE

Part C

Directions: Read the following texts carefully for comprehension. Each is followed by a number of questions or incomplete statements. Select the answer or completion that is best according to the text. Fill in the corresponding oval on the answer sheet.

Línea   La puerta oscilante se abrió. A esa hora no
había nadie en el café de José. Acababan de dar las
seis. José sabía que tenía que ser ella.
      —Hola, reina. —dijo José cuando la vio
(5) sentarse. Luego caminó hacia el otro extremo
del mostrador, limpiando con un trapo seco la
superficie de cristal.
      —¿Qué quieres hoy? —dijo.
      —Primero quiero enseñarte a ser caballero. —
(10) dijo la mujer. Cuando habló, subió el hombro para
que José notara el abrigo en que estaba envuelta.
      —Estás hermosa hoy, reina. —dijo José.
      —Déjate de tonterías. —dijo la mujer. —No
creas que eso me va a servir para pagarte.
(15)   —No quise decir eso, reina.
Apuesto que hoy te hizo daño el almuerzo. Te voy
a preparar un buen bistec. —dijo José.
      —Todavía no tengo plata. —dijo la mujer.
      —Hace tres meses que no tienes plata y siempre
(20) te preparo algo bueno. —dijo José.

59. ¿Dónde tiene lugar esta escena?

   (A) en un palacio

   (B) en una tienda

   (C) en un restaurante

   (D) en una casa

60. ¿Qué hacía José cuando la mujer entró?

   (A) limpiaba el mostrador

   (B) cocinaba el almuerzo

   (C) arreglaba sillas

   (D) contaba dinero

61. ¿Qué quería la mujer que hiciera José por ella?

   (A) que le diera el almuerzo

   (B) que le hablara

   (C) que le ayudara a quitarse el abrigo

   (D) que le dijera que era bonita

62. ¿Qué le ofrece José a la mujer?

   (A) abrazarla

   (B) darle plata

   (C) darle algo de comer

   (D) regalarle un abrigo

63. ¿Cuál es la relación entre estas dos personas?

   (A) Son rey y reina.

   (B) Son novios.

   (C) Son comerciante y cliente.

   (D) Son esposos.

GO ON TO THE NEXT PAGE

LA LIBERTAD EXISTE

ES UN EJERCICIO DIARIO
PEDRO FERRIZ DE CON

El ejercicio periodístico como acción transformadora.

Analizar, señalar, reconocer, denunciar; buscar el fondo

de las cosas y llevarlas al límite.

Infórmate con la visión de un hombre que cree en los jóvenes,

en la honestidad, en la construcción de un país distinto.

Escucha todos los días la experiencia y criterio

de Pedro Ferriz de Con, sólo en Imagen Informativa.

LUNES A VIERNES 6:50 A 11:00 HRS
90.5 FM 108 SKY

IMAGEN
INFORMATIVA
www.imagen.com.mx

64. Según el anuncio, ¿cómo es Pedro Ferriz de Con?

   (A) analfabeto
   (B) astuto
   (C) guapo
   (D) indolente

65. ¿En qué consiste el ejercicio diario de Pedro Ferriz de Con?

   (A) manejar los negocios del país
   (B) hacer comprensible las noticias del día
   (C) dirigir un programa para los jóvenes
   (D) nadar en el equipo Imagen Informativo

GO ON TO THE NEXT PAGE

Línea   Todos los años Las Fallas y la primavera
parecen llegar juntas a Valencia. En las plazas, en
los cruces de calles, en el más increíble espacio
urbano se levantan unas fallas, las grandes
(5) estructuras que pueden llegar hasta una altura
de 18 metros. Entre los actos más peculiares de
la semana fallera, que cada día del 16 al 19 de
marzo se anuncian con el comienzo del día, hay
fuegos artificiales y cohetes que lanzan los falleros
(10) detrás de los músicos que tocan. Entonces hay
procesiones que pasan por la calles hasta llegar
a la Plaza del Ayuntamiento donde se reciben
los premios por los monumentos falleros más
artísticos. Por la noche del último día, una gran
(15) multitud se congrega a las orillas del antiguo río
Turia, ahora sin agua, donde siempre hay los
más famosos fuegos de artificio del mundo. El 19
de marzo con la Noche de Fuego, terminan Las
Fallas. Es una noche mágica, cuando al fuego se le
(20) ofrecen Las Fallas como un homenaje.

66. ¿Qué son Las Fallas?

    (A) el nombre del Ayuntamiento

    (B) los habitantes de Valencia

    (C) una época de celebración

    (D) los visitantes de Valencia

67. ¿Dónde tienen lugar Las Fallas?

    (A) en una iglesia

    (B) en un centro urbano

    (C) en un río

    (D) en una chimenea

68. ¿Cómo se empieza cada mañana de la semana
fallera?

    (A) Se queman unos monumentos.

    (B) Lanzan cohetes a unas fallas.

    (C) Hacen ruido y tocan música.

    (D) Van al antiguo río Turia.

69. ¿Qué pasa en la última noche de Las Fallas?

    (A) Se queman las fallas.

    (B) Hay una lucha entre los falleros.

    (C) El público nada en el río.

    (D) Se construyen nuevas fallas.

70. Para los valencianos los días de Las Fallas
representan

    (A) una semana triste.

    (B) un rato olvidable.

    (C) un espectáculo religioso.

    (D) una época de gran alegría.

GO ON TO THE NEXT PAGE

Línea   En 1881, en lo que fuera la huerta del convento
de San Diego de Cuautla, se inauguró la estación
del ferrocarril. En ella, actualmente cada sábado
y domingo, como a las cuatro y media de la tarde,
(5) se aprovecha la oportunidad de vivir otra vez
tiempos pasados, de menos prisas: a esa hora se
echa a andar la máquina renovada, se saca de su
encierro y se acomoda, orgullosa, con sus dos
vagones de madera en el andén de la estación,
(10) pues a las cinco de la tarde inicia sus recorridos.
     El boleto para disfrutar de un viaje de apenas
un kilómetro cuesta cinco pesos ida y vuelta.
Ciertamente el recorrido es corto —por problemas
de vías y de terreno, comentan los encargados— y
(15) aunque algunos viajeros muestran su desacuerdo
diciendo que más tardan en sentarse cuando ya
tienen que bajar del vagón, otros piensan que es
preferible esto a que el tren siga abandonado y
olvidado.

71. ¿Dónde se queda el tren cuando no está en
servicio?

(A) en la estación
(B) en un jardín
(C) en refugio
(D) en el andén

72. El tren del que se habla en la selección es un
tren

(A) moderno.
(B) largo.
(C) abandonado.
(D) restaurado.

73. ¿Cómo era la vida en el pasado?

(A) tranquila
(B) apresurada
(C) incómoda
(D) lujosa

74. Los pasajeros en este tren probablemente son

(A) personas religiosas.
(B) gente vieja.
(C) trabajadores.
(D) aficionados a trenes.

75. ¿Cuándo hace el tren su recorrido?

(A) cada día por la tarde
(B) cada día por la mañana
(C) cada fin de semana por la tarde
(D) cada fin de semana por la noche

76. ¿Para qué toman el tren las personas que lo
usan?

(A) para ir lejos
(B) para recordar el pasado
(C) para ver el paisaje
(D) para visitar a parientes

77. Algunas personas que toman el tren se quejan
de que

(A) el boleto cuesta mucho.
(B) el tren no va lejos.
(C) las vías son malas.
(D) no se venden boletos de ida y vuelta.

GO ON TO THE NEXT PAGE

Línea Cuando iba por el puente con la torta entre las manos, oí otra vez a los muchachos. Y los vi allá abajo, nadando rápidamente hasta el centro del río para salvar una rata de agua, pues la pobre no
(5) podía nadar.

Los muchachos sacaron la rata y la depositaron sobre una piedra para que se secara al sol. Entonces fui a llamarlos para invitarlos a comer todos juntos la torta de chocolate, pues yo solo no
(10) iba a poder comer aquella torta tan grande.

De veras que los iba a llamar. Levanté las manos con la torta encima para mostrársela y todos vinieron corriendo. Pero entonces —puch— , me pasó el camión casi por arriba en medio de la
(15) calle que era donde, sin darme cuenta, me había parado.

Y aquí me ve usted: con las piernas blancas por y el yeso. Tan blancas como las paredes de este cuarto, donde sólo entran mujeres vestidas de
(20) blanco para darme una inyección o una pastilla también blanca. Y no piense que porque tengo un poco de fiebre, estoy diciendo mentiras, porque no es así. Y si usted quiere comprobar si fue verdad, vaya al puente, que seguramente debe estar todavía, sobre el asfalto, la torta grande que
(25) me regalaron las dos viejitas de la dulcería.

78. ¿Qué hacían los chicos cuando el narrador los llamó?

(A) Nadaban en un río.
(B) Corrían por la calle.
(C) Comían una torta
(D) Hablaban con el narrador.

79. ¿Qué llevaba el narrador en las manos?

(A) una rata
(B) una piedra
(C) comida
(D) yeso

80. ¿Por qué llamó el narrador a los chicos?

(A) Para decirles que no molestaran a la rata.
(B) Para avisarles de un peligro.
(C) Para decirles que tuvieran cuidado.
(D) Para invitarles a comer con él.

81. ¿Qué le pasó a la persona que narra la historia?

(A) Se cayó en el río.
(B) Sufrió un accidente en el puente.
(C) Se cayó en mitad de la calle.
(D) Se rompió las piernas en la cocina.

82. ¿Dónde está el narrador cuando narra esta historia?

(A) en una pastelería
(B) en casa
(C) en la calle
(D) en un hospital

83. ¿Quiénes son las mujeres vestidas de blanco?

(A) Son invitadas.
(B) Son cocineras.
(C) Son enfermeras.
(D) Son alucinaciones.

84. ¿Cómo se sentía el narrador al final?

(A) muy satisfecho
(B) entusiasmado
(C) un poco enojado
(D) muy perezoso

85. El narrador teme que el oyente de la historia

(A) no la crea.
(B) se sorprenda.
(C) se enoje.
(D) no la dude.

STOP!

**If you finish before time is up,
you may check your work.**

Answer Key
Diagnostic Test

Part A	Part B	Part C
1. D	33. A	59. C
2. A	34. B	60. A
3. D	35. D	61. C
4. B	36. C	62. C
5. B	37. D	63. C
6. B	38. D	64. B
7. C	39. B	65. B
8. D	40. B	66. C
9. A	41. B	67. B
10. D	42. D	68. C
11. C	43. D	69. A
12. B	44. D	70. D
13. A	45. C	71. C
14. B	46. B	72. D
15. B	47. B	73. A
16. D	48. D	74. D
17. C	49. B	75. C
18. C	50. B	76. B
19. A	51. D	77. B
20. C	52. A	78. A
21. D	53. C	79. C
22. A	54. B	80. D
23. C	55. A	81. B
24. C	56. C	82. D
25. B	57. C	83. C
26. D	58. D	84. C
27. A		85. A
28. A		
29. C		
30. A		
31. C		
32. D		

To score your Diagnostic Test, turn to chapter 10 (page 357) at the end of this book.

Part Two

Spanish Grammar Review

BEFORE WE BEGIN

This section of the book will review the basics of Spanish vocabulary and structures that might appear on the test. Each chapter in this section is dedicated to a different part of speech. The vocabulary study is integrated into the review of structures, because the best way to learn new words is to learn a few at a time and to use them.

Before we begin, let's look at some ways you can learn to recognize cognates.

- **In Spanish there is no *th* combination, so words that in English would have a *th*, have only a *t*.** The word "theater" becomes *teatro*; the word "theme" becomes *tema*, and "method" becomes *método*.

- **If an English word begins with *sc, sp, st, sch, spr, sl, sh*, then in Spanish, add the letter *e* in front.** The word "Spanish" becomes *español*, "school" becomes *escuela*, and "scene" becomes *escena*.

- **Frequently the letter *y* in English becomes the letter *i* in Spanish.** "Gymnasium" becomes *gimnasio*, and "type" becomes *tipo*.

- **The English combination of *ph* is always *f* in Spanish.** "Photography" becomes *fotografía*. "Geography" becomes *geografía*. The *ph* combination does not occur in Spanish except in words borrowed from English.

- **Most words in Spanish that use the letters *k* and *w* are borrowed from other languages.** In Spanish the *k* sound is produced by the letters *qu*, or by the letter *c* when followed by *a, o* or, *u*. For example, "frequent" becomes *frecuente*.

- **There are some diphthongs (vowel sounds) in Spanish that do not occur in English, and vice versa.** For example, Spanish *puerto* becomes "port" in English. *Encontrar* becomes "to encounter." The *o* in the infinitive becomes *ue* in some forms of stem-changing verbs. In Spanish the *ue* combination—where we use an *o* in English—is common.

- **There is no double *f* in Spanish.** In rare instances, the letters *s, n*, and *o* are doubled. The letters *rr* and *ll* in Spanish are considered a single character because they are pronounced differently than the single *r* and single *l*. Learn to distinguish vocabulary beginning with *l* and *ll*.

- **A word's ending can often indicate whether the word is a noun, adjective, or adverb.** If you have to guess about what a word means, this can be helpful.

- **It isn't always necessary to know the meaning of a word in order to answer a question. You can guess just by knowing the form that is required.** If you know that an infinitive verb is needed after a preposition, you'll just need to find the answer choice with an infinitive ending.

- **A word often has one stem with different endings for the various parts of speech.**

crecer	to grow, to raise (-*er* = verb)
crecimiento	growth (-*miento* = noun)
creciente	growing (-*iente* = adjective)

Chapter 3: **Nouns**

- Masculine Nouns
- Feminine Nouns
- Forming Plural Nouns
- Noun Endings

In Spanish, all nouns are either masculine or feminine. That is, all nouns have gender, whether they refer to people, places, things, abstractions, or concepts. You have to learn the gender of the noun when you learn the word itself. By knowing the gender of a noun, you'll be able to answer questions on adjective and noun agreement, and on pronouns.

Each adjective must have an ending of the same gender and number as the noun it modifies. If you don't know the gender of a noun, and there are no clues in the sentence or the passage, you might have to guess. Here are some rules that will help you guess more intelligently.

The gender of a noun is indicated by a preceding definite article (*the* in English).

> *el* = a masculine singular noun
>
> *los* = a masculine plural noun
>
> *la* = a feminine singular noun
>
> *las* = a feminine plural noun

There is no specific rule that governs which nouns are masculine and which ones are feminine, but there are some general rules.

MASCULINE NOUNS

3.1 Masculine nouns usually end with the letter -o, -or, or with -aje. (The one common exception to this rule is la mano.)

el abuelo	grandfather	el premio	prize
el ruido	noise	el boleto	ticket
el coraje	courage	el personaje	character
el chico	boy	el primo	cousin
el hielo	ice	el delito	crime
el traje	suit	el paisaje	countryside
el olor	smell	el dolor	pain
el partido	political party, game (sporting event)		

3.2 Some words that end in -ama, -ema, -ima, or -eta are masculine, even though they end with the letter -a. Some of these are words have come into the Spanish language from other languages.

> Many words ending in -ama, -ema, -ima, or -eta are masculine. Watch out for them.

el problema	problem	el planeta	planet
el programa	program	el tema	theme
el sistema	system	el mapa	map
el fantasma	phantom	el dilemna	dilemma
el día	day	el clima	climate
el drama	play, drama	el poema	poem
el telegrama	telegram	el atleta	athlete
el idioma	language		

3.3 Nouns that name the male of a species are masculine, no matter what the ending.

el caballo	horse	el caballero	gentleman
el yerno	son-in-law	el cura	priest
el león	lion	el padre	father
el macho	male (animal)	el marido	husband
el toro	bull	el buey	ox
el varón	male (person)	el cardenal	cardinal
el patriarca	patriarch	el poeta	poet
el héroe	hero	el actor	actor
el rey	king	el príncipe	prince
el conde	count	el duque	duke

If a noun that designates a male ends in an -a, the article indicates the gender.

el monarca	monarch	el centinela	sentinel

Note that the feminine gender of the above two nouns uses the article *la*, but the noun endings do not change.

3.4 Nouns that end in *-ista*, and *-ia*, but refer to men are masculine.

el recepcionista	recepcionist	el dentista	dentist
el especialista	specialist	el artista	artist
el periodista	reporter	el novelista	novelist
el espía	spy	el indígena	Indian

3.5 Infinitives, other parts of speech, and phrases are masculine when they are used as nouns.

El comprender es importante means:
Understanding is important.

El sí de las niñas es un drama famoso means:
The Girls' Consent is a famous play.

> Sometimes the only way to know the gender of a noun is to look at the article.

3.6 When referring to a mixed gender group, even if there is only one male in the group, the masculine article is used.

los padres	parents	los Díaz	Mr. & Mrs. Díaz
los chicos	boys and girls	los niños	children (boys and girls)

3.7 Most compound nouns are masculine, regardless of their ending.

el rascacielos	skyscraper	el parabrisas	windshield
el paraguas	umbrella	el altavoz	loudspeaker
el saltamontes	grasshopper	el abrelatas	can opener
el padrenuestro	Lord's Prayer	el tocadiscos	record player
el sordomudo	deafmute	el parachoques	bumper
el cumpleaños	birthday	el ferrocarril	railway

3.8 The names of days of the week and months are always masculine. (Notice that the first letters are not capitalized.)

el lunes	Monday	el martes	Tuesday
el miércoles	Wednesday	el jueves	Thursday
enero	January	marzo	March
agosto	August	septiembre	September

3.9 The names of cardinal points are masculine.

el norte	north	el sur	south
el este	east	el oeste	west
el oriente	east	el occidente	west

3.10 The proper names of oceans, rivers, mountains, and mountain ranges are masculine.

el Atlántico	Atlantic Ocean	el Tajo	Tagus River
el Orinoco	Orinico River	el Etna	Mt. Etna
el Amazonas	Amazon River	los Andes	Andes Mountains

3.11 The names of trees are masculine (but the fruit itself is feminine: *la banana, la naranja, la manzana.*)

el banano	banana tree	el naranjo	orange tree
el mango	mango tree	el manzano	apple tree
el roble	oak tree	el álamo	poplar tree
el acre	maple tree	el sauce	willow

3.12 For some masculine nouns, there is no clue, and you just have to memorize them.

el país	country	el ataúd	coffin
el rubí	ruby	el lápiz	pencil
el colibrí	hummingbird	el espíritu	spirit
el andén	train platform	el riel	railroad track
el ángel	angel	el hogar	hearth, home

FEMININE NOUNS

3.13 Most nouns that end in *-a* are feminine, except for those that end in *-ista* listed in 3.4.

la playa	beach	la pluma	pen, feather
la caja	box, cashbox	la novela	novel
la idea	idea	la lluvia	rain
la prensa	the press	la blusa	blouse
la brisa	breeze	la risa	laugh, laughter
la lana	wool	la seda	silk
la entrada	ticket to a show	la ola	wave
la madera	wood	la llave	key
la rama	branch (tree)	la rana	frog
la pata	paw, foot (of an animal)	la informática	data processing

3.14 Most words that end in -*ía*, -*ción*, -*dad*, -*ie*, -*tud*, -*umbre*, and -*sión* are feminine.

la zapatería	shoestore	la carnicería	butchershop
la nación	nation	la ciudad	city
la serie	series	la realidad	reality
la cumbre	peak	la muchedumbre	multitude
la lumbre	light	la certidumbre	certainty
la amistad	friendship	la penumbra	half light
la juventud	youth	la misión	mission
la superficie	surface	la caridad	charity
la tensión	tension	la virtud	virtue
la felicidad	happiness	la revolución	revolution
la libertad	liberty	la oscuridad	darkness

Notice that the endings -*ción* and -*sión* often correspond to -*tion* in English. And the endings -*tad*, -*dad* and -*umbre* often correspond to -*ty* and -*ness* in English.

3.15 Nouns that refer to women usually change the masculine -*o* ending to -*a*.

la abuela	grandmother	la chica	girl
la secretaria	secretary	la camarera	waitress
la criada	maid	la vecina	neighbor
la amiga	girlfriend	la cocinera	cook
la hechicera	spellcaster	la bruja	witch
la gata	cat (female)	la pasajera	passenger

3.16 Some nouns that refer to the female of the species are irregular and do not correspond to the masculine forms.

la mujer	woman	la vaca	cow
la hembra	female	la yegua	mare
la dama	lady	la esposa	wife
la madre	mother	la reina	queen
la nuera	daughter-in-law	la heroina	heroine
la gallina	hen	la actriz	actress
la emperatriz	empress	la condesa	countess

3.17 To make nouns that end in a consonant feminine, add -*a* to make them feminine.

la francesa	French lady	la española	Spanish girl
la vendedora	seller (f)	la diosa	goddess

> The letter *h* is never voiced in Spanish, so a noun beginning with a stressed *ha* will take a masculine article.

3.18 Some nouns are feminine, but take a masculine singular article because they begin with an accented or stressed -a. In the plural forms they take the feminine articles. All of the adjectives have to be feminine, regardless of the gender of the article used in the singular.

el agua	water	el hacha	axe
el águila	eagle	el ala	wing
el alma	soul	el alba	dawn
el hambre	hunger	el arte	art

3.19 Some nouns can be either masculine or feminine; the gender is indicated by the article. If you find one of these in a question, look for clues in the rest of the sentence.

la dependiente	clerk	la presidente	president
la mártir	martyr	la testigo	witness
la guía	guide	la joven	girl

3.20 Some feminine nouns end in -o. You can only tell that they're feminine by looking at other clues in the sentence.

la modelo	model	la reo	criminal
la testigo	witness	la víctima	victim

> Some nouns may fool you. They are feminine but use a masculine article in the singular form.

3.21 Nouns that end in -e can be either masculine or feminine. If you have to guess, you probably should guess that the noun is feminine.

el desfile	parade	la clase	class

3.22 Some nouns can be either masculine or feminine. They have no difference in meaning.

el, la dote	dowery, gift, talent	el, la mar	sea
			(The feminine form is usually poetic.)

3.23 Some nouns change meaning depending on their gender.

el cura	priest	la cura	cure
el cometa	comet	la cometa	kite
el cólera	cholera (disease)	la cólera	anger
el corte	cut, edge	la corte	court
el capital	money	la capital	the capital
el frente	front	la frente	forehead

FORMING PLURAL NOUNS

While you will not need to write these forms, it is useful to know how to construct plurals.

3.24 For nouns that end in a vowel, add -s. For nouns that end in a consonant, add -es.

el estacionamiento	parking place	los estacionamientos	parking places
el lugar	place	los lugares	places

3.25 For nouns that end with the letter z, change the z to c and add -es.

la luz	light	las luces	lights
la vez	time (a specific time)	las veces	times
la voz	voice	las voces	voices
el avestruz	ostrich	los avestruces	ostriches

3.26 For nouns that have an accent on the last syllable, drop the accent for the plural.

la manifestación	demonstration	las manifestaciones	demonstrations
el jardín	garden	los jardines	gardens

3.27 When the accent comes on a weak vowel like u or i, do not drop the accent.

el ataúd	coffin	los ataúdes	coffins
el baúl	trunk, chest	los baúles	trunks, chests

3.28 When a word ends with an accented vowel such as -i or -u, keep the accent and add -es.

el rubí	ruby	los rubíes	rubies
el hindú	Hindu	los hindúes	Hindus

3.29 For compound nouns that end with -s, the ending never changes. The plural form is indicated by the article.

el rascacielos	skyscraper	los rascacielos	skyscrapers
el guardafango	fender	los guardafangos	fenders

3.30 For days of the week that end with -es, the ending never changes. In order to indicate the plural, make the article el plural.

el lunes	Monday	los lunes	Mondays

KAPLAN

3.31 If a noun has an accent mark written over the third to last syllable, it stays where it is in the plural form.

el cuadrúpede   four foot (animal)   los cuadrúpedes   four footed (animals)

3.32 Some nouns add an accent mark when they are made plural.

el joven   young man   los jóvenes   young men
(and women, for a mixed group)

NOUN ENDINGS

Some endings, called *augmentatives* and *diminutives*, do not change the gender of the noun. Rather, they reflect the gender of the noun.

3.33 Augmentatives frequently mean that somebody or something is clumsy, coarse, or vulgar. The common augmentatives are:

-ón	as in **solterón**	bachelor
-ona	as in **solterona**	spinster
-ota	as in **besota**	big kiss
-azo	as in **cañamazo**	burlap, coarse material
	or **machetazo**	struck with a machete
-uca	as in **pajarraco**	ugly, old bird
-acho	as in **populacho**	common people

3.34 Diminutives often indicate that something or somebody is cute or pretty, or small. Or, it is used as a term of endearment. The common diminutives are:

-ito, -ita	as in **casita**	little house
	or **chiquito**	little boy
-illo, -illa	as in **cartelillo**	little poster, placard
-uelo, -uela	as in **mozuela**	pretty, young girl

However, the meaning of the last diminutive depends on the noun it is attached to:

-uelo, -uela	**mujerzuela**	a common woman

THINGS TO REMEMBER

- All nouns are masculine or feminine. Each adjective must have an ending of the same gender and number as the noun it modifies.
- Many words that end in *-ama*, *-ema*, *-ima*, and *-eta* are masculine.
- Most nouns that end in *-a* are feminine.
- The letter *h* is never voiced in Spanish, so a noun that begins with a stressed *ha* will take a masculine article.

REVIEW QUESTIONS

Set A: In the following exercise write the correct article, *el*, *la*, *los*, or *las* in the blank.

1. _____ área
2. _____ empleado
3. _____ limpiabotas
4. _____ barco
5. _____ español
6. _____ pensamiento
7. _____ reina
8. _____ paisaje
9. _____ vacaciones
10. _____ especie

11. _____ criatura
12. _____ riesgo
13. _____ magos
14. _____ angustia
15. _____ hambre
16. _____ lentitud
17. _____ ópera
18. _____ autoridad
19. _____ garaje
20. _____ costumbre

Set B: Select the article that completes the structure of the sentence, according to the gender of the noun. When there are two blanks in one sentence, choose your answer for the second blank from the second set of choices.

1. _____ alba es la precursora del día.

   A) El   B) Los   C) La   D) Las

2. _____ elefante que escapó del jardín zoológico es muy viejo.

   A) El   B) Los   C) La   D) Las

3. El dictador mostró _____ crueldad más terrible.

   A) el   B) los   C) la   D) las

4. ¿Quién puede medir _____ sabiduría del viejo hechicero?

   A) el   B) los   C) la   D) las

5. No me gusta _____ luz tan fuerte y blanca de _____ nuevos faroles.

   A) el   B) los   C) la   D) las
   A) el   B) los   C) la   D) las

6. ¿Es éste _____ sacacorchos que necesitas para abrir la botella?

   A) el   B) los   C) la   D) las

7. _____ crisis de ___ trabajadores fueron muy dolorosas.

   A) El   B) Los   C) La   D) Las
   A) el   B) los   C) la   D) las

8. Nunca se sabe si _____ esfuerzos tan fuertes valen _____ pena.

A) el   B) los   C) la   D) las

A) el   B) los   C) la   D) las

9. En mi colegio tenemos _____ varones más aplicados de _____ ciudad.

A) el   B) los   C) la   D) las

A) el   B) los   C) la   D) las

10. No me gusta _____ incertidumbre de no tener _____ diploma en _____ mano al graduarme.

A) el   B) los   C) la   D) las

A) el   B) los   C) la   D) las

A) el   B) los   C) la   D) las

Set C: Pick out the word that does not fit because the gender is different from the others in the group.

1. A) serie   B) realidad   C) programa   D) deuda

2. A) cumbre   B) planeta   C) rama   D) clase

3. A) mano   B) papel   C) hijo   D) padre

4. A) hermana   B) ciudad   C) diosa   D) día

5. A) nuera   B) rey   C) actriz   D) pared

6. A) tema   B) duque   C) lápiz   D) mujer

7. A) norte   B) Amazonas   C) virtud   D) lunes

8. A) llave   B) hogar   C) ángel   D) estudiar

9. A) idea   B) ataúd   C) especie   D) dama

10. A) colibrí   B) misión   C) amistad   D) librería

Set D: Make the following nouns plural.

1. el mapa _____

2. el jardín _____

3. el día _____

4. el poema _____

5. la actriz _____

6. el rubí _____

7. el viernes _____

8. el parabrisas _____

9. la botella _____

10. el joven _____

ANSWERS AND EXPLANATIONS

Set A

1. [el área.]

See 3.18.

2. [el empleado.]

See 3.1.

3. [el, los limpiabotes.]

See 3.7.

4. [el barco.]

See See 3.1.

5. [el español.]

See 3.17. Remember that if the noun adds -*a*, then the masculine form will not have the final -*a*.

6. [el pensamiento.]

See 3.1.

7. [la reina.]

See 3.15

8. [el paisaje.]

See 3.1. Make sure you read all parts of the rule, not just the first part.

9. [las vacaciones.]

See 3.14.

10. [la especie.]

See 3.14.

11. [la criatura.]

See 3.13. Do not assume that every blank will contain some irregular noun.

12. [el riesgo.]

See 3.1.

13. [los magos.]

See 3.24.

14. [la angustia.]

See 3.13.

15. [el hambre.]

See 3.18. The *h* is silent, so the *-a* is stressed here.

16. [la lentitud.]

See 3.14.

17. [la ópera.]

See 3.13.

18. [la autoridad.]

See 3.14.

19. [el garaje.]

See 3.1.

20. [la costumbre.]

See 3.14.

Set B

1. (A)

La precursora tells you that *alba* is feminine, but since it begins with a stressed *-a*, it takes the masculine article.

2. (A)

The adjective *viejo* tells you that *elefante* is masculine.

3. (C)

Nouns that end with *-dad* are feminine.

4. (C)

Words that end with *-ía* are usually feminine.

5. (C) and (B)

The adjective *blanca* tells you that *luz* is feminine. And for the second blank, the adjective *nuevos* tells you that *faroles* is masculine.

6. (A)

The demonstrative pronoun *éste* tells you that *sacacorchos* is masculine singular.

7. (D) and (B)

For the first blank, the plural verb *fueron* tells you that the noun is plural, and the adjective *dolorosas* tells you that the noun is feminine. As for the second blank, words that end with -ores are usually masculine plural.

8. (B) and (C)

Esfuerzos ends with *-os*, a masculine plural ending. For the second blank *la* is correct because *pena* ends with *-a*.

9. (B) and (C)

The adjective *aplicados* tells you that *varones* is masculine plural. *La* is the answer for the second blank because nouns that end with *-dad* are usually feminine.

10. (C), (A), and (C)

Nouns that end with *-umbre* are usually feminine. Nouns that end in *-oma* are usually masculine. For the third blank, *mano* is an irregular gender for a noun that you just have to memorize.

Set C

1. (C)

el programa. Words that end with *-ama*, *-ema*, and *-ima* are masculine. They come from Greek words. See 3.2.

2. (B)

el planeta. Some words that end in *-eta* are feminine, such as *la meta*, but this word is masculine. See 3.2

3. (A)

la mano. See 3.1.

4. (D)

el día. See 3.2.

5. (B)

el rey. The feminine form of this word is *la reina*. See 3.3 and 3.16.

6. (D)

la mujer. See 3.29.

7. (C)

la virtud. See 3.14.

8. (A)

la llave. See 3.21.

9. (B)

el ataúd. See 3.12.

10. (A)

el colibrí. See 3.12.

Set D

1.

los mapas. See 3.24.

2.

los jardines. See 3.26.

3.

los días. See 3.24.

4.

los poemas. See 3.24.

5.

las actrices. See 3.25.

6.

los rubíes. See 3.28.

7.

los viernes. See 3.30.

8.

los parabrisas. See 3.29.

9.

los múltiples. See 3.31.

10.

los jóvenes. See 3.32.

Chapter 4: **Adjectives**

- Placement of Adjectives
- Shortening Some Adjectives
- Gender Agreement
- Forming Plurals
- Other Rules for Adjectives
- Comparing Nouns
- Demonstrative Adjectives
- Possessive Adjectives
- Indefinite Adjectives
- Articles with the Neuter Article *Lo*

Adjectives modify nouns. In other words, they describe nouns, or say something about the nouns. Adjectives frequently end with *-o, -a, -able, -al, -ante, -ible, -iente, -oso, -dor, -or,* or *-ar*.

There are two kinds of adjectives: quantitative and qualitative. *Quantitative* adjectives limit the number of the noun. Words like *first, one,* and *several* are quantitative adjectives. *Qualitative* adjectives describe any other quality about the noun. *Beautiful* and *smart* are qualitative adjectives. In Spanish, quantitative adjectives usually come *in front of the noun*, and qualitative adjectives come *after the noun*. So when you see a blank right before or after a noun, it is quite possibly an adjective.

Be careful when you translate words from English into Spanish: You could be making a mistake. Unlike in English, in Spanish you cannot use a present participle (an *-ing* word in English) as an adjective. You could not describe a Cheshire cat as a "smiling cat." If you see a present participle (*-ando* or *-iendo* in Spanish), it is a distracter, an answer you might think is right if you didn't know the rules of Spanish grammar. You can eliminate that word without having to do any translation.

In Spanish, nouns do not describe other nouns directly. Spanish uses a prepositional phrase instead. For example, "a basketball player" becomes "un jugador de baloncesto." It helps to understand some of these structural differences between English and Spanish.

PLACEMENT OF ADJECTIVES

4.1 Some adjectives change meaning depending on where they are placed in a sentence. When they precede a noun, they mean something other than when they follow a noun.

	Before the Noun	After the Noun
antiguo, -a, -os, -as	old (former), old-time	old (ancient)
cierto, -a, -os, -as	certain	sure, true
grande, gran	great, grand	large, big
mismo _a mosmo_	same	him-, her-, yourself
nuevo _a vas vos_	another, different	new
pobre _es_	unfortunate	poor
simple _es_	simple, mere	silly

> Adjectives usually come right before or after the nouns they modify.

Before a noun, these adjectives imply that the noun is no different from all others like it. After a noun, they describe something about the noun that makes it different from all others like it.

Este pobre chico no tiene padres.   Este chico pobre no tiene padres.
This unfortunate (poor) boy has no parents.   This poor (penniless) boy has no parents.

In English some adjectives have more than one meaning. In the case of *poor* above, you would need more context to know the difference between the two sentences. But in Spanish the meaning is clear because of where the adjective is placed.

SHORTENING SOME ADJECTIVES

4.2 Some adjectives drop the final -*o* when they come before a masculine singular noun. This is called *apocopation*.

uno	un libro
bueno	un buen chico
malo	un mal programa
primero	el primer dia
tercero	el tercer piso
alguno	algún momento
ninguno	ningún deporte

But when a preposition like *de* comes between the adjective and the noun, do not drop the -*o* from the adjective.

Uno de los muchachos vino.	Un muchacho vino.
One of the boys came.	One boy came.
El primero de los muchachos salió.	El primer muchacho salió.
The first (one) of the boys left.	The first boy left.

Other adjectives that are shortened when they come before a noun are *grande*, *ciento*, and *Santo*.

Grande becomes *gran* before any singular noun, masculine or feminine.

Ella vive en una gran casa.	Ella vive en una casa grande.
She lives in a great (wonderful) house.	She lives in a large house.
Trabaja en un gran edificio.	Trabaja en un edificio grande.
He works in a great (marvelous) building.	He works in a large building.

Ciento becomes *cien* before a noun of either gender and number, and before the numbers *mil* and *millones*. Use the full form in front of any other number (*ciento doce*).

Cien músicos tocaban.
100 musicians were playing.

La raza humana cambió mucho en los últimos cien mil años.
The human race changed a lot in the last 100,000 years.

Santo is shortened before masculine names of saints, except for those beginning with *To-* or *Do-*. Think of the names of some U.S. cities: Santa Barbara, San Antonio, and San Francisco. But Santo Domingo, the capital of the Dominican Republic, and Santo Tomás show the exceptions.

GENDER AGREEMENT

4.3 Adjectives must always have endings that agree with the gender and number of the nouns they modify. If a noun is masculine singular, all the adjectives that go with it must have masculine singular endings.

> Adjectives must agree in gender and number with the nouns they go with.

As you can guess, the hard part is knowing the gender of the nouns. Try looking at the other words in the sentence, such as definite articles (*el, la, los, las*), indefinite articles (*un, una, unos, unas*), or demonstrative adjectives (*este, esta, estos, estas*), a proper name, or a pronoun. Remember that definite and indefinite articles are adjectives, too, so they have to agree in gender and number with the nouns they modify.

4.4 Adjectives that end in -o change to -a to go with feminine nouns; with masculine singular nouns, they stay the same.

Miguel es un amigo bueno.   Ángela es una amiga buena.
Miguel is a good friend.   Ángela is a good friend.

Miguel es un amigo bueno y guapo.   Angela es una amiga buena y bonita.
Miguel is a good and handsome friend.   Ángela is a good and a pretty friend.

In English, the words *good*, *handsome*, *pretty*, and *friend* have no gender. But in Spanish, since all nouns are masculine or feminine, all the adjectives must agree with them in gender.

4.5 Adjectives that end with -e stay the same for both masculine and feminine singular nouns.

Miguel es un alumno inteligente.   Ángela es una alumna inteligente.
Miguel is an intelligent student.   Ángela is an intelligent student.

In the first sentence above, you can tell that the noun is masculine by the -o on the end of *alumno*, so you have to use *un*. In the second sentence, you can tell by the -a on the end of *alumna* that the noun is feminine, so you have to use *una*.

El elefante es un animal enorme.   La reina es una mujer prudente.
The elephant is an enormous animal.   The queen is a prudent woman.

Miguel es un estudiante inteligente.   Ángela es una estudiante inteligente.
Miguel is an intelligent student.   Ángela is an intelligent student.

In the sentences above, the only way to determine whether you need to use *un* or *una* is by the student's name. Also, notice that *inteligente, enorme*, and *prudente* do not change because they end with -e.

4.6 For adjectives that end with -dor, add -a to make the feminine form.

Miguel es un estudiante trabajador.   Rosario es una estudiante trabajadora.
Miguel is a hard working student.   Rosario is a hard working student.

Do not be fooled by the -o ending on the name *Rosario*. The word *una* tells you that the noun *estudiante* is feminine, so you have to use *trabajadora* to agree with a feminine singular noun.

FORMING PLURALS

4.7 For adjectives that end with -o, -a, or -e, simply add an -s to make the plural forms agree with plural nouns.

Miguel y Ramón son alumnos buenos.
Miguel and Ramón are good students.

Both students are boys, so the noun ends in -os and the adjective does, too.

Ángela y María son alumnas buenas.
Ángela and María are good students.

Both students are girls, so the noun ends in -*as*. The adjective is also feminine plural.

Miguel y Ramón son alumnos inteligentes.
Miguel and Ramón are intelligent students.

The noun *alumnos* is masculine plural, but since the adjective ends with -*e*, you can only add -*s* to make it plural. The -*e* does not change.

Ángela y María son alumnas inteligentes.
Ángela and María are intelligent students.

Miguel y Ángela son alumnos buenos.
Miguel and Ángela are good students.

When there is a group of mixed gender, use the masculine form of nouns and adjectives.

Miguel y Ángela son alumnos inteligentes.
Miguel and Ángela are intelligent students.

Since the students are a boy and a girl, the masculine plural form of the noun *alumnos* is used. But since *inteligente* ends with -*e*, just add -*s* to make the word agree with the noun *alumnos*.

4.8 For all adjectives that end with a consonant, add -*es* to make the plural form of the adjective. It makes no difference what the gender of the noun is.

> To make plural those adjectives that end with a consonant, add -*es*.

Miguel y Ramón son alumnos populares.   **Ángela y María son alumnas populares.**
Miguel and Ramón are popular students.   Ángela and María are popular students.

OTHER RULES FOR ADJECTIVES

4.9 Adjectives are often formed from past participles (words ending in -*ado* or -*ido*). Even though a past participle is a principle part of a verb, it can be used as an adjective to describe nouns. When you see the past participle among possible answer choices, see if it is used as a verbal or an adjective.

Las señoras sentadas a la mesa charlaban.
The ladies seated at the table were chatting.

Sentadas comes from the verb *sentar*, but here it describes the ladies and is not used as a verb.

4.10 Some nouns have deceptive endings. Mano ends in -*o*, but is feminine (*la mano*). Similarly, nouns with the endings -*ama*, -*ema*, -*ima*, -*oma*, -*mna*, and *el día* seem to be feminine, but they're not. Use adjectives that agree with the gender of the noun and do not always rely on the ending of the noun to tell you which adjective form to use.

> Juan escribió un tema largo.
> Juan wrote a long theme.

Tema is masculine. You can tell that you need a masculine adjective by the article *un* in front of the noun.

> Juan escribió un tema interesante.
> Juan wrote an interesting theme.

In the sentence above, you simply have to know the gender of the noun to use *un*, because there are no clues in the ending of *interesante*.

> Juan escribe con la mano izquierda.
> John writes with his left hand.

> Los lunes parecen días muy largos.
> Mondays seem like long days.

Once again, you have to know the gender of *días* in order to make the adjective *largos* agree.

4.11 For nouns that begin with a stressed or an accented -*a* that take *el* in the singular form, make all the adjectives feminine (in spite of the article *el*).

> No me gusta nadar en el agua fría.
> I don't like to swim in cold water.

> El águila negra extendió el ala larga.
> The black eagle extended his long wing.

4.12 Some compound nouns are always plural, but take a singular article (*el*) for singular forms. Sometimes another word in the sentence will tell you whether to use a singular or plural adjective.

> El estudiante buscó el sacapuntas viejo que sabía estaba allí.
> The student looked for the old pencil sharpener that he knew was there.

In this sentence you would see a blank for either *el* or for *viejo*. These would indicate that the singular article *el* or the masculine singular adjective *viejo* was required.

COMPARING NOUNS

4.13 When two unequal nouns are compared or contrasted, use adjectives to indicate the difference. The adjective forms used in comparisons still follow the basic rules above. You can also use adverbs to compare actions, but we will look at that grammar in chapter 6.

4.14 To compare unequal nouns, use the adjectives *más* ("more"), or *menos* ("less") along with other adjectives. In Spanish there is no ending *-er* or *-ier*. The word *que* means "than" with a few exceptions.

> Mi hermano es más alto que mi hermana. Mi hermana es más alta que mi hermano.
> My brother is taller than my sister. My sister is taller than my brother.

For the first sentence, *alto* has an -o on the end to make it masculine singular to agree with *hermano*. For the second sentence, *alta* ends with -a to agree with *hermana*. Sometimes in a reading passage, the only way to know the gender of the narrator, or a person, is to notice the gender of an adjective used to describe him or her. That might be an important thing to notice!

To say that someone is shorter, you could also say *menos alto* instead of *más corto*. Think of the English expression "more or less." In Spanish you might hear, *Más o menos y más menos que más*, which means "More or less, and more less than more."

4.15 The verb used to make comparisons of inequality is most often a linking verb, a form of the verb "to be." But be prepared to recognize comparisons used with other verbs.

> Construyeron edificios más altos que las casas del barrio.
> They built taller buildings than the houses in the neighborhood.

Houses are a kind of building; one group of buildings is taller than the other.

4.16 When two groups of the same thing are compared, the noun may be omitted the second time. In these cases the adjective is used as a noun.

> Construyeron edificios más altos que los otros del barrio.
> They built taller buildings than the others in the neighborhood.

Since *los otros* is the same gender and number as *edificios*, you know it refers to *edificios* and the two are being compared. This is an elliptical use because the second noun is omitted. Adjectives are often used this way in order to avoid repetition of a noun.

> ¿Te gustan las blusas rojas o las blancas?
> Prefiero las blancas.

> Do you like the red blouses or the white ones?
> I prefer the white ones.

The adjectives used in this way will always agree in gender and number with the nouns that they describe.

4.17 When "more than" or "less than" is followed by a number, use *de*. However, when using the negative form, such as "no more" than, use *que*.

> En la clase había más de treinta estudiantes.
> In the class there were more than 30 students.

> En la clase no había más que treinta estudiantes.
> In the class there were no more than 30 students.

> Use *de* instead of *que* when you are comparing numbers. But use *que* if the expression is negative, i.e., *no más que*.

4.18 When two nouns are equal in quality, the structure is also invariable. You will also see this structure with adverbs. For the expression "as ... as" use a form of *tanto* that agrees with the noun for the first "as." Use *como* for the second "as."

> Tengo tantos libros como Vd.
> I have as many books as you.

Tantos above is masculine plural to agree with *libros*. *Tanto* always means "as much," or "as many." *Como* can mean a lot of things, but when used with a form of *tanto* means "as."

> La muchacha venía aquí tantos días como su hermana.
> The girl came here as many days as her sister.

> La muchacha sabía tanta biología como su hermano.
> The girl knew as much biology as her brother.

4.19 When you want to say that something is the "best" or the "greatest in its category," use an article (*el, la, los, las*) plus *más* or *menos* before the adjective. The English equivalent would be a word ending with *-est*. (Additionally, you can add *de*, which, in this structure only, means "in.")

> When comparing things that are equal, use *tan* or *tanto ... como*.

> Estos edificios son los más altos de la ciudad.
> These buildings are the tallest in the city.

Sometimes the only difference between the superlative and a comparative structure is the article. In these cases the comparative is implied, not explicitly stated.

> Estos edificios son más altos (que los otros).
>
> These buildings are taller (than the others).

> Estos edificios son los más altos (del barrio).
>
> These buildings are the tallest (in the neighborhood).

4.20 There are some important exceptions to the comparative and superlative adjectives given above.

bueno	good
mejor	better
el, la mejor los, las mejores	the best

Este estudiante es bueno.
This student is good.

Este estudiante es mejor (que otros).
This student is better (than others).

Este estudiante es el mejor (de todos).
Esta estudiante es la mejor (de todas).
This student is the best.

Este and *esta* (demonstrative adjectives) and the article before *mejor* will tell you whether the student is male or female. In both places the adjectives have to agree with the gender of the noun. When a noun ends with an -*e* or a consonant, then adjectives communicate important information.

> When something is the greatest or the best, use an article + *más* (or *menos*) + *de* before the noun. Think of *de* as meaning "in."

Estos estudiantes son los mejores (de todos).
These students are the best (of all).

Estas estudiantes son las mejores (de todos los estudiantes).
These students are the best (of all the students).

When *mejor* is used to describe somebody or something directly, it comes before the noun.

Ese chico es mi mejor amigo.
That boy is my best friend.

malo	bad
peor	worse
el, la peor los, las peores	worst, the worst

Ese chiste es malo.
That joke is bad.

Ese chiste es peor (que los otros).
That joke is worse (than others).

Ese chiste es el peor (de todos).
That joke is the worst (of all).

Estos cantantes son los peores (de todo el concierto).
These singers are the worst (in the whole concert).

Esas canciones son las peores (de todas).
These songs are the worst (of all songs).

When *peor* or *peores* is used to directly modify a noun, it comes in front of the noun.

El peor día de mi vida ocurrió ayer.
The worst day of my life occurred yesterday.

For the following group of adjectives, *mayor* refers to age in years or status. When you want to use *grande* to refer to size or height (physical aspects), use *más grande* or *menos grande*.

grande	great, big
mayor	greater, older
el, la mayor los, las mayores	the greatest, the oldest

Mi hermano es mayor (que su hermano).
My brother is older (than your brother).

Mi hermano es el mayor del grupo.
My brother is the oldest in the group.

Mis hermanos son mayores que mis hermanas.
My brothers are older than my sisters.

When *mayor* or *mayores* directly modifies a noun, it usually comes after the noun.

Mi hermano mayor ganó el partido con su gol.
My little brother won the game with his goal.

El/la menor and *los/las menores* refer to age or status. When you want to refer to size or height (physical aspects), use *más pequeño* (*-a, -os, -as*), or *menos pequeño* (*-a, -os, -as*).

pequeño	small
menor	minor, lesser, younger
el, la menor los, las menores	the least, the youngest

Ese profesor es el mayor de la facultad.
That teacher is the oldest on the faculty.

Esa estudiante es la mayor de su clase.
That student is the greatest in her class.

Simón Bolívar fue un gran hombre.
Simón Bolívar was a great man.

Ese señor es más grande que el otro.
That man is larger than the other (man).

Mi gata es más pequeña que su perro.
My cat is smaller than your dog.

4.21 When no comparison is involved, use muy plus an adjective. Alternatively, use the ending -ísimo (-a, -os, -as). Drop the last vowel on the adjective and add the ending.

> When there is no comparison between words, and something is "tops," look for -isimo.

La película es muy buena.
The movie is very good.

El hombre es muy alto.
The man is very tall.

La película es malísima.
The movie is very bad.

El jugador de baloncesta es altísimo.
The basketball player is very tall.

If the adjective ends with -co, change it to -qu. If it ends with -g, change it to to -gu. If it ends with -z, change it to -c when adding -ísimo. Rico becomes riquísimo, largo becomes larguísimo, and feroz becomes ferocísimo.

Ese restaurante está cerquísima.
That restaurant is very close.

El suelo de la cocina estaba sucísimo.
The kitchen floor was very dirty.

DEMONSTRATIVE ADJECTIVES

4.22 Demonstrative pronouns are easy to learn in Spanish.

este, esta	this
estos, estas	these
ese, esa	that (close by)
esos, esas	those (close by)
aquel, aquella	that (farther away)
aquellos, aquellas	those (farther away)

There are two forms for *that*: They indicate a difference in proximity.

Prefiero ese coche más que aquel coche.
I prefer that car (closer to me) to that car (way over there).

By selecting *ese* and *aquel*, you are saying that neither car is very close to you.

Demonstrative adjectives look exactly like pronouns, except that pronouns have accent marks.

POSSESSIVE ADJECTIVES

4.23 Some Spanish words that show possession indicate gender while others do not. And possessive adjectives agree with the nouns they modify (the person or thing that is possessed), not the person or thing that possesses something.

	Singular		Plural	
1st person	*mi, mis*	my	*nuestro, -a, -os, -as*	our
2nd person	*tu, tus*	your	*vuestro, -a, -os, -as*	your
3rd person	*su, sus*	his, her, its, your	*su, sus*	their, your

The singular forms and the third person plural do not indicate gender, but you can make them plural. The first and second person plural forms do indicate gender and number.

In the third person forms, two Spanish words are used to describe five different English words. Don't panic: You can usually determine what the word means from its context. Be careful in reading selections, however; make sure you can find the noun to which the possessive refers.

> **Puso su libro en la mesa.**
> He put his book on the table.
> She put her book on the table.
> He/She put your books on the table. (singular or plural "you")
> He/She put their books on the table.

> **Tomó sus libros.**
> He (she, you) took his books.
> He (she, you) took her books.
> He (she, you) took your books. (singular or plural "you")
> He (she, you) took their books.

Look at the difference between the second person and the third person possessive. This little difference can give you valuable information for a grammar question, like when you have to pick the correct verb form for another part of the sentence.

> **Miguel, pídele a tu papá el dinero.**
> Ask your father for the money.

If *pídele* were left blank, you would have to select the correct verb form. In this case you would want the familiar *tú* command. If this were a declarative sentence, there would be other correct answers, but since Miguel is set off by a comma, the name indicates that someone is talking directly to him. *Tu* tells you to use the familiar singular command form.

4.24 When a possessive adjective follows a noun, it takes a more emphatic form. You have heard it before in the expression "Dios mío." This, too, agrees in gender and number with the noun, and not the person or thing doing the possessing.

Singular	Plural
mío, mía, míos, mías	*nuestro, nuestra nuestros, nuestras*
tuyo, tuya, tuyos, tuyas	*vuestro, vuestra vuestros, vuestras*
suyo, suya, suyos, suyas	*suyo, suya suyos, suyas*

The context will indicate whether *suyo*, etc., refers to a singular or a plural possessor.

Esos amigos suyos no me llamaron antes de venir.
Those friends of yours didn't call before coming.

Estas canciones nuestras son mejores.
These songs of ours are better.

When you omit the noun and add an article to these emphatic forms of possessive adjectives, they become possessive pronouns.

INDEFINITE ADJECTIVES

4.25 There are positive and negative forms of indefinite adjectives. The negative form of an adjective is used when there is a negative in front of the verb. Ignore the rule that you would use in English. Double negatives are indeed the rule in Spanish.

Alguno and *ninguno* are indefinite adjectives. They always refer to a noun. They must agree in gender and number with the nouns they refer to.

Positive	Negative
algún, alguno, alguna	*ningún, ninguno, ninguna*
algunos, algunas	*ningunos, ningunas*

No vino ninguno de de los chicos.
None of the children came.

Algunos de los chicos vinieron.
Some of the children came.

¿Viste al presidente alguna vez?
Did you see the president at any time?

—No, no lo vi ninguna vez.
—No, I didn't see him at any time.

Or you can use a negative adjective in front of the verb, and it means the same thing.

Ningún chico vino esta mañana.
No boy came this morning.

¿Vino algún viajero esta mañana?
—No, no vino ninguno.
Did any traveler come this morning?
—No, none came.

ARTICLES WITH THE NEUTER ARTICLE *LO*

4.26 When an adjective is used with the neuter article *lo*, the adjective functions as a noun. The entire phrase refers to an abstract idea or concept.

Lo bueno del asunto es que aprendieron algo.
The good thing about the matter is that they learned something.

A veces es difícil distinguir entre lo bueno y lo malo.
Sometimes it is hard to distinguish between the good and the bad.

Since there is no noun to which the adjective refers, use *lo* plus the masculine singular form.

THINGS TO REMEMBER

- Adjectives modify nouns. In Spanish, adjectives often end with -o, -a, -able, -al, -ante, -ible, -iente, -oso, -dor, -or, or -ar.

- In Spanish, you cannot use an -ing word as an adjective as you do in English. You cannot say "a frowning boy." If you see this in an answer choice, eliminate it. It cannot be correct.

- Use de and not que when you compare numbers, as in, "There were more than 20 balloons." But use que if the expression is negative: "There were no more than 15 poodles."

- The difference between ese and aquel—which both mean that—is one of proximity. Ese is closer than aquel.

REVIEW QUESTIONS

Set A: In the following sentences, select the correct adjective form.

1. Cuando llegué al aeropuerto, vi ___ actividad.

   A) mucho   B) mucha   C) muchos   D) muchas

2. Anoche vi ___ programa interesante en la televisión.

   A) un   B) una   C) unos   D) unas

3. Mi paraguas ____ me protegió de la lluvia.

   A) rojo   B) roja   C) rojos   D) rojas

4. ____ mil aficionados asistieron al partido.

   A) Cien   B) Ciento   C) Cientos   D) Doscientas

5. Los amigos se vieron ___ veces ese verano.

   A) mucho   B) mucha   C) muchos   D) muchas

6. No vimos a ____ de los muchachos ayer.

   A) ningún   B) ninguno   C) alguno   D) algunos

7. ¡Qué ___ idea venir sin llamar!

   A) mal   B) malo   C) mala   D) malas

8. ¡Cuidado! Hoy es el ___ de abril.

   A) primer   B) primero   C) primera   D) primeros

9. Las ____ personas que llamen recibirán el premio.

   A) primer   B) primero   C) primera   D) primeras

10. Las mil y ___ noches cuenta unas leyendas árabes.

    A) un   B) una   C) unos   D) unas

11. Comieron porque tenían ___ hambre.

    A) mucho   B) mucha   C) muchos   D) muchas

12. Nunca hemos visto a ____ gente en un concierto.

    A) tan   B) tanto   C) tanta   D) tantos

13. Los muchachos saludaron a ___ amigo cuando lo vieron.

    A) su   B) sus   C) suyo   D) suyos

14. No es agradable nadar en el agua _____ del Océano Ártico.

    A) frío   B) fría   C) fríos   D) frías

15. Elena tiene sólo nueve años, es la ___ de sus hermanos.

    A) menos   B) menor   C) más   D) poca

16. Cuando llegamos a ___ Salvador, buscamos al agente.

    A) San   B) Santo   C) Santa   D) Santos

17. Una característica de las familias latinas es que son muy _____.

    A) unido   B) unida   C) unidos   D) unidas

Set B: For the following exercise, cover the English and see if you can translate the Spanish.

1. Cierta mañana de abril vi un espectáculo raro.

   On a certain (particular) day in April, I saw a rare sight.

2. La Gran Bretaña tuvo un imperio muy grande.

   Great Britain had a very large empire.

3. El pobre Juan tuvo muy mala suerte aquel día.

   Poor (unfortunate) John had very bad luck that day.

4. Fue un simple error de una muchacha simple.

   It was a mere mistake of a silly child.

5. Cuando vio a su antiguo novio, se sintió triste.

   When she saw her former boy friend, she felt sad.

6. ¿Quién lo hizo si no fue el ladrón mismo?

   Who did it if it was not the thief himself?

7. Ahora empezamos una nueva página en nuestra historia.

   Now we begin another page in our history.

8. Los nazcas tenían una civilización muy antigua.

   The Nazca had a very ancient civilization.

9. A veces he tenido la misma idea.

   At times I have had the same idea.

10. En los dibujos, Papá Noel es un hombre grande.

    In pictures, Santa Clause is a big man.

ANSWERS AND EXPLANATIONS

Set A

1. (B)

All nouns that end with -*dad* are feminine, so *mucha* is the answer. You can eliminate the plural forms (C) and (D) easily because you can tell that the noun is singular.

2. (A)

If you did not know that *programa* is masculine, you should review all masculine nouns that end with -*ma*. See 4.10.

3. (A)

Be careful of nouns that end in a plural form that are really masculine singular. *Mi* is singular, so you needed a singular adjective. You can immediately eliminate (C) and (D). See 4.12.

4. (A)

If you did not remember when to shorten *ciento*, go back and review it. See 4.2.

5. (D)

Veces is the plural form of *vez*, and it is feminine. *Vez* is a very common noun, so make sure you know it.

6. (B)

This adjective refers to *muchachos*, so you want a masculine form. Since there is a negative (No) before the verb, you have to use a form of *ninguno*. That means (C) and (D) are out. Do not shorten *ninguno*, though, because there is a word (*de*) between *ninguno* and the noun. See 4.25.

7. (C)

Idea is feminine, so you have to use *mala*. You know that the noun is singular, so (D) is out.

8. (B)

This is the date for the first of the month, so you have to use the full masculine singular form. But, also, since there is no noun directly after the blank, use the full form. See 4.2.

9. (D)

The blank is followed by a feminine plural noun, so you need a feminine plural form for the ordinal number. See 4.2.

10. (B)

This one is not shortened because the noun is feminine, *noches*. See 4.2.

11. (B)

Although *hambre* takes a masculine singular article (*el*), it's actually a feminine noun. See 3.18 in chapter 3.

12. (C)

For the gender of nouns like *gente*, See 3.21 in chapter 3. For the form to use, See 4.18.

13. (A)

Since the posessive adjective comes before the noun, you know to use a form of *su*. The adjective modifies *amigo*, not *muchachos*, so *su* is the answer. See 4.23.

14. (B)

This kind of question is common on the test, so make sure you know the feminine nouns that take a masculine singular article. Do not be fooled by the article *el*. See 3.18 in chapter 3.

15. (B)

Menor is the only possible answer here. (A) and (C) are adverbs. (D) is an adjective, but makes no sense here. The reference to age as well as the superlative structure of the article and the preposition *de* are clues that you need *menor*. Sometimes you'll see the adverb *más* modify an adjective, but you will not see it used in place of an adjective in a superlative structure.

16. (A)

In front of names beginning with anything except *-To* or *-Do*, *Santo* is shortened to *San.* See 4.2.

17. (D)

There are two nouns in this sentence, but since the verb son is plural, the adjective must refer to *familias*.

Chapter 5: **Verbs**

- Present Participles
- Past Participles
- Infinitives
- Conjugated Verbs
- Other Verb Forms
- Irregular Verbs
- Verbs in the Subjunctive Form
- Passive Voice Structures

Verbs are at the very heart of a sentence, so you should know how to use verbs well. On the SAT Subject Test: Spanish, you won't need to produce correct verb forms; you'll just have to be able to recognize the correct forms and their application. That means knowing how to conjugate verbs in any given tense. For instance, an accent on the final -o of a verb form makes it a preterite form of an -ar verb. Without an accent, it is a present indicative, first person singular form.

Verbs have four forms: present participle; past participle, infinitive, and the conjugated form.

PRESENT PARTICIPLES

5.1 A present participle is an -ing word in English. For -ar verbs, present participles end with -ando. For -er and -ir verbs, they end with -iendo. In Spanish, the present participle is called a gerundio.

5.2 A present participle can act as a verbal or as an adverb. First, it can be a verbal in progressive verb forms. We will address this in section 5.19.

Second, it can function as an adverb (though never as an adjective or noun, as it does in English). As an adverb, the present participle frequently follows verbs of motion, such as *salir* or *llegar*, and the verbs *andar*, *ir*, *seguir* and *continuar*. When used this way, it describes the action of the verb.

> **El chico vino corriendo para ver qué traía su padre.**
> The boy came running to see what his father was bringing.

Especially after *andar*, *ir*, *seguir*, and *continuar*, the verb indicates continuity of action, often translated as "to keep on" or "to go around -*ing*."

> **Los estudiantes seguían trabajando cuando entró el profe.**
> The students kept on working when the professor came in.

> **Las chicas andaban mirando cosas en las vitrinas.**
> The girls went around looking at things in the windows.

> **Muchachos, sigan escribiendo.**
> Children, keep on writing.

Sometimes the present participle indicates simultaneous action.

> **Escribió el tema, escuchando música popular.**
> He wrote the theme while listening to pop music.

> **Sonriendo, aceptó el trofeo.**
> Smiling, he accepted the trophy.

When expressing cause or condition, the present participle often comes at the beginning of the sentence, though it can be found in the middle.

> **Siendo hombre honesto, creyó todo lo que le dijeron.**
> Being an honest man, he believed everything they told him.

> **Estando en casa solo, no invitó a sus amigos a su casa.**
> Since he was home alone, he did not invite his friends over.

> **Muchos aprenden otra lengua mirando programas de televisión.**
> Many people learn another language watching TV programs.

> **Trabajando rápidamente, se acabará pronto con el proyecto.**
> Working quickly, one will finish quickly with the project.

In English, one could restate these last two examples by inserting the preposition *by* before the present participle, as in "By watching TV programs," or "By working quickly." But in Spanish no preposition is used in front of the present participle, because in such a case, you would have to use an infinitive.

PAST PARTICIPLES

5.3 A past participle is a word frequently ending in *-ed* in English. In Spanish most past participles end with *-ado* for *-ar* verbs, and *-ido* for *-er* and *-ir* verbs. Irregular past participles are listed in Section 5.20.

5.4 Past participles are only used verbally when they follow the verb *haber* as part of a compound (perfect) tense. Otherwise, they are used as adjectives, adjectives used as nouns, and in absolute constructions. See chapter Four on adjectives.

INFINITIVES

5.5 There are three kinds of infinitive endings: *-ar*, *-er*, and *-ir*. In English, the infinitive form consists of two words: "to + the verb." In Spanish, the infinitive form is one word, ending in *-ar, -er,* or *-ir.*

5.6 Infinitives are mainly used as nouns, either as subjects of verbs, or objects of verbs. As nouns, infinitives often correspond to *-ing* words in English.

Ver es creer.
Seeing is believing.

Escuchar la música es muy agradable.
Listening to the music is very pleasant.

Quiero aprender español.
I want to learn Spanish.

Debemos estudiar para aprender bien.
We ought to study in order to learn well.

Mis maestros me hicieron hacer la tarea.
My teachers made me do my homework.

Es difícil aprender toda esta materia rápido.
It's difficult to learn all this material quickly.

Another option is to use the infinitive after *al*, meaning "upon."

Al escuchar las noticias, sonrió alegremente.
Upon hearing the news, she smiled happily.

At times the infinitive is used with an indirect object pronoun to replace a dependent noun clause using the subjunctive. See section 5.29 for a more complete discussion of this use.

Infinitives are often used as the object of prepositions. Always use an infinitive when a verb follows a preposition.

> **Salí sin hablarles.**
> I left without speaking to them.

> **Para estar en buena forma, coma una dieta saludable.**
> In order to stay in shape, eat a healthy diet.

After the expressions *tener que*, *(haber) que*, *nada que*, *poco que*, *mucho que*, and *algo* you can use an infinitive. These are idiomatic expressions, and exceptions to the rule that after *que* you have to conjugate the infinitive.

> **Para salir bien, hay que tener confianza.**
> In order to do well, one has to have confidence.

> **Tienes que decirmelo todo; no puedo ir.**
> You have to tell me everything; I can't go.

> **Date prisa, tienes mucho que hacer.**
> Hurry up, you have a lot to do.

Infinitives are commonly used for commands, ads, or signs, concerning public health, traffic regulations, or the like.

> **No botar basura.**
> Don't litter.

> **No fumar.**
> No smoking.

> **¡Perder peso rápido! Adelgazará sin esfuerzo con nuestro programa.**
> Lose weight quickly! You'll slim down without effort with our program.

After a verb of perception, an infinitive can function as an adverb.

> **Últimamente lo vi correr calle abajo.**
> The last I saw of him was running down the street.

> **Les oí gritar al ver a su cantante favorito.**
> I heard them screaming upon seeing their favorite singer.

Finally, there is such a thing as a perfect infinitive. This form is used when the subject of the two actions is the same, but one action happens before the other in the past.

> **Debes de habérmelo dicho antes.**
> You ought to have told it to me before.

> **Nunca pareció haberle molestado ni un momento.**
> It never seemed to have bothered him even a moment.

CONJUGATED VERBS

5.7 There are five simple tenses in Spanish: present, preterite, imperfect, future and conditional. Combining *estar* with the present participle of each of these, you can form the progressive forms: present progressive, past progressive, future progressive and conditional progressive. Combining *haber* with the past participle, you can form the compound tenses.

To conjugate all verbs in the simple tenses, remove the infinitive ending (*-ar*, *-er*, -or *-ir*), and add the appropriate ending. This works for all tenses except the future and conditional. Add future and conditional endings to all regular, stem changing, and spelling change infinitives. Irregular verbs are different and you just have to memorize those forms. Use the following key:

1st person singular:	yo (I)
2nd person singular:	tú (you, familiar)
3rd person singular:	él (he, it, masculine)
	ella (she, it, feminine)
	Ud. or Vd.* (you, masculine or feminine, polite)
1st person plural:	nosotros/nosotras (we)
2nd person plural:	vosotros/vosotras** (you, familiar)
3rd person plural:	ellos (they, masculine)
	ellas (they, feminine)
	Uds. or Vds. (You, masculine and feminine, polite)

> Verbs can be divided into the following categories: regular, irregular, orthographic (spelling change), and radical (stem changing).

*Usted is abbreviated either as Ud. or Vd.

**This form is used mainly in Spain.

Chapter 7 will review more about the differences between the second and third persons singular and plural.

Present Tense

5.8 The present tense endings for each conjugation are:

	Singular			Plural		
	1st	2nd	3rd	1st	2nd	3rd
-ar	-o	-as	-a	-amos	-áis	-an
-er	-o	-es	-e	-emos	-éis	-en
-ir	-o	-es	-e	-imos	-ís	-en

As you can see, all the first person endings are -o, and all the -er and -ir endings are the same, except for the first and second persons plural.

> The only forms that have accent marks in the present are the second person plural forms.

Also notice that all the endings (except for the first person singular) begin with the same vowel as the infinitive ending. This is important to notice when you're trying to determine whether a verb form is in the indicative or the subjunctive. In most cases, you can also tell what the infinitive is from the ending used.

This simple tense can have several meanings in English. Look carefully at what the simple verb *hablo* can mean:

hablo =   I speak, talk, I am speaking, talking, I do speak, talk,
                 Am I speaking, talking...? Do I speak, talk...?

Exactly what a verb means within a sentence will depend on the context, so make sure to read the test questions carefully.

Preterite Tense

5.9 The preterite tense endings for each conjugation are:

	Singular			Plural		
	1st	2nd	3rd	1st	2nd	3rd
-ar	-é	-aste	-ó	-amos	-asteis	-aron
-er	-í	-iste	-ió	-imos	-isteis	-ieron
-ir	-í	-iste	-ió	-imos	-isteis	-ieron

Notice that the -er and -ir endings are exactly the same. When you compare the present and preterite endings, you'll see that the first person plural endings for -ar and -ir verbs are the same for the first person plural forms. When you come across these similar forms in a question, look at the context to see what tense is appropriate.

The first and third person singular preterite tense endings all have an accent except for irregular forms. In contrast, the first person singular present tense ending -o does not. The only difference between the first person singular present and the third person singular preterite, -ar verb form, is a little accent! Sometimes one or the other of these two forms will be a distracter among the possible answers, so remember that the preterite has the accent.

Imperfect Tense

5.10 The imperfect tense is the other simple past tense in Spanish. The endings are easy to learn.

	Singular			Plural		
	1st	2nd	3rd	1st	2nd	3rd
-ar	*-aba*	*-abas*	*-aba*	*-ábamos*	*-abais*	*-aban*
-er	*-ía*	*-ías*	*-ía*	*-íamos*	*-íais*	*-ían*
-ir	*-ía*	*-ías*	*-ía*	*-íamos*	*-íais*	*-ían*

As in the preterite, the *-er* and *-ir* conjugations have the same endings. In the *-ar* endings, only the first person plural form has an accent. This tense is hard to confuse with any other.

5.11 Distinguishing between the preterite and the imperfect can be difficult.
In many cases the two past tenses are translated the same way, but are not really interchangeable. Both may be grammatically correct in a given context, but may mean different things. It can be quite difficult to know which one to use. In a long selection, you will need to consider the whole context before deciding which one to use.

The preterite is called a *narrative* tense, while the imperfect is a *descriptive* tense. The preterite retells a past event that is over and done. When the speaker selects the preterite, he communicates that whatever was happening before no longer takes place. The preterite implies a specific beginning and end to an action or situation. The period of time does not have to be short, but the action does have to be completed.

> Los moros vivieron en España por casi ochocientos años. (preterite)
> The Moors lived in Spain for almost 800 years.

> Los moros vivían en España cuando empezó la Reconquista. (imperfect)
> The Moors were living in Spain when the Reconquest began.

In both cases above, the Moors no longer live in Spain, however each presents a separate idea. In the first sentence, with the preterite form of *vivir*, the speaker emphasizes that the Moors no longer live in Spain; they are long gone. "Vivieron" narrates what they did.

In the second sentence the fact that the "Moors were living in Spain" was an action in the process of happening when something else happened. *Vivían* describes what they were doing. They "were living." This is background information, setting the stage for something else that happens. That "something else" is *empezó la Reconquista*. The verb *empezó* is in the preterite because it refers to a specific moment when something began to happen. The speaker is not emphasizing when the Moors began to live in Spain or when they stopped living there. As you can tell, using the two tenses in Spanish creates a more dramatic effect.

The preterite and the imperfect are both past tenses: What matters is whether an event is considered over and done. If it is not considered over and done, it may even be ongoing into the present and the future.

Think of time in terms of a straight line: It goes from a point in the past to a point in the future. Wherever we are along that line at any given moment is the present. In other words, we relate everything to the present. In Spanish, instead of having a single past tense, there are two past tenses. The amount of time that a specific time took up in the past does not matter; what matters is whether a specific time/event can be considered "over and done." If it cannot, it may even be ongoing into the present and the future. Look at the following diagram.

(preterite)	**[past]**	**[present]**	**[future]**
(imperfect)	→ → → → → → →		

The preterite "brackets" an action in the past with regard to when it happened. The imperfect implies no specific time.

The Preterite:	The Imperfect:
1. specifies that an action began and/or ended in the past.	1. describes ongoing, continuous or habitual action.
2. narrates a series of actions that happened consecutively in the past.	2. sets the stage for an action or event that happened in the past.
3. narrates actions that occur at a specific moment.	3. describes emotional states of mind, or physical states of being.
	4. is used to tell time in the past.

5.12 Use the preterite when an action has a specific beginning and/or end.
Words commonly used in the preterite, by virtue of what they mean, are *empezar*, *comenzar*, and *decidir*, which in the past tense usually refer to a specific moment when an event takes place. For the same reason, *preguntar*, *decir*, and *ir* are often used in the preterite. There are also words or phrases that are cues that indicate the preterite. Some of the more common ones are:

de golpe	suddenly
de repente	suddenly
en seguida	suddenly
inmediatamente	suddenly, immediately
súbitamente	suddenly
ayer	yesterday
el verano pasado	last summer
la semana pasada	last week
anoche	last night
repentinamente	suddenly
cuando	when

These expressions usually indicate a specific moment in the past when something happened.

> **De repente mi mejor amigo entró en el cuarto.**
> Suddenly my best friend came into the room.

> **Anoche supe que mis parientes llegarían hoy.**
> Last night I found out that my relatives would come today.

> **Se despidió de los otros y salió inmediatamente.**
> He said goodbye and left immediately.

> **Cuando entró en la sala, me saludó.**
> When he came into the room, he greeted me.

Another clue to the preterite is a series of actions. On the test look at the other verbs in the sentence: If there is a string of three or more verbs, you should probably guess the preterite.

> **Ayer me desperté bien temprano, me levanté, y salí.**
> Yesterday morning I woke up early, got up, and left.

In passages, look for the conjunction *and*: If the verb in one part of the sentence is connected to another part with "and," they'll both be the same tense. And indicates parallel structures in which you need to use the same tense and mood.

> **Al despertarme, me levanté y me vestí rápidamente.**
> Upon waking up, I got up and got dressed quickly.

One word you'll want to watch for as an indicator of the preterite is *cuando*. Though in some cases you'll use the imperfect after *cuando*, you'll usually use the preterite. *Cuando* can also introduce a subordinate clause with the subjunctive; in past tenses, it usually indicates the preterite.

Sometimes it helps to think about what "specific moment," or "definite time" means. Think of it as "frozen time," as when you capture a moment in a photograph. When you take a picture in a snapshot, you freeze one particular moment. When you see the snapshot you have to imagine the actions or events or situations that come before or after the moment when the picture was taken, because they are not included in the snapshot.

5.13 There are five verbs that have a special meaning in the preterite: *saber*, *conocer*, *tener*, *querer*, and *poder*. They all refer to specific moments in time and have special meanings.

Saber: When you use *saber* in the preterite, you refer to a specific moment when you began to know, or found out, about something. So *saber*, when used in the preterite, means "to find out" or "to discover." Most often, for "knew," use the imperfect.

> **Al hablar con mi amiga, supe el secreto.**
> Upon talking to my friend, I discovered the secret.

Conocer: The moment when you first know somebody refers to when you met them. *Conocer* in the preterite means "to meet."

> **La conocí en la fiesta el sábado pasado.**
> I met her at the party last Saturday.

Tener: The start of having something is when you first get it, or receive it. *Tener* in the preterite refers to the time when it came into your possession.

> **Ayer tuve una carta de mi abuelo.**
> Yesterday I got a letter from my grandfather.

Querer: In the affirmative, the beginning of wanting is trying to do or get something. In the negative form, *querer* means "to refuse."

> **Anoche quise llamarte, pero no estuviste en casa.**
> Last night I tried to call you, but you weren't home.

> **No quiso hacer la tarea anoche.**
> He refused to do the homework last night. (Beyond not wanting to do it, he refused to do it.)

Poder: In the preterite, this verb is very subtle in its meaning: It implies a result to the action. It means "to manage to" or "to finally be able to" do something: A resultant action is implied. *Poder* usually takes the imperfect form when used in the past tense.

> **Quise llamarte anoche, pero no pude.**
> I tried to call you last night, but I could not. (And did not.)

Implied here is that, not only could I not call you, I did not; I could not manage to get hold of you by phone, for whatever reason.

5.14 Use the imperfect to describe actions or a state of being. In English we indicate this tense with "was ...ing," "used to ...," or even "would ...." The imperfect indicates habitual, repeated, or continuous action. It describes background information about an action or event. When a speaker selects the imperfect, he communicates that it's not important *when* the action began or ended in the past (if indeed, it ever ended).

Like the preterite, there are some words or phrases that are strong indicators of the imperfect. Some common ones are:

frecuentemente	frequently
a menudo	often
muchas veces	often, many times
a veces	sometimes
todo el tiempo	all the time

todas las tardes	every afternoon
todas las mañanas	every morning
todas las noches	every night
todos los días	every day
todos los años	every year
todos (unit of time)	every (unit of time)

Todos los días mi papá me llevaba a la escuela.
Every day my father used to take me to school. (or *would take me*, or *took me*, or even *was taking me to school*.)

Notice that there are various ways to translate a verb in the imperfect tense. All of them, however, relate the repeated, habitual nature of the action. The ongoing action in the example above is indicated by *todos los días*.

When something "happens" while something else is "going on," the preterite will tell "what happened," and the imperfect will describe the "goings on" (the background context or the ongoing situation). Or you can use the imperfect for all the verbs, to set the stage something else that happens.

Another word that commonly indicates the imperfect is *mientras*, which means "while."

Ella cantó mientras el público la aplaudía.
She sang while the public was applauding her.

Escuchaba la radio mientras estudiaba para el examen.
I listened to the radio while I was studying for the test. (was listening)

The difference between describing and narrating an action is subtle. Try to get an idea of the difference by looking at the following situation.

Esta mañana mientras manejaba a la escuela, pasaba por las calles tranquilas, escuchaba la radio del coche, miraba los semáforos, y leía el periódico, cuando de repente otro coche que me golpeó.
This morning while I was driving to school, I was going down the street, listening to the car radio, looking at the traffic lights, and reading the newspaper, when suddenly another car hit me.

All the action leading up to "suddenly" sets the stage for "another car hit me." All of the background action is described using the simple imperfect (past progressive in English), to indicate ongoing action. Using the imperfect for background information increases the dramatic impact of the added event about the other car. And though the action does not keep on going after the accident, it was ongoing when the accident happened.

The imperfect is also most often used to describe people, things or a state of mind. Usually this kind of information is background information. And if you think about it, an emotional or physical state of being does not typically have a specific moment when it begins and/or ends.

> Think of the imperfect tense as a moving video. The action is not frozen in a snapshot, but rather, it keeps happening, frame after frame. Using the imperfect indicates that the action had no definite end.

El cielo estaba de un azul profundo. Unas nubes como algodón pasaban lentamente por encima. La arena de la playa dulcemente calentaba los pies de los niños que jugaban en la orilla del mar tranquilo. Todos estaban muy contentos. Al momento todos querían pasar la eternidad allí.

The sky was a deep blue. A few clouds like cotton slowly passed by above. The beach sand deliciously warmed the feet of the children who were playing at the edge of the quiet sea. Everybody was quite happy. At that moment everybody wanted to spend eternity there.

One more case where you will almost always use the imperfect is telling time in the past. Think of this famous line of poetry: "Eran las cinco de la tarde," wrote Federico García Lorca, recounting the day a bullfighter died in the bullring. To emphasize that it happened at five o'clock in the afternoon, every other line in the poem is "Eran las cinco de la tarde." Then, at the end, it says "Eran las cinco en punto de la tarde./Eran las cinco en todos los relojes." ("It was five in the afternoon./It was five o'clock sharp in the afternoon./It was five o'clock on all the clocks.") You would think that saying it happened at 5:00 in the afternoon would be a specific time, but in fact it is background information. The action occurs when the bull gores the bullfighter with his horn. If you have trouble remembering to use the imperfect to tell time in the past, remember Garcia Lorca's line, "Eran las cinco de la tarde."

Future Tense

5.15 In English, the future is a two-word form: "will ..." or sometimes "shall. . . ." In Spanish the future takes a one-word form. The future perfect is two words: *haber* in the future tense plus the past participle. It is translated as "will have ...." Add the correct future ending to the infinitive.

To form the future tense, add these endings to the infinitive:

	Singular			Plural		
	1st	2nd	3rd	1st	2nd	3rd
-ar	-é	-ás	-á	-emos	-éis	-án
-er	-é	-ás	-á	-emos	-éis	-án
-ir	-é	-ás	-a	-emos	-éis	-án

As you can see, all of the future endings are the same for -ar, -er, and -ir verbs. And all except the first person plural have accent marks. It is important to notice these, especially in the third persons singular and plural, because the accent is all that distinguishes the future indicative from the imperfect subjunctive of -ar verbs.

Notice too, that the first person singular is -é, and the third person ending is -á. These two endings are frequently confused. Then, in the plural forms, the first and second persons plural begin with -e, and the third person begins with -a.

Don't do a literal translation from English to Spanish when dealing with the future; you're likely to miss the implied meaning. Remember that, in Spanish, the future tense often expresses wonder or conjecture (that exists in the present tense).

5.16 In Spanish when you wonder about or question something, the future is often used. In this context, the future expresses probability or possibility.

> No tengo reloj. ¿Qué hora será?
> I don't have a watch. I wonder what time it is?
> I don't have a watch. What time could it be?
> I don't have a watch. Would you be so kind as to tell me the time?

This question can be translated in different ways, all of which express probability or possibility.

Conditional Tense

5.17 The conditional tense communicates condition, and sometimes habitual action in the past. The simple translation in English is "would" (though "would" can mean other things, too). The conditional does not exist in English as a separate tense. To form the conditional tense, add these endings to the infinitive. Irregular verbs in the conditional use the same stems as the future, however.

	Singular			Plural		
	1st	**2nd**	**3rd**	**1st**	**2nd**	**3rd**
-ar	*-ía*	*-ías*	*-ía*	*-íamos*	*-íais*	*-ían*
-er	*-ía*	*-ías*	*-ía*	*-íamos*	*-íais*	*-ían*
-ir	*-ía*	*-ías*	*-ía*	*-íamos*	*-íais*	*-ían*

As in the future tense, all of the endings are the same for *-ar*, *-er*, and *-ir* verbs. Right away you see that these are the same endings as for *-er* and *-ir* verbs in the imperfect; the only difference is that they are added to the infinitive itself. Make sure you don't use the imperfect when you mean to use the conditional. Irregular verbs in the conditional use the same stems as the future, however.

Just as the future expresses probability in the present tense, the conditional expresses the same idea in the past tense.

> El tren andaba muy retrasado. ¿Cuándo llegaría?
> The train was running very late. When would it arrive?
> The train was running very late. I wondered when it would arrive?

Notice that one of the translations is "I wondered...," but there are no Spanish words that literally translate this sense of *wonder*. Conjecture is implied by the selection of the conditional tense.

5.18 In Spanish it is always better to use the conditional or the imperfect subjunctive when making a request of somebody. It is simply good manners. If you can recognize the situation, don't make the common mistake of using the simple present tense.

> Señorita, ¿podría mostrarme esa blusa azul?
> Miss, could you show me that blue blouse?

OTHER VERB FORMS

5.19 To make the progressive form, use the present participle after the verb *estar* in any simple tense. To make a present participle (an *-ing* word in English), just add *-ando* to an *-ar* verb, or *-iendo* to an *-er* or *-ir* verb. When the *-i* of the ending comes between two vowels, change the *-i* to *-y* as in *leyendo*.

> Estoy escribiendo.
> I am writing.
>
> Estoy hablando.
> I am talking.

Estar

present:	→	estoy	estás	está	estamos	estáis	están
imperfect:	→	estaba	estabas	estaba	estábamos	estabais	estaban
preterite:	→	estuve	estuviste	estuvo	estuvimos	estuvisteis	estuvieron
future:	→	estaré	estarás	estará	estaremos	estaréis	estarán
conditional:	→	estaría	estarías	estaría	estaríamos	estaríais	estarían

In the past tense you may see the preterite of *estar* used with a present participle. But most often the imperfect is used for the past progressive. Remember that a simple tense in Spanish has several different meanings in English. In Spanish, the progressive form is used only when something is in the process of happening.

5.20 Just like English has the auxiliary verb "to have" to form compound tenses, Spanish has the verb *haber*. To form a compound tense, conjugate *haber* in any simple tense and use a past participle (add *-ado* to an *-ar* verb, and *-ido* to an *-er* or *-ir* verb).

> He leído muchas páginas.
> I have read many pages.

Haber

present:	→	he	has	ha	hemos	habéis	han
imperfect:	→	había	habías	había	habíamos	habíais	habían
preterite:	→	hube	hubiste	hubo	hubimos	hubisteis	hubieron
future:	→	habré	habrás	habrá	habremos	habréis	habrán
conditional:	→	habría	habrías	habría	habríamos	habríais	habrían

Learn the irregular past participles listed below. Do not confuse past participles with present participles.

abierto	opened	vuelto	returned
cubierto	covered	envuelto	wrapped
descubierto	discovered	devuelto	returned
hecho	done	revuelto	scrambled
deshecho	undone	suelto	loose
satisfecho	satisfied	supuesto	supposed
dicho	said	escrito	written
muerto	dead	descrito	described
puesto	put, placed	impreso	printed
propuesto	proposed	visto	seen
opuesto	opposed	previsto	foreseen
resuelto	resolved	roto	broken

You will sometimes see a compound form among the answer choices in a grammar question. Compound forms often go together, so if it is in a single grammar sentence, see if there is a compound form in another part of the sentence. But sometimes, the simple tense might also make sense. To decide which one is right, translate the verb form and look at the sequence of tenses.

> I had thought you had come to the party, but I was wrong. (past perfect)
> I thought you came to the party, but I was wrong. (simple past)

"Had come" and "came" both make sense grammatically, so you would see only one of them listed in the answer choices. When in doubt, translate the other verb tenses to see if a compound tense makes the best sense. Or, look for the word *ya* in the sentence to signal the need for a compound tense: *Ya*, which means "already," indicates that something happened prior to the another moment indicated in the sentence. This is especially true for sentences in the future, e.g., "I will already have done this by the time you get here." Also, you will see past perfect tenses in the same sentence, and you will see the conditional perfect used with the pluperfect subjunctive in if-then statements ("If I had been there, I would have enjoyed the show, too."). Your clues about when to use the compound tenses are in the other verbs throughout the passage. If one of the answer choices is a compound verb form, translate the other verbs in the sentence to see which tense makes the most sense.

Back to the concept of time as a straight line, the compound tenses are specific points along the line: The present perfect refers to something that has happened just prior to the present moment, such as, "I have already seen that movie." The past perfect refers to something that happened prior to a point of time in the past, such as, "I had scarcely sat down, when the telephone rang." The conditional perfect refers to hypothetical situations (as in if-then statements), which do not refer to any particular moment in time, such as "If you had seen a ghost, you would have screamed, too." The future perfect refers a point in time after another moment in the future, such as, "By the time this test is done, I will have spent many hours preparing."

5.21 Expressions of time with the verb *hacer* can be confusing. Though they're easy to recognize, they are not translated literally.

Compound progressive forms (expressions of time with the verb *hacer)* are not common in Spanish. They are mentioned here only so that you will pay attention to another structure in Spanish.

> **Hace tres años que estudio español.**
> I have been studying Spanish for three years.

In the sentence above, the verb in English is "have been studying." "Have" is the helping verb, "been" is a past participle, and "studying" is a present participle. That makes this a present perfect progressive form. But look at the Spanish: First, it uses two simple verb forms: *hace* and *estudio*. Second, both of these verbs are in the present tense. And third, it does not contain the word "for;" it is implicit in the structure of the sentence.

> **Hacía tres años que estudiaba español.**
> I had been studying Spanish for three years.

The verbs above are in the imperfect tense, so the meaning in English is rendered in the past perfect progressive, "had" instead of "have."

> **Hace tres años que estudié español.**
> I studied Spanish three years ago.

Notice that *hace* is in the present tense, and *estudié* is in the preterite. Also notice that there's no need to literally translate *ago*. When you see *hacer* in an expression of time followed by *que*, make sure to use the correct tense. If *hacer* is in the present tense, use either the present or the preterite for the other verb in the sentence. If *hacer* is in the imperfect tense, use the simple imperfect for the other verb. There are alternatives to this, but these are the most common structures for expressing time.

¿Cuánto tiempo hace que ...? means "How long has (___) been ...ing on?" At times this is preceded by *desde*. *Tropezó con una silla que permanecía desde hacía seis años en el mismo sitio* means, "He bumped into a chair which had remained in the same place for six years." *Desde* is not translated literally, but conveys the length of time "since" something happened.

IRREGULAR VERBS

5.22 Some verbs do not follow any pattern. You just have to memorize these irregular verbs.

andar: to walk (andado, andando)

Andar is regular in all tenses except for the preterite, in which case it is like the verb *estar*.

preterite:	→	anduve	anduviste	anduvo	anduvimos	anduvisteis	anduvieron

caber: to fit (cabado, cabando)

Caber is irregular in all tenses except the imperfect.

present indicative:	→	quepo,	cabes,	cabe	cabemos	cabéis	caben
present subjunctive:	→	quepa	quepas	quepa	quepamos	quepáis	quepan

caer: to fall (caído, cayendo)

Caer is regular except for the first person singular present indicative, and all forms in the present subjunctive.

present:	→	caigo	caes	cae	caímos	caéis	caen
preterite:	→	caí	caíste	cayó	caímos	caísteis	cayeron
imperfect:	→	caía	caías	caía	caíamos	caíais	caían
future:	→	cabré	cabrás	cabrá	cabremos	cabréis	cabrán
conditional:	→	cabría	cabrías	cabría	cabriamos	cabríais	cabrían
present subjunctive:	→	caiga	caigas	caiga	caigamos	caigáis	caigan
imperfect subjunctive:	→	cupiera	cupieras	cupiera	cupiéramos	cupierais	cupieran

dar: to give (dado, dando)

present:	→	doy	das	da	damos	dais	dan
preterite:	→	di	diste	dio	dimos	disteis	dieron
imperfect:	→	daba	dabas	daba	dábamos	dabais	daban
future:	→	daré	darás	dará	daremos	daréis	darán
conditional:	→	daría	darías	daría	daríamos	daríais	darían
present subjunctive:	→	dé	des	dé	demos	deis	den
imperfect subjunctive:	→	diera	dieras	diera	diéramos	dierais	diera

decir: to tell, to say (dicho, diciendo)

present:	→	digo	dices	dice	decimos	decís	dicen
preterite:	→	dije	dijiste	dijo	dijimos	dijisteis	dijeron
imperfect:	→	decía	decías	decía	decíamos	decíais	decían
future:	→	diré	dirás	dirá	diremos	diréis	dirán
conditional:	→	diría	dirías	diría	diríamos	diríais	dirían
present subjunctive:	→	diga	digas	diga	digamos	digáis	digan
imperfect subjunctive:	→	dijera	dijeras	dijera	dijéramos	dijerais	dijera

estar: to be (estado, estando)

present:	→ estoy	estás	está	estamos	estáis	están
preterite:	→ estuve	estuviste	estuvo	estuvimos	estuvisteis	estuvieron
imperfect:	→ estaba	estabas	estaba	estábamos	estabais	estaban
future:	→ estaré	estarás	estará	estaremos	estaréis	estarán
conditional:	→ estaría	estarías	estaría	estaríamos	estaríais	estarían
present subjunctive:	→ esté	estés	esté	estemos	estéis	estén
imperfect subjunctive:	→ estuviera	estuvieras	estuviera	estuviéramos	estuvierais	estuvieran

haber: to have, with a past participle (habido, habiendo)

present:	→ he	has	ha	hemos	habéis	han
preterite:	→ hube	hubiste	hubo	hubimos	hubisteis	hubieron
imperfect:	→ había	habías	había	habíamos	habíais	habían
future:	→ habré	habrás	hará	habremos	habréis	habrán
conditional:	→ habría	habrías	habría	habríamos	habríais	habrían
present subjunctive:	→ haya	hayas	haya	hayamos	hayáis	hayan
imperfect subjunctive:	→ hubiera	hubieras	hubiera	hubiéramos	hubierais	hubieran

hacer: to do, to make (hecho, haciendo)

present:	→ hago	haces	hace	hacemos	hacéis	hacen
preterite:	→ hice	hiciste	hizo	hicimos	hicisteis	hicieron
imperfect:	→ hacía	hacías	hacía	hacíamos	hacíais	hacían
future:	→ haré	harás	hará	haremos	haréis	harán
conditional:	→ haría	harías	haría	haríamos	haríais	harían
present subjunctive:	→ haga	hagas	haga	hagamos	hagáis	hagan
imperfect subjunctive:	→ hiciera	hicieras	hiciera	hiciéramos	hicierais	hicieran

ir: to go (ido, yendo)

present:	→ voy	vas	va	vamos	vais	van
preterite:	→ fui	fuiste	fue	fuimos	fuisteis	fueron
imperfect:	→ iba	ibas	iba	íbamos	ibais	iban
future:	→ iré	irás	irá	iremos	iréis	irán
conditional:	→ iría	irías	iría	iríamos	iríais	irían
present subjunctive:	→ vaya	vayas	vaya	vayamos	vayáis	vayan
imperfect subjunctive:	→ fuera	fueras	fuera	fuéramos	fuerais	fueran

oír: to hear (oído, oyendo)

present:	→ oigo	oyes	oye	oímos	oís	oyen
preterite:	→ oí	oíste	oyó	oímos	oísteis	oyeron
imperfect:	→ oía	oías	oía	oíamos	oíais	oían
future:	→ oiré	oirás	oirá	oiremos	oiréis	oirán

conditional:	→	oiría	oirías	oiría	oiríamos	oiréis	oirán
present subjunctive:	→	oiga	oigas	oiga	oigamos	oigáis	oigan
imperfect subjunctive:	→	oyera	oyeras	oyera	oyéramos	oyerais	oyeran

poder: to be able (podido, pudiendo)

present:	→	puedo	puedes	puede	podemos	podéis	pueden
preterite:	→	pude	pudiste	pudo	pudimos	pudisteis	pudieron
imperfect:	→	podía	podáis	podía	podíamos	podíais	podían
future:	→	podré	podrás	podrá	podremos	podréis	podrán
conditional:	→	podría	podrías	podría	podríamos	podríais	podrían
present subjunctive:	→	pueda	puedas	pueda	podamos	podáis	puedan
imperfect subjunctive:	→	pudiera	pudieras	pudiera	pudiéramos	pudierais	pudieran

poner: to put, to place (puesto, poniendo)

present:	→	pongo	pones	pone	ponemos	ponéis	ponen
preterite:	→	puse	pusiste	puso	pusimos	pusisteis	pusieron
imperfect:	→	ponía	ponías	ponía	poníamos	poníai	ponían
future:	→	pondré	pondrás	pondrá	pondremos	pondréis	pondrán
present subjunctive:	→	ponga	pongas	ponga	pongamos	pongáis	pongan
imperfect subjunctive:	→	pusiera	pusieras	pusiera	pusiéramos	pusierais	pusiera

querer: to wish, to want, to love (querido, queriendo)

present:	→	quiero	quieres	quiere	queremos	queréis	quieren
preterite:	→	quise	quisiste	quiso	quisimos	quisisteis	quisieron
imperfect:	→	quería	querías	quería	queríamos	queríais	querían
future:	→	querré	querrás	querrá	querremos	querréis	querrán
conditional:	→	querría	querrías	querría	querríamos	querríais	querrán
present subjunctive:	→	quiera	quieras	quiera	queramos	queráis	quieran
imperfect subunctive:	→	quisiera	quisieras	quisiera	quisiéramos	quisierais	quisieran

saber: to know information (sabido, sabiendo)

present:	→	sé	sabes	sabe	sabemos	sabéis	saben
preterite:	→	supe	supiste	supo	supimos	supisteis	supieron
imperfect:	→	sabía	sabías	sabía	sabíamos	sabíais	sabían
future:	→	sabré	sabrás	sabrá	sabremos	sabréis	sabrán
conditional:	→	sabría	sabrías	sabría	sabríamos	sabríais	sabrían
present subjunctive:	→	sepa	sepas	sepa	sepamos	sepáis	sepan
imperfect subunctive:	→	supiera	supieras	supiera	supiéramos	supierais	supieran

salir: to leave, to go out (salido, saliendo)

present:	→	salgo	sales	sale	salimos	salís	salen
preterite:	→	salí	saliste	salió	salimos	salisteis	salieron
imperfect:	→	salía	salías	salía	salíamos	salíais	salían
future:	→	saldré	saldrás	saldrá	saldremos	saldréis	saldrán
conditional:	→	saldría	saldrías	saldría	saldríamos	saldríais	saldrían
present subjunctive:	→	salga	salgas	salga	salgamos	salgáis	salgan
imperfect subjunctive:	→	saliera	salieras	saliera	saliéramos	salierais	salieran

ser: to be (sido, siendo)

present:	→	soy	eres	es	somos	sois	son
preterite:	→	fui	fuiste	fue	fuimos	fuisteis	fueron
imperfect:	→	era	eras	era	éramos	erais	eran
future:	→	seré	serás	será	seremos	seréis	serán
conditional:	→	sería	serías	sería	seríamos	seríais	serían
pressent subjunctive:	→	sea	seas	sea	seamos	seáis	sean
imperfect subunctive:	→	fuera	fueras	fuera	fuéramos	fuerais	fueran

tener: to have, to possess (tenido, teniendo)

present:	→	tengo	tienes	tiene	tenemos	tenéis	tienen
preterite:	→	tuve	tuviste	tuvo	tuvimo	tuvisteis	tuvieron
imperfect:	→	tenía	tenías	tenía	teníamos	teníais	tenían
future:	→	tendré	tendrás	tendrá	tendremos	tendréis	tendrán
conditional:	→	tendría	tendrías	tendría	tendríamos	tendríais	tendrían
present subjunctive:	→	tenga	tengas	tenga	tengamos	tengáis	tengan
imperfect subjunctive:	→	tuviera	tuvieras	tuviera	tuviéramos	tuvierais	tuvieran

traer: to bring (traído, trayendo)

present:	→	traigo	traes	trae	traemos	traéis	traen
preterite:	→	traje	trajiste	trajo	trajimos	trajisteis	trajeron
imperfect:	→	traía	traías	traías	traíamos	traíais	traían
future:	→	traeré	traerás	traerá	traeremos	traeréis	traerán
conditional:	→	traería	traerías	traería	traeríamos	traeríais	traerían
present subjunctive:	→	traiga	traigas	traiga	traigamos	traigáis	traigan
imperfect subjunctive:	→	trajera	trajeras	trajera	trajéramos	trajerais	trajeran

valer: to be worth (valido, valiendo)

present:	→	valgo	vales	vale	valemos	valéis	valen
preterite:	→	valí	valiste	valió	valimos	valisteis	valieron
imperfect:	→	valía	valías	valía	valíamos	valíais	valían
future:	→	valdré	valdrás	valdrá	valdremos	valdréis	valdrán

conditional:	→	valdría	valdrías	valdría	valdríamos	valdríais	valdrían
present subjunctive:	→	valga	valgas	valga	valgamos	valgáis	valgan
imperfect subjunctive:	→	valiera	valieras	valiera	valiéramos	valierais	valieran

ver: to see (visto, viendo)

present:	→	veo	ves	ve	vemos	veis	ven
preterite:	→	vi	viste	vio	vimos	visteis	vieron
imperfect:	→	veía	veías	veía	veíamos	veíais	veían
future:	→	veré	verás	verá	veremos	veréis	verán
conditional:	→	Vería	verías	vería	veríamos	veríais	verían
present subjunctive:	→	vea	veas	vea	veamos	veáis	vean
imperfect subjunctive:	→	viera	vieras	viera	viéramos	vierais	vieran

venir: to come (venido, viniendo)

present:	→	vengo	vienes	viene	venimos	venís	vienen
preterite:	→	vine	viniste	vino	vinimos	vinisteis	vinieron
imperfect:	→	venía	venías	venía	veníamos	veníais	venían
future:	→	vendré	vendrás	vendrá	vendremos	vendréis	vendrán
conditional:	→	vendría	vendrías	vendría	vendríamos	vendríais	vendrían
present subjunctive:	→	venga	vengas	venga	vengamos	vengáis	vengan
imperfect subjunctive:	→	viniera	vinieras	viniera	viniéramos	vinierais	vinieran

Stem-Changing Verbs

5.23 All radical (stem-changing) verbs that end in *-ar* and *-er* change only in the present, in the first, second, and third persons singular, and the third person plural. They change *-e* to *-ie* and *-o* to *-ue*.

encontrar (ue): to meet

| | encuentro | encuentras | encuentra | encontramos | encontráis | encuentran |

Verbs that end with *-ir* can change in one of two ways: from *-e* to *-ie*, and from *-o* to *-ue*; or from *-e* to *-i*. Either way, these changes occur in the present tense, in first, second, third person singular, and third person plural. These *-ir* verbs also change from *-e* to *-i* or *-o* to *-u* in the third persons of the preterite.

While you won't have to come up with these forms for the test, you will need to recognize them. In fact, knowing the stem changes can help you identify the infinitive. This is especially true in the subjunctive.

sentar: to seat

| present indicative: | → | siento | sientas | sienta | sentamos | sentáis | sientan |
| present subjunctive: | → | siente | sientes | siente | sentemos | sentéis | sienten |

sentir: to feel

| present indicative: | → | siento | sientes | siente | sentimos | sentís | sienten |
| present subjunctive: | → | sienta | sientas | sienta | sintamos | sintáis | sientan |

As you can see, the present indicative of *sentar* has some similarities with the present subjunctive of *sentir*. And the present subjunctive of *sentir* looks like *sentar* in some forms.

Spelling Change Verbs

5.24 Some verbs change spelling in order to keep the conjugated forms sounding like the infinitive. This has major implications on the pronunciation of three consonants: -c,-g, and -z. These three consonants have two sounds, depending on the vowel that follows. (In Latin America the *-z* generally sounds like *-s*, so you just have to memorize the spelling of those few verbs that end with *-zar*.)

In the case of these spelling change verbs (called *orthographic verbs*), changes usually occur in the first person singular present indicative. Some verbs also change in the first person singular preterite. And for those verbs that change spelling in the first person singular present and preterite, all the present subjunctive forms change accordingly.

Let's review the most common spelling changes. Notice that the only difference between the spelling change verbs in the first person singular preterite and the present subjunctive is the accent. Pay attention to accents on these verb forms among the answer choices; frequently they are distracters.

Verbs ending with *-car* change c to *qu* in the first person singular in the preterite.

buscar: to look for

present:	yo busco
preterite:	yo busqué, tú buscaste, etc.
present subjunctive:	yo busque, tú busques, etc.

Verbs ending with *-cer* change c to *zc* in the first person singular in the present.

conocer: to know, to be acquainted with

present:	yo conozco, tú conoces, etc.
preterite:	conocí
present subjunctive:	yo conozca, tú conozcas, etc.

Verbs ending with *-ucir* change in the present like *-cer* verbs (only in the first person singular), and in the preterite change to irregular endings in all six forms.

traducir: to translate

present:	yo traduzco, tú traduces, etc.
preterite:	yo traduje, tú tradujiste, etc.
present subjunctive:	yo traduzca, tú traduzcas, etc.

Verbs ending in *-gar* change *g* to *gu* in the first person singular preterite, and all six forms of the present subjunctive.

llegar: to arrive

present: yo llego

preterite: yo llegué, tú llegaste, etc.

present subjunctive: yo llegue, tú llegues, etc.

Verbs ending in *-ger* change *g* to *j* in the first person singular present indicative and in all six forms of the present subjunctive.

escoger: to choose

present: yo escojo, tú escoges, etc.

preterite: yo escogí, etc.

present subjunctive: yo escoja, tú escojas, etc.

Verbs ending in *-guir* drop the *u* after the *g* in the first person singular present indicative, and all six forms of the present subjunctive.

seguir: to follow

present: yo sigo, tú sigues, etc.

preterite: yo seguí

present subjunctive: yo siga, tú sigas, etc.

Verbs ending in *-uir* add a *y* between the *u* and the ending in all forms in the present indicative and present subjunctive.

huir: to flee

present: yo huyo, tú huyes, etc.

preterite: yo huí, tú huiste, él (ella, Vd.) huyó, nosotros huimos, vosotros huisteis, ellos (ellas, Vds.) huyeron

present subjunctive: yo huya, tú huyas, etc.

Verbs that end with *-zar* change *z* to *c* in the first person singular preterite.

empezar: to begin

present: yo empiezo

preterite: yo empecé, tú empezaste

present subjunctive: yo empiece, tú empieces, etc.

There are other spelling change verbs, but it is unlikely you will see them. If you come to a verb form you do not recognize, you might be able to deduce what the infinitive is if it has an ending like the ones listed above. And if you're stuck trying to identify the correct subjunctive form in a compound sentence, look for an accent to distinguish the preterite form from the present subjunctive. This isn't the case with every verb, but it is for many. In all cases, generalize from the examples above. The rules apply to all verbs that end with *-car, -cer, -ucir, -gar, -ger, -guir, -uir*, and, finally, *-zar*.

VERBS IN THE SUBJUNCTIVE FORM

5.25 To form the present subjunctive mood tenses, use the first person singular present indicative stem and drop the -o. For -ar verbs, add the present tense endings for -er verbs. For -er and -ir verbs, add the endings for -ar verbs. It's that simple.

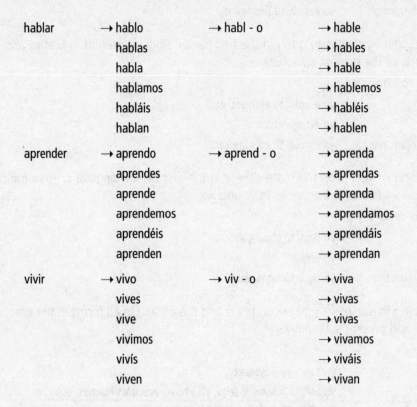

hablar	→ hablo	→ habl - o	→ hable
	hablas		→ hables
	habla		→ hable
	hablamos		→ hablemos
	habláis		→ habléis
	hablan		→ hablen
aprender	→ aprendo	→ aprend - o	→ aprenda
	aprendes		→ aprendas
	aprende		→ aprenda
	aprendemos		→ aprendamos
	aprendéis		→ aprendáis
	aprenden		→ aprendan
vivir	→ vivo	→ viv - o	→ viva
	vives		→ vivas
	vive		→ vivas
	vivimos		→ vivamos
	vivís		→ viváis
	viven		→ vivan

These rules apply to forming the present subjunctive in irregular, stem-changing and spelling-change verbs, too. For the stem-changing verbs, all you need to know is that -ar and -er verbs change the same way in the present subjunctive that they do in the indicative: first, second, and third person singular, and third person plural. Don't be confused by the fact that there is no future subjunctive—just use the present subjunctive.

empezar: to begin

present subjunctive: → empiece empieces empiece empecemos empecéis empiecen

volver: to return

present subjunctive: → vuelva vuelva vuelva volvamos volváis vuelvan

Verbs that end in -ir change a bit differently. Verbs that change -e to -ie or -o to -ue in the present, and -e to -i and -o to -u in the preterite have those changes in the present subjunctive, but some of them also change in the first and second persons plural. The most common verbs that make these changes in the present subjunctive are: *sentir, sentirse, divertirse, referir, preferir, dormir, morir, sugerir,* and *consentir.*

sentir: to feel

present subjunctive: → sienta sientas sienta sintamos sintáis sientan

dormir: to sleep

present subjunctive: → duerma duermas duerma durmamos durmáis duerman

5.26 There are seven common verbs that are completely irregular in the present subjunctive: *dar, estar, haber, hacer, ir, saber, ser.* Remember that *haber* is an auxiliary verb used in compound tenses, and with the expression *hay*, *había*, etc. (meaning "there is, there was, etc.").

dar: to give

present subjunctive: → dé des dé demos deis den

estar: to be

present subjunctive: → esté estés esté estemos estéis estén

haber: to have

present subjunctive: → haya hayas haya hayamos hayáis hayan

hacer: to do, to make

present subjunctive: → haga hagas haga hagamos hagáis hagan

ir: to go

present subjunctive: → vaya vayas vaya vayamos vayáis vayan

saber: to know

present subjunctive: → sepa sepas sepa sepamos sepáis sepan

ser: to be

present subjunctive: → sea seas sea seamos seáis sean

5.27 To form the imperfect subjunctive, take the third person plural form of the preterite and drop the *-on*. Then add: *-a, -as, -a, -amos, -ais, -an*.

hablar	→ hablaron	→ hablar-on	→ hablara
aprender	→ aprendieron	→ aprendier-on	→ aprendiera
vivir	→ vivieron	→ vivier-on	→ viviera

No matter what that stem is in the preterite, it is the same for the imperfect subjunctive, regular, irregular, stem-changing, and spelling change verbs included. The only thing you have to look for is an accent mark on the first person plural, where the whole ending is *-iéramos*. There is another set of endings that end in *-se*, instead of *-ra*. These endings would look like this:

hablar: to speak

hablase   hablases   hablase   hablásemos   hablaseis   hablasen

aprender: to learn

aprendiese   aprendieses   aprendiese   aprendiésemos   aprendieseis   aprendiesen

vivir: to live

viviese   vivieses   viviese   viviésemos   vivieseis   viviesen

All you need to do is recognize these forms on the test. For all practical purposes, the two forms are completely interchangeable.

5.28 Think of the subjunctive as a mood, not a tense. It captures a feeling about issues that are uncertain, unproven facts, things that may not really exist. In many cases, the structure of the sentence will tell you whether or not to use the subjunctive.

There are only two simple tenses in the subjunctive mood and two compound tenses. For the most part you will only see the subjunctive in present subjunctive, present perfect subjunctive (the present subjunctive of *haber* plus the past participle), past (imperfect) subjunctive, and pluperfect (imperfect of *haber* plus a past participle) subjunctive. Theoretically, you could also use it in progressive forms, too.

Let's divide the uses of the subjunctive into four categories: noun clauses; adjective clauses; adverb clauses; and miscellaneous uses. Each category has its own rules for using the subjunctive.

5.29 When a main clause expresses desire, emotion, doubt, or observed reality, the noun clause that follows almost always takes the subjunctive. Some verbs that indicate use of the subjunctive are: *esperar*, *querer* (when it means to want), *pedir*, *exigir*, *recomendar*, *mandar*, *requerir*, *aconsejar*, *sugerir*, and *preferir*.

In the following sentences, the main clauses express some type of emotion or observed possibility.

> Mi amigo espera que salga bien en el examen. (desire)
> My friend hopes that I do well on this test.

> Mi amigo se alegraba que yo saliera bien. (emotion)
> My friend was happy that I did do well.

> Mi amigo dudaba que yo saliera mal. (doubt)
> My friend doubted that I would do poorly.

> Es posible que salga bien en el examen. (observed possibility)
> It is possible that I will do well on the test.

When considering use of the subjunctive, look for:
- The verbs: *esperar*, *querer*, *pedir*, *exigir*, *recomendar*, *mandar*, *aconsejar*, *sugerir*, or *preferir*
- "Que" to introduce the dependent clause
- A change of subject in the verb in the dependent clause

Notice that the noun clauses are all introduced by the word "that" ("that I do well"; "that I did do well," etc.). In Spanish you'll see the word *que*. If *que* is not in the sentence, look for an infinitive, because that is what you would use as the object of the verb. In English we often use an infinitive instead of a dependent clause with the subjunctive. In Spanish you can do the same thing, though it is less common when there is a change of subject.

> **Pidió que yo viniera lo más pronto posible.**
> **Me pidió venir lo más pronto posible,**
> He asked me to come as soon as possible.

> **Fue imposible que viniera ayer.**
> **Me fue imposible venir ayer.**
> It was impossible for me to come yesterday.

Sometimes the verb in the main clause is a command form, but it still requires the subjunctive in the dependent clause. Use the present subjunctive after these command forms.

> **Pídale que venga lo más pronto posible.**
> Ask him to come as soon as possible.

> **Diles que vengan a la fiesta.**
> Tell them to come to the party.

Now, read the following sentences and see if you can understand their meanings.

> **Fue mejor que no saliera con ellos este fin de semana.**
> It was better that I not go out with them this weekend.

> **Mis amigos quieren que los acompañe este fin de semana.**
> My friends want me to go with them this weekend.

> **Mi amigo me pidió que lo acompañara al cine.**
> My friend asked me to go with him to the movies.
> (My friend asked that I go with him to the movies.)

> **Sería una buena idea que estudiaras con tus amigos.**
> It would be a good idea (for you) to study with your friends.

In the last sentence, even though *for you* is not translated, it is the subject of the verb in the dependent noun clause.

• *Desire*

When used in the subjunctive form, desire communicates more than just "wanting"; it communicates a broader sense of request, command, communication, or suggestion. In addition to the obvious verbs (*esperar, pedir, requerir, recomendar, sugerir, sentir*), *decir* can also indicate the subjunctive mood: When it implies a command or a request, it takes the subjunctive. In this sense, it expresses desire on one's part. When *decir* communicates a simple statement of fact, it takes the indicative mood.

> **Me dijo que viniera esta tarde. (a command/request)**
> He told me to come this afternoon.

> **Me dijo que vendría esta tarde. (a statement of fact)**
> He told me she would come this afternoon.

• *Emotion*

Common verbs of emotion are *temer, alegrarse de, tener miedo, tener vergüenza, estar orgulloso de, sentir, arrepentirse de,* and *avergonzar.*

> **Temo que no le guste el regalo.**
> I am afraid she does not like the gift.

• *Doubt*

In clauses that express doubt, the main verbs to look for are *negar, dudar,* and *no creer.* Be careful, though: If *dudar* is negative ("no dudar"), then it means something is certain and is not an expression of doubt. When you say, "I do not doubt," you're saying that you believe something is possible. Don't use the subjunctive when you are stating a fact.

> **No creo que llueva esta tarde.**
> I do not believe it will rain this afternoon.

> **Dudo que llueva esta tarde.**
> I doubt that it will rain this afternoon.

> **Creo que no va a llover esta tarde.**
> I believe that it is not going to rain this afteroon.

> **No dudo que va a llover esta tarde.**
> I do not doubt that it is going to rain this afternoon.

> **No niego que va a vender el coche.**
> I do not deny that he is going to sell the car.

At times you may see the indicative after *no creer* in a question. In these cases the speaker anticipates an affirmative response to the question, so *creer* takes the indicative. If the speaker anticipates a negative response, *no creer*, then the subjunctive is used.

• *Observed Reality*

> Many expressions of observed reality begin with *It* plus a form of *ser* plus *que.*

Most expressions of observed reality begin with the verb *ser,* though you might see words like *Basta, Vale,* or *Importa* at the start of one of these expressions.

> **Basta que le dé cinco dólares y se va.**
> It is enough to give him five dollars and he goes away.

The English translation is rather awkward: We would more likely say, "All you have to do is give him five dollars and he will go away."

> **Vale que estudies un poco antes del examen.**
> It is worth a good bit for you to study a little before the test.

This, too, is an awkward translation. "It would be a good idea for you to study a little before the test" is better.

Expressions of observed reality require the indicative. Like the verbs of doubt or denial, these expressions introduce clauses in which the speaker states a fact.

Ser plus *claro / seguro / obvio / evidente* takes the indicative:

> **Es obvio que el subjuntivo no es muy difícil.**
> It is obvious that the subjunctive is not very difficult.

> **Es evidente que es posible hacerlo.**
> It is clear that it is possible to do it.

No cabe duda takes the indicative:

> **No cabe duda que yo puedo hacer esto.**
> There is no doubt that I can do this.

By the same token, the opposite of these expressions requires the subjunctive, because they do express uncertainty.

> **No es obvio que todos sepan esta materia.**
> It is not obvious that everybody knows this material.

> **No es claro que siempre digan la verdad.**
> It is not clear that they always tell the truth.

5.30 If the thing or person described by an adjective clause does not exist with certainty, use the subjunctive mood. If the thing or person does exist, use the indicative. An adjective clause modifies a noun. In other words, it describes or gives information about a particular noun.

The indicative mood is used with phrases of certainty. Similarly, use the indicative after the verb *pensar*. Anything that someone thinks or believes is stated in the indicative.

> **Vi a un hombre, que hablaba bien el español.**
> I saw a man, who spoke Spanish well.

The subjunctive mood is used if there is less certainty about the noun; that is, if the thing or person described by the adjective clause does not exist or if the speaker is uncertain it exists (or, if the speaker wishes to communicate that the thing or person is hypothetical).

Busco un coche que sea barato y funcione bien.
I am looking for a car that is cheap and runs well.

Busco el coche que es barato y funciona bien.
I am looking for the car that is cheap and runs well.

In the first sentence above, the speaker is not sure that such a car exists. In the second sentence, the speaker knows it does exist, he just has to find it (wherever it is). Notice that the article in front of the noun is *a* in the first sentence, and *the* in the second sentence. You need to look carefully at the articles, then at the meaning of the sentence to see if the noun is known or unknown to the speaker.

When the noun is a person, sometimes you can tell if it is known or unknown to the speaker by the personal *a*, or its absence in front of the noun. (Remember that if the object of a verb is a person, Spanish uses the word *a* before the objective noun, though not after the verb *tener*.) If there is no personal *a*, then use the subjunctive in the adjective clause.

Busco al hombre que habla español.
I am looking for the man who speaks Spanish.

Busco a un hombre que hable español.
I am looking for a man who speaks Spanish.

Tengo un amigo que habla español.
I have a friend who speaks Spanish.

Quiero tener un amigo que hable español:
I want to have a friend who speaks Spanish.

In sentence one of the second set, there is no personal *a*, because it is not used after the verb *tener*.

Another group of antecedents that an adjective clause can modify are words that end with *-quiera*. If used as an indefinite person, place, thing, or time, these would take the subjunctive. Though in some cases these antecedents can take the indicative, the subjunctive is more common.

quienquiera	whoever	(quienesquiera in the plural form)
dondequiera	wherever	
cuandoquiera	whenever	
comoquiera	however	
cualquiera	whichever	(cualesquiera, in the plural form)
quequiera	whatever	

> The subjunctive is a mood that communicates uncertainty. If an action has happened, it is certain. If it has not yet happened, it is uncertain that it will actually take place.

Quienquiera que venga, lo acomodaremos.
Whoever comes, we will accommodate him.

Cuandoquiera que puedas venir, dímelo y te encontraré.
Whenever you can come, let me know and I will meet you.

There is another type of adjective clause, the *...por .... que ....* structure, that always takes the subjunctive. Any adjective can go after *por*, and the subjunctive must be used after *que*.

Por mucho que sepa, nunca sabrá demasiado.
No matter how much you know, you will never know too much..

Por interesante que sea el programa, no quiero hacerlo.
No matter how interesting the program may be, I don't want to do it.

El chico no gana, por rápido que corra.
The little boy is not winning, no matter how fast he runs.

5.31 Adverb clauses describe the action of the verb. They almost always take the subjunctive form. Conjunctions expressing purpose or proviso always take the subjunctive in the subordinate clauses.

Purpose: *para que* = in order that, so that
              a fin de que = in order that, so that

Proviso: *con tal (de) que* = provided that
              sin que = without
              en caso (de) que = in case
              a menos que = unless
              a no ser que = unless

Lo hizo para que sus amigos lo admiraran,
He did it so that his friends would admire him.

Lo hizo sin que sus amigos lo supieran.
He did it without his friends knowing about it.

Les da el dinero en caso que lo necesiten.
He give them money in case they need it.

Harían el trabajo a menos que les dijera que no.
They would do the work unless he told them not to (do it).

Additionally, the following conjunction about time always takes the subjunctive:

antes (de) que = before

Hizo el trabajo antes que le dijera hacerlo.
He did the work before being told to do it.

It is not easily apparent from a direct English translation whether the subjunctive is needed for the Spanish, so be careful. English expresses the subjunctive in various ways: It can use the infinitive or a gerund.

> When deciding whether to apply the subjunctive, do not rely on how you would translate the sentence into English. Oftentimes there is no way to express the subjunctive in English.

Adverbial conjunctions of time are a little trickier. At times they take the indicative, and at times they take the subjunctive. Conjunctions of time introduce clauses in which an action has either happened or not, in relation to the time in the main clause. If the action has not happened, use the subjunctive. If it has happened, use the indicative. Usually, if the tense used in the main clause is in the future or future perfect (or possibly in the present), you'll need the subjunctive in the adverbial clause. If the past tense is used, you'll use the indicative, because the action has already happened.

Conjunctions of time that commonly take the subjunctive when the action has not happened are:

> *en cuanto* = as soon as
>
> *tan pronto como* = as soon as
>
> *luego que* = as soon as
>
> *así que*   = as soon as
>
> *hasta que* = until

In some cases *cuando* and *mientras* can introduce a subordinate clause using the subjunctive, but you need to look carefully at the sentence.

Te llamaré tan pronto como llegue. (subjunctive)
I will call you as soon as I arrive.

Llámame tan pronto como llegues. (subjunctive)
Call me as soon as you arrive.

Me llamó tan pronto como llegó. (indicative)
He called me as soon as he arrived.

In the first sentence the speaker has not arrived yet, so the subjunctive is used after *tan pronto como*. In the second sentence, the verb in the main clause is a command form, but since the action in the subordinate clause has not happened yet, the subjunctive is used.

In the third sentence, the person arrived and called, so it is a fact that has happened. The action in the subordinate clause happened before the action in the main clause, so the indicative is used.

The last category of conjunctions can take either the indicative or the subjunctive, depending on the broader context of the sentence. When the subjunctive is used, the speaker does not know for certain if something actually will happen or happened as he thought it might.

aunque = although, even though

de modo que = in such a way that, so that

de manera que = in such a way that, so that

Habló de modo que todos lo entendieran. (subjunctive)
He spoke in such a way that everyone could understand him.

Habló de modo que todos lo entendieron. (indicative)
He spoke in such a way that everyone understood him.

Aunque llueva mañana, no iré. (subjunctive)
Even though it may rain tomorrow, I will not go.

Aunque llueve mañana, no iré. (indicative)
Even though it is going to rain tomorrow, I will not go.

Always Use the Subjunctive	Depending on Tense Use the Subjunctive	Depending on Context Use the Subjunctive
para que	*tan pronto como*	*aunque*
a menos que	*luego que*	*de modo que*
sin que	*en cuanto*	*de manera que*
en caso (de) que	*así que*	
con tal que	*hasta que*	
a fin (de) que	*mientras*	
antes (de) que	*cuando*	

5.32 If-then statements sometimes require the subjunctive. In many cases, when there is a condition in the "then" clause, the subjunctive is used in the "if" clause. There is no word in Spanish that translates the word *then*, but it is implied using the conditional tense.

Si tengo el dinero, voy a España. (indicative)
If I have the money, I will go to Spain.

Cuando he tenido el dinero, he ido a España. (indicative)
When I have had the money, I have gone to Spain.

Si tuviera el dinero, iría a España. (subjunctive)
If I had the money, I would go to Spain.

Si hubiera tenido el dinero, habría ido a España. (subjunctive)
If I have had the money, I would have gone to Spain.

In the present and the present perfect tenses, the subjunctive is not used because no statement is made about whether or not the event will take place. Using the subjunctive implies a resultant event, but only if the if condition is true. On the test, you can use the imperfect subjunctive after *si*, but not the present subjunctive. (Some cases do require the present subjunctive after *si*, but in those cases *si* usually mean something other than *if*.)

5.33 A few additional cases require the subjunctive.

Quizás and Tal Vez: Quizás (sometimes spelled *quizá*) and *tal vez* both mean "perhaps." You may see the subjunctive after these expressions, but it is not required by the grammar. Whether the subjunctive is appropriate depends on how much uncertainty the speaker wishes to communicate.

Ojalá: After the expression *ojalá*, you must use the subjunctive. The expression is translated several ways: "I hope that...," "With luck...," or "God willing...." You can use present, past, present perfect, or past perfect subjunctive, depending on the context.

> Ojalá que vengan mis amigos a mi fiesta.
> I hope my friends come to my party.

> Ojalá que ganemos el campeonato.
> With luck we will win the championship.
>
> I hope that we win the championship.

Sentences that begin with Que: When *Que...* begins a sentence, the subjunctive is used with the meaning of "Would that...," or "Let ...," or "Why don't...."

> Que vengan Vds. esta tarde para visitarme.
> Why don't you come over this afternoon to visit me.

> ¡Qué coman tortas!
> Let them eat cake!

> ¡Que pudieran verme ahora mis amigos!
> Oh that my friends could see me now!

In all of these statements, the subjunctive communicates a wish or something uncertain; in other words, nonfacts. If the clause begins with *Que*, it is an elliptical statement: Part of the sentence is omitted, but it is stated as if it were a whole sentence. The omitted part is a main clause that would require the subjunctive in the subordinate or dependent clause.

Softened Statements: Sometimes you will want to express a wish or request of someone without seeming too aggressive. Use the imperfect subjunctive in these situations.

> Un día un hombre entró en una tienda para comprar algo, pero
> el dependiente estaba ocupado. Para llamar la atención del depen-
> diente, el hombre dijo:
> —¿Señor, pudiera ayudarme, por favor?
> —A sus órdenes, señor. ¿En qué puedo servirle?
> —Quisiera ver esa guayabera que tiene allí.
> —Sí, señor. Aquí la tiene.

Although this example expresses exaggerated politeness, you get the idea that the customer treats the salesperson with respect. He could have easily used the conditional tense in place of the imperfect subjunctive. The simple present tense would be considered very rude.

Command Forms

5.34 All forms of the subjunctive, with the exception of the first person, can be used in a command. Since *you* accounts for the second and third persons singular and plural, each of those forms can be a command form.

A command form is nothing more than a dependent noun clause, with the main clause omitted. "Do your homework" really means "I want you to do your homework." The first part ("I want you") is omitted.

In addition to the subjunctive verb forms, there are some special forms to use in the affirmative second persons, singular and plural forms. If you already know how to form the subjunctive of all verbs, plus the six verbs that do not end in o in the first person singular present, then you have most of the information you need.

> The first person plural can also be used as an indirect command (a subjunctive form), and is usually translated "Let's...."

The forms that are used for commands are:

tú: For affirmative (positive) commands, use the third person singular present indicative. This is a crucial form to recognize.

> **Mira, tú y tu hermano van a recibir un premio.**
> Look, you and your brother are going to receive a prize.

The phrase *tú y tu* here is the only indicator of what person and number command form is required.

> **Pídele a tu padre el dinero.**
> Ask your father for the money.

Tu is the only word that indicates the subject of the command is "tú." Remember that the affirmative *tú* command does not end with the usual subjunctive ending. For the negative *tú* command, use the second person singular present subjunctive.

> **¡No me digas!**
> You don't say!

> **No me pidas otra vez que te dé dinero.**
> Don't ask me again to give you money. (The only clue is *te* in front of *dé*)

> **No escuches las tonterías de tu hermano.**
> Don't listen to your brother's silliness.

Remember that *tú* is the correct form to use between friends. It is not considered appropriate to use it with anyone more formal, though some parents will use the third person, formal, or polite *usted* with their children. *Usted* indicates a more formal relationship.

Usted: The third person singular is commonly used with anyone other than your peers.

>   **Dígame lo que quiere, señor.**
>   Tell me what you want, sir.

>   **Mire Vd., señor, tengo mucha prisa.**
>   Look here, mister, I'm in a hurry.

Nosotros: This first person plural is an indirect command. The negative form is the same as the affirmative one. Look at the following examples and compare the Spanish verb forms with the English translation to fix it in your mind.

>   **Escuchemos lo que dice el político antes de decidir.**
>   Let's listen to what the politician says before deciding.

>   **No nos quedemos en casa esta noche. Salgamos ahora.**
>   Let's not stay home tonight. Let's go out now.

>   **¿Debemos ponernos las chaquetas?**
>   **—Sí, pongámonoslas.**
>
>   Should we put on our jackets?
>   —Yes, let's put them on.

Notice that the pronouns go on the end of the affirmative command forms. And the final *s* from the ending *pongamos* has been dropped before the pronoun *nos*. *Las* refers to "chaquetas." Also, there is an accent on the ending of the form, but you would not see this kind of form with pronouns without an accent.

Vosotros: You probably won't see this form on the test in a grammar sentence, but you might see it in a reading selection. *Vosotros* verb forms are used in Spain as the plural of *tú*. In Spanish America it is common to use the third person plural, *ustedes*, instead of the second person plural, *vosotros*. To make the affirmative *vosotros* command, drop the *r* from the infinitive ending and add *d*. For reflexive verbs, drop the final *s* from the -*mos* ending, and add the pronoun, *os*.

>   **Volved tan pronto como podáis.**
>   Come back as soon as you can.

>   **Por favor, sentaos aquí cerca de vuestra abuela.**
>   Please, sit here next to your grandmother.

Idos, for the verb *ir*, is the only exception to the above rule. It is irregular because it does not drop the *d*.

> *Nosotros* was made famous in Old West films, when the sheriff gathered his posse and called out the command, ¡Vámonos, hombres! ("Let's go, men!") Of course, vámonos is an irregular verb in the first person plural.

To make the negative *vosotros* command, use the second person plural present subjunctive.

> **No volváis hasta que lo tengáis hecho.**
> Don't come back until you have it finished.

Ustedes: The affirmative and negative forms of *ustedes* use the third person plural of the present subjunctive. There are no exceptions.

> **Digan Vds. la verdad.**
> Tell the truth.

> **No fumen en el restaurante.**
> Don't smoke in the restaurant.

It is common to include the pronoun *usted* or *ustedes* (or their abbreviations) after the third person commands, but *tú* is not usually added in second person singular commands. In fact, when the pronoun *Ud./Vd.* or *Uds./Vds.* appears after a verb, that's one indication that it may be a command form. Commands are imperative sentences, so the verb is in a different place from declarative sentences. But remember, that in questions too, the subject also follows the verb. Read the sentence carefully to see where the verb appears in relation to the subject.

> The abbreviations Ud. and Vd. are used for singular you (*usted*).
>
> The abbreviations Uds. and Vds. are used for plural you (*ustedes*).

5.35 Of the irregular verbs, pay particular attention to *dar*, *decir*, *ir*, and *ver* in the affirmative familiar command forms. You will notice that *sé*, the command for *ser*, is the same as the first person singular of *saber*.

Infinitive	Affirmative	Negative
decir	Di	*No digas*
hacer	Haz	*No hagas*
ir	Ve	*No vayas*
poner	Pon	*No pongas*
salir	Sal	*No salgas*
ser	Sé	*No seas*
tener	Ten	*No tengas*
venir	Ven	*No vengas*

Dime cuando vayas para que pueda encontrarte allí.
Tell me when you go so that I can meet you there.

Dame el libro cuando lo termines.
Give me the book when you finish it.

Vete rápido para llegar antes que los otros.
Go quickly in order to get there before the others.

Mira el arco iris en el cielo. Es señal de buena suerte.

Look at the rainbow in the sky. It's a sign of good luck.

5.36 Six verbs do not end in -*o* in the first person singular present indicative. The command forms of these six verbs are as follows. You will recognize them as present subjunctive forms.

Infinitive	Affirmative	Negative
dar	Dé Vd.	No des (tú)
	Den Vds.	No dé Vd. No den Vds.
estar	Esté Vd.	No estés (tú)
	Estén Vds.	No esté Vd. No estén Vds.
ir	Vaya Vd.	No vayas (tú)
	Vayan Vds.	No vaya Vd. No vayan Vds.
saber	Sepa Vd.	No sepas (tú)
	Sepan Vds.	No sepa Vd. No sepan Vds.
ser	Sea Vd.	No seas (tú)
	Sean Vds.	No sea Vd. No sean Vds.

Verbs with Unusual Structure

5.37 Some verbs use sentence stuctures that are quite different from their English translations. These verbs include *gustar, faltar, quedar, bastar, agradar, parecer, placer, sobrar,* and *tocar* (when it means "to be one's turn").

Some verbs turn the object in the English sentence into the subject in the Spanish sentence. *Gustar*, for example, means "to be pleasing to." In "I like tacos," *tacos* is the object. For the Spanish translation, *tacos* becomes the subject, and "I" is changed into an indirect object pronoun. The ending of *gustar* would agree with *tacos*, third person plural, instead of "I." So "I like tacos" becomes *Me gustan los tacos*. Literally, that means, "The tacos are pleasing to me."

PASSIVE VOICE STRUCTURES

All of the sentence structures reviewed so far in this chapter have been in the ACTIVE VOICE. In the ACTIVE VOICE, the subject of the verb acts upon the object. When the subject is acted upon by the object, the sentence is in the PASSIVE VOICE. It is fairly easy to determine just by looking at a sentence whether it is in ACTIVE or PASSIVE VOICE. In Spanish, though, there is more than one way to express the PASSIVE VOICE. There is the TRUE PASSIVE, and there is the *SE SUBSTITUTE* for the TRUE PASSIVE VOICE.

5.38 To spot the TRUE PASSIVE VOICE **structure by looking for: the subject + *ser* ("to be") + past participle + por ("by") + agent.**

> El tema fue escrito por el estudiante.
> The paper was written by the student.

In English the person doing the action does not have to be explicitly stated or even strongly implied. If *ser* is followed by a past participle, and the subject is being acted upon, it is the PASSIVE VOICE.

> The paper was written.

Normally in Spanish the agent is explicitly expressed. The important cues to look for are the verb "to be" and the preposition "by" after the past participle. In these structures the past participle functions as an adjective, not a verbal, so its ending agrees in gender and number with the subject, the noun it modifies, or describes. In the example above, *tema* is a masculine noun, so *escrito* is masculine singular. Notice how the past participle changes in the following examples, according to the gender and number of the subjects.

> La composición fue escrita por el estudiante.
> Los temas fueron escritos por el estudiante.
> Las composiciones fueron escritas por el estudiante.

The verb form also changes from singular to plural. Theoretically, the verb "*to be*" can occur in any person and number, but third person forms are most common. *Ser* can be in any tense, also.

> Las lecciones han sido aprendidas por los estudiantes.
> The lessons have been learned by the students.

In this example the verb *ser* is in the present perfect tense, so *ser* is a past participle, functioning as a verbal, because it comes after a conjugated form of *haber*. Remember that the past participle after *haber* always ends with -*o*. But the verb *ser* in the PASSIVE VOICE must also be followed by a past participle. The word *aprendidas* refers to the subject, *lecciones*, so it agrees in gender and number; it is feminine plural. *Aprendidas* functions as an adjective.

There are some cases in which the preposition *por* is replaced by the preposition *de*, when the agent is a person. This construction is used especially when the verb in the PASSIVE VOICE stresses an emotional attitude, such as *temer*, *odiar*, *aborrecer*, and *amar*.

El profesor fue odiado de todos.
The teacher was hated by all.

5.39 When the agent is neither expressed nor important, Spanish uses the SE SUBSTITUTE. In these cases, the speaker wishes to emphasize the action done to the subject.

Se ve la montaña a lo lejos.
The mountain is seen in the distance.

Se ven las montañas a lo lejos.
The mountains are seen in the distance.

Notice that the Spanish translations do not even use the verb *to be*. Rather, they use the pronoun *se* plus a conjugated form of the verb that in English is a past participle. In this case, that is "seen." When the subject is singular, use a third person singular verb; when the subject is plural, use a third person plural verb. The focus of the sentence is on the act of seeing the mountain.

Sometimes you will see infinitives used as nouns. When there is one infinitive, it is the same as a masculine singular noun. When there are two or more infinitives, treat them as masculine plural nouns. Another important thing to notice is that in Spanish the verb comes before the rest of the sentence.

Se practican hablar y escribir en la clase.
Speaking and writing are practiced in the class.

We would seldom use these structures in English. We would say something like:

You/One/They can see the mountain in the distance.
In class we practice speaking and writing.

In the above examples, *You*, *One*, and *They* do not refer to anyone in particular, and as such, are called "impersonal subjects." Sometimes it is difficult even for English speakers to understand that the subject is not specific. In all of these cases, however, Spanish normally uses the *se* substitute instead of the ACTIVE VOICE. One of the best ways to remember this structure is to remember an example: Think of a store sign you might have seen: *Aquí se habla español*, which means "Spanish is spoken here."

You may wonder how to distinguish the SE SUBSTITUTE construction from a reflexive *se*. When a reflexive verb is used in the PASSIVE VOICE, generally *uno* is used also.

Uno se levanta inmediatamente al despertarse.
One gets up immediately upon awakening.

THINGS TO REMEMBER

- The preterite and imperfect are both past tenses. What matters is whether an even is considered *over* and *done* (preterite). If it is ongoing in the present and into the future, use the imperfect.
- When making a request of somebody in Spanish, use the conditional or imperfect subjunctive. Don't use the simple present tense.
- Think of the subjunctive as a mood, not a tense. It captures a feeling about issues that are uncertain. When a main clause expresses desire, emotion, doubt, or observed reality, the noun clause that follows almost always takes the subjunctive.
- Use *se substitute* when you want to emphasize the action done to the subject: *Se ven las montaña a lo lejos*. (The mountains are seen in the distance.)

REVIEW QUESTIONS

Set A: In the following exercise, circle the correct answer that completes the meaning of the sentence.

1. Cuando _____ a la fiesta anoche, vimos a todos nuestros amigos.

    A) llegamos   B) llegan   C) llegábamos   D) llegaban

2. Al subir la escalera el pobre hombre se ___ y se le rompió el dedo.

    A) caí   B) caía   C) cayó   D) caería

3. No _____ la respuesta hasta hablar con la profesora, entonce ella me la dijo.

    A) supe   B) supo   C) sabían   D) sé

4. Cuando vi a Elena esta mañana, ella _____ muy cansada.

    A) estuve   B) estuvo   C) estaba   D) estuviera

5. Mientras los pájaros _____ en los árboles, yo gozaba del día.

    A) cantaron   B) canté   C) cantaran   D) cantaban

6. Perdón, señor, ¿___ decirme cómo se llega a la Calle Ocho?

    A) Puede   B) Pudiera   C) Pudo   D) Pueda

7. ¡Qué lástima! Parece que ayer Juan _____ un accidente terrible.

    A) sufre   B) sufría   C) sufrió   D) sufriría

8. ¿Elena? Sí, la recuerdo bien. _____ muy bonita cuando era niña.

    A) es   B) era   C) fue   D) será

9. En la fiesta anoche, todos mis amigos ___ cuando entré.

    A) charlan   B) charlaban   C) charlaban   D) charlaran

10. Estoy segura que mañana no ___ a la escuela porque estoy muy enferma hoy.

    A) iba   B) fue   C) iré   D) vaya

11. Llovía a cántaros cuando de repente alguien ___ a la puerta.

    A) llama   B) llamaba   C) llamó   D) llamaría

12. ___ en España cuando empezó la guerra.

    A) Vivo   B) Vivía   C) Viviera   D) Viviría

13. Lo sabía porque ya _____ con mi hermano ayer.

    A) hablo   B) ha hablado   C) había hablado   D) habría hablado

14. ¿Cuántas veces antes de ésta te ___ que no interrumpas a tu tío?

    A) digo   B) diré   C) he dicho   D) estoy diciendo

15. Con suerte el año que viene nosotros ___ de vacaciones a Chile.

    A) vamos   B) íbamos   C) hemos ido   D) iremos

16. De veras, si me ___ acompañarte al cine esta noche, no iré.

    A) pides   B) pidas   C) pedirías   D) pidieras

17. Obviamente, será importante que nosotros ___ un poco.

    A) estudiamos   B) estudiemos   C) estudiaremos   D) estudiáramos

18. No saldrá al aeropuerto hasta que ___ cuándo llega el vuelo.

    A) sabe   B) supo   C) sabrá   D) sepa

19. Les diremos las noticias cuando ___ esta noche.

    A) llegan   B) llegaban   C) llegarán   D) lleguen

20. Si ___ un millón de dólares, compraría una gran casa de campo.

    A) tengo   B) tenía   C) tendría   D) tuviera

21. Dile a Miguel que ___ tan pronto como sea posible; necesito su ayuda.

    A) viene   B) venía   C) venga   D) vendré

22. Nadie me dijo nada después de que ___ a la reunión.

    A) llego   B) llegaba   C) llegué   D) llegara

23. Niño, recomiendo que ___ tu tarea para aprender más.

    A) haga   B) haces   C) hagas   D) harías

24. Mi hijo invitó a nuestros amigos para que ___ asistir a la boda también.

    A) pueden   B) pudieron   C) podrían   D) pudieran

25. Si él ___ que ellos querían venir, los habría invitado también.

    A) sabría   B) habría sabido   C) había sabido   D) hubiera sabido

26. Antes de ingresar en la universidad, sería mejor ___ un poco de dinero.

    A) gana   B) ganará   C) gane   D) ganar

27. Juanito, ___ acá en seguida y no toques la mercancía.

    A) van   B) venga   C) ven   D) ve

28. Luis leyó la revista antes de que su hermano se la _____ a su cuarto.

    A) lleva   B) llevaría   C) llevará   D) llevara

29. Ojalá que mi hermana _____, siempre le gustaba visitarlos.

    A) está   B) estaba   C) estaría   D) estuviera

30. Siempre sentía que no ___ para verlo otra vez antes de que saliera.

    A) fui   B) iría   C) habría ido   D) hubiera ido

31. Prefiero asistir a una universidad que ___ muchos latinos.

    A) tiene   B) tenga   C) tuviera   D) tuvo

32. Dondequiera que _____, siempre recordarás tu país nativo.

    A) irá   B) fuiste   C) vayas   D) irías

Set B: For the following exercise, see if you can translate the Spanish.

1. Me pidieron que trajera refrescos a la fiesta.

2. Cuandoquiera que quieras venir, ven y estaré esperándote.

3. Fue muy difícil terminar por mucho que trabajáramos.

4. El muchacho entró a medianoche sin que sus padres lo oyeran.

5. Haz la tarea, entonces habrás terminado con lo más difícil.

6. Nos aconsejan que sigamos estudiando un poco más.

7. ¿Qué harías si ganaras un millón de dólares?

8. Ve a casa tan pronto como puedas para despedirte de tu abuela.

9. Asistía a la Universidad de Valencia mientras vivía allá.

10. Esta mañana cuando me desperté no me sentía bien.

11. Me dijeron que los muchachos ya habían venido por la casa.

12. ¿Quién te ha dicho que el subjuntivo es fácil?

13. ¿No crees que mañana será buen día para salir?

14. No hay sabio que sepa todo.

15. Hice todo el trabajo ayer para que él lo tuviera hoy.

16. Me aconsejaron que hiciera el viaje con ellos a menos que uno de ellos estuviera enfermo cuando saliera el grupo.

17. Basta que lo viera una vez para averiguar que estaba enfermo.

ANSWERS AND EXPLANATIONS

Set A

1. (A)

Cuando most often introduces the preterite. Do not be confused that the preterite and the present indicative forms look alike in the first person plural. See 5.8 and 5.9.

2. (C)

Even if you did not recognize that the situation takes the preterite, you could tell that it takes the preterite from the conjunction *y* ("and"), which indicates a parallel structure. The verbs in both clauses joined by *y* will be in the same tense. This is a good rule of thumb to remember. See 5.12.

3. (A)

Supe means "found out," or "discovered." You need to use the first person singular instead of the third person. Irregular preterites have *-o* as a third person ending, not a first person ending. See 5.13.

4. (C)

The imperfect describes a mental, emotional, or physical state of being. Though the speaker saw Elena at a specific time, there is no indication of when she began to be tired. See 5.11.

5. (D)

This verb describes what was going on, so use the imperfect. It is background information. See 5.11.

6. (B)

Remember the polite, or softened request? The speaker is asking directions of a stranger, and does not want to be too pushy. See 5.33.

7. (C)

The word *ayer* should tip you off to the preterite here; it narrates what happened. See 5.12.

8. (B)

This verb describes what Elena looked like, without regard to a specific time in the past. "When she was a girl" is a general time frame, so use the imperfect. See 5.11.

9. (C)

This verb communicates background information about something that was going on when something else happened. The ongoing action is in the imperfect, and the event that happened, or is narrated, is in the preterite. See 5.11.

10. (C)

Mañana tells you that you need to use the future. See 5.15.

11. (C)

The preterite is used in this case to narrate an action, indicated by the words *de repente,* meaning "suddenly." See 5.12.

12. (B)

This is background information about what was going on when something else happened. Your only other correct option would have been a preterite form, which was not an answer choice. See 5.14.

13. (C)

The pluperfect is indicated by the word *ya,* and by the imperfect tense of *sabía.* The pluperfect indicates a time before a moment in the past. See 5.20.

14. (C)

Don't be confused by *antes de.* It is not followed immediately by the verb, and there is no *que* before the verb to make a subordinate clause. You have to use the present perfect. In the adverbial phrase *antes de ésta, ésta* refers to *vez,* just before the present. When you are not sure, translate the tense of the verb into English. See 5.20.

15. (D)

Because the speaker is referring to the future, *el año que viene,* you need to use the future of *ir.* Make sure you recognize the forms of the future and remember that the first person plural of the future tense does not have an accent. See 5.15.

16. (A)

You need to use the present tense, even though this is an *if-then* statement. You usually only use the imperfect subjunctive after *si,* not the present subjunctive. See 5.32.

17. (B)

Use the present subjunctive after the impersonal expression. *Ser* will not always be in the present tense; it can be in any tense. See 5.29.

18. (D)

Hasta que is an adverbial conjunction of time that takes the subjunctive when the action has not yet happened, and the indicative when it has. For a cue to use the subjunctive, look for the future tense in the main clause, or a command form or sometimes the present. For the cue to use the indicative mood, look for a past tense in the main clause. See5.31.

19. (D)

Whenever you see *cuando,* be careful. Even though you have learned to look for the preterite after *cuando,* you need to pay attention to the tenses of other verbs in the sentence. *Diremos* is the future of *decir,* so *cuando* is going to take the present subjunctive. In this sentence it introduces a subordinate clause in which the action has not yet happened. *Cuando* is an adverbial conjunction of time that introduces the present subjunctive in such cases. See 5.31.

20. (D)

Even before you began to translate the sentence, after seeing *si*, you should have looked in the rest of the sentence for the conditional tense. It tells you that this is probably an *if-then* statement and you will need the imperfect subjunctive in the *if* portion. If you were to translate this sentence from English to Spanish you could quite likely miss the subjunctive, because you would translate the verb as a simple past tense. See 5.32.

21. (C)

Di is a form of *decir*, followed by *que* and a change of subject in the following noun clause. Use the present subjunctive because the speaker is making a request. The speaker is not stating a fact, but wants Miguel to do something. Use the subjunctive in noun clauses after verbs that indicate a request, a command, a wish, or anything that shows one person trying to influence another. See 5.29.

22. (C)

After *después que*, use the indicative in the past tense. See 5.31.

23. (C)

Use the subjunctive after *recomendar* because it is a verb that communicates influence of one person on another in the noun clause that follows it. See 5.29.

24. (D)

You have to use the subjunctive after *para que*. Use the imperfect subjunctive because the other verb in the sentence is in the preterite. See 5.31.

25. (D)

Once again, after seeing *si,* look for the conditional tense somewhere in the sentence. You would see it in the conditional perfect, *habría invitado*. Usually when you see a compound tense in these sentences, use the compound tense in the other clause, too. See 5.32.

26. (D)

If the word *que* does not come before the verb, then you probably want to use the infinitive. See 5.6.

27. (C)

Do not confuse *ir* with *ver*. When you see the other verb in the sentence, *toques*, you will recognize the familiar negative command, too, and remember that *ir* is irregular in the affirmative familiar form. See 5.35.

28. (D)

Antes (de) que always requires the subjunctive in both the past and the present tenses. Look at the other verbs in the sentence to determine whether to use past or present subjunctive. See 5.31.

29. (D)

Ojalá always takes the subjunctive. Look at the rest of the sentence to determine past or present tense. The verb *gustaba* tells you to select the past subjunctive as the correct answer. See 5.33.

30. (D)

You need the subjunctive in the noun clause after a verb of emotion. *Sentir* is a verb of emotion. See 5.29.

31. (B)

This is an adjective clause, modifying an indefinite antecedent. The speaker is not certain that the university exists, so the verb in the adjective clause is in the subjunctive. See 5.30.

32. (C)

This is also an adjective clause. *Quiera* at the end of any word usually means that the antecedent is unknown to the speaker. Any time you see any of the indefinite antecedents listed in 5.30, you can quickly find the subjunctive among answer choices. See 5.30.

Set B

1. They asked me to bring refreshments to the party.

2. Whenever you want to come, come on and I'll be here waiting.

3. It was hard to finish, no matter how hard we worked.

4. The boy came in at midnight without his parents hearing him.

5. Do the work, then you will have finished with the hardest part.

6. They advise us to keep studying a little more.

7. What would you do if you won a million dollars?

8. Go home as soon as you can to say good-bye to your grandmother.

9. I was attending the University of Valencia while I was living there.

10. This morning when I woke up I didn't feel well.

11. They told me that the boys had already come by the house.

12. Who has told you that the subjunctive is easy?

13. Don't you think that tomorrow will be a good day to go?

14. There is no wise man who knows everything.

15. I did all the work yesterday so he would have it today. See 5.12 and 5.31.

16. They advised me to make the trip with them unless one of them happened to be sick when the group left.

17. You only had to look at him once to see that he was sick. (One look was enough to see that he was sick.)

Chapter 6: **Adverbs**

- Types of Adverbs
- Adverbial Rules

An adverb describes a verb, adjectives, or another adverb. It can communicate information about how or where something happens. Sometimes an entire clause describes something about the verb: It is a subordinate adverbial clause.

Where adverbs are placed in a sentence varies a lot, though they usually the follow the verb. For emphasis they precede the verb, but most often they follow.

Frequently in English adverbs end with *-ly*. That suffix, *-ly*, corresponds to *-mente* in Spanish. When a word ends with *-mente*, it is likely to be an adverb. Adding the suffix can cause spelling changes to the base word, though, so you need to be able to make the appropriate changes. For an adjective that ends with a consonant, simply add *-mente* at the end, as in *fácilmente*. Notice that the accent stays in the same place. Do the same thing for an adjective that ends in -e. For an adjective that ends with -o, drop the -o and add *-amente*, as in *rápidamente*.

When two adverbs that end with *-mente* appear in a sentence, the first one drops the ending, but retains a feminine adjective ending if it ends with -o. If one of the two adverbs does not end in *-mente*, it comes before the longer regular adverb form. The two adverbs are connected with a comma.

> **La pareja se quejaba ruidosa y amargamente.**
> The couple complained loudly and bitterly.

> **Los niños salieron alegre y rápidamente.**
> The children left happily and quickly.

TYPES OF ADVERBS

6.1 Adverbs of place tell where something takes place.

abajo	below	bajo	under
debajo	beneath	arriba	up, above
encima	on top	adentro	inside
dentro	inside	afuera	outside
fuera	outside	atrás	back, behind
detrás	back, behind	delante	ahead, in front
ante	before	adelante	ahead, in front
lejos	far	cerca	near
acá	(over) here	aquí	here
allí	there	allá	(over) there
ahí	(there, allí)	donde	where

The distinction in use between some of these adverbs is subtle. In general, *aquí* and *acá* refer to static placement. *Allí* and *allá* are used with verbs of motion. In addition *acá* and *allá*, in general, refer to locations closer or farther, respectively, from the speaker. These adverbs are sometimes followed by *de*.

Esos chicos por allá lo hicieron.
Those boys over there did it.

¡Juanito, ven acá ahora!
Johnny, come here right now!

Among the words that are variations of "above" and "below," *arriba* and *debajo* (de) have more literal meanings than *encima*, *abajo*, and *bajo*. And *encima* and *debajo* may even imply some physical contact because of proximity.

Los vecinos que viven arriba hacen mucho ruido.
The neighbors who live upstairs make a lot of noise.

La carta está debajo del libro que está encima de la mesa.
The letter is underneath the book that is on top of the table.

Lo hicieron bajo los ojos del nuevo jefe.
They did it under the eyes of the new boss.

Similarly, *detrás* has a more literal interpretation of "behind" than does *atrás*, which is used more figuratively.

El guante perdido estaba en el suelo detrás de la puerta.
The lost glove was on the floor behind the door.

Lo dejaron atrás cuando salieron.
They left him behind when they left.

Do not confuse *ante*, meaning "before," with *antes*, which also means "before." *Ante* refers to placement, and is an adverb of place, while *antes* is an adverb of time, meaning "before" in time.

El ladrón apareció ante el juez para confesar su crimen.
The thief appeared before the judge to confess his crime.

When adverbs of place are combined with a preposition, usually *de* or *a*, or when *a* is placed as a prefix in front, they take on subtle changes in meaning.

abajo	**Los niños corrían calle abajo.** The children were running down the street.
bajo	**Bajo su supervisión acabamos el trabajo.** Under his supervision we finished the work.
adelante	**Vamos a seguir adelante.** We are going to go ahead.
delante de	**Ponga la letra delante del número.** Put the letter in front of the number.
adentro	**Las señoras estaban sentadas adentro.** The ladies were seated inside.
dentro de	**Puse la carta dentro del sobre.** I put the letter inside the envelope.
afuera	**Niños, salgan afuera para jugar.** Children, go outside to play.
fuera de	**La fruta estaba fuera de su alcance.** The fruit was outside of his reach.
alrededor	**Miraron alrededor, pero no vieron nada.** They looked around, but didn't see anything.
alrededor de	**La zorra corría alrededor de la gallinera.** The fox ran around the chicken house.
atrás	**Atrás en al autobús, los niños dormían.** In the back of the bus, the children slept.
detrás de	**Un carro estaba estacionado detrás del otro.** One car was parked behind the other one.
cerca	**La tienda está cerca, no más de un kilómetro.** The store is nearby, no more than a kilometer.
cerca de	**Mis abuelos viven cerca de nosotros.** My grandparents live near us.
debajo	**Antes de salir, lo pusieron debajo.** Before leaving, they put it underneath.
debajo de	**Puso los zapatos debajo de la cama.** He put his shoes underneath the bed.

encima	Antes de poner la mesa, puso el mantel encima.
	Before setting the table, she put the tablecloth on top.
encima de	El pájaro grande voló por encima de la casa.
	The big bird flew above (over) the house.
enfrente	La casa de enfrente es la mía.
	The house in front is mine.
enfrente de	Enfrente de la iglesia, hay una plaza.
	In front of the church is a plaza
lejos	Fuimos lejos para asistir al colegio.
	We went a long way (far away) to go to school.
lejos de	Mi escuela está lejos de mi casa.
	My school is far from my house.

6.2 Adverbs of time are used frequently, so should be easy to remember. In addition to the phrases *alguna vez*, *la última vez*, and *la primera vez*, the primary one word adverbs of time are:

ahora	now	anoche	last night
ayer	yesterday	anteayer	day before yesterday
mañana	tomorrow	hoy	today
cuando	when	mientras	while
entonces	then, so then	luego	then
nunca	never	jamás	never, ever
antes	before(hand)	después	after(wards)
aún	still, yet	todavía	still, yet
ya	already	ya no	no longer
temprano	early	tarde	late
recién	recently, just	pronto	soon

Tarde and *mañana* can be an adverb or a noun. Look at how the word functions in the sentence to determine which form it takes. *Pasado mañana* means "day after tomorrow."

Siempre, *nunca*, and *jamás* are usually studied with indefinite adjectives and pronouns, but they are adverbs. The distinction between *nunca* and *jamás* is that *jamás* is more emphatic, with the meaning of "never, ever." You could remember it from the name of Never, Never Land in the story of Peter Pan, too.

Los niños perdidos vivían en la Tierra de Nunca Jamás.
The lost boys lived in Never, Never Land.

In any sentence *nunca* functions like all the other negative indefinite adjectives and pronouns: Use it as a double negative if it follows the verb, or place it in front of the verb to negate the verb.

En aquel entonces no vi nunca a mi mejor amiga.
In those days, I never saw my best friend.

En aquel entonces, nunca vi a mi mejor amiga.

In those days, I never saw my best friend.

You might have difficulty distinguishing *aún* from *aun*. Though you do not see this adverb often, *aún* has the meaning of *todavía*; they are practically synonymous. But *aun* without the accent means "even."

Aun hoy en día los acueductos romanos aún llevan agua.

Even today the Roman aqueducts still carry water.

Todavía and *ya* tend to cause confusion, because at times it appears that their use is idiomatic.

No quiero ver esa película, *ya* la vi.

I don't want to see that movie, I already saw it.

Todavía no he visto esa película, pero quiero verla.

I have not seen that movie yet, but I want to see it.

Todavía escribe a su antiguo novio.

She still writes to her former boy friend.

Ya no escribe a su antiguo novio.

She no longer writes to her former boyfriend.

6.3 Adverbs of manner describe how something is done.

así	thus, like this, like that, such, so
bien	well, really, thoroughly
mal	badly
como	like
según	accordingly, it depends

The adverbs *bien* and *mal* are especially easy to confuse with the adjectives *bueno* and *malo*.

Salí bien en el examen.

I did well on the exam.

El examen fue bueno; todos salieron bien.

The exam was good; everybody did well on it.

¿Cómo estás hoy?

—Estoy mal.

"How are you today?"

—"I am not well."

Aunque las instrucciones eran malas, los estudiantes buènos entendieron bien lo que tenían que hacer.

Although the instructions were bad, the good students understood well what they had to do.

In Spanish people rarely make the mistake so common in conversational English. *Bueno* is an adjective describing the character of the subject. *Bien* is the adverb describing how one feels in response to the question, "How are you today?" Notice that the verb *estar* is used in the question.

Bien has the additional meaning of "well, " "really," or "thoroughly."

> ¿Cómo prefieres la carne de res?
> —Bien cocida, por favor.

> How do you like your beef cooked?
> —Well done, please.

> **Esta mañana, me levanté bien temprano.**
> This morning I got up really early.

Así is highly idiomatic in the way it is used. You will probably see it in a context something like the one below.

> ¿Cómo se hace eso?
> —(Lo hace) así. Lo hace según las direcciones.

> How do you do that?
> —You do it this way. (You do it like this.) You do it according to the directions.

Some adverbs that describe how something is done are irregular: They do not end with -*mente*.

despacio	slowly
de prisa	quickly
a prisa	quickly
rápido	quickly, rapidly

Rápido has a full form, *rápidamente*, but in conversation, especially, a shorter form is preferred. The others do not have forms that end with -*mente*.

6.4 Adverbs of degree relate to comparative quantities, or degree of similarity or difference. Some are used in invariable structures like comparisons of inequality.

algo	somewhat, rather, a bit
apenas	barely, scarcely
bastante	enough. really, rather
demasiado	too much
casi	almost
cuanto	as much
más	more, very
menos	less
poco	little

sólo	only
medio	half
mucho, muy	very
tan	as
tanto	as much

The adverb *sólo*, meaning "only," has an accent, unlike the adjective *solo*. One way to remember *sólo* is that the accented form is a shortened form of *solamente*.

Apenas is an adverb that frequently introduces the preterite when narrating stories in the past tense.

Apenas entramos en la casa cuando empezó a llover.
We scarcely got inside the house when it started to rain.

Algo is used idiomatically. It can also be an indefinite pronoun, so make sure you understand how it functions in a sentence.

Esta tarde estaba algo cansada cuando llegué a casa.
I was somewhat (rather) tired when I got home this afternoon.

Do not expect to see the word *demasiado* used as often as it is in English. The meaning "too" is quite often implicit in the structure of the sentence. You would, however, see it to describe something that is excessive.

Es temprano para que venga.
It is too early for him to come.

Este chico es muy joven para conducir solo.
The boy is too young to be driving alone.

Hace mucho calor para estar en la playa hoy.
It's too hot to be at the beach today.

Esa mujer habla demasiado.
That woman talks too much.

You will recognize some of these adverbs, such as *muy*, *más*, and *menos*, from adjective structures of inequality. As adverbs they modify adjectives.

Mi amigo es muy alto.
My friend is very tall.

Mi mejor amigo es más alto que yo.
My best friend is taller than I.

Mi mejor amigo es menos alto que yo.
My best friend is shorter (less tall) than I.

The only place you will *never* use the adverb *muy* is in front of *mucho*. The way to say "very much" is *muchísimo*.

Tan will come in front of an adjective or another adverb to make a comparison.

> Los gatos son tan inteligentes como los perros.
> Cats are as intelligent as dogs.

> Los gatos corrieron tan rápido como los perros.
> Cats run as fast as dogs.

In the first sentence, *inteligentes* is an adjective. It agrees in number (it cannot agree in gender), with the noun *gatos*. *Tan* modifies *inteligentes*. In the second sentence, *rápido* is an adverb; if it were an adjective, it would agree in gender and number with *gatos*. So *tan* modifies *rápido*, another adverb.

Tanto is also frequently seen in structures of equality, where two nouns are compared. The difference it has with the adverbial comparisons above, however, is that with *tan* the two things compared are verbals. When you use *tanto* as an adverb, it is not followed by a noun, but rather by *como*, meaning "as."

> Nosotros estudiamos tanto como otros estudiantes.
> We study as much as other students.

> Los gatos corren tanto como los perros.
> Cats run as much as dogs.

6.5 Adverbs of conjecture, doubt or negation communicate a variety of meanings. Many are used conversationally, communicating the attitude of the speaker.

acaso	perhaps, maybe, by chance
bueno	okay, yes
no	no, not
sí	yes, certainly, definitely
quizá(s)	perhaps
tal vez	perhaps
también	also, as well
tampoco	neither, either
ya	yes, sure, indeed, of course

Three of these adverbs, *acaso*, *quizás*, and *tal vez* often can take the subjunctive, depending on the degree of uncertainty the speaker wishes to communicate. The subjunctive is frequently used to communicate uncertainty, but it is not grammatically necessary to use it.

The other adverbs communicating attitude are *también* and *tampoco*, which are often used with indefinite negative words. If *tampoco* does not precede the verb itself, it takes a negative in front of the verb it accompanies. For that reason, it can mean "either," because in English that is how we sometimes translate double negatives.

No quiero hacer la tarea esta noche.

—Ni yo tampoco.

I don't want to do the homework tonight.

—Me neither. (I don't either.)

The word *no* is an adverb, not an adjective. Adverbs do not come directly in front of nouns like they do in English.

Though *bueno* is an adjective, there are times when it functions as an adverb.

¿Te traigo algo?

—Bueno, un café con leche, por favor.

Can I bring you anything?

—Well, coffee with milk, please.

¿Te llamo mañana?

—Bueno.

Shall I call you tomorrow?

—Okay.

Sometimes the word *sí* is used in the middle of a sentence. In these cases, it emphasizes an affirmative attitude or response. Similarly, the word *ya* communicates agreement in a response.

Pero yo sí quería hacer la tarea.

But I did (indeed) want to do the homework.

¿Terminaste la tarea?

—Ya. (La terminé.)

Did you finish your homework?

—Yes. (It's already done.)

ADVERBIAL RULES

6.6 When an adverbial phrase is too cumbersome or long, a prepositional phrase can replace the adverb ending with *-mente*. *Con* and *sin* are the most common prepositions to use with nouns.

Hizo el examen sin miedo.

He took the test fearlessly.

Terminó el trabajo sin esfuerzo.

He finished the work effortlessly.

Nos habló con paciencia.

He spoke to us patiently.

Nos habló con gran paciencia.

He spoke to us very patiently. (with great patience)

Ellos corrían locamente, pero él les hablaba con calma.

They was running around crazily, but he was speaking to them calmly.

Sometimes *sin* plus an infinitive can have the meaning of an adverb.

> El pobre dejó caer el vaso sin querer.
> The poor fellow dropped the glass unintentionally.

Other adverbs used with prepositions are idiomatic; you just have to learn them separately.

en seguida	immediately (inmediatamente)
por desgracia	unfortunately (desgraciadamente)
por completo	completely (completamente)
en serio	seriously (seriamente)
de súbito	suddenly (súbitamente)
de repente	suddenly (repentinamente)

Some common expressions combine prepositions and adverbs.

a gusto	at ease, comfortably
a medias	half, halfway
a menudo	often, frequently
al final	at the end
en alguna parte	somewhere
en fin	finally, in the long run
en resumen	in conclusion
no... hasta	not until
por cierto	certainly; by the way; as a matter of fact
por fin	finally
por poco	almost

6.7 Some adverbial conjunctions always require the subjunctive, while others require it only at times.

Always Use the Subjunctive with:

para que	Se lo dije para que lo supieras.
	I told it to you so (that) you would know.
a fin de que	Lo hizo a fin de que pudiera ir.
	He did it so that he could go.
a menos que	A menos que lo haga, no irá.
	Unless he does it, he will not go.
salvo que	Salvo que lo haga, no irá.
	Unless he does it, he will not go.
a no ser que	A no ser que lo vea, no diré nada.
	Unless I see him, I will not say anything.
antes (de) que	Antes de que se fuera, se lo dije.
	Before he left, I told it to him.

con tal que   Con tal que fuera, iría.
                 Provided that he went, I would go.

sin que   Entró sin que nadie le oyera.
                 He came in without anyone hearing him.

en caso que   En caso que fuera, le di dinero.
                 In case he were going, I gave him money.

The following adverbial conjunctions sometimes take the subjunctive, depending on the context. See chapter Five to review use of the subjunctive.

Sometimes Use the Subjunctive with:

cuando   Le diré cuando venga.
                 I will tell him when he comes.
                 Le dije cuando vino.
                 I told him when he came.

en cuanto   Le diré en cuanto llegue.
                 I will tell him as soon as he comes.
                 Le dije en cuanto llegó.
                 I told him as soon as he arrived.

tan pronto como Le diré tan pronto como llegue.
                 I will tell him as soon as he arrives.
                 Le dije tan pronto como vino.
                 I told him as soon as he came.

a pesar de que   A pesar de que no lo quiera, se lo daré.
                 In spite of not wanting it, I'll give it to him.
                 A pesar de que no lo quería, se lo di.
                 In spite of not wanting it, I gave it to him.

después (de) que Después de que vaya, se lo diré.
                 After he goes, I will tell you.
                 Después de que se fue, recordé otra cosa.
                 After he left, I remembered something else.

mientras   Mientras estén aquí, no saldré
                 While they are here, I will not leave.
                 Mientras estaban aquí, no salí.
                 While they were here I did not leave.

hasta que   Hasta que vuelva, lo esperaré.
                 Until he comes back, I will wait.
                 Hasta que volvió, esperé.
                 Until he returned, I waited.

de modo que	Habla de modo que lo comprendan.
	He speaks in such a way that they may understand him.
	Habla de modo que lo comprenden.
	He speaks in such a way that they understand him.
de manera que	Lo hizo de manera que nadie lo viera.
	He did it in such a way that nobody might see it.
	Lo hizo de manera que nadie lo vio.
	He did it in such a way that nobody saw it.
aunque	Aunque llueva, iré.
	Even though it may rain, I will go.
	Aunque llueve, iré.
	Even though it is raining, I will go.

THINGS TO REMEMBER

- The distinction between some adverbs is subtle. In general, *aquí* and *acá* refer to static placement. *Allí* and *allá* are used with verbs of motion.
- Do not confuse *ante*, which means "before" in terms of place, with *antes*, which means "before" in the sense of time.
- The adverbs *bien* and *mal* are easy to confuse with the adjectives *bueno* and *malo*. *Bueno* describes the character of the subject. *Bien* would be your response to the question, "How are you today?"

REVIEW QUESTIONS

Set A: In the following exercise, circle the adverb that completes the meaning of the sentence.

1. Los hombres salieron ___ silenciosamente como entraron.

   A) tanto   B) tanta   C) tantos   D) tan

2. Las alumnas contestaron ____ y vagamente.

   A) distraídas   B) distraído   C) distraídamente D) distraída

3. Quiénes trabajan ___ alcanzarán lo que quieren.

   A) duro   B) duros   C) duras   D) dura

4. ___ los caballos empezaron a correr.

   A) Bueno   B) De repente   C) Demasiado   D) Todavía

5. Me gustaría acompañarte, pero no puedo ___.

   A) también   B) algo   C) nada   D) tampoco

6. Después de tanto trabajo me acosté ___ temprano.

   A) tanto   B) así   C) bien   D) recién

7. Entraba lentamente en el cuarto cuando ___ algo me dio en la cara.

   A) en serio   B) de repente   C) por completo   D) a veces

8. ____ llegué cuando se me acercó para darme las noticias.

   A) Como   B) Apenas   C) Siempre   D) Acaso

9. Por la mañana no me gusta levantarme ___ temprano.

   A) bueno   B) ya   C) tal   D) tan

10. En el amor tanto como en la guerra, vale esforzarse ___.

    A) mal   B) casi   C) bien   D) poco

11. No sé quién llamó. ____ fue su amigo.

    A) Apenas   B) Tal vez   C) Ya   D) Aún

12. ____ recuerdo las tortas que preparaba mi mamá.

    A) Como   B) Solo   C) Bastante   D) Todavía

Set B: Select the correct adverbial conjunction that best completes the sentence.

1. Le di las noticias ___ otra persona pudiera decírselas.

   A) mientras   B) después de que   C) antes que   D) cuando

2. El año pasado estaba en casa ___ ocurrió el desastre.

   A) antes que   B) sin que   C) después que   D) con tal que

3. Le señora le envolvió el regalo ___ pudiera dárselo a su novia.

   A) a menos que   B) a fin de que   C) a no ser que   D) cuando

4. El estudiante salió bien ___ nadie le ayudara.

   A) sin que   B) después que   C) mientras   D) hasta que

5. ___ hacer el examen, estudia para aprender todo lo que puedas.

   A) Después de   B) Con tal que   C) A menos que   D) Antes de

Set C: Select the adverb of place that completes the sentence.

1. Estoy en el quinto piso, y mi amigo trabaja ___ , en el segundo.

   A) debajo   B) bajo   C) abajo   D) debajo de

2. Le gustará esa casa, tiene un jardín elegante ___ .

   A) afueras   B) fuera de   C) detrás   D) atrás

3. La mujer lentamente puso ek pendiente ___ de la caja.

   A) adentro   B) dentro   C) bajo   D) tras

4. No pudieron dormir a causa del tráfico de los aviones ___ .

   A) encima   B) arriba   C) lejos   D) alrededor de

5. En el sexto período, ella se sentaba ___ mí.

   A) delante de   B) cerca   C) enfrente   D) atrás

ANSWERS AND EXPLANATIONS

Set A

1. (D)

Use the shortened form of *tanto* in front of adverbs. You use only the longer form in front of nouns. See 6.4.

2. (D)

Use the feminine form of the adjective when there are two adverbs.

3. (A)

This is an adjective used as an adverb, in the same way that *rápido* is used when it is an adverb and does not end in *-mente*.

4. (B)

You need an adverb of time that *empezaron* will follow. *Todavía* is the only other adverb of time, but it makes no sense in this sentence. See 6.2.

5. (D)

The only adverb that makes any sense is *tampoco*, because of the negative before the verb. *Nada* and *algo* are pronouns that make no sense. They can be used as adverbs, but in this sentence they do not fit. *Algo* used as an adverb has the meaning of "rather," and *nada* is usually preceded by *por* when used as an adverb.

6. (C)

Bien in this sentence has the meaning of "very." See 6.3.

7. (B)

You need an adverb that will be followed by the preterite. An adverb meaning "suddenly" is the only choice that works here.

8. (B)

Scarcely is the adverb that sets up the preterite in this sentence. No other adverb makes sense. *Siempre* would refer to more than one time in the past, so it does not fit. The others are not adverbs of time. See 6.2 and 6.4.

9. (D)

You want an adverb that means "so." The only one that fits is *tan*. The negative of the verb eliminates *ya* as a possibility.

10. (C)

Though the other adverbs fit grammatically, *bien*, meaning "well," the best answer. If *poco* had been *un poco*, you could have correctly chosen it.

11. (B)

The first sentence makes perhaps the best choice. No other answer choice makes sense. See 6.4.

12. (D)

To make *solo* an adverb, you need to have an accent. Otherwise, it is an adjective. That makes "still" the best answer. See 6.2.

Set B

1. (C)

The verb *pudiera* indicates the need for an adverbial conjunction that requires the subjunctive. *Mientras* and *cuando* are adverbial conjunctions of time, but they take the indicative if the action in the subordinate clause has already happened. The action takes place in the past, so these two adverbial conjunctions do not work here. *Antes que* always takes the subjunctive, in the past, present, and future. See 6.2.

2. (C)

The past tense in the subordinate clause tells you that you cannot use *con tal que*, *antes que*, or *sin que* because they always take the subjunctive. *Después que* is the only possibility. See 6.7.

3. (B)

The most common adverbial conjunction of purpose is *para que*, but in fact *a fin de que* means the same thing. Sometimes the preposition *de* is omitted in the phrase. In the context of the sentence, the adverbial conjunction of condition, *a menos que* and *a no ser que* do not make any sense. *Cuando* is an adverbial conjunction of time that does not make any sense here. See 6.7.

4. (A)

Después que, *mientras*, and *hasta que* all would take the indicative because of the past tense in this sentence. *Sin que* is the answer choice that always takes the subjunctive.

5. (D)

You should have recognized the familiar command in *estudia*, meaning that this sentence communicates some instructions about a test. The only adverbial conjunction that makes any sense, then, is *antes de*. There is no conjugated verb in the subordinate clause, so the two choices that end with *que* are not correct. They would not work grammatically. That leave *antes* and *después*. While you could say "After taking the final exam, study to learn as much as you can," it does not make much sense. "Before" is a more logical answer.

Set C

1. (C)

You want the choice that means "downstairs," which is *abajo*. *Debajo* means "below" more than it means "downstairs." See 6.1.

2. (D)

"In the back" is the meaning of *atrás*. The other alternatives have to do with the out of doors, but that doesn't make much sense, since that is where gardens usually are. *Afuera* would have worked, but not *afueras*, which means "outskirts," as of a city or town.

3. (B)

You want to say "inside" of the box. *Adentro* means "inside" in the sense of "indoors." *Bajo* means "beneath" or "under" in a figurative sense, so it makes no sense. *Tras* is the same as *detrás de*, which would be redundant, because *de* follows the blank.

4. (B)

Encima indicates close proximity between the places or things named in the sentence, or the sense of "on top of." The meaning here is "overhead," which is *arriba*. *Lejos* makes no sense, because airplanes in the distance would not cause a lack of sleep. Airplanes do not normally fly around places where people sleep, either, so *alrededor* is not a good choice.

5. (A)

"In front of" is the only possibility. *Atrás* means "in *the back*," which does not work here. The other two adverbs have no preposition after them, which means the first noun is not set in a specific place in relation to another person or object.

Chapter 7: **Pronouns**

- Personal Pronouns
- Prepositional Pronouns
- Indirect Object Pronouns
- Direct Object Pronouns
- Verbs That Change Meaning According to Pronoun
- Indefinite Pronoun *Lo*
- Reflexive Pronouns
- Demonstrative Pronouns
- Possessive Pronouns
- Interrogative Pronouns
- Indefinite Pronouns
- Relative Pronouns

Pronouns can be very confusing, but they don't have to be your downfall. First, the basics: Pronouns replace nouns. All nouns have gender and number, so pronouns must be the same person, number, and gender of the nouns they replace. Pronouns can replace proper nouns, names, or common nouns, nouns for people, things, or concepts. In Spanish there are five main types of pronouns: personal, object of the preposition, indirect object, direct object, and reflexive.

Word order is important with pronouns, and they are placed differently than they are in English. The placement of a pronoun in a sentence depends on the kind of pronoun it is.

7.1 Personal pronouns (subjects of verbs) generally come before conjugated verbs. Reflexive, indirect, or direct object pronouns come *before* conjugated verb forms in declarative, interrogative, and exclamatory sentences, as well as before negative commands. They come *after* (and are attached to) affirmative commands, infinitives, and present participles.

These rules for placement are invariable. When there is a combination of an indirect and a direct object pronoun, the indirect object pronoun always precedes the direct object pronoun. When there is a reflexive and a direct object pronoun, the reflexive pronoun always comes first.

When the verb is a compound form, a progressive form, or an expression that includes an infinitive, the pronouns may come either in front of the conjugated verb or at the end of the infinitive or present participle. Pronouns are never added to past participles.

When two pronouns are added to the end of an infinitive, an accent mark is written over the vowel where the stress falls before the pronouns are added. For infinitives, this would be over the vowel in the infinitive ending. When a pronoun is added to an affirmative command or present participle, an accent mark is written over the syllable where the stress falls before the pronoun is added. For first, second, third singular and third person plural verb forms, this syllable would be the second to last syllable of the conjugated verb form. For first and second persons plural, this would be over the first vowel of the ending. This is important to know to help you recognize command forms.

Prepositional pronouns, demonstrative, and possessive pronouns are much more variable in where they come in a sentence. Usually they appear in the same places that they do in English sentences.

PERSONAL PRONOUNS

7.2 With personal pronouns, use the second person familiar "you" with people you would call by their first name. The third person "you" is more formal.

	Singular		Plural	
1st person	yo	I	nosotros nosotras	we
2nd person	tú	you (familiar)	vosotros vosotras	you (familiar)
3rd person	él ella usted (Vd.)	he, it (m) she, it (f) you (polite)	ellos ellas ustedes (Vds.)	they (m) they (f) you (polite)

In Spanish, *tú, vosotros, usted,* and *ustedes* all mean "you." But the second persons *tú* and *vosotros* are more informal than the third persons *usted* and *ustedes.* Using the second person indicates familiarity; you show that you are close friends. (There is even a verb for this, *tutear,* meaning "to talk in the second person.")

In the third person, "it" has a masculine and a feminine form, because all nouns are of one gender or the other. When you substitute third person pronouns for nouns, you must select *él* or *ella.* These pronouns can refer to persons or things, so don't be confused when you see them and are trying to identify a subject of a verb.

Any combination of *yo* plus a noun or pronoun makes the subject *nosotros* or *nosotras*, depending on the gender of the two subjects. In Spanish America *tú* plus another subject will be the third person *ustedes* instead of *vosotros*. But don't overlook *vosotros* just because it may not be a point of grammar on the test. It may appear in a reading selection, and is used in Spain.

Subject pronouns usually precede the verb in declarative sentences, the most common kind of sentence. In interrogative sentences (questions) and exclamatory sentences, the subject pronouns tend to follow the verb. Keep this in mind when we begin looking at other kinds of pronouns.

7.3 When the ending on a verb form indicates the person and number of the subject, no personal pronoun is necessary. This is true especially for the first and second persons singular and plural. The third person forms, however, each have three or four possible subjects, so a subject pronoun is commonly used for those. Usually a noun or subject pronoun is used and then not repeated unless there is a change of subject or the speaker wishes to emphasize the subject. Keep this in mind when you are trying to figure out who or what the subjects of the verbs are. When you listen to spoken Spanish, using subject pronouns indicates emphasis that is often communicated in English with intonation or voice pitch.

PREPOSITIONAL PRONOUNS

7.4 When a pronoun follows a preposition, use a prepositional pronoun. Prepositional pronouns are:

	Singular		Plural	
1st person	*mí* *commigo*	me	*nosotros* *nosotras*	us
2nd person	*ti* *contigo*	you (familiar)	*vosotros* *vosotras*	you (familiar)
3rd person	*él* *ella* *Vd.*	him, it (m) her, it (f) you (polite)	*ellos* (m) *ellas* (f) *Vds.*	them them you (polite)

Except for the first and second persons singular, these pronouns are the same as the personal pronouns. Notice also that the first person singular has an accent mark; that little mark distinguishes *mí* from *mi*. One form is a pronoun (*mí*), and the other is a possessive adjective (*mi*). It is important to know this distinction.

Also notice that after the preposition *con* there is an irregular form, *conmigo, contigo,* and *consigo*. There is a third person form, *consigo*, but it does not replace *con él, ella, Vd.* as the first and second person does. *Consigo* means "with him, her, or you," but is not common.

The hard part about prepositional pronouns, or object of the preposition pronouns, is not learning the forms, it's remembering the two exceptions with *con* (in the first and second persons singular), remembering the accent on *mí*, and recognizing a preposition when you see one. There is a whole chapter on prepositions, but let's look at some common prepositions here. Whenever you see these—either alone or with other words such as *por encima de*—think about using the correct pronoun, if a pronoun is needed.

a	to, at
con	with
de	from, of
en	in, on
por	by, through, for
para	for, in order to
hacia	toward
sobre	over, on, about
bajo	under, below
desde	from, since
hasta	until, up to, even
entre	between
sin	without

The neuter pronoun, *ello*, is used after prepositions when the antecedent is a situation, idea, or condition.

> No pienses más en ello.
> Don't think any more about it.

INDIRECT OBJECT PRONOUNS

7.5 The indirect object is the person or thing receiving the direct object, or being acted upon by the subject. Indirect object pronouns tell to whom, for whom, from whom, or by whom something is done. There are two forms of the indirect object pronouns: stressed and unstressed. The stressed form is optional, since it serves to call attention to the pronoun by repeating the person and number of the pronoun. The unstressed form is not optional.

The *unstressed forms* (not optional) for indirect object pronouns are as follows. You must use the unstressed forms instead of a literal translation in a sentence when using the indirect object pronoun.

	Singular		Plural	
1st person	*me*	me	*nos*	us
2nd person	*te*	you (familiar)	*os*	you (familiar)
3rd person	*le*	him, it, you (m) her, it, you (f)	*les*	them, you (m) them, you (f)

Since the third person indirect object pronouns, *le* and *les*, have several possible referents (such as to him, to you, to it), you'll often see in Spanish a prepositional phrase in addition to the indirect object pronoun. Prepositional phrases such as *a él, a ella, a Vds.* serve only to clarify the referent.

For example, you would say:

Estoy pidiéndole (a Vd.) traer sus discos al baile.
I am asking you to bring your cds to the dance.

You want to use *a Vd.* to show who is supposed to bring the cds. If you don't use *a Vd.*, it could mean *a él* or *a ella*, meaning you were asking "him" or "her" to bring the cds.

Vamos a darles (a ellos) un regalo cuando vengan.
We are going to give them a gift when they come.

In the example above, you need to include *a ellos*, because even though *les* means "to them," it can also mean "to you." Including it clarifies to whom you are giving the gift.

Here are some additional examples:

Llamele Vd. (a él) esta noche para decirle las noticias.
Call him this aftrnoon to tell him the news.

No les digan (a ellos) todos nuestros secretos.
Don't tell them all of our secrets.

Frecuentemente les daba dulces cuando los veía.
I frequently gave them candy whenever I saw them.

The *stressed forms* are optional and are used for emphasis and clarity. They use the preposition *a* or *de,* followed by the appropriate prepositional pronoun. They are used only for emphasis, since inflection of voice in Spanish does not communicate emphasis the way it does in English.

—¿Te llamó a ti?
—*Sí, a mí,* or *Me llamó a mí.*

7.6 Several verbs take the indirect object pronoun, because their meaning is not translated literally. *Gustar* is the most common; the indirect object pronoun will tell you to *whom* something is pleasing. Other verbs are *faltan, parecer, quedar, agradar, bastar, hacer falta, sobrar*, and sometimes *tocar*.

What is in English the object of the verb becomes the subject in Spanish. Again, with *gustar,* "to be pleasing to," the indirect object pronoun refers to what is in English the subject. In Spanish "The play is pleasing to me" becomes *Me gusta el drama.* The ending on the verb is *-a,* a third person singular ending, while the indirect object pronoun is in the first person singular, *me,* and comes before the noun. Note that *me* is an indirect object pronoun, not a personal pronoun.

Me gusta el drama.
The play is pleasing to me. (I like the play.)

This seems simple enough, until we try out the third person structure.

A los muchachos les gustan las muchachas.
A ellos les gustan ellas.
The boys like the girls. (The girls are pleasing to the boys.)

It is a little harder to tell who likes whom when the nouns are replaced with pronouns. *A* replaces *A los muchachos*, and *ellas* replaces *las muchachas*. You know who likes whom by the personal *a* in front of *ellos*, indicating the indirect object, and the personal *a* that is absent in front of *ellas*. *Ellas* with no personal *a* means that *ellas* is the subject of the verb *gustan*: "Girls are pleasing to boys," or "Boys like girls." If you were to eliminate all of the pronouns except the indirect object pronoun, you would have "They like them." The context would have to tell you who liked whom.

Nos quedan diez minutos hasta que salga el avión.
We have ten minutes left until the plane leaves.

Le faltó a él una página para terminar el libro.
He had one page left in order to finish the book.

Les hacía falta la práctica para poder hablar mejor.
They were lacking practice to be able to speak better.

Te toca a ti traer el desayuno para la reunión.
It's your turn to bring breakfast for the meeting.

The indirect object pronoun also commonly substitutes for a possessive adjective when speaking of a part of the body or an article of clothing.

Me duele la cabeza esta mañana.
My head hurts this morning.

Me duelen los pies de tanto caminar ayer.
My feet hurt from walking so much yesterday.

> Some people use *la* as an indirect object pronoun (*leísmo, laísmo*), though the practice is not common. You will not see it on the SAT Subject Test: Spanish.

In both of these cases, the subject of the verb is a part of the body. In English, we say "my" and then name whatever part. In Spanish the tendency is to avoid using the possessive. There are some instances where it is permissible, but most often it is not.

7.7 An indirect object pronoun plus an infinitive can act as an object of a verb to replace the subjunctive in dependent noun clauses. Put the indirect object pronoun that corresponds to the person and number of the subject in the dependent clause. Drop *que*, and add the infinitive in place of the conjugated verb.

Me aconsejaron ir a una escuela cerca de casa.
They advised me to go to a school close to home.

Me aconsejaron que fuera a una escuela cerca de casa.

They advised that I go to a school close to home.

7.8 It is possible to use an indirect object pronoun even when the objective complement is also used. Don't be thrown off by this use of the pronoun when the noun is also used. The indirect object pronoun is used redundantly especially when the subjunctive is used in a subordinate or dependent clause.

Le dio al niño unos dulces calmarlo.

He gave the boy some candy to calm him.

Le dio al niño unos dulces para que se calmara.

He gave the boy some candy so that he would calm down.

DIRECT OBJECT PRONOUNS

7.9 Direct objects receive the direct action of the subject. They answer the questions "Who?" or "What?"

	Singular		Plural	
1st person	*me*	myself	*nos*	us
2nd person	*te*	you (familiar)	*os*	you (familiar)
3rd person	*lo* *la*	him, it, you (masc.) her, it, you (fem.) itself yourself	*los*	them, you (masc.) them, you (fem.)

The first and second persons singular and plural are the same as the indirect object pronouns. The third person pronouns are different. It is probably helpful to know that in Spain, the pronoun le is used as a direct object pronoun when it refers to a male.

Mi novio me dio un regalo para mi cumpleaños.

My boyfriend gave me a gift for my birthday.

Mi novio me lo dio para mi cumpleaños.

My boyfriend gave it to me for my birthday.

Pide a tu padre el dinero que quieras.

Ask your father for the money you want.

Pídeselo a tu padre.

Ask your father for it.

As per the last examples, you do not need both a direct and an indirect object pronoun to use one or the other. Similarly, when you substitute a pronoun for a noun, you drop all of the modifiers, even the adjective clauses. Without the noun, "you want," which modifies "money," is dropped.

Sometimes you will see a direct object pronoun used redundantly, though the practice is not as common as with indirect object pronouns. With direct object pronouns, this is especially true when the object noun comes in front of the verb, instead of after it where is normally comes.

Las manzanas las usé en un pastel.
I used the apples in a pie.

A la señora no la vi al salir.
I did not see the woman when I left.

You will also see the direct object pronoun when *todo (toda, todos, todas)* is used as a direct object. Since *todo* refers to a specific noun, it will agree in gender and number with that noun.

Los saludamos a todos.
We greeted all (of the guests).

Las comimos todas esta mañana. (las manzanas)
We ate them all up this morning

Aside from these cases it is not common to use the direct object pronoun redundantly.

VERBS THAT CHANGE MEANING ACCORDING TO PRONOUN

7.10 A few verbs take the indirect object in Spanish, but do not follow the standard rules. *Ayudar*, *invitar*, and *preguntar* take the indirect object pronoun, even though they do not do so in *English*.

Le pregunté si quería acompañarme.
I asked him if he wanted to accompany me.

Le ayudó a preparar la lección.
I helped her prepare the lesson.

A verb can take either the direct or indirect object, though each will mean different things.

Le robó ayer.   **Lo robó del banco.**

He robbed him yesterday.   He stole it (the money)
from the bank.

Le pegó ligeramente.   **Lo pegamos en la pared.
(el cartel)**

He hit him lightly   We stuck it on the wall.

INDEFINITE PRONOUN *LO*

7.11 It isn't always clear where the referent for *lo* is. You know that all nouns have gender, and pronouns replace nouns. But sometimes *lo* doesn't seem to refer to anything in particular. In these cases, the referent is considered neuter in gender, and refers to an idea contained in a whole clause. It is frequent with short, one syllable sentences.

> Lo siento, señor. No hay remedio.
> I'm sorry (about that), sir. There is no helping it.

> ¿Has oído que no tenemos clases mañana?
> —Sí, lo sé. ¡Cuánto me alegro! Estoy cansadísimo.

> Have you heard that we don't have classes tomorrow?
> —Yes, I know. How glad I am! I'm really tired.

Lo has no particular referent in the first example; it refers to a situation, commonly expressed in English as "about that." In the last example, *lo* refers to the news about not having classes. *Lo* does not have an English equivalent in such a case.

In other cases *lo* is used as a complement to replace adjectives, pronouns, or nouns, when used with the verbs *ser*, *estar*, and *parecer*. There is no word in English that translates this use of *lo*; the meaning is usually communicated through inflection of voice.

> Tú siempre mientes. ¡Eres mala conmigo!
> —No, ¡no lo soy! Sólo que siempre exageras las cosas.

> When there is no specific referent, the indefinite *lo* is neuter in gender. It refers to an idea expressed in a whole clause instead of a single word.

REFLEXIVE PRONOUNS

7.12 Reflexive pronouns are common in Spanish with some verbs. They are not translated literally, however. Reflexive means that the action is "reflected" back on the subject, or that the subject does the action to him or herself. The pronoun and the verb ending are the same person and number, as in *Me pregunto qué pasa,* "I ask myself what is happening." These types of verbs are not common in English.

Like the indirect and direct object pronouns, the first and second persons singular and plural are the same, so you just have to learn the third persons.

		Singular		Plural
1st person	*me*	myself	*nos*	ourselves
2nd person	*te*	yourself (familiar)	*os*	yourselves (familiar)
3rd person	*se*	himself	*se*	themselves
		herself itself yourself (polite)		yourselves (polite)

The reflexive pronoun can be used for the same reason that the indirect object pronoun is used with parts of the body or articles of clothing: to avoid the possessive adjective. *Me lavo las manos* ("I wash my hands") for example, uses the reflexive pronoun instead of the pronoun for "my."

Other times it is understood that the subject acts upon itself, though the reflexive pronoun is not included in the English translation. *Me siento en la silla* ("I sit down in the chair") uses a reflexive pronoun to show that the subject seats himself (or herself). Without the pronoun, someone else seats the person. *El mozo sentó a la señora a la mesa* ("The waiter seated the lady at the table") does not use the reflexive pronoun. If a pronoun were used in this last example, you would say *La sentó a la mesa*, meaning "He seated her at the table."

levantar	to raise, lift	levantarse	to get up
enfadar	to anger	enfadarse	to get angry
desmayar	to dismay	desmayarse	to faint
sentar	to seat	sentarse	to sit down
alegrar	to gladden	alegrarse	to be glad
avergonzar	to shame, to make ashamed	avergonzarse	to be ashamed
acercar	to place near, to bring near	acercarse	to approach, to come near
alejar	to move away	alejarse	to move away, to distance
mejorar	to improve	mejorarse	to improve, to get better
mojar	to wet	mojarse	to get wet
secar	to dry	secarse	to dry off
desatar	to untie	desatarse	to become untied
casar	to wed	casarse	to marry, to get married
regocijar	to gladden	regocijarse	to rejoice

In English, we often add another word: "to become," "to get," etc. If you can't remember which verbs take a reflexive pronoun, look for the pronoun that is the same person and number as the subject of the verb, and look at the context to see if you need a reflexive pronoun.

7.13 When an action is reciprocal, with a subject and object acting upon each other, the reflexive pronoun is used. In English we use the phrase "each other." In such cases the reflexive pronoun can be used with verbs that are not normally used reflexively, such as *Nos vemos mañana*, meaning, "We'll see each other tomorrow."

Los dos amantes se miraron y él le sonrió.
The two lovers looked at each other and he smiled at her.

7.14 When something happens suddenly or accidentally, it is common to use the reflexive pronoun and an indirect object pronoun to depersonalize the event. The object acts upon itself, as it were, to present the person (indicated with the indirect object pronoun) as an innocent bystander. In such cases the verb is a third person singular or plural form, depending on the number of the subject.

> **Se me ocurrió una idea brillante.**
> A brilliant idea occurred to me.
>
> **Se le cayó el vaso al mozo.**
> The waiter dropped the glass.
>
> **Se me rompió la computadora.**
> The computer crashed (malfunctioned) on me.

This may appear to be a variation of the PASSIVE VOICE, in which *se* indicates that the subject is acted upon by an agent. The reflexive pronoun indicates the PASSIVE VOICE and the indirect object pronoun indicates to whom the action is done. The ACTIVE VOICE is more common. The examples below illustrate how *se* is used passively with an indirect object pronoun. In either case, the agent is indefinite, irrelevant in the information communicated.

> **Se le nombró líder del grupo.**
> He was named leader of the group.
>
> **Le nombraron líder del grupo.**
> They named him leader of the group.

In the substitute construction for the PASSIVE VOICE, using *se*, the agent is an irrelevant piece of information. The focus of the structure is on the action, not the perpetrators of the action.

7.15 When a singular or plural third person indirect object pronoun is followed by a third person singular or plural direct object pronoun, the indirect object pronoun always changes to *se*. There are no exceptions to this rule. It only applies to third person object pronouns.

When this situation appears, look carefully at the antecedents to figure out to whom or what the indirect object pronoun refers. The *se* in this case is not reflexive.

La niñera le lavó la cara al niño.	**La niñera le lavó la cara a él.**
The babysitter washed the child's face.	The babysitter washed his face.
Ella le lavó la cara a él.	**Ella se la lavó a él.**
She washed his face.	She washed it for him.
	Ella se la lavó.
	She washed it for him.

La niñera is the subject of the verb *lavó*. *La cara* is the direct object of *lavó*. *Al niño* is the indirect object. When substitutions are made for the nouns, *ella* is used for *la niñera*, *la* is used for *la cara*, *le* is used for *al niño*.

In the last sentence *a él* is omitted, but the meaning is still there because *se* functions as an indirect object pronoun. The prepositional phrase that clarifies the indirect object pronoun is not necessary, but the indirect object pronoun is. So you need to use *se* for *le*. You would have to tell from the context to whom *se* referred.

Now compare the final sentence above with the final sentence at the end of this series.

La niñera se lavó la cara.
The baby sitter washed her (own) face.

Ella se lavó la cara.
She washed her face.

Ella se la lavó.
She washed it.

The last two sentences are identical in Spanish, *Ella se la lavó*, but they have different meanings depending on how you interpret *se*. You would have to rely on the context of the sentence to tell what "it" means.

7.16 Synopsis of personal, prepositional, indirect, direct, and reflexive pronouns.

	Personal	Prepositional	Indirect Object	Direct Object	Reflexive
1st person	*yo*	*mí, conmigo*	*me*	*me*	*me*
2nd person	*tú*	*ti*	*te*	*te*	*te*
3rd person	*él* *élla* *Vd.*	*él* *ella* *Vd.*	*le*	*lo* *la*	*se*
1st person	*nosotros* *nosotras*	*nosotros* *nosotras*	*nos*	*nos*	*nos*
2nd person	*vosotros* *vosotras*	*vosotros* *vosotras*	*os*	*os*	*os*
3rd person	*ellos* *ellas* *Vds.*	*ellos* *ellas* *Vds.*	*les*	*los* *las*	*se*

Pay particular attention to the third person pronouns. And even though personal and prepositional pronouns are similar, unless you recognize the prepositions, it is easy to misidentify the function of the pronoun.

DEMONSTRATIVE PRONOUNS

7.17 The difference between demonstrative adjectives and demonstrative pronouns is that the pronouns with adjectival equivalents have accent marks.

éste	ésta	ése	ésa	aquél	aquélla
éstos	éstas	ésos	ésas	aquéllos	aquéllas

"One" is sometimes implied in the meaning of these pronouns.

> Me gusta esta blusa más que ésa.
> I like this blouse more than that one.

> Me gustan esos zapatos deportivos más que aquéllos.
> I like those sneakers (there) more than those over there.

Unlike adjectives, there is a neuter form of the demonstrative pronoun: It works much the same way as *lo* in referring to an idea or concept.

> ¡Eso es! Ahora sé cómo voy a resolver el problema.
> That's it! Now I know how I am going to solve the problem.

> Esto es lo que tenemos que hacer.
> This is what we need to do.

In both cases above the referent for *eso* and *esto* is indefinite. The first one refers to an idea the speaker has had. The second refers to a concept. *Aquello* can also be used to refer to something indefinite and remote, either in time or place. Notice that none of the neuter forms takes an accent.

POSSESSIVE PRONOUNS

7.18 Possessive pronouns are like one of the forms of possessive adjectives. Like adjectives, they agree in gender and number with the nouns they modify. though unlike adjectives, they take an article.

el mío	los míos
la mía	las mías

el tuyo	los tuyos
la tuya	las tuyas

el suyo	los suyos
la suya	las suyas

el nuestro	los nuestros
la nuestra	las nuestras

el vuestro	los vuestros
la vuestra	las vuestras
el suyo	los suyos
la suya	las suyas

Finding the noun that these pronouns replace is not usually hard: Look for a noun that is the same person, number, and gender of the pronoun.

> **Miguel lleva unos zapatos nuevos hoy, y los compró en la misma tienda en que tú compraste los tuyos.**
> Michael bought some new shoes today, and he bought them in the same store where you bought yours.

> **¡Qué simpáticos eran! Invitaron a los padres de Elena a la fiesta, y también a los nuestros.**
> How nice they were! They invited Elena's parents to the party, and ours, too.

> **Estaba tan cansado ayer que apenas pude acabar mi trabajo, mucho menos ayudarles con el suyo.**
> I was so tired yesterday that I could scarcely finish my work, much less help them with theirs.

As you can see, there can be a lot of ambiguity in the third person singular and plural. For that reason, there is another set of structures used to clarify who has what. For *el suyo*, you can substitute *el de él, el de ella, el de Vd.* or *el de ellos, el de ellas, el de Vds.* The article used (*el, la, los, las*), is the same gender and number of the noun it replaces. *Él, ella, Vd., ellos, ellas* or *Vds.* tells whose something is. In the last example above, you can replace *el suyo* with *el de ellos*, in which case *el* replaces *el trabajo*, and *de ellos* tells whose work. The sentence would read:

> **Ayer estaba tan cansado que apenas pude acabar con mi trabajo, mucho menos con el de ellos.**

Be on the lookout for masculine nouns like *programa* that end with *-a*, and feminine nouns like *mano* that end with *-o*.

Cuyo

7.19 Cuyo is a relative possessive pronoun meaning "whose." It usually refers to people. In questions, it is replaced by *¿de quién?* Since it is a possessive pronoun, it agrees in gender and number with the thing that is possessed, not with the antecedent.

> **El hombre, cuya hermana está aquí, es español.**
> The man, whose sister is here, is Spanish.

> **El estudiante, cuyo tema leí esta mañana, es muy bueno.**
> The student, whose theme I read this morning, is very good.

> **¿De quién es este abrigo?**
> Whose coat is this?

INTERROGATIVE PRONOUNS

7.20 Questions usually begin with interrogative pronouns. All interrogative pronouns have accents; when they do not have accents, they function in other ways (usually as adverbs).

Note: When an interrogative pronoun comes after direct address, or within a sentence, the first letter is not capitalized. The upside down question mark is used instead at the beginning of the question.

> Pero nunca me preguntaron, —Hombre, ¿qué pasó?
> But they never asked me, "Well, what happened?"

The most common interrogative pronouns are listed below.

¿Qué?	What? Which?
¿Por qué?	Why? (For what reason?)
¿Para qué?	Why? (For what purpose?)
¿De qué?	From what?
¿Con qué?	With what?
¿Quién?	Who?
¿Cuánto?	How many?
¿Cuánta?	
¿Cuántos?	
¿Cuántas?	
¿Dónde?	Where?
¿Cuál?	Which?
¿Cuáles?	
¿Cuándo?	When?
¿De quién?	Whose?
¿De quiénes?	
¿Para quién?	For whom?
¿Para quieenes?	

Many simple prepositions can precede these pronouns: *¿Qué?; ¿Quién?; ¿Dónde?; ¿Cuándo?;* and *¿Cuál?* Note that in Spanish, prepositions never appear at the end of a sentence.

Interrogative pronouns can also appear in a declarative sentence when it communicates an implied question.

> No sé por qué me preocupo tanto por eso.
> I don't know why I worry so much about that.

> Me preguntaron cuándo vendría esa noche.
> They asked me when I would come that night.

¿Cuál? Versus ¿Qué?

Both *¿Cuál?* and *¿Qué?* mean "which," but *¿Cuál?* implies a choice or selection. Both pronouns are used before nouns, though in spoken Spanish *¿cuál?* is used in front of nouns with a preposition (usually *de*) or a verb. Especially with the verb *ser*, *¿Cuál?* is used instead of *¿Qué?* except for definitions.

> ¿Cuál de estos vestidos prefieres?
> Which of these dresses do you prefer?
>
> ¿Cuál prefiere Vd.?
> Which do you prefer?
>
> ¿Cuál es la capital de México?
> What is the capital of Mexico?
>
> ¿Qué es la vida?
> What is life?
>
> ¿Qué hora es?
> What time is it?

¿Para qué? Versus ¿Por qué?

¿Para qué? asks what purpose something or somebody serves. *¿Por qué?* asks the reason why something exists or happens: The answer explains *why* something is. This goes back to one of the basic distinctions between *por* and *para*.

> —Mamá, ¿para qué hay veinte dólares en la mesa?
> —Para hacerme recordar algo. Necesito huevos para una torta pero estoy ocupada. ¿Puedes ir a la tienda para comprarme algo?
> —Pero, Mamá, ¿por qué tengo que ir yo?
> —Porque no puedo ir y tu hermano está ocupado.

The first question asks "the purpose" for the money being on the table. Mama answers that the purpose is "to remind herself of something." And when Mama asks the child to help out by running an errand, the child asks "why" she has to go.

INDEFINITE PRONOUNS

7.21 Different words exist for affirmative and negative indefinite pronouns. Those that are negative require a double negative if they follow a verb. If they precede a verb, no other negative is needed.

alguien	nadie
somebody	nobody, no one
todo	nada
everything	nothing

In English we do not use double negatives, so *nada* is translated as "anything" when there's another negative in the sentence. In Spanish, however, if a verb is negated by the word "no" (or another type of negative), you must use the negative indefinite pronoun, adverb, or adjective.

Alguien me dijo que nadie venía.	Alguien me dijo que no venía nadie.
Somebody told me that no one was coming.	Somebody told me that no one was coming.
Para mi cumpleaños nadie me dio nada.	Para mi cumpleaños no me dio nada nadie.
For my birthday nobody gave me anything.	For my birthday, nobody gave me anything.

Cualqiera and *quienquiera,* meaning "whichever" and "whoever" are also indefinite pronouns. The plural forms are *cualesquiera* and *quienesquiera.* When these words are used as pronouns, they do not drop the final -*a*. They cannot agree in gender with the nouns to which they refer, but they do agree in number. These indefinite pronouns that end in -*quiera* often take the subjunctive in dependent adjective clauses modifying the indefinite pronouns.

RELATIVE PRONOUNS

7.22 Relative pronouns are most often viewed as "those words" at the beginning of clauses. The most common ones are: *que, quien, quienes, cuyo (-a, -os, -as), el cual, la cual, los cuales, las cuales, el que, la que, los que, and la que.* A relative pronoun introduces a dependent or subordinate clause and joins it to the preceding noun or pronoun that is its antecedent. It can function as a subject of a subordinate clause, or as a subjective or objective complement.

Few points of grammar are as confusing as relative pronouns. Which form to use in Spanish depends on the person, gender, and number of the noun, as well as how the relative pronoun functions in the sentence. Often direct translation is not a reliable indicator. Pay attention to the punctuation, as well as to the pronoun's antecedent to see the relationship between the dependent or subordinate clause and the noun. In Spanish the relative pronoun is never omitted, as is sometimes the case in English.

> In English, the most common relative pronouns are: "that," "who," "whom," "whose," "which," and "that which."

Que

7.23 By far the most common relative pronoun in Spanish is *que*. As it can replace nouns for people and things, it can mean "who," "whom," and "that." *Que* is invariable: It is the same no matter the gender and number of the noun it replaces. *Que* often introduces a restrictive clause, one not set apart by commas.

El *libro que* estoy leyendo es muy útil.
The *book (that)* I am reading is very useful.

El *profesor que* me enseña es muy inteligente.
The *teacher who* is teaching me is very intelligent.

No me gusta el *libro que* me has traído.
I don't like the book (*that*) you have brought me.
(The book you have brought me is not pleasing to me.)

Think of the relationship between the clauses as two sentences that have been combined. In the first example, the distinct sentences would say "I am reading a book" and "The book is very useful." When they are put together, one sentence becomes a clause that describes the book. Notice that there is no comma to set the clauses apart.

Quien and *Quienes*

7.24 *Quien(es)* **means "who" or "whom." It refers only to people, not things. Use *quien* in place of *que* when you see commas, which indicate a nonrestrictive clause.**

El perro del señor, quien es mi vecino, me mordió.
The dog of the man, who is my neighbor, bit me.

El papel que interpretó el actor, quien está con nosotros esta noche, fue creado específicamente para él.
The role that the actor, who is with us tonight, played was created especially for him.

When the noun is the object of the verb, the relative pronoun takes the personal *a*.

La *chica, a quien* conoció anoche, es una actriz famosa.
The *girl, whom* you met last night, is a famous actress.

Los *hombres, con quienes* fuimos, nos dieron buenos consejos.
The *men, with whom* we went, gave us good advice.

Always use *quien* or *quienes* if a simple preposition (such as *a*, *con*, or *de*) precedes a relative pronoun meaning "who" or "whom." If the preposition is compound (such as *delante de* or *al lado de*), you should look for a form of *el cual*. See 7.26.

La *chica, con quien* me encontraré mañana, es muy amable.
The *girl, with whom* I am meeting tomorrow, is very nice.

La *bibliotecaria, de quien* escribí, vendrá mañana.
The *librarian, about whom* I wrote, is coming tomorrow.

La *biblioteca, cerca de la cual* estacioné, es muy grande.
The *library, near which* I parked, is very large.

When *quien* or *quienes* is used as the subject of the verb, it means *the one who*. This meaning is common in proverbs or sayings.

Quien busca, encuentra.
He who seeks, finds.

Quienes estudian, salen bien en los exámenes.
Those who study do well on tests.

El Que, La Que, Los Que, and *Las Que*

7.25 It is usually harder to recognize situations which require *el que, la que, los que*, or *las que*, which means "who," "whom," "that," or "which." Most often *que* is used to mean "who." *El (la, los, las) que* is a more literary form. For example, it is correct to say, *Vivía en el tercer piso de la casa, el que se vino abajo a causa del terremoto*. In the sentence *el que* refers to *el tercer piso*. However, in conversation, you would most likely hear simply, *Vivía en el tercer piso de la casa, que se vino abajo a causa del terremoto*. Whether the relative pronoun refers to *el tercer piso* or *la casa*, the fact remains that all floors and the house came down in the earthquake.

In nonrestrictive clauses, a clause set off by commas, you can use *el que, la que, los que*, or *las que* when there is a selection implied. The person singled out is one of a group.

Ese *hombre, el que* es mi amigo, me ayudó.
The *man, who* is my friend, helped me.

In general use *el (la, los, las) que* after a short preposition such as *a, con, de*, or *en*.

La *casa en la que* vivimos ya no está allí.
The *house in which* we lived is no longer there.

The masculine forms of *el que* can be used in place of *quien* when the pronoun functions as the subject of the verb.

El que busca, encuentra.
He who seeks, finds.

Los que estudian, salen bien en los exámenes.
Those who study do well on tests.

El Cual, La Cual, Los Cuales, and *Las Cuales*

7.26 This relative pronoun is commonly used to distinguish between antecedents when the referent is ambiguous. This is the same use as for *el que*.

La *hija* del presidente, *la cual* nos habló anoche, es abogada en San Francisco.
The president's *daughter*, who spoke to us last night, is a lawyer in San Francisco.

After the prepositions *por, para* and *sin*, a form of *el cual* is preferred to avoid confusion with the expressions *porque, para que*, and *sin que*.

La *puerta* por *la cual* salimos anoche hoy está cerrada.
The *door* through which we left last night is closed today.

El *niño* para *el cual* compraste el juguete está muy feliz.
The *boy* for whom you bought the toy is very happy.

After compound prepositions use the appropriate form of *el cual*.

El *edificio* al lado *del cual* estacioné el coche es muy alto.
The *building* next to *which* I parked the car is very tall.

La *bolsa* dentro de *la cual* puse los libros está en la mesa.
The *bag* in *which* I put the books is on the table.

Lo Que and Lo Cual

7.27 When the antecedent for a relative pronoun is a situation, a previously stated idea, or something not yet stated, use *lo que* or *lo cual*. The two forms are practically interchangeable, although *lo cual* tends to be a more literary form. *Lo que* is more common in spoken Spanish.

Lo que más me gusta es hablar con mis amigos.
What I like most is talking to my friends.

No sé lo que haría en tal situación.
I don't know what I would do in a situation like that.

Hablamos con ellos, después de lo cual fuimos a casa.
We spoke with them, after which we went home.

Cuanto

7.28 *Cuanto* is used as a neuter *pronoun*, meaning *todo lo que*, "all that" or "everything."

Cuanto me dijo anoche fue muy interesante.
Everything you told me last night was very interesting.

THINGS TO REMEMBER

- When there is no specific referent, the indefinite *lo* is neuter in gender. It refers to an idea expressed in a whole clause instead of a single word: *Lo siento* means, "I'm sorry [about that]."
- *Cuyo* is a relative possessive pronoun meaning "whose." It usually refers to people. If used in a question, it changes to *¿de quién?*: *¿De quién es este abrigo?* ("Whose coat is this?")
- Both *¿Cuál?* and *¿Qué?* mean "which," but *¿Cuál?* implies a choice or a selection.
- *¿Para qué?* asks what purpose something has or somebody serves. *¿Por qué?* explains why something is.

REVIEW QUESTIONS

Set A: In the following exercise, circle the correct pronoun that acts to substitute the underlined noun.

1. El niño se puso <u>la gorra</u>. El niño se ___ puso.

    A) ella   B) le   C) lo   D) la

2. Nos gustan <u>programas interesantes</u>. Nos gustan ___.

    A) nosotros   B) ellos   C) ellas   D) las

3. Lo dimos <u>al pobre</u>. ___ lo dimos.

    A) El   B) Le   C) Se   D) Ello

4. Ella va a darlo <u>a mi hermana y a mí</u>. Ella va a ___.

    A) dármelo   B) dártelo   C) dárnoslo   D) dárselo

5. <u>Los turistas</u> visitaron el museo. ___ visitaron el museo.

    A) Ellos   B) Ellas   C) Se   D) Los

6. Conocí <u>al señor</u> anoche. ___ conocí anoche.

    A) El   B) Lo   C) La   D) Ello

7. Puse el dinero en <u>la mesa</u>. Puse el dinero en ___.

    A) él   B) la   C) lo   D) ella

8. Tengo <u>una entrada</u> para el concierto. ___ tengo para el concierto.

    A) El   B) La   C) Lo   D) Ella

Set B: Select the appropriate interrogative pronoun for each of the following questions.

1. ¿ ___ hace ese señor con quien hablabas?

    A) Quién   B) Cuál   C) Para qué   D) Qué

2. ¿ ___ veces tengo que decirle que estudie más?

    A) Cuándo   B) Cuánto   C) Cuántos   D) Cuántas

3. ¿ ___ sirve esta máquina? La usamos para cortar madera.

    A) Qué   B) Quién   C) Para qué   D) Por qué

4. ¿ ___ programa prefiere ver esta noche?

    A) Qué   B) Cuánto   C) Para qué   D) Cuál

5. ¿ ___ viste ayer en la oficina?

    A) De quién   B) Para quién C) A quién   D) Quién

6. ¿ ___ viniste esta noche? Había mucha congestión en las calles.

   A) Dónde   B) Cómo   C) Quién   D) Adónde

7. ¿ ___ fueron estos hombres enmascarados?

   A) De dónde   B) Dónde   C) A quiénes   D) Cuánto

8. ¿ ___ es el perro que siempre viene a la puerta?

   A) Con qué   B) Dónde   C) Cuáles   D) De quién

Set C: Select the most appropriate answer to complete the sentences.

1. Voy a llevar los regalos ___ cuando voy a la fiesta.

   A) hacia mí   B) conmigo   C) sin mí   D) a mí

2. ¿Quién ___ pidió que lo trajeras?

   A) tú   B) se   C) te   D) él

3. ¡No puedo creer ___ me dijeron!

   A) que   B) cuál   C) lo que   D) el que

4. Antes de limpiar la mesa, quité los platos de ____.

   A) la   B) él   C) ellos   D) ella

5. ___ vio a mi hermano, ¿verdad?

   A) Me   B) Yo   C) Tú   D) Él

6. Cuando llegué no vi a ____.

   A) alguien   B) alguno   C) ningún   D) nadie

7. Por suerte ____ de ellas llegaron temprano.

   A) algún   B) algunos   C) alguna   D) algunas

8. Cuando le pedí un dólar, me dijo que no tenía ____.

   A) no   B) ninguno   C) ninguna   D) ningún

9. Se fue sin pagar, y fue ____ lo que me preocupó tanto.

   A) eso   B) éste   C) ése   D) ésta

10. Miguelito, ____ las manos antes de sentarte a la mesa.

    A) lava   B) lávate   C) lávese   D) lávense

11. Ángela, no sé por qué siempre ___ olvida llevar tu mochila.

    A) te   B) se me   C) se te   D) se le

12. Muchos estudiantes ____ comunican por correo electrónico hoy.

   A) les   B) ellos   C) se   D) los

13. Llevaré mis maletas al tren, pero tienes que llevar ____.

   A) las mías   B) los suyos   C) las tuyas   D) el suyo

Set D: Combine the following sentences using a relative pronoun. There may be more than one grammatically correct way to combine the sentences.

   1. Vivía en Buenos Aires. Es una ciudad muy cosmopolita.

   2. ¿Irás a la fiesta esta noche? La fiesta será en el club.

   3. Invité a un amigo. El amigo tiene una hermana hermosa.

   4. ¿Viste la película? La película se estrenó anoche.

   5. No conozco a esa mujer. La mujer lleva un sombrero grande.

   6. El hombre que trabaja duro duerme bien.

   7. Voy a viajar este verano. Me gusta viajar.

   8. El coche de mi amigo es viejo. Compró el coche el año pasado.

ANSWERS AND EXPLANATIONS

Set A

1. (D)

You need a direct object pronoun because *la gorra* is the direct object of the verb. *Se* is a reflexive pronoun, with which you can use a direct object pronoun.

2. (B)

Programas is a masculine noun and is the subject of *gustar*, so you need to use a subject pronoun. Do not be confused by the pronoun you would use if you were to translate this into conversational English.

3. (C)

The indirect object pronoun *le* becomes se in front of another third person object pronoun.

4. (C)

When the first person is combined with any other subject, you must use the first person plural pronoun.

5. (A)

Look at the article to tell the gender of a noun that ends with *-ista*. Then use a subject pronoun. *Visitar* is not a reflexive verb, nor does it make any sense used reflexively in this sentence. Remember that *los* is not a subject pronoun, so it does not make any sense.

6. (B)

The personal a does not indicate an indirect object; it is used in front of direct as well as indirect objects. When in doubt ask if the object answers the question, "to whom?" or "whom?" In this case it tells who the speaker met, so use a direct object pronoun.

7. (D)

After the preposition en, an object of the preposition pronoun is required. *Ella* is the only choice that is the correct gender and number to replace *mesa*.

8. (B)

You need a feminine singular direct object pronoun to replace *entrada*.

Set B

1. (D)

No choice makes sense except for *¿Qué?* There is no selection implied, so *¿cuál?* doesn't make sense.

2. (D)

In order to use the correct form of this interrogative pronoun, you need to know the gender of the noun it precedes. In this case *veces* is feminine plural.

3. (C)

There is only one possibility for this question: The answer will tell what purpose the machine serves. Although *¿Por qué?* could be a possibility, it answers a question about *why* it is used, rather than for what purpose.

4. (A)

¿Cuál? is usually separated from a noun by a verb or by the preposition de. *¿Qué?* can also mean "Which?"

5. (C)

You have to use a in front of *quién* when the antecedent to the pronoun is a person and the object of the verb.

6. (B)

The second sentence makes clear that there was a traffic problem that caused problems. The question asks how something happened.

7. (A)

Fueron makes this a tricky question. Without the preposition a it must be a form of "to be." And since it is "to be," the only interrogative pronoun that makes sense is "from where?" Remember that *¿a quiénes?* can only be used when the noun is an objective complement.

8. (D)

This question asks whose dog is at the door. *¿Dónde?* cannot be used because the noun is not an event that takes place in a certain physical location.

Set C

1. (B)

The preposition *con* is your only possible answer here. Used with the first person singular prepositional pronoun, it becomes *conmigo*.

2. (C)

The subject of the verb in the dependent clause is second person singular, so *te* is the correct answer. *Tú* and *él* are subject pronouns, both of which are wrong because *quién* is the subject of the verb. *Se* makes no sense at all.

3. (C)

Without a specific antecedent you have to use *lo que*.

4. (D)

After *en* you have to use a prepositional pronoun that agrees in gender and number with the noun to which it refers, in this case, *mesa*. *Ella* is the only pronoun that agrees with *mesa*.

5. (D)

With the noun after the verb and no redundant pronoun among the answer choices, a personal pronoun is the only correct answer. Do not be fooled by the irregular preterite verb form that has no accent. The -o ending does not indicate a first person verb form here. In the third person a personal pronoun is often used for clarification.

6. (D)

With the negative before the verb, you have to use an indefinite negative pronoun.

7. (D)

Since *llegaron* is plural and *ellas* is feminine, *algunas* is the only possible answer.

8. (B)

In this sentence *ninguno* is used in place of *dólar*. The indefinite negative is needed because of the negative before the verb.

9. (A)

There is no antecedent for "that," which refers to the whole idea of leaving without paying. The neuter pronoun is the only possibility.

10. (B)

Use the second person singular command. Remember to use a reflexive pronoun because *manos* is a part of the body.

11. (C)

You cannot just use a reflexive pronoun here because the verb ending is third person. This ending, taken with the second person possessive adjective *tu* means that the passive construction with an indirect object pronoun is the only correct answer.

12. (C)

This is the reciprocal use of the reflexive pronoun.

13. (C)

The possessive pronoun refers to *maletas*. *Tienes* indicates the second person singular owner of the suitcases.

Set D

There are several possible answers for each question. The most obvious are listed.

1. *Vivía en Buenos Aires, que es una ciudad muy cosmopolita.*

   In this sentence *que* refers to Buenos Aires and functions as the subject of *es*.

2. *¿Irás a la fiesta la que será al club esta noche?*

   The pronoun *la que* refers to *fiesta*, and has the meaning of "the one that," implying that there are going to be several parties. One of them will take place at the club, so there is a selection implied.

3. *Invité a un amigo, cuya hermana es hermosa.*
   In this sentence *cuya* means "whose." It is feminine because *hermana* is feminine, even though it refers to *amigo*.
   Invité a un amigo, quien tiene una hermana hermosa.
   Invité a un amigo, el que tiene una hermana hermosa.
   In both of these sentences *quien* and *el que* occur in the nonrestrictive clauses. They have the meaning of "the one who."

4. *¿Viste la película que se estrenó anoche?*

    Que in this sentence refers to *película* and is the subject of *estrenó*. The pronoun occurs in a restrictive clause; you can tell because there are no commas.

    ¿Viste la película, la que se estrenó anoche?

    La que implies that there were several films that one could have seen last night. The speaker distinguishes one movie from the others by using *la que* to mean "the one that."

5. *No conozco a esa mujer que lleva el sombrero grande.*

    Que occurs in a restrictive clause.

    No conozco a esa mujer, la que lleva un sombrero grande.

    No conozco a esa mujer, quien lleva un sombrero grande.

    Both of these sentences have non-restrictive clauses that take *quien* or *la que*, meaning "the one who." Look for commas.

6. *El que trabaja duro duerme bien.*

    Quien trabaja duro duerme bien.

    The pronouns function as the subject of the verb in the main clause in these sentences. The subject is indefinite so a relative pronoun is used.

7. *Voy a viajar este verano, lo que me gusta.*

    Voy a viajar este verano, lo cual me gusta.

    In both of these sentences it is the action of traveling that is pleasing, so the neuter relative pronoun is used.

8. *El coche de mi amigo, el que compró el año pasado, es viejo.*

    El que is used to specify the antecedent. If the friend had been the antecedent, *quien* would have been used.

Chapter 8: **Prepositions**

- The Preposition *A*
- The Preposition *En*
- The Preposition *De*
- The Preposition *Con*
- *Por* and *Para*
- Other Prepositions

Perhaps no other point of grammar is as hard to master as the use of prepositions. The way prepositions are used is highly idiomatic, which means that you have to simply memorize them in many cases. You cannot always rely on translation from one language to another.

A preposition is a word that relates a noun or its equivalent to another noun, to a verb, or to the rest of a sentence. In the sentence *El regalo es para mi novia*, the preposition *para* links the subject of the verb *regalo* with the object of the preposition, *novia,* a noun. In *La puerta fue abierta por él*, the preposition *por* links *puerta* with *él*, a pronoun.

This chapter will deal with simple prepositions and specific prepositions that come after particular verbs. These main prepositions are: *a, con, de, en, hacia, por, para, sin,* and *sobre*. We have already reviewed the compound prepositions in chapter 6, though the most important ones are repeated here.

> Whenever a verb follows a preposition, the verb always takes the infinitive form. Remember this simple yet important rule.

8.1 Some verbs have the preposition included in their meaning. As a result, these verbs are not followed by prepositions.

agradecer	Les agradezco su amable atención.
	I thank you *for* your kind attention.
buscar	Busco un libro que lo explique todo.
	I am looking *for* a book that explains everything.
mirar	Miró el espectáculo increíble.
	He looked *at* the incredible show.

esperar	Esperamos el autobús de las cinco.
	We are waiting *for* the five o'clock bus.

In Spanish, there is no apostrophe to show ownership as there is in English. Instead, Spanish uses the preposition *de* to show possession and ownership. *La madre del niño está aquí* means "The child's mother is here." Nor is it possible for one noun to modify another directly. *El jugador de baloncesto es muy alto* means, "The basketball player is very tall." In addition to showing ownership, *de* functions in a sentence as a linking word.

THE PREPOSITION *A*

8.2 In general, *a* indicates place, time, manner, and condition. It is usually used after verbs of motion, beginning, and learning.

8.3 *A* is also used as the personal *a*, which specifies when an objective complement is a person. This is especially useful when the subject and object both follow the verb. Though the subject normally precedes the verb, at times you will see it, along with the object, follow the verb. In fact, for questions, both items follow the verb.

> Also use the personal *a* before indefinite pronouns such as *alguien nadie*, *alguno*, *ninguno*, and *cualquiera* when they refer to people.

> Regaló el hombre algo especial a su novia.
> ¿Vio su hermano a mi hermana en la fiesta?

Without the personal *a* to indicate that *novia* is the indirect object above, you might be confused. Similarly, without the personal *a* you would not know that *hermana* was the direct object in the second example.

In some cases, the personal *a* is not used. After the verb *tener* you do not use a personal *a*.

> No tengo hermanos.
> I don't have any brothers.

Nor do you need a personal *a* with indefinite objects: The absence of the personal *a* indicates that the object is unknown or uncertain, meaning that the subjunctive is needed in the adjective clause.

> Buscan a la estudiante que salió bien en el examen.
> They are looking for the student who did well on the test. (indicative)

> Buscan un estudiante que haya salido bien.
> They are looking for a student who may have done well. (subjunctive)

8.4 After verbs of motion, the preposition *a* indicates direction toward something or some place. Some common verbs of motion are *ir, venir, llegar, bajar, subir, acercarse, alejarse,* and *caminar*.

> Fuimos a España el verano pasado.
> We went to Spain last summer.

> Llegaron a la escuela a tiempo.
> They got to school on time.

When the verbs *empezar* and *comenzar* are followed by an infinitive, the preposition *a* precedes the infinitive. Similarly, when verbs of learning like *aprender* and *enseñar* are followed by another verb, use the preposition *a*.

> **Empecé a estudiar después de cenar.**
> I began to study after eating supper.

> **Después de mucha práctica aprendí a jugar bien al tenis.**
> After a lot of practice, I learned to play tennis well.

Other verbs that take the preposition *a* when followed by an infinitive are:

acostumbrarse a	to be accustomed to
apresurarse a	the hurry
asistir a	to attend
atreverse a	to dare
invitar a	to invite
ir a	to be going to
negarse a	to refuse
ponerse a	to begin
resignarse a	to resign oneself to
volver a	to (do something) again

The preposition *a* is also used with expressions of time, to tell when something will happen. In using this structure with telling time of day, you have to use the definite article, *las*, with the number, in order for the expression to mean "o'clock." Use *de* when a specific hour is given. When no specific hour is mentioned, the preposition *por* is used.

> **Cuando tengo clases por la mañana, me levanto a las ocho de la mañana.**
> When have classes in the morning I get up at 8 o'clock A.M.

Also, *a* refers to a period of time after which something happened, as well as a measure of distance.

> **En aquella época se casaban a los tres o cuatro años de cortejar.**
> In those days they used to get married after three or four years of courtship.

> **La casa queda a unos kilómetros de la escuela.**
> The house is a few kilometers from the school.

8.5 Beyond these general situations which require *a*, there are very many expressions for which there is no literal translation. These expressions are common and should be familiar to you.

a causa de	because of **No fueron a causa de la lluvia.** They did not go because of the rain.
a eso de	about (in time) **Llegaron a eso de las nueve de la noche.** They arrived around nine o'clock at night.

a fondo	in depth
	Necesitamos estudiar esto más a fondo.
	We need to study this in more depth.
a fuerza de	through (great effort)
	Aprobé el examen a fuerza de trabajar duro.
	I passed the test by (dint of) working hard.
a la vez	at the same time
	Todos hablaron a la vez.
	Everybody spoke at once. (at the same time)
al menos	at least
a lo menos	**Nos quedan al menos cinco minutos.**
	We have at least five minutes left.
a lo mejor	maybe
	A lo mejor podemos verlo cuando sale.
	Maybe we can see him when he leaves.
a mano	by hand
	Se hacen los sombreros a mano.
	The hats are made by hand.
a pie	on foot
	Fuimos del hotel al restaurante a pie.
	We went on foot (walked) from the hotel to the restaurant.
a caballo	on horseback
	Subieron la montaña a caballo.
	They went up the mountain on horseback.
a ojo	guessing (by eye)
	No estoy seguro, a ojo diré que queda a media milla.
	I'm not sure, but I'd guess it is about half a mile away.
a tiempo	on time
	Vale llegar a tiempo a las clases.
	It is a good idea to get to classes on time.

Notice the difference between *a causa de* and *porque*. Also, in the expression, *a mano*, you can substitute other nouns for *mano* to indicate what manner or method is used to make something, like *a máquina*. In the expression, *a pie* and *a caballo*, both indicate a way of getting somewhere.

8.6 The preposition *a* plus the masculine singular article *el* always becomes *al*. The preposition *a* plus the pronoun *él* never changes (except when *el* is part of a title). When *al* precedes a verb form, the verb is always in the infinitive.

Al is often used to indicate simultaneous action, and replaces a clause with a conjugated verb. Do not be misled by translating what you would say in English into Spanish. Look carefully at the following sentences, as this point of grammar is commonly tested.

Al ver a su antiguo vecino, lo saludó amablemente.
Upon seeing his former neighbor, he greeted him warmly.

Todos se callaron *al observar* al profesor entrar en la sala.
Everyone got quiet *upon seeing* the teacher enter the room.

Al oír las noticias, el chico decide regresar a casa.
Upon hearing the news, the boy decides to go home.

THE PREPOSITION *EN*

8.7 The preposition *en* is primarily used with reference to place, though it can be used to indicate time, method, and cause. It is also used in some expressions with adverbial conjunctions, as well as with some verbs when followed by another verb.

En tells where something takes place or is physically located. This might be translated as "inside" or "on top of." *En* is used with the verb *estar* to designate placement of something or somebody. However, *en* is not normally used with *ser,* except when it means "to take place."

La fiesta está *en* casa de Elena.
The party is *at* Helen's house.

Los papeles que buscas están *en* la mesa.
The papers you are looking for are *on* the table.

El pájaro *en* la jaula cantaba toda la tarde.
The bird *in* the cage was singing all afternoon.

When *en* refers to time, it indicates a given time when something occurs. There are two exceptions to this rule: Do not use *en* with days of the week. Instead, use only the article. And do not use *en* when a specific hour of the day is given. Instead use *a* to mean "at," or *de* to mean "in."

En aquel entonces, todos estaban viviendo *en* México.
At that time, everybody was living *in* Mexico.

En ese mismo instante, sonaron las campanas de la iglesia.
At that very moment, the church bells rang.

Las clases empiezan a las ocho de la mañana.
Classes begin at 8:00 in the morning.

Use *en* after the word *último* or any ordinal number (first, second, etc.), when the number is followed by an infinitive.

Fue el último *en* salir de la sala.
He was the first to leave the room. (in leaving the room)

The verbs that normally take the preposition *en* are given below.

consentir en	to consent to
consistir en	to consist of
convertir en	to convert into
convertirse en	to become, to be converted into
empeñarse en	to insist on
entrar en	to go in, to enter
especializarse en	to major in (in school)
fijarse en	to notice
influir en	to influence
insistir en	to insist
pensar en	to think of, to meditate about (This does not mean to have an opinion.)
tardar en	to take (a long) time

Below are the most important expressions that use *en*.

en cambio	however, on the other hand
	Ella no escribió un tema; en cambio preparó un discurso.
	She did not write a theme; however she prepared a speech.
en cuanto a	with respect to, in regard to
	En cuanto al examen, será fácil.
	In regard to the test, it will be easy.
en lugar de	instead of, in place of
en vez de	**En vez de estudiar, el muchacho jugó con sus amigos.**
	Instead of studying, the boy played with his friends.

Of course, you remember the adverbial conjunction, *en cuanto*, meaning "as soon as." Similarly, you will remember the adverb of place, *enfrente de*, meaning "in front of," and the adverb of time, *en seguida*, meaning "immediately."

THE PREPOSITION *DE*

8.8 *De* is a very versatile word in Spanish. It shows possession, origin or nationality, material composition, and time. It designates function or state (condition), location, cause, use, physical characteristics, and passive voice construction at times. And finally, *de* can serve as a substitute for *si* in an if-then statement.

• Possession

Spanish does not use an apostrophe to show possession, as does English. Using the word *de* indicates possession.

> **La mochila *de* María está en la silla.**
> Mary's backpack is on the chair.

• Origin

When *de* shows origin, the verb *ser* is usually used with it. In addition to names of countries, you can use any noun that shows origin, such as east, west, north, south, the other side of the planet, from the moon.

> **Ese señor es *de* Costa Rica, es costarricense.**
> That man is *from* Costa Rica, he is Costa Rican.

> **Esos muchachos son *del* barrio este.**
> Those boys are *from* the neighborhood to the east.

• Material Composition

To indicate material or substance from which something is made, use *de*.

> **Me gustan las casas *de* madera.**
> I like houses made *of* wood. (wooden houses)

> **El reloj es *de* oro.**
> The watch is (*made of*) gold.

• Time

When used in expressions of time, *de* indicates a specific hour.

> **Los españoles cenan a las diez *de* la noche.**
> Spaniards eat dinner at 10 o'clock *at* night.

• Function or State

When *de* indicates a condition, function, or state, it frequently means "as" or "like." Another possible word for this is *como*. When used in this manner, *de* may be harder to figure out.

> **Para el programa la muchacha se vistió *de* reina.**
> For the program the girl dressed *as* a queen. (*like* a queen)

> **El muchacho trabajó un verano *de* jardinero.**
> The boy worked one summer *as* a gardener. (in the capacity *of* gardener)

> **De niña, vivía en Honduras.**
> *As* a child, I used to live in Honduras. (*When I was* a child)

• Location

De can indicate location instead of a preposition for "on."

> Entró en la tienda *de* la esquina para comprar un refresco.
> He went in the store *on* the corner to buy a drink.

• Cause

After an adjective *de* can express cause of an action or a state of being.

> Me muero *de* hambre.
> I'm dying *of* hunger.

> Al fin del día estaba muy contento *del* trabajo que hice.
> At the end of the day I was very happy *about* the work I did.

• Use

De can indicate what something is supposed to be used for. It can be confusing, especially when a phrase has two possible meanings.

> Casi nadie usa una máquina *de* escribir ahora.
> Almost no one uses a typewriter (machine *for* writing) now.

> Pidió una taza *de* café.
> She asked for a cup *of* coffee.

> Pidió una taza *de* café en una taza *de* té.
> She asked for a cup of coffee in a teacup.

• Physical Characteristics

De can indicate physical characteristics. This avoids the repetition of verbs describing what someone looks like.

> Me enamoré de la muchacha *de* los ojos verdes.
> I fell in love with the girl *with* the green eyes.

• Passive Voice Construction

In the passive voice you can use *de* when the agent is a person(s), and the action deals with strong emotion.

> El dictador fue temido *de* la gente.
> The dictator was feared *by* the people.

In passive voice type constructions that contain verbs meaning "to be," *de* is used to mean "by." The verbs used in this type of construction introduce the apparent agent. Some of these verbs are: *acompañar, preceder, rodear,* and *seguir.*

> La casa estaba rodeada de árboles.
> The house was surrounded by trees.

Los elefantes vienen seguidos de los payasos.
The elephants are coming followed by the clowns.

A number of expressions that begin with *de* typically follow *estar*. One of those is *de pie*. While *a pie* means "on foot," *de pie* means "standing."

de pie	standing **Todos estaban de pie para el himno nacional.** Everyone was standing for the national anthem.
de rodillas	kneeling **Encontró al hombre de rodillas en la iglesia.** He found the man kneeling in the church.
de luto	in mourning **La viuda se vistió de luto después de la muerte de su esposo.** The widow dressed in mourning after her husband died.
de acuerdo (con)	in agreement **Estoy de acuerdo contigo; deben ir ahora.** I agree with you; they ought to go now.
de buen (mal)	in a good (bad) mood **Todos estaban de buen humor al salir bien.** Everyone was in a good mood upon doing well.
a favor de	in favor of **Muchas personas votaron a favor de la ley.** Many people voted in favor of the law.
en contra de	against **Más personas votaron en contra que a favor de la ley.** More people voted against than for the law.
de huelga	on strike **Los empleados están de huelga, no trabajan.** The employees are on strike, they aren't working.
de vacaciones	on vacation (notice the Spanish is always plural) **Mis vecinos están de vacaciones.** My neighbors are on vacation.
de viaje	on a trip **El jefe de la oficina no viene, está de viaje.** The boss isn't coming, he is on a trip.
de vuelta	to be back, on return **No saben cuándo estarán de vuelta.** They do not know when they will be back.
de regreso	to be back, on return **De regreso pasaré por su oficina.** On my return I will come by your office.

• *Substitute for "Si" in an If–Then Statement*

In *if–then* statements, *de* replaces *si* and is followed by an infinitive. These statements can be in any tense, not just the conditional and imperfect subjunctive. The clause that is replaced in the past tense is the one containing the subjunctive. In the present tense, it replaces an indicative verb form.

> De verte otra vez, te daré los apuntes.
> Si te veo otra vez, te daré los apuntes
> If I see you again, I will give you the notes.

> De verte otra vez, te daría los apuntes.
> If I were to see you again, I would give you the notes.

> De haberte visto otra vez, te habría dado los apuntes.
> If I had seen you again, I would have given you the notes.

8.9 The following verbs normally require *de* when they are followed by another verb.

acabar de	to just (+ verb)
	to finish
	to have just (done something)
acordarse de	to remember
alegrarse de	to be glad
arrepentirse de	to regret
avergonzarse de	to be ashamed
burlarse de	to make fun of
darse cuenta de	to realize (become aware of)
dejar de	to stop
depender de	to depend on
despedirse de	to say good-bye
enamorarse de	to fall in love
enterarse de	to find out about
estar enamorado de	to be in love with
olvidarse de	to forget
pensar de	to think about (have an opinion)
quejarse de	to complain about
terminar de	to finish, to have just
tratar de	to try
tratarse de	to be about, to deal with

Be careful with some of the verbs above. When *olvidarse* is a reflexive verb, it will use *de*, but when you do not use the reflexive, don't use *de*. *Pensar* plus *de* is "to have an opinion about something," which is different from meditating about something. *Tratarse de* relates to what something deals with.

> Esa película trata de la vida de los cubanos en la Florida.
> That film is about the life of Cubans in Florida.

Another important verb to recognize is *darse cuenta de*, meaning "to realize." There is another verb that means "to realize," *realizar*, when it means "to fulfill," as in "He realized his dream of becoming a movie star."

> Cuando ganó la lotería, realizó su sueño de independencia financiera.
> When he won the lottery, he realized his dream of financial independence.

8.10 The following expressions using *de* are quite common.

de buena gana	willingly
	Hicimos el trabajo de buena gana.
	We did the work willingly.
de mala gana	unwillingly
	Nos acompañó de mala gana.
	He went with us unwillingly.
de vez en cuando	from time to time
de cuando en cuando	**De vez en cuando descansamos.**
	From time to time we rest.
de veras	really
	Nos gusta hacer exámenes de veras.
	We really like to take tests.
de nuevo	again, over again
	Lo hicieron de nuevo.
	They did it again.(over again)
de esta manera	this way, in this manner
	Se hace el ejercicio de esta manera.
	One does the exercise this way.

You will also remember the adverbial conjunctions and phrases that begin with *de*: *de modo que*, *de manera que*, *de repente*, *de golpe*, and *de pronto*.

THE PREPOSITION *CON*

8.11 *Con* is used to express accompaniment, to replace adverbs with a prepositional phrase, to indicate a person by something that he or she has, or to indicate some kind of concession.

•Accompaniment

When *con* indicates accompaniment, it tells "with what" or "with whom" something or someone goes.

> Nos gusta el chile con carne.
> We like chile with meat.

> Venga con nosotros al cine esta noche.
> Come with us to the movies tonight.

•Replacing Adverbs

You have already reviewed prepositional phrases used in place of adverbs in chapter 6. When the adverb is a long word, the tendency in conversation is to use the prepositional phrase, though words are not avoided simply because they are long. Look at the following sentences to see how prepositional phrases have a different sound. In some cases the adverb ending with *-mente* does work better.

> Los padres señalaron a su hijo *muy orgullosamente*.
> The parents pointed to their son *very proudly*.

> Los padres señalaron a su hijo *con mucho orgullo*.
> The parents pointed to their son *with great pride*.

•Indicating a Person

Con can also distinguish one person from another by indicating an object he has in his possession.

> Hable Vd. con el señor *con* el libro allí.
> Speak to the gentleman *with* the book over there.

> El cantante es el hombre *con* la guitarra.
> The singer is the man *with* the guitar.

•Indicating a Concession

Con meaning "concession" means to take something into consideration. The expression can be translated in a variety of ways.

> Se creería que lo harían *con* todo el tiempo que tienen.
> You would think they would do it *given* all the time they have.

8.12 When the following verbs are followed by an infinitive, *con* usually follows the verb to introduce the infinitive.

casarse con	to get married
encontrarse con	to meet
enojarse con	to get mad at
	to get angry with

meterse con	to get involved
	to get mixed up with
quedarse con	to keep
soñar con	to dream about

Remember that some of these verbs have a different meaning when they are not reflexive. *Casar*, for example, means "to marry." *Encontrar* is followed by the preposition *a* when it is not reflexive. One of the most common mistakes is *soñar*, which always takes *con* when it means "to dream about." *Quedar* is also used commonly without the reflexive pronoun, and means "to stay" or "to remain."

8.13 There is one common expression with *con*.

Con respeto al asunto, no podré decirle más.
With respect to the issue, I cannot tell you more.

The only other expression is *con tal que*, an adverbial conjunction that you have already reviewed. It means "provided that."

POR AND *PARA*

8.14 Perhaps no two prepositions cause more problems for Spanish students than *por* and *para*. *Para* is most commonly used to show purpose. *Por* has more varied uses. Among other things, it is used to express reason and cause, method or manner, and an idea or action that is pending.

8.15 *Para* is used to indicate purpose, destination, use of something, or comparison. It is also used as a substitute for "according to" and to indicate an employer. No verb requires the preposition *para*.

• *Purpose and Destination*

Para is most commonly used to show purpose (as opposed to reason). It is frequently needed to introduce an infinitive. In English the meaning would be "in order (to)" though these words are often omitted in the English translation.

El monumento es *para* conmemorar la guerra.
The monument is (*in order*) to commemorate the war.

Lo hice todo *para* ti.
I did it all *for* you.

¿*Para* qué hiciste eso?
—*Para* molestarte.
"*What* did you do that *for*?"
—"Just (*in order*) to bother you."

Para salir bien, se necesita estudiar un poco.
In order to do well, one needs to study a little.

In a sense, purpose *is* destination, so these two uses are related. When something has a specific purpose, it is directed toward something. And when something has a destination, it is directed toward someone or some place. *Para* indicates that direction. After verbs of motion, *para* can indicate movement toward a thing or place, even in simple terms of where something is physically located.

> **Salieron *para* la gran selva tropical.**
> They left *for* the great tropical forest.

> **Este regalo es *para* mi nieto *para* su cumpleaños.**
> This gift is *for* my grandson *for* his birthday.

Destination in time is another way of thinking of a deadline. When something is due by a certain time, use *para*.

> **Ahora hago la tarea *para* mañana.**
> Now I am doing homework *for* tomorrow. (The homework *is due* tomorrow.)

> **No hay problema. Lo tendremos hecho *para* mañana.**
> Don't worry. We will have it done *by* tomorrow.

• *Use of Something*

Para tells what something is used for, somewhat like the preposition *de*, but more commonly used to show purpose, or functionality of something.

> **Este tenedor es para comer ensalada, ése es *para* postre.**
> This fork is *for* eating salad, that one is *for* dessert.

• *Comparison and "According to"*

To make a comparison, use *para*. In a related manner, use *para* as a substitute for *según*, "in the opinion of" or "according to."

> **Habla bien el español *para* un norteamericano.**
> He speaks Spanish well *for* a North American. (*compared to* other North Americans)

> ***Para* muchos, lo único que cuenta es ganar.**
> *For* many people, the only thing that counts is winning.

• *Indicating an Employer*

When you want to indicate an employer or the person for whom you work, use *para*.

> **Hace muchos años que trababa para el gobierno.**
> He has been working *for* the government for many years.

8.16 There are just a few expressions with *para*.

estar para	to be about to (in Spain)
	No puedo hablar ahora, estoy para salir.
	I can't talk now, I'm about to leave.
no ser para tanto	To not be that bad
	Hija, no llores. No es para tanto.
	My child, don't cry. It's not that bad.
no estar para bromas	to not be in the mood for jokes
	No hagas eso; no estoy para bromas.
	Don't do that; I'm in no mood for jokes.
para siempre	forever
	Nada se pierde para siempre.
	Nothing is lost forever.

8.17 *Por* has a large variety of meanings, not all of which seem closely related. Its meanings range from reason and cause to duration of time. When used with an infinitive, it indicates that something is pending.

• *Reason and Cause*

Reason explains why something happens or why something is the way it is. *Por* signifies reason or cause for something. This use is very similar to *a causa de*, meaning "because of."

Por trabajar tarde, no llegó a casa hasta la medianoche.
Because of working late, he didn't get home until midnight.

Por querer aprobar el examen, estudió muchas horas.
Out of wanting to pass the test, he studied many hours.

Fuimos en su coche *por* la lluvia.
We went in his car *because* of the rain.

• *Indefinite Time or Place and Duration of Time*

The last example above could also mean "We went in his car *through* the rain." At times, *por* can mean "through." The context will tell you which meaning is intended. In these cases, *por* indicates passage through time or space. Passing through time is a way of expressing duration of time.

Al volver a casa, fueron *por* el parque.
Upon returning, they went *through* the park.

Estudié *por* tres horas antes de hacer el examen.
I studied *for* three hours before taking the test.

> If you're stuck deciding between *para* and por, make *por* your default preposition. *Para* has fewer uses, so if you do not see any reason to use it, go with *por*.

For the last example, you could also use the structure *hacer* plus a unit of time plus *que* plus a verb to communicate how long something has been going on. With this structure, there is no word that translates "for."

> **Hace tres horas que estudio para el examen.**
> I have been studying for three hours for the exam.

• *Method or Manner*

When the preposition indicates method or manner, use *por*. This often relates to modes of transportation or means of communication. In this structure, *por* emphasizes what means of transportation or communication you use.

> **Fuimos *por* coche *por* la lluvia.**
> We went *by* car *because of* the rain.

> **Nos hablamos todos los días *por* teléfono.**
> We talk to each other every day *by* telephone.

• *Passive Voice Construction*

The agent in a true passive voice structure is the preposition *por*. When you see *por* and an agent, or someone doing the action, look for *ser* to see if it is really the passive voice.

> **La carta vale mucho porque fue escrita por un escritor famoso.**
> The letter is worth a lot because it was written by a famous writer.

• *Exchange and Acting on Behalf of Someone*

Use *por* when something is exchanged for something else. This category includes something as concrete as a store purchase or as abstract as a feeling.

> **Se vendió la casa por un millón de dólares.**
> The house was sold for a million dollars.

> **No sé cuánto daría *por* poder dormir por toda una noche.**
> I don't know what I would give (in exchange) to be able to sleep through the night.

Similarly, when someone does something on some else's behalf or because of someone else, use *por*.

> **Lo hice todo por ti.**
> I did it all for you. (in your place, instead of your having to do it)

• *Quantity*

Por can indicate quantity.

> **Se compran los huevos *por* docenas.**
> Eggs are bought *by* the dozen.

> *Por* indicates the idea of exchange or substitution. Reason (*por*), explains why something is done for someone else. *Para* suggests that someone receives something. There is no exchange, no reciprocal action. Purpose (*para*) implies a destination.

Manejó en exceso del límite de 80 kilómetros *por* hora.

He exceeded the speed limit of 80 kilometers (*per*) an hour.

• Object of a Search or Request

Although this use is often overlooked, *por* indicates the object of a search. When the preposition designates the object of a search, look for verbs like *venir, volver, ir, regresar, enviar,* or *mandar*. And when the preposition designates the object of a question or a request, look for a verb related to communication.

Cuando estaba enfermo, mi mamá llamó *por* el médico.

When I was sick, my Mom called *for* the doctor.

Fui al supermercado *por* leche.

I went to the supermarket *for* milk.

Cuando vi a María anoche, ella preguntó *por* ti.

When I saw Mary last night, she asked *about* you.

• Pending Action

When you want to indicate that something is not yet complete but still to be done, use *por*. In these cases, an infinitive follows *por* (as is required following any preposition). Verbs commonly used in this sense are *quedar, tener*, and *faltar*.

Aún tengo unos capítulos por estudiar.

I still have some chapters left to study.

Me faltan unas páginas por escribir.

I have a few pages yet to write.

8.18 Only a few verbs require *por*.

esforzarse por	to make an effort
interesarse por	to be interested in
preocuparse por	to worry about
tomar por	to take (someone) for (something)

Remember that *esforzar* is a stem-changing verb. And *tomar por* does not mean literally "to take someone" to some place. It implies mistaking someone for something other than what he is. *Lo tomaron por alemán* means, "They took him for a German," when he may not have been German.

8.19 There are not many expressions that use *por*. In addition to those listed below, remember *por ... que*, which means "however much" or "no matter how (much)," followed by an adjective and a verb. The verb is usually in the subjunctive mood, but its use depends on the degree of uncertainty in the speaker's mind.

por eso, esto	therefore, that (this) is the reason
	No tengo dinero, por eso no fui.
	I don't have any money, therefore I didn't go.

por fin	finally
	Por fin comprendí la diferencia.
	I finally understood the difference.
por lo general	in general, as a rule
por lo común	**Por lo general estudio antes de hacer un examen.**
	In general I study before taking tests.
por supuesto	of course
	Por supuesto quiero salir bien.
	Of course I want to do well.
por otra parte	on the other hand
	Por otra parte me cuesta mucho trabajo preparar.
	On the other hand it is a lot of work for me to get ready.
por poco	almost
	Por poco me caí cuando me levanté.
	I almost fell down when I got up.
por lo menos	at least
	Tardó por lo menos una semana en llegar.
	It took at least a week for it to arrive.

OTHER PREPOSITIONS

8.20 Other important prepositions are *ante, bajo, hasta, entre, hacia, sobre,* and *sin*.

Ante: Do not confuse *ante* with *antes* the adverb. *Ante* means "before" in the sense of location, literally, and "in the face of."

La vista hermosa se extendió *ante* el viajero.
The beautiful sight spread out *before* the traveler. (or "in front of")

Todos temblaban *ante* el peligro de la inundación.
Everybody trembled *in the face of* the flood.

Bajo: When *bajo* is used as a preposition, it can indicate a physical position below, underneath, or beneath something. *Bajo* can also have a figurative meaning.

Almorzamos *bajo* los árboles.
We ate lunch *beneath* the trees.

Bajo el reinado de Juan Carlos España se modernizó.
Spain modernized *under (during)* the reign of Juan Carlos.

Desde and *Hasta*: Although *desde* is an adverb, it can also mean "from." In this sense, it refers to a point of departure, whether it be place or *time*.

Desde la Revolución, la sociedad ha cambiado mucho.
Since the Revolution, society has changed a lot.

Desde lejos se veía el tren acercándose.
From afar you could see the train coming closer.

With *desde* marking the beginning, *hasta* indicates the end.

Desde la medianoche *hasta* las seis dormí bien.
From midnight *until* six o'clock I slept well.

You probably know *Hasta mañana* and other similar expressions. *Hasta* has other meanings too. It can function as an adverb, meaning "even," but it is more common as a preposition. It marks the end or destination in time or space.

Me acompañó *hasta* la esquina.
She accompanied me *as far as* the corner.

Hasta encontrar a Enrique, no conocía a un millionario.
Until meeting Henry, I never knew a millionaire.

Entre: To indicate a point between two extremes, either in time or space, use *entre*. It can be used literally or figuratively.

El Lago Yojoa está *entre* San Pedro Sula y Tegucigalpa.
Lake Yojoa is *between* San Pedro Sula and Tegucigalpa.

Entre nosotras, creo que llegarán entre la una y las dos.
Between us, I believe they will arrive between one and two o'clock.

Hacia: Used infrequently, *hacia* is a preposition showing direction. It means "toward." Though it looks like the imperfect of the verb *hacer*, it has no accent. Use an object of the preposition pronoun after *hacia*.

Lo reconocí a medida que venía *hacia* mí.
I recognized him as he was coming *toward* me.

Sobre: *Sobre* has a variety of meanings related to location. In addition, it is used in idiomatic expressions to relay approximations. It is quite commonly seen in *sobre todo*, which means "above all" or "most of all."

Escríbame un tema *sobre* la música popular latina. (or *de* la música)
Write me a theme *about* popular Latin music.

Las ventanas de mi apartamento daban sobre la plaza.
The windows of my apartment looked out over the plaza. (looked upon)

Sobre todo es importante descansar cuando se trabaja duro.
Above all it is important to rest when you work hard.

Sin: The preposition *sin* means "without," that something is lacking. When used with an infinitive, it can mean something was not finished, expressed with a past participle in

English. Alternatively, when used with an infinitive and a present participle in English, it indicates something did not happen.

> **No hay éxito *sin* esfuerzo.**
> There is no success *without* effort.

> **Los turistas salieron *sin* visitar el museo.**
> The tourists left *without* visiting the museum.

> **El problema de la contaminación del aire está *sin* resolver.**
> The problem of air pollution is *un*resolved.

Looking at the last two examples above, in English the preposition is followed by the present or past participle. In Spanish, however, the preposition *sin* must be followed by an infinitive.

THINGS TO REMEMBER

- Whenever a verb follows a preposition, the verb *always* takes the infinitive form.
- Some verbs have the preposition included in their meaning, and so no extra preposition is required: *Buscar* means "to look for."
- In Spanish, there is no apostrophe to show ownership as there is in English. In Spanish, you must use the preposition *de* to show possession and ownership: *Le madre del niño* is "the child's mother."

REVIEW QUESTIONS

Set A: In each of the following groups, select the one infinitive that cannot take the same preposition that the other three infinitives can take. In other words, three infinitives could be followed by the same preposition, while the fourth infinitive could not. Select the one infinitive that requires a different preposition.

1. A) enojarse   B) casarse   C) encontrar   D) soñar

2. A) pensar   B) invitar   C) comenzar   D) aprender

3. A) atreverse   B) pensar   C) olvidarse   D) enamorarse

4. A) enterarse   B) fijarse   C) insistir   D) tardar

5. A) preocuparse   B) preguntar   C) interesarse   D) despedirse

Set B: Circle the correct preposition.

1. No me gusta cuando unos chicos se burlan ____ otros.

   A) a   B) sobre   C) por   D) de

2. Él sabía que era amor ____ primera vista cuando ella le sonrió.

   A) a   B) de   C) en   D) con

3. No lo supe ____ ayer porque no recibí la carta.

   A) a   B) hasta   C) desde   D) hacia

4. ____ lo general prefiero dormir tarde los sábados.

   A) En   B) Para   C) Por   D) Con

5. Enviaron ____ una vecina para quedarse con la chica enferma.

   A) de   B) hasta   C) para   D) por

6. ____ falta de un caballo, se perdió la guerra.

   A) En   B) Sin   C) De   D) Por

7. ____ decir una palabra, la mujer salió del cuarto.

   A) Con   B) Sin   C) Por   D) En

8. ¿Ves ____ esa chica? Es mi hermana.

   A) a   B) hasta   C) sobre   D) de

9. Trabajaron ____ poder descansar los fines de semana.

   A) de   B) en   C) para   D) desde

10. La pintura será hecha ___ un artista famoso.

   A) por   B) de   C) hacia   D) a

11. Nunca hemos vista a un jugador ___ baloncesto tan alto.

   A) para   B) de   C) en   D) con

12. Muchos estudiantes tardan ___ empezar a estudiar.

   A) a   B) de   C) en   D) con

13. El público depende ___ gobierno para mantener las calles.

   A) al   B) del   C) en el   D) con el

14. Creo que este presidente es muy bueno. ¿Qué piensas ___ él?

   A) a   B) de   C) en   D) por

15. No reconozco este sombrero. ¿ ___ quién será?

   A) A   B) Con   C) De   D) Sobre

16. ¿Cuánto me darás ___ esta mesa antigua? Vale mucho.

   A) para   B) sobre   C) en   D) por

17. Ten cuidado, Juanito. ___ un chico pequeño eres muy atrevido.

   A) Por   B) A   C) De   D) Para

18. El avión hizo escala en Chicago ___ Nueva York y San Francisco.

   A) sobre   B) a   C) entre   D) para

19. Aunque es de Buenos Aires, ahora vive ___ Tejas.

   A) de   B) con   C) en   D) por

20. ___ salir bien en este examen, podría adelantarme un semestre.

   A) En   B) Para   C) De   D) Desde

21. Esa muchacha ___ pelo largo es muy hermosa.

   A) de   B) en   C) a   D) por

22. Me preocupo de vez en cuando ___ los problemas ambientales.

   A) de   B) en   C) por   D) con

23. Muchos adolescentes no están avergonzados ___ sus padres.

   A) de   B) en   C) por   D) sobre

24. Nadie quiere tener que presentarse ___ un juez por ninguna razón.

   A) de   B) antes   C) ante   D) sobre

25. Al comprar un billete, avise al agente ___ cuándo lo necesita.

   A) para   B) ante   C) dentro   D) después de

26. Siempre debe tomar las medicinas ___ control médico.

   A) en   B) debajo   C) bajo   D) a

27 Muchas personas se acostumbran ___ tomar vitaminas a diario.

   A) a   B) bajo   C) con   D) de

28. ___ una semana terminaré con las clases del verano.

   A) A   B) Dentro   C) Dentro de   D) Hasta

29. Habla bien la lengua, casi lo toman ___ español.

   A) a   B) por   C) para   D) en

30. Hoy más de veinticinco millones ___ habitantes viven en la ciudad.

   A) a   B) para   C) con   D) de

ANSWERS AND EXPLANATIONS

Set A

1. (C)

Encontrar a. The other verbs take *con*. In order to use *con* with *encontrar* you need the reflexive pronoun.

2. (A)

Pensar en or de. The other verbs take *a*.

3. (A)

Atreverse a. The other verbs take *de*.

4. (A)

Enterarse de. The other verbs take *en*.

5. (D)

Despedirse de. The other verbs take *por* (though *preguntar* could be followed by other prepositions as well).

Set B

1. (D)

De always follows *burlarse* when the expression is followed by another verb.

2. (A)

Amor a primera vista is an expression: "Love at first sight."

3. (B)

Hasta has the meaning of "until" in this sentence. See 8.20.

4. (C)

Por lo general is an expression. If the phrase did not contain *lo*, *en* would be a possibility. See 8.19.

5. (D)

When a search is implied, use *por* to indicate the object of the search.

6. (D)

The meaning of *por* in this case is "because of" or "out of," indicating a reason.

7. (B)

In this context, *sin* is the only word that fits the meaning of "without." See 8.20.

8. (A)

When the object of the verb is a person or something the speaker wishes to personify, the personal *a* is required.

9. (C)

The context of the sentence requires a preposition indicating purpose.

10. (A)

Passive voice structures, indicated by *ser*, a past participle, and an expressed agent, means that you must use *por.* See 8.17.

11. (B)

Baloncesto is a noun that describes *jugador*. The preposition *de* links the two since a noun cannot modify another noun in Spanish.

12. (C)

Use *tardar* plus *en* when the expression is followed by another verb. See 8.7.

13. (B)

De always follows *depender* when the expression is followed by another verb. *De* plus *el* (from *gobierno*) is *del*.

14. (B)

When *pensar* is used to mean an opinion, use *de*. The other preposition you can use after *pensar* is *en*, which indicates "to think about" in the sense of meditating about something.

15. (C)

De indicates possession in this case.

16. (D)

Por has the meaning of "in exchange for" in this sentence.

17. (D)

Para indicates an implied contrast. The implication is that most small children are not daring. This particular child has received a warning because perhaps he has overestimated his abilities. He is being told, "For a small child, you are very daring."

18. (C)

Entre, meaning "between," is the only preposition that fits the context.

19. (C)

Although *de* is used in the first part of the sentence, telling origin, *en* is required in the second part. That's because "now he lives in Texas."

20. (C)

Though you may have chosen *para*, it will not work here: The two clauses would not make sense together with "in order to" at the beginning of the first clause. Using (C), *de* takes the place of *si* and a conjugated verb in an *if-then* statement. The conditional in the *then* portion should indicate that the imperfect subjunctive would be used in the *if* clause if *de* were not used. See 8.8.

21. (A)

De in this sentence indicates a personal characteristic.

22. (C)

Use *preocuparse* plus *por* when the expression is followed by another verb. See 8.18.

23. (A)

De is the preposition that normally follows *estar avergonzado*.

24. (C)

Do not confuse *ante* with *antes*, an adverb. The only preposition meaning "before" is *ante*. See 8.20.

25. (A)

Para is used to indicate a deadline, or destination in time.

26. (C)

Bajo means "under" in an abstract sense here, as opposed to meaning "beneath" in the sense of physical location. See 8.20.

27. (A)

A follows *acostumbrarse* when the expression is followed by another verb.

28. (C)

"Within" is *dentro de. Dentro* means "inside," which does not fit the context here.

29. (B)

"To be taken for" is por.

30. (D)

After the number *millón* or *millones*, use *de* before the following noun.

Chapter 9: **Conjunctions and Transitional Phrases**

- Conjunctions for Equal Parts
- Conjunctions of Subordination
- Transitional Phrases

Conjunctions connect words, phrases, or clauses. In other words, a conjunction can link a list of words all in the same category: nouns, verbs, adjectives, or adverbs. For example, "I saw a man, a woman, and their children at the gate" joins words of equal value. Or, in a compound sentence, a conjunction can link two clauses, each of which could stand alone as a complete sentence, into one sentence. For example, "You can go to the party or you can stay home." Additionally, a conjunction can introduce a clause whose importance is secondary to the main thought of the sentence (called a dependent or subordinate clause). For example, "You can go to the party, unless you have homework to do." The most common conjunctions are:

y	and
o	or
ni	nor
o ... o	either ... or
ni ... ni	neither ... nor, either ... or
pero	but
mas	but (notice there is no accent mark)
porque	because
sino	but rather plus a noun
sino que	but rather plus a clause with a verb
no sólo ... sino	not only ... but
como	as, like, as a result, since
como resultado	
puesto que	since, as
ya que	
debido a que	

CONJUNCTIONS FOR EQUAL PARTS

9.1 To join equal parts, conjunctions are used in essentially the same way as in English.

> En el jardín zoológico vi a monos, elefantes, y jirafas.
> At the zoo I saw monkeys, elephants, and giraffes.

> El constante ir y venir de gente causó gran conmoción.
> The constant coming and going of people caused a lot of commotion.

And

There is nothing difficult about using "and," the Spanish word *y*. The only exception is when *y* immediately precedes a word that begins with the sound *i*: Since that combination of sounds would be very confusing, you change the *y* to *e*. This includes words that begin with *h*, because *h* is never sounded in spoken Spanish. (However, if a word begins with *hie-*, as in *hielo*, the *y* is not changed to *e*, because *ie* is a diphthong with the *e* more strongly pronounced than the *i*.)

> Español e italiano son idiomas parecidos.
> Spanish and Italian are similar languages.

> Viniendo e yendo constantemente, terminaron pronto.
> Coming and going constantly, they soon finished.

> Las calles cubiertas de nieve y hielo son peligrosas.
> The streets covered with snow and ice are dangerous.

Or

For the word "or," (the Spanish word *o*), a similar rule applies. If the word following "or" begins with *o-* or *ho-*, change the *o* to *u*. Don't worry about any diphthongs with *o*.

> Vimos a siete u ocho personas allí.
> We saw seven or eight people there.

> Contratamos a mujeres u hombres para este empleo.
> We hire women or men for this job.

> Los chicos jugaron al tenis, o se quedaron en casa.
> The children played tennis, or they stayed inside.

Nor

When *o* follows a negated verb or a verb preceded by a negative indefinite pronoun, adverb or adjective, use *ni*.

> Nadie estudió, escuchó, ni miró la pizarra.
> Nobody studied, listened, or looked at the blackboard.

Either-Or

In constructions where the meaning is "either ... or," use *o ... o.*

> U hombres o mujeres pueden hacer este trabajo.
> Either men or women can do this work.
>
> O te vas con migo en el coche O te vas caminando.
> Either you come with me in the car or you have to walk.

Neither-Nor

Just as you use *ni* for *o* when the verb is negated, use *ni ... ni* in place of *o ... o.*

> No les gustan ni, ni ladrones, ni tramposos.
> They don't like either, thieves or cheaters.
> (They like neither, thieves nor cheaters.)

But

The word *pero* has the same uses as in English: It is used only to connect two clauses. When "but" is followed by a word or phrase only, the clause is elliptical, meaning that one clause is understood even though it contains just a few words. *Pero* indicates something that is contrary to what is expressed in the other clause.

> Se dice que la clase es difícil, pero no lo creo.
> They say that the class if difficult, but I don't believe it.

The word *mas* is used just like *pero.* Notice that it has no accent, which is what distinguishes it from the adjective *más.*

> Me dijo que iría, mas no fue.
> He told me he would go, but he didn't (go).

Because

As a conjunction, *porque* is spelled as one word, with no accent. Since there are few synonyms for it, *porque* is a common conjunction. It indicates cause and motive. That is, it explains the reason for something.

> No queremos ir porque estamos cansados.
> We don't want to go because we are tired.
>
> Porque era muy rico, prestó dinero a sus amigos.
> Because he was very rich, he loaned money to his friends.

But rather

Sino means "but," except that it is used *after a negative* to indicate an alternative to whatever precedes it. When the clause following *sino* contains a verb, use *sino que*.

> No vendían ropa, sino sólo zapatos en la tienda.
> They didn't sell clothes, but only shoes in the store.
>
> Me dijo que no iría, sino que me esperaría aquí.
> He told me he would not go, but rather would wait for me here.

Not only . . . but

When a sentence contains *no sólo*, meaning "not only," then *sino también* serves to connect the two parts in a positive way.

> No sólo los adultos vinieron, sino también sus niños.
> Not only the adults came, but also their children.

As / Like / As a Result / Since

The word *como* has various meanings. It is commonly used as an adverb and in many idiomatic expressions. As a conjunction it connects two clauses, and it frequently indicates cause and condition. When it indicates cause, it means "since" or "as."

> Como te dije antes, me fascina la cultura española.
> Like (as) I told you before, Spanish culture fascinates me.
>
> Como tenía sueño, se acostó.
> Since he was sleepy, he went to bed.
>
> No le hablé. Como resultado no vino.
> I didn't speak to him. As a result he did not come.

When you want to say "as if," use *como si* plus the imperfect subjunctive in the clause beginning with *como si*. Using the subjunctive indicates that it is hypothetical and contrary to fact.

CONJUNCTIONS OF SUBORDINATION

9.2 The most common conjunction is *que* ("that"), which is never omitted in Spanish, but frequently omitted in English. Almost every clause that contains a conjugated verb has *que* in the conjunction that introduces the clause.

> Quiero que vengas a la fiesta.
> I want you to come to the party. (that you come)

> Pay attention to the transitional phrases that are false cognates, meaning they mean something other than their English sound-alike words.

Hable más alto, por favor, que oigo mal.

Please speak louder, I don't hear well.

¿Quieres venir?

—¡Claro que sí!

"Do you want to come?"

—"But of course!"

TRANSITIONAL PHRASES

9.3 Transitional phrases can communicate a chronological order or logic of events, where and how things happen, and even attitudes. Many transitional phrases begin with prepositions or are part of an adverbial conjunction, as you have seen in earlier chapters.

no obstante	nevertheless, yet, however
sin embargo	No los veo a menudo. No obstante hablamos una vez a la semana.
	I don't see them often. Nevertheless, we talk once a week.
casi	almost, almost always, almost never
casi siempre	Casi me olvidé de decirle.
casi nunca	I almost forgot to tell her.
	Casi siempre hacía la tarea.
	I almost always did the homework.
entonces	then
	Llamé a la puerta y entonces entré.
	I knocked at the door and then entered.
en lo tocante	with respect to
	En lo tocante al trabajo, lo tendré para mañana.
	With regard to the work, I will have it for tomorrow.
en primer lugar	in the first place
	En primer lugar, se necesita venir a la clase.
	In the first place, you need to come to class.
en segundo lugar	in the second place
	En segundo lugar, se necesita estudiar.
	In the second place, you need to study.
por ejemplo	for example
	Tiene mucha libertad. Por ejemplo, puede ir y venir cuando quiera.
	He has a lot of freedom. For example, he can come and go as he wishes.
en gran parte	in large part, to a great extent
	Su éxito se debe en gran parte a su trabajo.
	Her success is due in large part to her work.

cada vez más	more and more
	Cada vez más se ven a los hispanos en las universidades.
	More and more one sees Hispanics at the universities.
cada vez menos	less and less
	Cada vez menos se oyen críticas del presidente.
	Less and less you hear criticism of the president.
por suerte	luckily, fortunately
	Por suerte, el conductor no se hirió en el accidente.
	Fortunately, the driver was not hurt in the accident.
por desgracia	unfortunately
	Por desgracia, sufrió un accidente ayer.
	Unfortunately, he had an accident yesterday.
por otro lado	on the other hand
en cambio	
	Por otro lado, tuvo mucha suerte en salir con vida.
	On the other hand, he was lucky to escape with his life.
por consiguiente	thus, therefore, then
	No fuimos; por consiguiente perdimos una gran oportunidad.
	We didn't go, therefore we lost a great opportunity.
de hecho	in fact, as a matter of fact, really
	De hecho, nunca he querido ir allí.
	In fact, I never have liked to go there.
en realidad	actually
	En realidad, nadie quería ir.
	Actually, nobody wanted to go.
actualmente	presently, nowadays
	Actualmente la situación se ha puesto mejor para los obreros en la fábrica.
	Nowadays the situation has gotten better for the workers at the factory.
hoy en día	nowadays
	Hoy en día no muchos viven en el campo.
	Nowadays not many (people) live in the country.
además	in addition
	Además de visitar a los abuelos, vimos a todos los tíos también.
	In addition to seeing the grandparents, we saw all the aunts and uncles, too.
de veras	really
	De veras, me gusta escribir.
	Really, I like to write.
para resumir	in conclusion, to summarize
	Para resumir, estas expresiones son muy importantes.
	In conclusion, these expressions are very important.

de lo anterior	from the above
	De lo anterior se ve que hay muchas expresiones útiles.
	From the above you can see that there are many useful expressions.
en todo caso	in any case
	En todo caso, es importante estudiarlos.
	In any case, it is important to study them.
a fin de cuentas	in the end, all in all
al cabo	**A fin de cuentas, lo que cuenta es lo que se sabe.**
	In the end, what counts is what you know.
al fin y al cabo	after all, when all is said and done
	Al fin y al cabo, lo que cuenta es que cada uno se sienta feliz consigo.
	After all, what counts is that every one feels happy with himself.

THINGS TO REMEMBER

- Use of the word "and" is rather straightforward in Spanish. The only exception is when it comes right before a word that begins with the sound *i*: Since that combination of sounds would be very confusing, you change the *y* to *e*. This includes words that begin with *h*, since *h* is never sounded in spoken Spanish.
- When *o* ("or") follows a negative verb, use *ni* ("nor") instead.
- The most common conjunction is *que* ("that"), which is *never* omitted in Spanish, but often omitted in English: *Quiero que vengas a la fiesta*. ("I want you to come [that you come] to the party.")

REVIEW QUESTIONS

Set A: Circle the answer choice that is a synonym to the word listed.

1. como

   A) quizás   B) no obstante   C) de hecho   D) ya que

2. tal vez

   A) por lo menos   B) en gran parte   C) a lo mejor   D) porque

3. actualmente

   A) hoy en día   B) en realidad   C) de hecho   D) desde

4. en lo tocante a

   A) por lo general   B) a pesar de   C) sin embargo   D) en cuanto a

5. pero

   A) menos   B) cada vez menos   C) tal vez   D) mas

6. por consiguiente

   A) desde   B) después   C) entonces   D) de lo anterior

7. por otra parte

   A) cada vez más   B) sin embargo   C) en cambio   D) de hecho

8. u

   A) ni   B) sino   C) o   D) y

9. a fin de cuentas

   A) al cabo   B) después   C) desde   D) puesto que

10. acaso

   A) apenas   B) por otra parte   C) a pesar de   D) quizás

Set B: Select the word or phrase that completes the meaning of the sentence. Read the entire sentence before making your choice.

1. No tenían mucho dinero, ___ no fueron al cine.

   A) sino   B) como   C) por consiguiente   D) o

2. ___, los que salen bien son los que trabajan mucho.

   A) Ni   B) Puesto que   C) Además   D) Desde

3. ___ no pude oír al conferenciante, salí.

   A) Como   B) Además   C) Pero   D) También

4. Me faltan unas cosas para la escuela, ___ un cuaderno.

    A) en cambio   B) sino   C) por ejemplo   D) actualmente

5. ___ querían ver a su héroe, sino hablar con él.

    A) Ni   B) O   C) No sólo   D) También

6. Me llamó para invitarme a la fiesta, ___ no estuve en casa.

    A) o   B) sino que   C) desde   D) pero

7. ___ los dos se casaron y vivían felizmente para siempre.

    A) Ya que   B) Porque   C) Al fin y al cabo   D) Según

8. ___ se ven tantas camionetas como coches en los caminos.

    A) Cada vez más   B) Según   C) En lo tocante   D) Sino

9. A medida que se me acercaron, vi que eran hombre ___ hijo.

    A) y   B) e   C) o   D) u

10. No fue a la conferencia ___ se sentía mal esa noche.

    A) también   B) o   C) porque   D) apenas

11. Entró en la sala de clase. ___ se sentó en la mesa.

    A) Pero   B) Entonces   C) Casi   D) Como

12. ___ mi hermana ___ su amiga jamás supo mi secreto.

    A) O ... o   B) Ni ... ni   C) No sólo ... sino   D) Y ... y

13. Seguramente no irá hoy, ___ casi nunca nos acompaña a visitarla.

    A) para resumir   B) sino   C) porque   D) desde

14. Corrió ___ le persiguiera un tigre.

    A) como   B) desde   C) de hecho   D) como si

15. Vamos al parque ___ que llueva mañana.

    A) entonces   B) en cuanto   C) a pesar de   D) además

16. ___, siguieron asistiendo a la escuela.

    A) Porque   B) De todos modos C) Desde   D) Como

17. ___ mi amigo tuvo que volver a casa solo.

    A) No sólo   B) En lo tocante a C) Por desgracia   D) Ya que

ANSWERS AND EXPLANATIONS

Set A

1. (D)

Ya que means "since."

2. (C)

A lo mejor means "perhaps."

3. (A)

Actualmente is a false cognate: You might think it means "actually." In fact, it means "nowadays" or "presently," which in Spanish, is how you would also translate *hoy en día*.

4. (D)

En cuanto a means "with regard to."

5. (D)

Mas without an accent means "but."

6. (C)

Entonces can mean "thus" or "therefore," but "then" is its most common meaning.

7. (C)

En cambio means "on the other hand," like *por otra parte*.

8. (C)

Remember that *u* replaces *o* when it precedes a word beginning with *o-* or *ho-*.

9. (A)

Al cabo means "in the end," just like *al fin y al cabo*, *por fin*, and *a fin de cuentas*.

10. (D)

Acaso and *quizás* both mean "maybe" or "perhaps." Remember that *quizás* (sometimes spelled *quizá*) takes the subjunctive in the verb, though *acaso* takes either the indicative or the subjunctive.

Set B

1. (C)

Por consiguiente, meaning "therefore," is a transitional phrase that connects the two ideas. No other conjunction makes sense. Although the verb in one clause is negated, *sino* does not work because the ideas in each clauses are not contrasted. That means (A) is out. The conjunction *o*, choice (D), cannot be used, because you would not use it before *no*. The sentence says, "The didn't have much money, (therefore/so) they didn't go to the movies."

2. (C)

Además means "in addition." The other answer choices would be used to introduce subordinate clauses or another independent clause. This sentence contains two adjective clauses describing *los que*, so no conjunction is needed. *Desde* (D), can be an adverb, like *además*, but "since" makes no sense here. Choice (B), *puesto que*, also means "since" or "because," so it can be eliminated as well. The sentence says, "In addition, those who do well are those who work hard."

3. (A)

This is a compound sentence, with a conjunction that indicates reason. *Como* is the only word that fits. *Además* or *también* would work, except that there's no other conjunction in front of *salí*, so (B) and (D) are out. The sentence says, "Since I couldn't hear the speaker, I left."

4. (C)

Un cuaderno is one item that the subject doesn't have, so it is an example. (D) means "nowadays" or "presently," so it does not fit. (B) is a conjunction that would introduce another clause, but the ideas are not contrasting, and the verb in the main clause is not negated. The sentence says, "I am lacking some things for school, for example, a notebook."

5. (C)

Sino should be a clue that you need (C) *No sólo* at the start of the sentence. No other answer choice makes sense. The sentence says, "Not only did they want to see their hero, but rather to speak with him."

6. (D)

Pero is the only conjunction that makes any sense: The sentence says, "He called me to invite me to the party, but I was not at home."

7. (C)

"In the end" is the only phrase that makes any sense. This is a compound sentence, with two parts connected by *y*, so you just need a transitional phrase at the beginning of one clause. *Según* is a transitional phrase, but doesn't work in this sentence, which says, "In the end the two got married and lived happily every after."

8. (A)

Cada vez más is a transitional phrase that introduces the idea. (C) *en lo tocante* is usually set apart from the sentence by a comma. *Según*, meaning "according to," makes no sense here. And *sino* (D) doesn't fit because the verb in the sentence is not negated. The sentence compares the number of pickup trucks with cars, but without the negative, *sino* makes no sense. If the sentence had said, "One does not see many trucks, but rather cars," then you could have used *sino*.

9. (B)

Remember that *y* changes to *e* when followed by a word that begins with *i, y*, or *hi-*.

10. (C)

You need a conjunction that indicates reason, so *porque* is the answer. (A) *También*, meaning "also," might make sense, except that for it to be used in this blank, it would need to be set apart with commas. *O* makes no sense, and can't be used because the first clause is negative, so (B) is wrong, as is (D) *apenas*, which means "scarcely." The sentence says, "She did not go to the lecture because she felt bad that night."

11. (B)

An adverb must start off the second sentence in order to continue the chronological sequence. *Entonces* is the only word that makes sense. The sentences say, "He entered the class room. Then he sat down at the table."

12. (B)

The word *jamás* makes *No sólo ... sino* and *o ... o* nonsensical in this sentence. With the correct *Ni ... ni*, the sentence reads, "Neither my sister nor my friend ever found out my secret."

13. (C)

Neither *para resumir* nor *sino* makes sense, so (A) and (B) are wrong. *Desde* (D) means "since" in a temporal sense. The sentence says, "Surely he will not go today, because he almost never goes with us to visit her." *Porque* is correct because it introduces the reason why he is not going.

14. (D)

The imperfect subjunctive that follows the blank tells you that *como si* is the only possible answer. It expresses something contrary to fact. The sentence says, "He ran as if a tiger were chasing him."

15. (C)

The subjunctive after the adverb means you need either *aunque* or *a pesar de*. (B) *en cuanto*, "with regard to," is an adverbial conjunction that introduces the subjunctive, but is not usually followed by *que* and then the subjunctive.

16. (B)

De todos modos is the only possible choice because this is not a compound sentence. The other choices are all conjunctions that introduce subordinate clauses. The sentence says, "Anyway, they kept on attending the school."

17. (C)

Por desgracia is the only expression that makes sense. The sentence says, "Unfortunately my friend had to return home alone." *En lo tocante a*, choice (B), makes no sense, nor does *No sólo*, choice (A), because the other half of the expression is not used. *Ya que* doesn't work, either, because this is not a compound sentence.

Part Three

Practice Tests

- There are five tests in this section. Tests 1 through 4 are Spanish Tests, while Test 5 is a Spanish with Listening Test. Answers and explanations follow each test.

- Your answer sheet is a generic answer for sheet for the SAT Subject tests. Therefore, it has five columns. For the Spanish Test, use *only* columns A, B, C, and D.

- For the Spanish with Listening Test, there is no CD. There are scripts, however, so you can get an idea of the kinds of selections you will hear, and the structure of the questions.

- Take the tests in a quiet room with no distractions. Bring some No. 2 pencils. Use the answer sheets provided to mark your answers.

- Time yourself. Spend no more than one hour on each test.

- Scoring instructions are in the "Scoring Your Practice Tests" section (page 357).

Practice Test 1

Answer Grid
Practice Test 1

1. Ⓐ Ⓑ Ⓒ Ⓓ Ⓔ
2. Ⓐ Ⓑ Ⓒ Ⓓ Ⓔ
3. Ⓐ Ⓑ Ⓒ Ⓓ Ⓔ
4. Ⓐ Ⓑ Ⓒ Ⓓ Ⓔ
5. Ⓐ Ⓑ Ⓒ Ⓓ Ⓔ
6. Ⓐ Ⓑ Ⓒ Ⓓ Ⓔ
7. Ⓐ Ⓑ Ⓒ Ⓓ Ⓔ
8. Ⓐ Ⓑ Ⓒ Ⓓ Ⓔ
9. Ⓐ Ⓑ Ⓒ Ⓓ Ⓔ
10. Ⓐ Ⓑ Ⓒ Ⓓ Ⓔ
11. Ⓐ Ⓑ Ⓒ Ⓓ Ⓔ
12. Ⓐ Ⓑ Ⓒ Ⓓ Ⓔ
13. Ⓐ Ⓑ Ⓒ Ⓓ Ⓔ
14. Ⓐ Ⓑ Ⓒ Ⓓ Ⓔ
15. Ⓐ Ⓑ Ⓒ Ⓓ Ⓔ
16. Ⓐ Ⓑ Ⓒ Ⓓ Ⓔ
17. Ⓐ Ⓑ Ⓒ Ⓓ Ⓔ
18. Ⓐ Ⓑ Ⓒ Ⓓ Ⓔ
19. Ⓐ Ⓑ Ⓒ Ⓓ Ⓔ
20. Ⓐ Ⓑ Ⓒ Ⓓ Ⓔ
21. Ⓐ Ⓑ Ⓒ Ⓓ Ⓔ
22. Ⓐ Ⓑ Ⓒ Ⓓ Ⓔ
23. Ⓐ Ⓑ Ⓒ Ⓓ Ⓔ
24. Ⓐ Ⓑ Ⓒ Ⓓ Ⓔ
25. Ⓐ Ⓑ Ⓒ Ⓓ Ⓔ
26. Ⓐ Ⓑ Ⓒ Ⓓ Ⓔ
27. Ⓐ Ⓑ Ⓒ Ⓓ Ⓔ
28. Ⓐ Ⓑ Ⓒ Ⓓ Ⓔ
29. Ⓐ Ⓑ Ⓒ Ⓓ Ⓔ

30. Ⓐ Ⓑ Ⓒ Ⓓ Ⓔ
31. Ⓐ Ⓑ Ⓒ Ⓓ Ⓔ
32. Ⓐ Ⓑ Ⓒ Ⓓ Ⓔ
33. Ⓐ Ⓑ Ⓒ Ⓓ Ⓔ
34. Ⓐ Ⓑ Ⓒ Ⓓ Ⓔ
35. Ⓐ Ⓑ Ⓒ Ⓓ Ⓔ
36. Ⓐ Ⓑ Ⓒ Ⓓ Ⓔ
37. Ⓐ Ⓑ Ⓒ Ⓓ Ⓔ
38. Ⓐ Ⓑ Ⓒ Ⓓ Ⓔ
39. Ⓐ Ⓑ Ⓒ Ⓓ Ⓔ
40. Ⓐ Ⓑ Ⓒ Ⓓ Ⓔ
41. Ⓐ Ⓑ Ⓒ Ⓓ Ⓔ
42. Ⓐ Ⓑ Ⓒ Ⓓ Ⓔ
43. Ⓐ Ⓑ Ⓒ Ⓓ Ⓔ
44. Ⓐ Ⓑ Ⓒ Ⓓ Ⓔ
45. Ⓐ Ⓑ Ⓒ Ⓓ Ⓔ
46. Ⓐ Ⓑ Ⓒ Ⓓ Ⓔ
47. Ⓐ Ⓑ Ⓒ Ⓓ Ⓔ
48. Ⓐ Ⓑ Ⓒ Ⓓ Ⓔ
49. Ⓐ Ⓑ Ⓒ Ⓓ Ⓔ
50. Ⓐ Ⓑ Ⓒ Ⓓ Ⓔ
51. Ⓐ Ⓑ Ⓒ Ⓓ Ⓔ
52. Ⓐ Ⓑ Ⓒ Ⓓ Ⓔ
53. Ⓐ Ⓑ Ⓒ Ⓓ Ⓔ
54. Ⓐ Ⓑ Ⓒ Ⓓ Ⓔ
55. Ⓐ Ⓑ Ⓒ Ⓓ Ⓔ
56. Ⓐ Ⓑ Ⓒ Ⓓ Ⓔ
57. Ⓐ Ⓑ Ⓒ Ⓓ Ⓔ
58. Ⓐ Ⓑ Ⓒ Ⓓ Ⓔ

59. Ⓐ Ⓑ Ⓒ Ⓓ Ⓔ
60. Ⓐ Ⓑ Ⓒ Ⓓ Ⓔ
61. Ⓐ Ⓑ Ⓒ Ⓓ Ⓔ
62. Ⓐ Ⓑ Ⓒ Ⓓ Ⓔ
63. Ⓐ Ⓑ Ⓒ Ⓓ Ⓔ
64. Ⓐ Ⓑ Ⓒ Ⓓ Ⓔ
65. Ⓐ Ⓑ Ⓒ Ⓓ Ⓔ
66. Ⓐ Ⓑ Ⓒ Ⓓ Ⓔ
67. Ⓐ Ⓑ Ⓒ Ⓓ Ⓔ
68. Ⓐ Ⓑ Ⓒ Ⓓ Ⓔ
69. Ⓐ Ⓑ Ⓒ Ⓓ Ⓔ
70. Ⓐ Ⓑ Ⓒ Ⓓ Ⓔ
71. Ⓐ Ⓑ Ⓒ Ⓓ Ⓔ
72. Ⓐ Ⓑ Ⓒ Ⓓ Ⓔ
73. Ⓐ Ⓑ Ⓒ Ⓓ Ⓔ
74. Ⓐ Ⓑ Ⓒ Ⓓ Ⓔ
75. Ⓐ Ⓑ Ⓒ Ⓓ Ⓔ
76. Ⓐ Ⓑ Ⓒ Ⓓ Ⓔ
77. Ⓐ Ⓑ Ⓒ Ⓓ Ⓔ
78. Ⓐ Ⓑ Ⓒ Ⓓ Ⓔ
79. Ⓐ Ⓑ Ⓒ Ⓓ Ⓔ
80. Ⓐ Ⓑ Ⓒ Ⓓ Ⓔ
81. Ⓐ Ⓑ Ⓒ Ⓓ Ⓔ
82. Ⓐ Ⓑ Ⓒ Ⓓ Ⓔ
83. Ⓐ Ⓑ Ⓒ Ⓓ Ⓔ
84. Ⓐ Ⓑ Ⓒ Ⓓ Ⓔ
85. Ⓐ Ⓑ Ⓒ Ⓓ Ⓔ

Practice Test 1

Directions: Select the most appropriate word to complete the sentence and fill in the corresponding oval on the answer sheet.

1. Anoche al ___ a casa conocí a mi vecino nuevo.

    (A) llorar
    (B) llover
    (C) llegar
    (D) llevar

2. Es mejor que los estudiantes ___ a una escuela en su propio barrio.

    (A) atiendan
    (B) asistan
    (C) revuelvan
    (D) entreguen

3. El cartero me dio la ___ con las noticias del nacimiento de mi primera sobrina.

    (A) letra
    (B) película
    (C) firma
    (D) carta

4. No sólo los niños se divertían en la feria, ___ también los padres.

    (A) sin
    (B) sin que
    (C) sino
    (D) pero

5. Miguel quería venir a la fiesta, pero no le dijo ___ a qué hora sería, y no vino.

    (A) algo
    (B) nadie
    (C) ningún
    (D) alguno

6. Mi hermana estará conmigo, nosotras siempre viajamos ___.

    (A) juntado
    (B) juntos
    (C) junta
    (D) juntas

7. A Raúl le gusta mucho ___ para ver los peces en el magnífico mundo submarino.

    (A) esquiar
    (B) bucear
    (C) merendar
    (D) cruzar

8. Para recibir el máximo beneficio del curso, se necesita hacer la ___ cada noche.

    (A) asignatura
    (B) conferencia
    (C) lectura
    (D) escuela

GO ON TO THE NEXT PAGE

9. Enrique, ¿tienes tus maletas? El botones ya vino por ___.

   (A) las
   (B) suyas
   (C) ellos
   (D) las mías

10. Antes de ___ los pasajeros tienen que abrocharse los cinturones de seguridad.

   (A) embarcar
   (B) abordar
   (C) despegar
   (D) enterrar

11. El conjunto que ___ para el quinceañero de mi hija es muy bueno.

   (A) asistirá
   (B) jugará
   (C) tocará
   (D) tomará

12. El profesor pidió que sus estudiantes le ___ los papeles.

   (A) entregan
   (B) entregaban
   (C) entregaron
   (D) entregaran

13. Alguien me dio unas entradas ___ para el concierto.

   (A) gratis
   (B) libras
   (C) frecuentes
   (D) duras

14. Me sorprendió verla ___ a la cabeza de la mesa.

   (A) sentado
   (B) sentados
   (C) sentada
   (D) sentando

15. Juanito, recuerda lavarte las manos con ___ para limpiarlas bien.

   (A) fresas
   (B) jabón
   (C) sopa
   (D) carne

16. Nos llamará antes de que ___ para que sepamos cuándo vendrá.

   (A) salga
   (B) saldrá
   (C) sale
   (D) salir

17. Es difícil quedarse tranquilo cuando todos a su ___ están volviéndose locos.

   (A) rodeo
   (B) alrededor
   (C) circunstancia
   (D) frontera

18. No pienso ir al cine esta noche, ___ he visto esa película.

   (A) todavía
   (B) ya no
   (C) no sólo
   (D) ya

19. Porque llegó tarde a la parada, ___ el autobús porque ya se había ido.

   (A) vio
   (B) acompañó
   (C) extrañó
   (D) perdió

20. Esta carne no es muy tierna, necesito un ___ bien afilado para cortarla.

   (A) cuchillo
   (B) cuchara
   (C) tenedor
   (D) clavo

GO ON TO THE NEXT PAGE

21. Cuando leí la noticia se me ocurrió ___ obvio que fue todo el asunto.

    (A) el
    (B) la
    (C) lo
    (D) le

22. ____ tengo mucha tarea esta noche, puedo salir por un ratito.

    (A) A pesar de que
    (B) No obstante
    (C) Por fin
    (D) A menos que

23. Hijito, al cruzar la calle, tienes que mirar ___.

    (A) ruidosamente
    (B) cuidadosamente
    (C) precisamente
    (D) actualmente

24. Con dificultad los coches manejan por las calles ___ del pueblo viejo.

    (A) estrechas
    (B) amplias
    (C) flacas
    (D) adecuadas

25. Arriba se ve la montaña, abajo el lago, y el reflejo de la cumbre en el agua de ___.

    (A) lo
    (B) la
    (C) ella
    (D) él

26. A esta hora mañana cuando yo lo vea, ___ el trabajo.

    (A) termino
    (B) terminé
    (C) habré terminado
    (D) haya terminado

27. El hombre iba ___ tras el autobús que acababa de salir sin él.

    (A) corría
    (B) corrió
    (C) correr
    (D) corriendo

28. Me gusta nadar ___ esquiar porque se hacen las dos actividades en el agua.

    (A) como
    (B) igual
    (C) lo mismo
    (D) tanto como

29. De niño uno de mis libros favoritos era *Las mil y ___ noches*.

    (A) Un
    (B) Uno
    (C) Una
    (D) Unas

30. Parece que a los estudiantes hoy les ___ el tiempo y la voluntad para estudiar.

    (A) falta
    (B) faltan
    (C) falten
    (D) ha faltado

31. ¡Qué lástima que ustedes no ___ venir hasta hoy!

    (A) han podido
    (B) habrán podido
    (C) habrían podido
    (D) hayan podido

32. Antes de salir, ___ adónde vas y déjame un número de teléfono.

    (A) dime
    (B) dígame
    (C) me dice
    (D) me dices

GO ON TO THE NEXT PAGE

Part B

Directions: First read through the entire paragraph. Then, for each numbered blank, choose the completion that is most appropriate given the context of the passage. Fill in the corresponding oval on the answer sheet.

Atrás parecen haber (33) los tiempo en los que los niños (34) con la pelota regular, la muñeca que habla, o la bicicleta como sus máximos (35) . Estas últimas Navidades lo han reflejado claramente: la computadora, el vídeo e (36) la moda con los nuevos objetos del (37) de los niños.

Estas cosas son lo que quieren porque los niños van al colegio, sus (38), ven la televisión, algunos duermen ocho horas al día y nada más. No tienen tiempo libre para jugar. Todo lo cual hace que (39) por computadores, vaqueros, y zapatos deportivos de marca (40) de los juguetes.

33. (A) quedado
    (B) llegado
    (C) apreciado
    (D) prevenido

34. (A) se dirigían
    (B) se atrevían
    (C) se conformaban
    (D) se enfadaban

35. (A) grifos
    (B) regalos
    (C) regateos
    (D) mercados

36. (A) incluido
    (B) inclusivo
    (C) incluir
    (D) incluso

37. (A) arte
    (B) suceso
    (C) partido
    (D) deseo

38. (A) deberes
    (B) muebles
    (C) molestias
    (D) paces

39. (A) se interesan
    (B) se interesen
    (C) se interesarían
    (D) se interesarán

40. (A) a pie
    (B) a la vez
    (C) en vista
    (D) en vez

GO ON TO THE NEXT PAGE

Cuando fue (41) por el equipo nacional, en (42) Víctor pensó que iba a estar muy lejos de su familia y que en el norte hacía mucho frío. No le importó que le (43) el número 77. El 75, que (44) ha usado, lo lleva el portero Jamian Stephens. Todavía no firma su (45) . Dice que su agente le (46) que el bono por firmar sería de (47) 130 mil y 140 mil dólares, (48) 210 mil por la primera temporada. Le (49) sobrevivir a los tres cortes previos a la temporada que se llevarán (50) en junio, julio y agosto.

41. (A) elegido
    (B) erguido
    (C) guiado
    (D) puesto

42. (A) ese año
    (B) esa vez
    (C) esa temporada
    (D) ese momento

43. (A) dé
    (B) dio
    (C) habrían dado
    (D) dieran

44. (A) cuando
    (B) siempre
    (C) hasta
    (D) todavía

45. (A) contrato
    (B) argumento
    (C) estancia
    (D) tratamiento

46. (A) habrá dicho
    (B) ha dicho
    (C) diga
    (D) haya dicho

47. (A) hacia
    (B) hasta
    (C) sobre
    (D) entre

48. (A) ya
    (B) más
    (C) pues
    (D) menos

49. (A) falta
    (B) pregunta
    (C) arriesga
    (D) facilita

50. (A) a cabo
    (B) consigo
    (C) en cambio
    (D) en la actualidad

GO ON TO THE NEXT PAGE

Por la noche, mientras __(51)__ aburridamente en la gran mesa del __(52)__, con el abuelo, oí ruidos en la cocina y se me despertó la curiosidad. __(53)__ terminé de comer, besé al abuelo y fingí subir a acostarme. __(54)__, muy al contrario, bajé a la cocina, donde Elisa, la cocinera, y las criadas, __(55)__ con el mandadero Lucas el Gallo, se reían de los alambradores, que allí estaban. El viejo contaba algo, sentado junto a la lumbre, y el niño miraba con sus ojos negros, __(56)__ dos agujeros muy profundos, el arroz que le servía Elisa en una escudilla de barro. Me acerqué silenciosamente, __(57)__ a la pared como yo sabía, para que nadie se __(58)__ en mí.

51. (A) ceno
    (B) cené
    (C) cenamos
    (D) cenaba

52. (A) dormitorio
    (B) comedor
    (C) desván
    (D) sótano

53. (A) Además
    (B) Aun
    (C) Apenas
    (D) Acaso

54. (A) Pero
    (B) Sino que
    (C) También
    (D) A pesar

55. (A) junto
    (B) consigo
    (C) aislado
    (D) pelado

56. (A) tanto
    (B) todavía
    (C) como
    (D) así

57. (A) asomada
    (B) atada
    (C) notada
    (D) pegada

58. (A) recorriera
    (B) aconsejara
    (C) fijara
    (D) entrara

GO ON TO THE NEXT PAGE

Part C

Directions: Read the following texts carefully. Then, for each question that follows, select the best answer according to the text. Fill in the corresponding oval on the answer sheet.

—¡Te vas a morir de tanto dulce!

—¿Y qué?

La niña mira despacio. Acaricia los dulces con una mirada de gran catador. Va de un puesto al otro; costales llenos de monedas de chocolate, arcones de cacahuates garrapiñados, una cueva de paletas de oro y miel que relampaguean en los tablones de madera y brillan hasta la calle; hasta el Anillo de Circunvalación.

—¿A cómo los cacahuates?

—A tres por diez

Los cacahuates se alinean en fila india, entubados en papel celofán. Cada tubito lleva por lo menos ocho o nueve cacahuates.

—¿Y los chocolates?

Al preguntárselo, sueña con saborear cada uno de ellos a medida que se los come, dejándolos disolver en la boca lentamente.

—Depende... ¿de cuáles quieres?

59. ¿En qué tipo de tienda tendrá lugar esta escena?

(A) una taquería

(B) una tintorería

(C) una peluquería

(D) una dulcería

60. La niña hablaba con

(A) una amiga.

(B) su mamá.

(C) una maestra.

(D) un dependiente.

61. ¿Cómo miraba los productos la niña?

(A) amargamente

(B) codiciosamente

(C) con odio

(D) con ansiedad

62. ¿Sobre qué aspecto del producto preguntaba la niña?

(A) el sabor

(B) el precio

(C) el tamaño

(D) la cantidad

63. ¿En qué se encontraban los cacahuates?

(A) envueltos en bolsas grandes

(B) sueltos en el puesto

(C) en cilindros metálicos

(D) en pequeños paquetes

64. ¿Cómo comería el chocolate?

(A) Piensa devorarlo rápidamente.

(B) Lo tomaría sólo para el olor delicioso.

(C) Guardaría una parte para otro día.

(D) Lo comería despacio, disfrutándolo.

GO ON TO THE NEXT PAGE

Creamos el auto perfecto. Aunque el resto del mundo, no lo sea.

El Nuevo Passat

65. Según la propaganda, ¿qué ha creado la compañía que produce este coche?

(A) un coche ideal
(B) un mundo perfecto
(C) un auto inadecuado
(D) unas calles congestionadas

GO ON TO THE NEXT PAGE

Línea   A 15 kilómetros de la isla más cercana, El Bajo
está formado por una serie de pináculos dentados
que alcanzan profundidades de más de 60 metros.
La corriente de la marea provoca que las aguas
(5) profundas fluyan hacia la superficie atravesando
peces vela, atunes y tiburones.
   Estábamos en busca de tiburones martillo.
Debíamos ser cautelosos si queríamos ver a los
martillos, pues una vez que se les avista son muy
(10) tímidos; si uno hace movimientos bruscos ellos
desaparecen. Súbitamente, entre un cardumen
de atunes, apareció un gigantesco tiburón. Yo
llevaba una cámara y quería tomarle una foto.
Mis compañeros pensaron que no era una buena
(15) idea, pues sacaron un gran cuchillo...por si acaso.
Parecía como si el tiburón nos estuviera probando.
Mi acelerado corazón presentía que nos quería
como plato fuerte para la cena y, a pesar de que
me sentía algo asustado; nadé despacio hacia el
(20) animal.
   Recorrí unos tres metros y él giró y desapareció
casi instantáneamente. Como me tomó por
sorpresa, no pude tomarle la foto; de haberme
quedado quieto, seguramente se hubiera acercado
(25) aún más a nosotros.

66. Cuando el narrador vio el tiburón estaba en

   (A) un restaurante.
   (B) una isla.
   (C) las montañas.
   (D) el mar.

67. El narrador de este relato es

   (A) peregrino.
   (B) buceador.
   (C) cocinero.
   (D) carnicero.

68. ¿Qué buscaba el narrador?

   (A) un viaje relajado
   (B) un pez extraño
   (C) trabajo divertido
   (D) comida para la cena

69. ¿Cómo se sentía el narrador al ver el tiburón
de cerca?

   (A) ansioso
   (B) avergonzado
   (C) cobarde
   (D) valiente

70. Cuando el hombre vio el tiburón, ¿qué se le
ocurrió?

   (A) Pensaba que sería difícil sacar una foto
del animal.
   (B) Se preguntó si el animal tenía mucha
hambre.
   (C) Pensaba que sus compañeros no eran
muy valientes.
   (D) Se le ocurrió que él podía cenar tiburón
esa noche.

71. Al fin y al cabo, ¿qué hizo el tiburón?

   (A) Se quedó quieto para una foto.
   (B) Huyó del encuentro lentamente.
   (C) Atacó al narrador.
   (D) Se fue cuando el narrador se le acercó.

72. El narrador quería que

   (A) hubiera tenido más paciencia.
   (B) el tiburón no lo hubiera comido.
   (C) se hubiera escapado del tiburón.
   (D) lo hubiera matado con el cuchillo.

GO ON TO THE NEXT PAGE

Línea   Desde nuestro origen y bajo cualquier latitud, los pueblos indígenas hemos considerado a la tierra como algo sagrado. Ella nos da la vida y es parte fundamental de nuestra cosmovisión,
(5)   por lo que la respetamos y la veneramos. Hemos heredado de nuestros abuelos una convivencia armoniosa con la naturaleza, lejos de pretender someterla como si fuéramos sus dueños.

La tierra es raíz y fuente de nuestra cultura,
(10)   a la cual tenemos que acudir diariamente para regenerarnos. Ella contiene nuestra memoria, ella acoge a nuestros antepasados y requiere, por lo tanto, que la honremos y le devolvamos con ternura y respeto los bienes que nos brinda.
(15)   A lo largo de estos últimos años, nuestra madre naturaleza ha sufrido un deterioro, en numerosos casos irreversibles. Sin embargo, a pesar de esa marcha acelerada de la todopoderosa modernidad hambrienta de espacios y pulmones siempre
(20)   menos vírgenes, diversas iniciativas impulsadas por personas, instituciones y movimientos interesados en la conservación de la vida han logrado, en muchos casos, crear las llamadas áreas protegidas y frenar la despiadada destrucción que
(25)   parecía encaminada hacia un trágico destino.

73.   ¿Cuál es el tema de esta selección?

(A) el valor del ecoturismo

(B) la importancia de desarrollar recursos naturales

(C) las creencias tradicionales de los indígenas

(D) un anuncio de un desastre ecológico

74.   Según esta autora, los indígenas creían que

(A) la tierra importa tanto como la gente.

(B) la gente debe todo a la tierra.

(C) el hombre es dueño de la tierra.

(D) Dios mandó al hombre dominar la tierra.

75.   ¿Qué requiere la tierra de la gente?

(A) Dice a la gente que entierren los muertos en la tierra.

(B) Manda que se cuide de la naturaleza.

(C) Hay que regar la tierra regularmente.

(D) Quiere que la gente no tome los bienes que le da.

76.   En esta selección la sociedad moderna se caracteriza por

(A) su avaricia devoradora en cuanto a los recursos naturales.

(B) un buen entendimiento de la naturaleza.

(C) la armonía con la que coexiste con la naturaleza.

(D) una actitud abierta con respeto a las tradiciones indígenas.

77.   Esta autora parece estar

(A) contenta con el estado del mundo.

(B) pesimista en cuanto al futuro.

(C) enojada con la sociedad moderna.

(D) orgullosa de su origen indígena

GO ON TO THE NEXT PAGE

Línea   Fue ahí, frente al fuego, donde recibí de mi
madre las primeras lecciones de lo que era la
vida. Fue ahí donde Saturnina, una sirvienta
recién llegada del campo, a quien cariñosamente
(5)   llamábamos Sato, me impidió un día pisar un
grano de maíz tirado en el piso porque en él estaba
contenido el Dios del Maíz y no se le podía faltar
al respeto de esa manera. Fue ahí, en el lugar más
común para recibir visitas, donde yo me enteré
(10)   de lo que pasaba en el mundo. Fue ahí donde mi
madre sostenía largas pláticas con mi abuela, con
mis tías y de vez en cuando con algún pariente
ya muerto. Fue ahí, pues, donde atrapada por el
poder hipnótico de la llama, escuché todo tipo de
(15)   historias, pero sobre todo, historias de mujeres.
        Más tarde, tuve que salir, me alejé por completo
de la cocina. Tenía que estudiar, prepararme para
mi actuación futura en la sociedad. La escuela
estaba llena de conocimientos y sorpresas. ¡Uf,
(20)   cuántas cosas aprendí! En esa época, me sentía tan
superior a las pobres mujeres que pasaban su vida
encerradas en la cocina. Sentía mucha lástima de
que nadie se hubiera encargado de hacerles saber,
entre otras cosas, que el Dios del Maíz no existía.
(25)   Con mi título en una mano y el germen de la
revolución en la otra el mundo se abría para mí.

78.   ¿Cuándo ocurrió lo que recuerda la narradora?

(A) el año anterior

(B) el mes pasado

(C) hace mucho años

(D) hace tres años

79.   ¿Por qué le gustaba tanto la cocina?

(A) Porque era un mundo seguro.

(B) Porque tantas cosas ocurrieron allí.

(C) Porque los hombres no entraron allí.

(D) Porque hacía mucho calor en la cocina.

80.   La actitud de la narradora empieza a rechazar
la cocina porque

(A) ella se internó en una escuela.

(B) ella se aburrió de todas las historias.

(C) no recibió el respeto que quería.

(D) su mamá hablaba con espíritus allí.

81.   Lo que recuerda más sobre Saturnia es que era

(A) una criada crédula.

(B) una mujer mezquina.

(C) una sacerdotisa sabia.

(D) una cocinera muy inteligente.

82.   En la cocina la narradora aprendió

(A) las recetas que usaba su madre.

(B) a mantener el fuego del hogar.

(C) a platicar con sus parientes.

(D) los buenos modales de una señora.

83.   ¿Qué sueño tenía la narradora?

(A) Quería ser gran cocinera fuera de casa.

(B) Soñaba con una carrera fuera de la casa.

(C) Quería enseñar a Sato que el Dios del
Maíz no existía.

(D) Esperaba ser una gran dama en la
sociedad.

84.   La narradora parecía sentirse superior porque

(A) estaba aburrida.

(B) era más rica que las mujeres de la cocina.

(C) estaba más enterada del mundo de fuera.

(D) estaba más complacida consigo.

85.   ¿Qué actitud parecía tener la narradora al final?

(A) Anhelaba el pasado perdido.

(B) Sentía gran antipatía para con las
mujeres de su familia.

(C) Le dio lástima que su madre no asistiera
a la escuela también.

(D) Se sentía muy superior a las mujeres de
su antiguo hogar.

STOP!

**If you finish before time is up,
you may check your work.**

Answer Key
Practice Test 1

Part A	Part B	Part C
1. C	33. A	59. D
2. B	34. C	60. D
3. D	35. B	61. B
4. C	36. D	62. B
5. B	37. D	63. D
6. D	38. A	64. D
7. B	39. B	65. A
8. C	40. D	66. D
9. D	41. A	67. B
10. C	42. D	68. B
11. C	43. D	69. A
12. D	44. B	70. B
13. A	45. A	71. D
14. C	46. B	72. A
15. B	47. D	73. C
16. A	48. B	74. B
17. B	49. A	75. B
18. D	50. A	76. A
19. D	51. C	77. D
20. A	52. B	78. C
21. C	53. C	79. A
22. A	54. A	80. A
23. B	55. A	81. A
24. A	56. C	82. D
25. D	57. D	83. B
26. C	58. C	84. C
27. D		85. A
28. D		
29. C		
30. B		
31. D		
32. A		

ANSWERS AND EXPLANATIONS

Part A

1. **(C)** All of these words begin with *ll* and it is easy to confuse them. You need to focus on more than just the first few letters. In the sentence, look for the word(s) that would go with one of the four choices. The word *conocí* tells you that the answer could have something to do with movement, and *vecino* tells you that it has to do with a person. The sentence says, "Last night upon arriving at home I met my new neighbor." The answer is *llegar*.

2. **(B)** You can tell from the word *estudiantes* that the topic has to do with school. Be wary of false cognates, however: There is a distracter in this set of answer choices: It is the word *atender*, which means "to attend to." The other infinitives are *asistir*, "to attend school or an event," *revolver*, "to revolve, to spin," and *entregar*, "to hand in, to turn over."

3. **(D)** This set of answer choices also contains a common distracter: *letra*. Remember that there are different kinds of letters, and in Spanish, different words for each. *Carta* is a letter that someone writes. *Letra* is a letter of the alphabet. *Firma* is a signature and *firmar* means "to sign," as in to write your name on something.

4. **(C)** Do not use *que* after *sino* unless there is a conjugated verb after it. You might also think that you could use *pero*, but you cannot because of *No sólo* at the beginning of the sentence. When you see *no sólo*, also look for *sino también* somewhere else in the sentence.

5. **(B)** When you see a set of answer choices containing a negative indefinite word, look at what the sentence says. You can see right away that you need a pronoun because the blank comes before a conjugated verb with no obvious subject. (C) and (D) are adjectives, and there is no noun that they refer to, so they can be eliminated. (A) and (B) are possibilities: You could use *alguien*, except that the verb is preceded by *no*, meaning you need a negative indefinite pronoun. The reason Miguel did not come was because nobody told him, so *nadie* is the correct answer.

6. **(D)** You might be tempted to automatically look for *juntos*. But notice that the subject pronoun is feminine, *nosotras*. When the subject is feminine plural, use an adjective that agrees in gender and number, *juntas*. The adjective means "together," describing the subject.

7. **(B)** This is a vocabulary question. *Bucear* is "to dive," which is the correct answer. *Merendar* is "to snack," so it does not work. *Esquiar* is also associated with water, but on the surface, not under water. You might associate *cruzar* with a similar word *crucero*, meaning a "cruise," but once again, it is not what you would do to see fish underwater.

8. **(C)** *Asignatura* means "course of study in a discipline"; in other words, a subject in school. Once again, watch out for false cognates. *Conferencia* means "lecture," and *lectura* means "reading." The only answer that makes sense is the reading you ought to do to get ready for class. Make sure that you know the difference between these words.

9. **(D)** You need a possessive pronoun here, but since it replaces *maletas*, you need a feminine plural pronoun. The element that makes *mías* a pronoun is the article, *las*, in front of it. After the preposition *por* you have to use a prepositional pronoun or a possessive pronoun. The only prepositional pronoun among the choices is *ellos* which does not agree with *maletas* anyway, so it cannot be the answer.

10. (C) You fasten your seat belt before taking off, so *despegar* is the only correct answer. *Embarcar* and *abordar* also have to do with traveling by plane, but make no sense in the chronology of the activities. Pay attention to *antes de*, which means "before."

11. (C) *Tocar* means "to play" a musical instrument. Do not confuse it with *tomar*, meaning "to take," or with *jugar*, which means "to play" a game.

12. (D) Seeing that all the answer choices are different forms of the same verb, this is a grammar question. Given that fact, look at the verbs first, then the subjects, and then the conjunctions. The verb in the main clause is *pidió*, past tense. There's also a change of subject from the first verb to the second one, *profesor* and *estudiantes*. You need to use the imperfect subjunctive because of the verb *pedir*, *que*, and the change of subjects. You do not even need to know what the words mean.

13. (A) *Libras* looks something like *libre*, which is literally translated to mean "free," but does not really work here. *Libre* ends with an *e*, which means that it would not change the ending except to agree with plural nouns. *Libras* is a noun, meaning "pounds," so it makes no sense here. *Gratis* is the word commonly used in Spanish to mean that something does not cost anything.

14. (C) Look at the pronoun after *ver*. You need to use a feminine singular adjective here. You might be tempted to use a present participle, *sentando*, except that you cannot use a present participle as an adjective in Spanish. If you remember this simple rule, you will avoid common mistakes.

15. (B) There is a common false cognate in this sentence. *Sopa* means "soup," and *jabón* means "soap." Make sure you know these two words.

16. (A) This sentence should take no time at all. You don't need to translate anything, just notice that *antes de que* comes right before the verb. When you see that adverbial phrase, you know you need the subjunctive. *Salga* is the only possibility, then. If you made the mistake of translating directly from English to Spanish, you might have used the future indicative or present tense instead, because there is nothing in the English to indicate the need for the subjunctive in Spanish.

17. (B) This is not such an obvious answer. You may have to translate some things, even after you have the general idea about the meaning of the sentence. You may just have to know that *alrededor* means "around," or in this case, "vicinity." It is the only word that makes sense, although *rodeo* and *circunstancias* also have to do with relative proximity. Only a translation will do here.

18. (D) The sentence states that the speaker does not want to go see a movie. Here, you need to ask the reason why. The present perfect, *he visto*, tells you that the speaker has already seen the movie, so look for the conjunction that means "already." (B) doesn't work, because the negative of the verb makes no sense with the first part of the sentence. (A) is commonly confused with *ya*, but *todavía* has more of the meaning of "still" or "yet," so it would not work here.

19. (D) The sentence states that because the speaker arrived late at the bus stop, he missed the bus. *Parada* may look like the English word "parade," but the word *autobús* should tip you off that this sentence is not about parades. If you did not understand the word *parada* you might have guessed (A), but that would not be correct: The sentence says the bus had already gone. Similarly, (B) is wrong. The two words that mean "to miss" are *extrañar* and *perder*. *Extrañar*, however, means to miss someone. *Perder* means to miss a ride on some mode of transportation.

20. (A) The answer is *cuchillo*, inducated by the phrase *bien afilado* and the word *cortarla*.

21. **(C)** When you see the blank in front of an adjective like *obvio*, look for the noun to which it refers. Here, there is no noun with *obvio*, so you should use *lo*. With (D) *le*, you would never use the indirect object pronoun just before an adjective, so you can eliminate it.

22. **(A)** This is simple vocabulary. Of all of these phrases, only *A pesar de que*, meaning "in spite of," makes any sense. Go back to the grammar section and review these phrases if you missed this question.

23. **(B)** The distracter in this set of four is the word *actualmente*. It means "presently," so it makes no sense here. You could associate *ruido* with street traffic, but it makes no sense with *cruzar*, so it is not correct. *Precisamente* does not make sense either. You may recognize the word from the verb *cuidarse de*, meaning "to take care of," or from the expression *tener cuidado*, meaning "to be careful." *Cuidadosamente* is the answer.

24. **(A)** The words *con dificultad* tell you that for some reason cars cannot negotiate the streets in old villages. *Estrechas* means "narrow," so it is the best answer.

25. **(D)** When you see the blank after a preposition, *de*, in this case, and a set of articles and pronouns, you probably need to translate the sentence. You need to find the pronoun to which the answer will refer. The sentence is, "Above is seen the mountain, below the lake, and the reflection of the peak in the water of it." The water has to be the lake. *Él* is the correct answer.

26. **(C)** The only verbal tense that makes sense here is the future perfect because the time referred to in the blank is in the future, but before another time in the future. The sentence says, "By this time tomorrow when I see you, I will have finished the work." *Vea* and *mañana* tell you that the action has not yet happened.

27. **(D)** After a verb of motion, such as *iba*, you often use a present participle as an adverb. If there were a preposition, *a*, then you would use an infinitive.

28. **(D)** The sentence presents a comparison, and because *tanto* is not in the sentence, (A) makes no sense. *Tanto* would be needed somewhere else to use *como* by itself. (B) and (C) are wrong because there is no *que* after the blank. The only choice that makes sense is *tanto como*, which means "as much as."

29. **(C)** *Una* must agree with *noches*.

30. **(B)** The subject of the verb *faltar* is *tiempo y voluntad*.

31. **(D)** *Qué lástima* is an impersonal expression that requires the subjunctive. The only possible choice here is *hayan podido*. If there had been two subjunctive answer choices, you would have had to consider the phrase *hasta hoy*.

32. **(A)** You may have correctly thought you needed a command form. And when you looked for a command form, perhaps you went for the subjunctive form, *dígame*. That is not a bad strategy, except that you need to consider the person and number of the subject, as well as the verb you are using. *Decir* is irregular, and the subject is familiar "you," so you need to look for an irregular *tú* command form. The only correct choice, then, is *dime*. *Me dice* would not have been a bad guess: At least you saw that the *tú* command form, affirmative, is the third person singular verb form. But in this case, the pronoun before the verb should have told you that (C) is incorrect. Pronouns go after and attached to affirmative commands. (D) might work, except that the conjunction y indicates a parallel structure. You normally use the same form in both parts and the second part contains the affirmative command, *déjame*.

Part B

33. (A) The passage deals with how times have changed. *Atrás* should have tipped you off that the first sentence deals with time gone by, not with time to come. *Quedado* is the only choice that places time in the past. *Llegado* would deal with the present or future. Notice the contrast between normal balls, bicycles, talking dolls, and computers, videos, and new fashions. (C) doesn't work, because children apparently want new things instead of the standard things given as gifts in the past.

34. (C) The only word that makes sense is *conformarse*, meaning "to be satisfied with." While you might associate *dirigirse* with *bicicleta*, the verb does not work with the other items in the list of standard old gifts. *Atreverse*, "to dare," makes no sense, so (B) is out. And the passage does not say anything about how the children react to the gifts, so (D) can be eliminated as well.

35. (B) All of the objects mentioned would be appropriate as gifts, *regalos*. No other choice makes sense.

36. (D) All of the answer choices are a form of the verb *incluir*, so you want a part of speech that will fit the structure. An infinitive will not work as an adverb. (D) can be an adjective, but it would agree in gender and number with a noun, in this case *moda*, which is feminine. (A) and (B) are adjectives, too, but don't work for the same reason. *Incluso* can also be an adverb, however, and would end in -*o*. It is the correct answer.

37. (D) *Arte* often appears after the word *objeto*, but this paragraph does not talk about art. It deals with what children want most. The word *deseo*, meaning "desire," is the correct answer.

38. (A) When the children go to school, they do their work, *sus deberes*, watch television, sleep, and nothing more. They have no time for anything else. They could make *muebles*, "furniture," but the text doesn't indicate that this is a design school. (C) *molestias* does not make sense, because the work they do is why they are there, not the distractions they may have. *Hacer las paces* is "to make up," or "to make peace," which makes no sense, so (D) is out. Since infinitives can be used as nouns, *deberes* (the plural form) means "duty," in the sense of homework.

39. (B) The verb *hace* is used here to mean wishing, wanting, or necessity, followed by *que*. That clause (with a verb of volition) is followed by a dependent noun clause, so you need the subjunctive.

40. (D) Notice the parallel structure in this passage: The items listed up front are typical toys, *juguetes*, while the items mentioned later are things children would want for their schoolwork. These are not things children would use to pass free time. (A), meaning "standing," is wrong, because it has nothing to do with having brand name shoes instead of toys. *En vista* does not make any sense in this context.

41. (A) The subject matter is professional football. Players are selected in the draft, so (A) is correct. *Puesto* would work, except that the passage does not say when the player entered the draft.

42. (D) You need to pick the correct expression of time. You may be tempted to use *vez*, but that wouldn't work here because *vez* refers to a specific time, or time in a series, so (B) is out.

43. (D) The subjunctive is needed after an impersonal expression like *no importó*. Use the past subjunctive, because the passage is told in the past.

44. (B) The passage indicates that Víctor used to have the number 75. In the sentence *lo lleva el portero Jamian*, "lo" refers to the number. (A) and (C) do not fit between *que* and the conjugated verb in this adjective clause. *Todavía* means "still," and in the context of the paragraph, does not make sense, so (D) is wrong.

45. (A) This vocabulary question contains some false cognates. *Argumento* means "plot." *A tratamiento* is a "treatment," but you don't sign one. *Estancia* means various things, but not a contract, or anything one would sign. *Firmar* means "to sign."

46. (B) Look at the structure of the sentence: You can tell this part is a dependent clause, as it comes after *dice que*. The sentence contains a noun clause, and there is a change of subject, so you need to see if the subjunctive is required. But a translation of the main clause and the dependent clause tells you that Víctor is making a statement of fact, so you have to use the indicative instead. You cannot use the future perfect, because Víctor is talking about something his agent has just told him, not something he will tell him in the future.

47. (D) Don't be fooled by the preposition *de*. You can use an adverb after it, which is the case here. Look for the conjunction *y* or *o* between the numbers. If the numbers are written out, make sure to look for *u* instead of *o* in front of the number *ocho*. Without the two numbers, you could have picked *hasta* or *sobre*, depending on the phrase.

48. (B) You want a word that means "plus." *Más* is the only word that makes any sense.

49. (A) It helps to know that *cortes* means "cuts," but you should have some idea of that from the word *sobrevivir*. Even if you didn't know that, you could figure it out by taking it apart. *Sobre* means "above" or "beyond." Combined with "to live," it means "to survive." You might think that *pregunta* is a possibility, except that *preguntar* has more of a meaning of "to question," than "to ask for," so (B) is out.

50. (A) The expression *llevar a cabo* means "to carry out," in the sense of accomplishing something. Although you may associate *llevar* with carrying something along with you, the reflexive pronoun and the context should tip you off to another meaning. You would not carry anything in June, July, and August, anyway. (C) doesn't make sense, nor does (D), which means "in the present time."

51. (D) The passage begins with *mientras*. Of all the possibilities, only the imperfect will work here.

52. (B) If you relate *cenar*, meaning "to dine," with *mesa*, then *comedor* is the only correct answer. Though you might find a *mesa* in another room of the house, a *gran mesa* would indicate a dining table, found in a dining room.

53. (C) *Scarcely* is the only word that fits. If is often followed by a verb in the preterite tense. (D) is frequently followed by the subjunctive, so it can be eliminated.

54. (A) Though *sino que* means "but rather," in this case it would be redundant with *al contrario* and *fingir*. (B) is out. *También* doesn't fit with *al contrario*, and *a pesar* makes no sense, so (C) is out.

55. (A) *Junto* is an adverb in the expression *junto con*. If it were an adjective, it would end in a feminine plural form, to agree with the nouns, *las criadas* and *la cocinera*. You might be tempted to use *consigo*, but that makes no sense, because it means "with himself, herself, yourself."

56. (C) The only word that makes any sense here is *como*, because you need a word that sets up a simile, a word to link *ojos* with *agujeros profundos*.

57. (D) From the context in this passage, the narrator seems to be someone who is trying to be stealthy, someone sneaking around. But you cannot always take words literally. *Pegada* means "stuck to," but it is the best choice. *Atada* means "tied," which would work, except that the narrator could not then move along the wall. *Asomar* is usually used in connection with an opening in a wall, such as a window, but not with the wall itself.

58. (C) This answer is a common false cognate. In some cases it means "to fix," but when it is reflexive as it is here, it means "to notice." The more common word for to fix is *reparar* or *arreglar*.

Part C
Questions 59–64

This passage speaks of a little girl looking at stacks of candy in a store. The stacks contain various kinds of sweets, nuts, and chocolates.

59. (D) Since there are sweets in the store, you know it must be a candy shop, (D). Remember that if you remove the ending *-ería*, you will frequently find a noun that indicates what the shop sells. *Dulce*, meaning "sweet," is the subject of the little girl's interest. The store is neither a *taquería* nor a *peluquería* (hair salon). If you do not recognize *tintorería*, you have still narrowed down your choices for a good guess.

60. (D) One would expect the little girl to be with her mother, but you can tell from her discussion that she is not. The person with whom she is speaking has information about the merchandise, so it would be a clerk, *un dependiente*.

61. (B) *¿Cómo?* asks how she looks at the sweets. *Codiciosamente* means "greedily," as is indicated by her conversation. She clearly wants to buy some, but perhaps does not have much money to spend. She is looking for the best buy, while savoring how all of the sweets would taste.

62. (B) The girl thinks about all of these aspects—the flavor, the price, the size, and the quantity—but asks about only the price.

63. (D) Some of these answer choices pick up synonyms for words in the passage, but do not answer the question. *Tubitos* are little tubes, sort of like *cilindros*, but they are not metallic, they are tubes of cellophane. *Costales* are large bags, but they do not contain *cacahuates*. *Sueltos* means "loose," so it is not a good choice. "Little packages" is the best answer. Look for the description of the little tubes of peanuts, containing just a few peanuts.

64. (D) The girl spends the whole last paragraph talking about how she would consume the chocolates. *Sabor* means "taste," and *lentamente* means "slowly." She will not hold on to them to enjoy the smell, so (B) is out, nor will she keep some for another day. (C) is out as well.

Question 65

65. (A) The caption states "the car is perfect, even though (*aunque*) the rest of the world is not." *Crear* means "to create." Do not confuse it with *creer*, "to believe." Do not be fooled by the word *auto* in one of the answer choices: A word that has been lifted from a text is unlikely to be the correct answer. Look for a synonym for *auto*. That word is *coche*. Look for a synonym for *perfecto*, and that word is *ideal*.

Questions 66–72

This passage talks about a diving experience. The diver is looking for sharks, but comes across one so unexpectedly that he is somewhat unnerved by the experience. He wants to take a picture of it, but is unsuccessful because he hasn't thought through what he is doing.

66. (D) There are a lot of references at the beginning to topographical features on land, but *aguas*, *corriente*, and *fluir* refer to underwater locations. Also *tiburones* are "sharks," which live only in water. So in spite of all the nouns pertaining to land, this short narrative takes place in the sea. Of course, if you know *tiburón*, then you know that it has to take place underwater.

67. (B) *Buceador* is the word for "diver," as in a scuba diver. Even though he talks about food, he is neither a cook nor a butcher, at least in his role as narrator of the passage.

68. (B) Do not be distracted by the word *divertido*. He certainly has an interesting and entertaining experience, but it is not work. He is on a trip, but he is hardly "relaxed" about seeing sharks. All the talk about food is a distracter.

69. (A) If you were looking for a word for "nervous," you might get confused on this sort of question. You should anticipate what the right answer should be, but don't fixate on one word. Be prepared to look for synonyms in Spanish.

70. (B) All the talk about food is his conjecture about what the shark could be thinking. He thinks he could be a tempting bite for the shark, so he wonders if the shark is hungry. *Preguntarse* means "to ask oneself," or "to wonder."

71. (D) The word *desapareció* tells you that the shark went away. *Huyó* could seem a good choice, except that *lentamente* is not *instantáneamente*. The narrator did not get his picture, which leaves only (D).

72. (A) All of these answers contain the subjunctive, meaning that they are things the narrator wished. He did not wish that the shark had eaten him, nor that he had gotten close for a picture, nor that he had killed the shark. He did wish that he had had more patience.

Questions 73–77

The selection is a little more philosophical. It deals with the perspective of indigenous people of Latin America and their sense of connection to the environment. Don't be put off by words like *cosmovisión*. You can figure out what the selection is about even if you don't understand some big words. Usually with this topic, there are lots of cognates. It is not unusual to find a selection dealing with a cultural topic on the SAT Subject Test: Spanish.

73. (C) The author does talk about natural resources, *recursos naturales* in a general way, but usually in connection with the attitudes of indigenous people. She also says that there has been some irreversible damage, though *sin embargo* indicates a hopeful tone. This piece does not focus on the dire consequences of ecological damage, but rather on the healthy relationship indigenous people have always had with the environment.

74. (B) You can use the process of elimination here. The author is saying that people owe everything to the earth. You get that idea from the words *ella nos da la vida*. The rest of the sentence, *y es parte de nuestra cosmovisión*, is an elaboration on the idea that life comes from the earth. The words *la respetamos y la veneramos* indicate the attitude toward the earth. It is sacred, greater than people. In (B), *debe* is the word that indicates the correct answer. *Deber* means "to owe."

75. (B) The answer is in the second paragraph. You can find the word *requiere*, but you have to find other words to paraphrase what comes after *requiere*. You will recognize *honrar*, but remember that *devolver* means "to give back." *Ternura* and *respeto* also indicate the idea of taking care of something. The only answer with that meaning is the one with *cuidarse*.

76. (A) You only need to know that *avaricia* is "avarice" or "greed." *Devoradora* goes with *hambrienta*, from the word *hambre*. Remember that *-ienta* is an ending for an adjective. Don't be sidetracked by other words lifted from the passage.

77. (D) She is not exactly content with things, otherwise she would not be writing the piece, so (A) is out. She is not pessimistic about the future, either, nor does she use any words of anger, so (B) and (C) are wrong as well. She does, however, point to the healthy attitude held by indigenous people.

Questions 78–85

This passage deals with a writer reminiscing about her mother's kitchen. It was a welcoming place where she learned more than cooking. In this piece she does not talk about recipes, but rather the people and place.

78. (C) Buried in the passage are the words *En esa época*. *Esa* indicates some time ago. *Época* indicates a period of time, as a stage of her life. Although there is no other mention of time, it is apparent from the rest of the passage that she means that time before she went off to school, thinking about the future ahead of her in some place other than the kitchen. It would even be more than three years, because she talks about having received a diploma.

79. (A) The kitchen was a secure place. The repetition of *Fue ahí* in the first paragraph indicates that she is remembering all the great things about it. It is the combination that she remembers, that, when taken all together, make it a comfortable place, *un mundo seguro*. She talks about things that happened in the kitchen with Saturnina, but she focuses on one thing only.

80. (A) All you need to know to answer this question is the word *internarse*, meaning "to enroll" or "to matriculate." If you do not recognize that word, however, you can eliminate the other choices. (D) is true; she does say her mother communicates with spirits, but that is not the reason the narrator wants to leave that world of the kitchen behind her. School represented new opportunities and broader horizons.

81. (A) The word *crédula* means "credulous," meaning that she believed easily. The story about the God of Corn would be an example of a sincere belief. The narrator does not believe in such a deity, but in hindsight, she can see that the fact that Sato believed in the God of Corn is an example of a person who is sincere in what she believes. She does not think that Sato is stupid for believing in deities inhabiting things in nature. If you do not know *crédula*, you can eliminate some of the other choices. *Mezquina* means "mean," which certainly is not the case. Though she talks about gods, she is not a priestess, nor does the text say that she is a cook. *Criada* is another word for *sirvienta*.

82. (D) *Modales* in answer choice (D) means "manners" or "ways," and these indeed are what the narrator learned in the kitchen. She did not tend to the fire in the home, she only looked at it, so (B) is wrong. And she does not speak in this text about any recipes she learned from her mother, so (A) is out. *Recetas* means "recipes" (although *recetar* means "to prescribe" so *receta* has other meanings as well.)

83. (B) The last sentence tells you that she was looking for opportunities away from the kitchen. The *otro mundo* was waiting for her. She does use the word *sociedad*, though not in the sense that she wants to be a great lady in society, so (D) is not correct.

84. (C) She felt superior because she knew more about the world outside of the kitchen. The kitchen bored her, but that would not make her feel superior, so (A) is wrong. *Complacida* in (D) means "content," so that would not be a correct answer. And when she refers to the "poor women" in the text, she means that they are pitiable, not penniless, so (B) is wrong. *Enterarse de* in (C) means "to be knowledgeable about," which would make her feel superior, so it is the answer.

85. (A) *Anhelar* means "to yearn," "to long for." The tone of the passage reveals a certain nostalgia for what she learned in the kitchen.

Practice Test 2

Answer Grid
Practice Test 2

1. (A) (B) (C) (D) (E)
2. (A) (B) (C) (D) (E)
3. (A) (B) (C) (D) (E)
4. (A) (B) (C) (D) (E)
5. (A) (B) (C) (D) (E)
6. (A) (B) (C) (D) (E)
7. (A) (B) (C) (D) (E)
8. (A) (B) (C) (D) (E)
9. (A) (B) (C) (D) (E)
10. (A) (B) (C) (D) (E)
11. (A) (B) (C) (D) (E)
12. (A) (B) (C) (D) (E)
13. (A) (B) (C) (D) (E)
14. (A) (B) (C) (D) (E)
15. (A) (B) (C) (D) (E)
16. (A) (B) (C) (D) (E)
17. (A) (B) (C) (D) (E)
18. (A) (B) (C) (D) (E)
19. (A) (B) (C) (D) (E)
20. (A) (B) (C) (D) (E)
21. (A) (B) (C) (D) (E)
22. (A) (B) (C) (D) (E)
23. (A) (B) (C) (D) (E)
24. (A) (B) (C) (D) (E)
25. (A) (B) (C) (D) (E)
26. (A) (B) (C) (D) (E)
27. (A) (B) (C) (D) (E)
28. (A) (B) (C) (D) (E)
29. (A) (B) (C) (D) (E)

30. (A) (B) (C) (D) (E)
31. (A) (B) (C) (D) (E)
32. (A) (B) (C) (D) (E)
33. (A) (B) (C) (D) (E)
34. (A) (B) (C) (D) (E)
35. (A) (B) (C) (D) (E)
36. (A) (B) (C) (D) (E)
37. (A) (B) (C) (D) (E)
38. (A) (B) (C) (D) (E)
39. (A) (B) (C) (D) (E)
40. (A) (B) (C) (D) (E)
41. (A) (B) (C) (D) (E)
42. (A) (B) (C) (D) (E)
43. (A) (B) (C) (D) (E)
44. (A) (B) (C) (D) (E)
45. (A) (B) (C) (D) (E)
46. (A) (B) (C) (D) (E)
47. (A) (B) (C) (D) (E)
48. (A) (B) (C) (D) (E)
49. (A) (B) (C) (D) (E)
50. (A) (B) (C) (D) (E)
51. (A) (B) (C) (D) (E)
52. (A) (B) (C) (D) (E)
53. (A) (B) (C) (D) (E)
54. (A) (B) (C) (D) (E)
55. (A) (B) (C) (D) (E)
56. (A) (B) (C) (D) (E)
57. (A) (B) (C) (D) (E)
58. (A) (B) (C) (D) (E)

59. (A) (B) (C) (D) (E)
60. (A) (B) (C) (D) (E)
61. (A) (B) (C) (D) (E)
62. (A) (B) (C) (D) (E)
63. (A) (B) (C) (D) (E)
64. (A) (B) (C) (D) (E)
65. (A) (B) (C) (D) (E)
66. (A) (B) (C) (D) (E)
67. (A) (B) (C) (D) (E)
68. (A) (B) (C) (D) (E)
69. (A) (B) (C) (D) (E)
70. (A) (B) (C) (D) (E)
71. (A) (B) (C) (D) (E)
72. (A) (B) (C) (D) (E)
73. (A) (B) (C) (D) (E)
74. (A) (B) (C) (D) (E)
75. (A) (B) (C) (D) (E)
76. (A) (B) (C) (D) (E)
77. (A) (B) (C) (D) (E)
78. (A) (B) (C) (D) (E)
79. (A) (B) (C) (D) (E)
80. (A) (B) (C) (D) (E)
81. (A) (B) (C) (D) (E)
82. (A) (B) (C) (D) (E)
83. (A) (B) (C) (D) (E)
84. (A) (B) (C) (D) (E)
85. (A) (B) (C) (D) (E)

Practice Test 2

Part A

Directions: Select the most appropriate word to complete the sentence and fill in the corresponding oval on the answer sheet.

1. En esta época un aguacero puede ___ los arroyos con una inundación inesperada.

   (A) llegar
   (B) llenar
   (C) llevar
   (D) llover

2. Seguramente no vamos a ___ las montañas que se ven a lo lejos.

   (A) alcanzar
   (B) arrastrar
   (C) quedar
   (D) enterrar

3. Si necesitas dinero puedes tomar un ___ de cinco dólares de mi cartera.

   (A) boleto
   (B) billete
   (C) pasaje
   (D) peso

4. Vamos al parque ___ se dice que va a llover esta tarde.

   (A) quien
   (B) que
   (C) aunque
   (D) mientras

5. Me gusta cuando no tengo ___ que hacer.

   (A) algo
   (B) alguien
   (C) nada
   (D) nadie

6. Prefiero los huevos ___ para el desayuno.

   (A) apagados
   (B) envueltos
   (C) girados
   (D) revueltos

7. La pierna quebrada me duele mucho; por eso el médico me recetó unas ___.

   (A) piezas
   (B) pastillas
   (C) palizas
   (D) pastas

8. Esta noche es el último ___ entre los Metros y los Cosmos para el campeonato regional.

   (A) deporte
   (B) partido
   (C) equipo
   (D) parto

9. Éste es el señor, ___ esposa me envió una invitación a la reunión.

   (A) cuyo
   (B) quien
   (C) cuya
   (D) suyo

GO ON TO THE NEXT PAGE

10. Ojalá que ___ más calor, no llevo un abrigo conmigo.

    (A) esté
    (B) haga
    (C) sea
    (D) tenga

11. ¡Qué lástima que mis amigos no me ___ al parque en estas vacaciones!

    (A) acompañen
    (B) lleguen
    (C) salgan
    (D) alojen

12. Si ___ despejado, iríamos al parque esta tarde.

    (A) está
    (B) estaba
    (C) estuvo
    (D) estuviera

13. El turista gritaba en voz ___, irritando a todo el mundo.

    (A) mojada
    (B) alta
    (C) gorda
    (D) erguida

14. María, ___ la televisión, por favor. Quiero ver las noticias.

    (A) apaga
    (B) encierra
    (C) pon
    (D) torna

15. Por ganar el campeonato, los jugadores recibieron ___ y la admiración de todos.

    (A) la prisa
    (B) la prima
    (C) la medalla
    (D) el precio

16. No se nada en ese río porque ___ bien frío todo el año.

    (A) es
    (B) está
    (C) hace
    (D) tiene

17. Puesto que mi hermana está en la universidad ahora, sólo la veo ___.

    (A) de vez en cuando
    (B) por última vez
    (C) en aquel entonces
    (D) a larga distancia

18. No vimos a ningunos indios porque ___ vivían en esa región.

    (A) además
    (B) pues
    (C) todavía
    (D) ya no

19. Los turistas en el tren tenían ___ maletas como personas en la familia.

    (A) tan
    (B) tantos
    (C) tanta
    (D) tantas

20. En caso de emergencia, busque Vd. ___ más cerca.

    (A) el éxito
    (B) la salsa
    (C) la salida
    (D) la ensalada

21. Fue increíble ___ bonito que eran todas las flores del prado montañero en verano.

    (A) el
    (B) la
    (C) lo
    (D) las

GO ON TO THE NEXT PAGE

22. Los trenes largos pasaban ___ porque subían cuesta arriba y pesaban mucho.

    (A) rápidamente
    (B) lentamente
    (C) mansamente
    (D) actualmente

23. A veces es difícil encontrar estacionamiento en el centro ___ de toda la gente.

    (A) a causa
    (B) a lo mejor
    (C) porque
    (D) por consiguiente

24. El ___ problema del parque es el número de visitantes que tiene cada verano.

    (A) grande
    (B) más
    (C) mayor
    (D) mejor

25. Esta mañana cuando me desperté, ___ olvidó cepillar los dientes.

    (A) se
    (B) se me
    (C) me
    (D) me lo

26. Sólo cinco clientes estaban ___ en la pensión, pero todos pasaron un buen rato.

    (A) se alojan
    (B) alojado
    (C) alojarse
    (D) alojándose

27. El parque ___ declarado monumento nacional el año que viene.

    (A) es
    (B) fue
    (C) será
    (D) fuera

28. ¿No le gustan los exámenes? Ni a mí, ___.

    (A) también
    (B) demasiado
    (C) siempre
    (D) tampoco

29. Hay muchos ___ libros en esa biblioteca.

    (A) cientos
    (B) mil
    (C) miles de
    (D) millón de

30. No me ___ más que tres fotos en este rollo; no puedo sacar más.

    (A) quedo
    (B) queda
    (C) quedan
    (D) queden

31. Será buena idea que ___ bronceador si vas a tomar el sol a la playa.

    (A) te pongas
    (B) solicites
    (C) laves
    (D) cubras

32. Al principio acampamos para que ___ viajar más, pero ahora lo hacemos por gusto.

    (A) podemos
    (B) podamos
    (C) podíamos
    (D) pudiéramos

GO ON TO THE NEXT PAGE

Part B

Directions: First read through the entire paragraph. Then, for each numbered blank, choose the completion that is most appropriate given the context of the passage. Fill in the corresponding oval on the answer sheet.

Cuando (33) a la casa a la una de la tarde, el sol pega duro sobre la casa blanca y barrida de Cri-Crí en Texcoco. Afuera, ni un (34) sonido, (35) el gallo siquiera. En la (36) de la mesa de la cocina está Cri-Crí. A un lado, el brasero que mandó construir "(37) a mí me gustan los braseros; (38) uno en la cocina de mi casa cuando era niño."

Cri-Crí dice que es una de esas (39) personas que tienen la llave para volver a la infancia. Dice que todavía es la época en que (40) con las hormigas, que las deja entrar a la azucarera, que es su club social, y todas las noches va a verlas.

33. (A) llegamos
    (B) llegábamos
    (C) hemos llegado
    (D) lleguen

34. (A) otro
    (B) solo
    (C) bueno
    (D) cualquier

35. (A) no
    (B) también
    (C) ni
    (D) más

36. (A) pierna
    (B) pata
    (C) cabecera
    (D) superficie

37. (A) para que
    (B) aunque
    (C) porque
    (D) pero

38. (A) hay
    (B) habían
    (C) hubieron
    (D) había

39. (A) tristes
    (B) lástimosas
    (C) afortunadas
    (D) generosas

40. (A) se casa
    (B) se divierte
    (C) se equivoca
    (D) se despide

GO ON TO THE NEXT PAGE

La parte más difícil de viajar con niños es mantenerlos (41). Sin embargo, para ello se puede empacar material que los mantenga ocupados (42) el trayecto. Lo recomendable es (43) que tus hijos lleven algunos juguetes. No olvides meter una (44) de dulces y un paquete de calcomanías neón de superhéroes. (45) materiales que se aconsejan son: libreta, marcadores o (46) de color, y unas figuras de acción. Las mochilas (47) a tus hijos distraídos durante las primeras horas del viaje. De ahí (48), puede ser que tengas que (49) en tu reserva de emergencia con adivinanzas y concursos de " (50) lo encuentra primero."

41. (A) aburridos
    (B) entretenidos
    (C) dormidos
    (D) engañados

42. (A) mientras
    (B) hacia
    (C) como
    (D) durante

43. (A) dejar
    (B) dejando
    (C) dejado
    (D) deje

44. (A) ganga
    (B) pieza
    (C) bolsa
    (D) barca

45. (A) Ningunos
    (B) Tantos
    (C) Algunos
    (D) Cuántos

46. (A) luces
    (B) botellas
    (C) manchas
    (D) lápices

47. (A) mantendrán
    (B) regalarán
    (C) despertarán
    (D) supondrán

48. (A) frente
    (B) en adelante
    (C) atrás
    (D) afuera

49. (A) respaldarte
    (B) convertirte
    (C) consentirte
    (D) tardar

50. (A) que
    (B) cuánto
    (C) quién
    (D) cuyo

GO ON TO THE NEXT PAGE

Fernando Botero está indignado. Las (51) de dos de sus esculturas de pequeño formato están a la (52) en un almacén ubicado en Miami. Las esculturas que aparecen firmadas por Botero y con un sello de la fundación italiana falso están (53) por un precio muy rebajado.

Tanto la persona que consignó las obras (54) la propietaria del almacén en (55) momento han (56) que se trata de dos obras originales del artista colombiano, pero sí (57) un malestar (58) los expertos del arte por las obvias señales en las esculturas que no respetan el perfeccionismo característico del trabajo de Botero.

51. (A) obras
    (B) réplicas
    (C) pinturas
    (D) pruebas

52. (A) renta
    (B) mano
    (C) venta
    (D) forma

53. (A) dañadas
    (B) ladradas
    (C) preguntadas
    (D) exhibidas

54. (A) como
    (B) que
    (C) así
    (D) pues

55. (A) ningún
    (B) alguno
    (C) no
    (D) nada

56. (A) decir
    (B) diciendo
    (C) dicho
    (D) dichos

57. (A) se creó
    (B) se convirtió
    (C) se acabó
    (D) se transformó

58. (A) además
    (B) ante
    (C) entre
    (D) hasta

GO ON TO THE NEXT PAGE

Part C

Directions: Read the following texts carefully. Then, for each question that follows, select the best answer according to the text. Fill in the corresponding oval on the answer sheet.

En la tarde regresan a sus casas con prisa. "¡Tengo ganas de ver la tele! ..." Invitan a sus amigos y se están horas enteras echados absortos frente a la televisión. Como era de esperarse, no hacen la tarea.

En la noche, a la hora de dormir, empiezan las apuras. Los padres deciden que "la salud es lo primero", que ante todo el niño tiene que tener su sueño completo.

—¡Vamos, ya duérmete! ¿Dónde dejaste la mochila?

El niño no alcanza a contestar. Mientras tanto la mamá busca la mochila y entre los dos, papá y mamá, se quiebran la cabeza con los quebrados de la tarea.

59. ¿Qué hace el niño cuando vuelve a casa por la tarde?

(A) Se pone a trabajar.

(B) Se relaja con compañeros.

(C) Habla con sus padres al mirar la tele.

(D) Duerme la siesta antes de hacer la tarea.

60. ¿Cuál es la actitud de los niños al regresar a casa?

(A) Están muy animados al llegar.

(B) Están muy cansados.

(C) Están aburridos.

(D) Tienen mucha hambre.

61. A la hora de acostarse, ¿qué pasa?

(A) Todos se acuestan tranquilos.

(B) Los padres regañan al hijo.

(C) Los padres y el hijo miran la televisión.

(D) El niño se apura para hacer su tarea.

62. El razonamiento de los padres es que

(A) los niños necesitan hacer la tarea.

(B) el sueño importa sobretodo.

(C) la tarea no es muy importante.

(D) es importante mirar la televisión.

63. Cuando los padres empiezan a buscar la mochila, ¿qué hace el niño?

(A) Les dice a sus padres que hagan la tarea.

(B) Sigue mirando la televisión.

(C) Los mira sin decir nada.

(D) Ayuda a los padres a buscarla.

64. Según esta selección, al final los padres

(A) se alegran del buen trabajo del hijo.

(B) se esfuerzan en hacer la tarea del niño.

(C) están muy enojados con el niño.

(D) están muy orgullosos del niño.

GO ON TO THE NEXT PAGE

65. ¿Quiénes serán los consumidores de este producto?

   (A) clientes de un club social
   (B) jóvenes en busca de entretenimiento
   (C) personas que reparan su casa
   (D) parejas que buscan alojamiento

66. Según el anuncio, el producto ofrece

   (A) nuevos negocios para el empresario.
   (B) protección de la lluvia y fuego.
   (C) mejoramiento de relaciones sociales.
   (D) compañeros con quienes salir.

GO ON TO THE NEXT PAGE

Línea Muchísimos reportajes, así como numerosos campeonatos mundiales y competencias, han contribuido a crear la fama de un rincón dominicano que sirve de refugio a los apasionados
(5) de las olas y el viento. Sin embargo, no todos conocen la historia de Cabarete. Dos amigos me pusieron al tanto.

Con la idea de experimentar nuevos lugares para practicar su deporte que no fueran Hawai ni
(10) Florida, en 1985, los dos buscaban algún destino en el Caribe que sirviera a sus propósitos y no fuera muy caro. Entonces se fueron probando playa por playa hasta llegar a Cabarete.

Volvieron al otro día con las tablas y luego
(15) alquilaron una cabaña. ¡Se volvieron locos! Había una brisa increíble y podían practicar su deporte a cualquier hora. En esos años apenas había otro turista norteamericano en el lugar, la gente andaba en burro y no había teléfono. Con el
(20) tiempo, los amigos abrieron una escuela de tabla y vela. Fue así como poco tiempo después empezaron a llegar los mejores deportistas del mundo.

67. ¿A qué se debe la fama de Cabarete hoy?

   (A) Nadie se interesa en deportes acuáticos.
   (B) No tiene ningunos turistas.
   (C) Está lejos de Hawaii y Florida.
   (D) Tienen carreras acuáticas allí.

68. Inicialmente, al llegar los dos amigos

   (A) hicieron unas investigaciones.
   (B) buscaron un buen hotel turístico.
   (C) gastaron mucho dinero.
   (D) hicieron un recorrido de la costa.

69. A consecuencia de establecerse en Cabarete los dos amigos

   (A) sufrieron gran inestabilidad mental.
   (B) se alegraban de encontrar el campo abierto.
   (C) se mantenían despiertos día y noche.
   (D) se empobrecieron al alquilar una habitación.

70. Actualmente muchas personas vienen a Cabarete para

   (A) gozar del ambiente rural.
   (B) practicar su deporte favorito.
   (C) encontrar a otros turistas.
   (D) alejarse de teléfonos.

71. Según el artículo, el narrador al final es

   (A) un periodista de vacaciones.
   (B) un deportista de tabla y vela.
   (C) un empresario de tabla y vela.
   (D) un maestro de una escuela.

GO ON TO THE NEXT PAGE

Línea   El desprecio a la supervivencia se nota en
cualquier aspecto de la vida ciudadana. La
despreocupación con que se dejan abiertos
agujeros en la calzada, exponiendo al transeúnte a
(5) la caída o al automovilista al golpe, es una muestra
de la indiferencia con que el posible daño físico es
visto por los responsables.

   Un día, yendo en coche, salí de una curva para
encontrarme inesperadamente con un árbol en
(10) mitad de la carretera. Lo acababan de derribar
unos leñadores que me miraron asombrados
cuando yo bajé del coche. No comprendían
nada porque usábamos idiomas distintos. Yo les
hablaba de su inmensa responsabilidad moral y
(15) ellos me contestaron que tenían un permiso del
Ayuntamiento. «¿Pero no se dan cuenta que al
no poner a alguien con una bandera en la curva,
cualquiera puede estrellarse contra el árbol?» No
se les había ocurrido. Luego me preguntaron si
(20) me había asustado y me ofrecieron un vaso de
vino. Era la clásica diferenciación cultural entre
lo jurídico y lo personal. La posibilidad de que el
señor X, se estrellase contra el obstáculo no había
llegado a su imaginación. Pero cuando el señor
(25) X cobraba forma humana, estaban dispuestos a
hacer de todo para ayudarle.

72. ¿Cuál es el tema de esta selección?

  (A) la falta de cortesía en la sociedad

  (B) los peligros de conducir

  (C) los problemas de comunicación

  (D) responsabilidad individual para
      sobrevivir

73. ¿Qué le paso un día al autor?

  (A) Se desvió en una curva.

  (B) Atropelló a unos leñadores.

  (C) Almorzó con unos trabajadores.

  (D) Se paró repentinamente en el camino.

74. ¿Cómo reaccionaron los leñadores al autor?

  (A) Se burlaron de él.

  (B) Lo disculparon.

  (C) Lo miraron perplejos.

  (D) No le hicieron caso.

75. Según el autor, la actitud de los leñadores
era que

  (A) los conductores necesitaban protección.

  (B) eran responsables de avisar al público del
      peligro.

  (C) no tenían que hacer nada a menos que
      alguien se lo dijera.

  (D) no era posible avisar a cada
      automovilista personalmente.

76. Según el autor, los leñadores no habían hecho
lo que debían porque les faltaba

  (A) imaginación.

  (B) educación.

  (C) tiempo.

  (D) energía.

77. A fin de cuentas, todos los hombres

  (A) se entendieron mal.

  (B) brindaron por una nueva amistad.

  (C) llamaron a las autoridades.

  (D) se despidieron súbitamente.

GO ON TO THE NEXT PAGE

Línea   Yo quería saber si valía la pena seguirla
escribiendo porque ya no veía nada; tenía la
impresión de que no había en el mundo más que
lo que escribía y quería poner los pies sobre la
(5) tierra. Me senté a leer en el escenario iluminado;
la platea con "mi" público seleccionado,
completamente a oscuras. Empecé a leer, no
recuerdo bien qué capítulo, pero yo leía y leía y a
partir de un momento se produjo un tal silencio
(10) en la sala y era tal la tensión que yo sentía, que me
aterroricé. Interrumpí la lectura y traté de mirar
algo en la oscuridad y después de unos segundos
percibí los rostros de los que estaban en primera
fila y al contrario, vi que tenían los ojos así—los
(15) abren muy grandes—y entonces seguí mi lectura
muy tranquilo.
        Realmente la gente estaba como suspendida;
no volaba una mosca. Cuando terminé y bajé
del escenario, la primera persona que me abrazó
(20) fue Mercedes, con una cara...¡con una cara!...
Ella tenía por lo menos un año de estar llevando
recursos a la casa para que yo pudiera escribir y el
día de la lectura la expresión en su rostro me dio
la gran seguridad de que el libro iba por donde
(25) tenía que ir.

78. ¿Quién habla?

(A) un actor

(B) un novelista

(C) un profesor

(D) un interlocutor

79. El hablante probablemente está en

(A) una sala de estar.

(B) un cine.

(C) una sala de clase.

(D) un anfiteatro.

80. ¿Qué cuenta la selección?

(A) el ensayo de un drama

(B) una producción de televisión

(C) una conferencia

(D) la lectura de una novela

81. ¿Por qué interrumpió el hablante lo que hacía?

(A) Esperaba oír el aplauso del público.

(B) Las luces le molestaban.

(C) Querían mirar al público.

(D) Estaba cansado de lo que hacía.

82. El público, al presenciar la función

(A) se aterrorizó.

(B) se maravilló.

(C) se asustó.

(D) se regocijó.

83. Al principio el narrador

(A) dudaba de sí mismo.

(B) no hacía caso del público.

(C) quería asombrar al público.

(D) se arrepintió de haber venido.

84. ¿Por qué reaccionó Mercedes de tal manera?

(A) Estaba muy desilusionada por la
reacción del público.

(B) Llevaba mucho tiempo sola en casa.

(C) Compartía la alegría del narrador.

(D) Estaba muy sorprendida del éxito.

85. Al final el hablante experimentó un
sentimiento de gran

(A) desahogo.

(B) confusión.

(C) sorpresa.

(D) rencor.

STOP!

**If you finish before time is up,
you may check your work.**

Answer Key
Practice Test 2

Part A		Part B		Part C	
1.	B	33.	A	59.	B
2.	A	34.	B	60.	A
3.	B	35.	C	61.	B
4.	C	36.	C	62.	B
5.	C	37.	C	63.	C
6.	D	38.	D	64.	B
7.	B	39.	C	65.	C
8.	B	40.	B	66.	B
9.	C	41.	B	67.	D
10.	B	42.	D	68.	D
11.	A	43.	A	69.	B
12.	D	44.	C	70.	B
13.	B	45.	C	71.	A
14.	C	46.	D	72.	D
15.	C	47.	A	73.	D
16.	B	48.	B	74.	C
17.	A	49.	A	75.	C
18.	D	50.	C	76.	A
19.	D	51.	B	77.	B
20.	C	52.	C	78.	B
21.	C	53.	D	79.	C
22.	B	54.	A	80.	D
23.	A	55.	A	81.	C
24.	C	56.	C	82.	B
25.	B	57.	A	83.	A
26.	D	58.	C	84.	C
27.	C			85.	A
28.	D				
29.	C				
30.	C				
31.	A				
32.	D				

ANSWERS AND EXPLANATIONS

Part A

1. (B) Even if you do not know exactly what *aguacero* or *inundaciones* means, you should be able to deduce that it has to do with water. (D) has to do with water, but doesn't work in the context of the sentence. You want the word "to fill," which is *llenar*.

2. (A) If you are not careful, you could mistake *enterrar* for a correct answer. *Entrar* would work here, but it is quite different from *enterrar*, which means "to bury." *Quedar* is not followed by any preposition, so (C) will not work. You want a verb of motion. *Alcanzar* is the answer. It means "to achieve," as in reaching someplace you want to go.

3. (B) *Billete* and *boleto* both mean "ticket" in different parts of the Spanish speaking world. But a *billete* also means a "bill" of money. A *boleto* is a ticket that allows you entrance to some place. A *peso* is a unit of currency, so a *peso* of five dollars means nothing, so (D) is out.

4. (C) *Aunque*, "although," is the only word that combines the contrasting thoughts in this sentence. Take note that *se* precedes the verb *dice* in this sentence. This is a SE SUBSTITUTE structure, meaning "they say." However, "they" does not refer to anyone in particular. This construction is much more common in Spanish than in English.

5. (C) You need a negative indefinite pronoun to be the object of the verb. You cannot use *algo* because *no* comes before the verb, so (A) is wrong. *Alguien* and *nadie* refer to people, neither of which makes sense.

6. (D) *Revueltos* comes from the verb *revolver*, "to revolve." It does not mean "to return." *Huevos revueltos* are "revolved eggs" or "scrambled eggs." *Girar* also means "to spin around," but is not used to describe the preparation of eggs. *Envolver* means "wrapped up," and *apagados* makes no sense.

7. (B) *Pastillas* or *pildoras* are "pills." Don't confuse all the words that begin with the same letter.

8. (B) *Partido* has a number of meanings. It is a "game" between two teams, as in this sentence, or it is a party, as in a political party. If you guessed *equipo*, at least you associated the word with sports, which is the topic of the sentence. But the question is about the last game, a regional championship, not the last team.

9. (C) *Cuya* agrees in gender and number with the noun it modifies, *esposa*.

10. (B) When you are talking about weather being hot or cold, use *hacer*. You know that this sentence deals with weather because the speaker says that he did not bring a coat. The word *ojalá* always takes the subjunctive. If the speaker had said that he was cold, you would have needed *tener*. If the air had been cold, you would have used *estar*. And if you were describing something like ice being cold, you would have used *ser*.

11. (A) *Acompañar*, relates to "accompany." Don't be distracted by the grammar of the sentence here. (C) is wrong: You do "go out" with friends, but *salir* makes no sense because of the pronoun *me* in front of the blank.

12. (D) When you see *si*, scan the sentence for the conditional tense. If you do not see it, use the indicative. If you do see the conditional, use the imperfect subjunctive.

13. (B) You may not think of *alta* with voice, but that is the way to express "loud voice."

14. (C) The speaker wants Maria to turn on the television. *Pon* is the affirmative familiar *tú* command for *poner*. *Tornar* means "to turn" but not "to turn on." *Apagar* is a common verb. It means "to turn off," which is wrong here.

15. (C) This vocabulary question includes several nouns that are easy to confuse: *prisa*, "haste," *prima*, "cousin," and *precio*, "price." *Medalla* is a cognate.

16. (B) Use *está* because the verb describes the temperature of the water. Even though the water is cold all year, the context here refers to the water's condition, not its generally accepted characteristic. If you said, "El agua helada *es* fría," the use of *ser* would define the ice water. In this sentence, the cold state of the water is not a definitive characteristic, but rather a state of being, or how it feels to the touch.

17. (A) This is a vocabulary question about expressions that have no literal translation. *De ... en* means "from ... to," as in "from time to time." *A larga distancia* could be related to the speaker's sister being at the university, but the expression does not fit. One does not see someone at a university at a long distance.

18. (D) "No longer" is the expression that makes sense here. The first part of the sentence makes the other answer choices nonsensical.

19. (D) This structure deals with a comparison of equality. Make *tanto* agree with the noun it precedes. If you were comparing adverbs, then you would use *tan*.

20. (C) Look out for false cognates. *Salida* is "exit," as you may have noticed on signs near many emergency exits. *Éxito* means "success," so (A) is wrong.

21. (C) You cannot use any article that indicates gender or number here, because *bonito* does not modify any specific noun. When you see a blank in front of an adjective, always look to see if it goes with a noun. If there is no noun, then use *lo*. The meaning of the expression is "how," as in "It was incredible how pretty it was with all the flowers..." In other cases, it could mean "the pretty thing about," though the word "thing" is not translated into Spanish.

22. (B) *Lento* means "slow." Even if you do not know *cuesta arriba*, you know that *arriba* has to do with going "up" somehow. *Cuesta arriba* means "up hill." *Largo* means "long," and the verb *pesar* means "to weigh." *Rápidamente* is grammatically correct, but goes against the laws of physics to actually happen.

23. (A) This grammar question expresses a common mistake. When you want to say "because of," you need to use *a causa de*. Since *de* is after the blank, you cannot use any other choice.

24. (C) You cannot use *grande* in front of a masculine singular noun, so (A) is incorrect. *Más* makes no sense grammatically; and it is improbable that one would speak of the "best" problem. The best choice is *mayor*. Remember that it can mean "greatest" and well as "oldest."

25. (B) *Olvidar* takes *se* and an indirect object pronoun to deflect responsibility for something happening. One does not want to admit forgetting something, so in English you would say, "It slipped my mind." You know that the speaker is first person, *yo*, but the verb ending is third person singular, olvidó. So *me* makes no sense. *Se* doesn't make sense either, because you want to indicate the subject somehow. You also notice that *los dientes* uses an article "the" instead of a possessive adjective "my." You need an indirect object pronoun to indicate possession of parts of the body. *Se* plus *me* communicates that "brushing my teeth slipped my mind," and is the correct answer. Also note that when *olvidar* is followed by *de* it is always reflexive: *Olvidarse de* means "to forget."

26. (D) Here you need to use the present participle after *estar* to form the present progressive. You can use a past participle, but it would have to agree with the noun it modifies. *Alojado* should be *alojados* if it modified *clientes*. You will not use an infinitive after *estar* the way you can after ser, so (C) is out. (A), the conjugated verb makes no sense: You will not have two conjugated verbs in a row, unless there are two different subjects.

27. (C) This is a true passive voice construction. *El año que viene* is "next year," indicating that the future is the only possible answer.

28. (D) This is a common expression. You have to use the negative form, the opposite of *también*, because of *ni*. The other choices make no sense.

29. (C) *Ciento*, *miles*, and *millones* take *de* when you refer to a number "of" items. While you do say *mil veces* for "a thousand times," you will say *miles de veces* for "thousands of times." Before other numbers, use *mil*. Remember that *ciento* is shortened to *cien* before all nouns, singular and plural. *Millón* would have to be plural in this sentence after *unos*.

30. (C) Look for the subject behind the verb. The subject is *fotos*. You know that *me* is not a subject pronoun, so *quedo* is not correct. There is no reason to use the subjunctive, so *queden* is wrong as well.

31. (A) All the verb forms are in the subjunctive, but don't be confused by the grammar. The sentence talks about putting on *bronceador*, "tanning lotion." If you don't know that word, you could look at *tomar el sol a la playa* to get the idea of putting something on your skin. *Te pongas* is the only choice that works here. *Solicitar* means "to apply," but in the sense "to put in an application somewhere." *Cubrir* might be tempting, since it means "to cover," but you don't "cover tanning lotion."

32. (D) You need the subjunctive after *para que*, so just look for some indication of whether to use the present or past subjunctive. *Acampamos* can be present or preterite, so that won't help. The word *ahora* sets up a comparison of then and now, however, so even though it would be tempting to just guess the present subjunctive form, look at the time frame of each clause. You would see that *Al principio* refers to the past, so *acampamos* is a preterite form. *Ahora* indicates the present, in contrast to the past.

Part B

33. (A) All the verbs in the sentence are in the present tense, so that's what you need to use. You might also try the present perfect, but after trying out the meaning, you would see that it makes no sense with the present tense *pega*. The subjunctive is incorrect after *cuando*, since the action has already taken place.

34. (B) *Un* is never used in front of *otro*, so (A) is definitely wrong. *Un* never comes before *cualquier*, either, so (D) is out. *Bueno* is wrong because before a masculine singular noun it should be shortened to *buen*. *Solo* means "single," or "lone," and is the correct answer.

35. (C) Whenever you see *siquiera*, the word *ni* is somewhere close by. *Ni siquiera* means "not even." In this case the noun comes between these two words.

36. (C) Tables do have legs (A), but when you are talking about where someone is sitting, you need to use *cabacera*, choice (C). From scanning the passage, you learned that Cri-Crí is a person, and the sentence indicates where he was sitting. One does not sit on the table top, either, so *superficie* is incorrect as well.

37. (C) You cannot use (A) because the verb that follows is in the indicative. *Para que* is always followed by the subjunctive. (B) makes no sense in the context of the passage. The speaker is talking about why he likes *braseros*, not expressing any qualifications about liking them. (D) makes no sense because he is not offering a contrary view about *braseros* or saying that he has had one built in his kitchen, but he does like them. *Porque* is the only logical choice.

38. (D) The third person singular form of this verb can be used to mean "there is" or "there was," so you have to just select the present or the past. *Habido* is a correct form in other contexts, as in *ha habido*, "there has been," or *habiendo*, meaning "having." It is never used in the plural form when it means "there is, are, was, were, will be, would have been, etc." Even if the noun following the verb is plural, this is singular. You would say *hay braseros* or *había braseros* to mean, "There are hearths" or "There were hearths" in the plural. From the rest of the passage you can see that you need the imperfect because of *era* later in the sentence.

39. (C) From the context you can see that this man considers himself a fortunate person to be able to return to his childhood. He delights in an imaginative world. *Afortunada* conveys the sense of delight. *Lastimosa* means "pitiful." *Generosa* does not fit here.

40. (B) Do not confuse *despedirse* with *divertirse*, which means "to have a good time." *Equivocarse* means "to be mistaken."

41. (B) *Entretener*, "to entertain," is the only logical way to travel peacefully with children.

42. (D) *Durante* is "during." *Como*, meaning "as," does not fit with the noun *trayecto*. You could move "toward" a *trayecto*, but in this context, the noun refers to being on a trip. That means (B) is out.

43. (A) Here you must find the correct part of speech to follow *ser*. You need to use a verb as a noun, and the only possible form is an infinitive. In English a gerund, ending in *-ing*, is a verb used as a noun, but you can never use a present participle as a noun in Spanish. Resist the temptation to translate literally. You can use a past participle after *ser*, but in such cases, the verb form is used as an adjective, not a noun.

44. (C) You need to name something in which you carry candy. A *bolsa* is a "bag" or a "sack," so it is the correct answer. A *bolsa* can also mean a stock market, depending on the context.

45. (C) The only word that works is *algunos*. *Cuántos* would be a possibility, except that it has an accent mark, making it an interrogative pronoun. You can't use *ningunos* because the statement is positive. *Tantos* does not make sense because it means "so much," or "as many," implying a comparison.

46. (D) You need a noun that describes something that has different colors. *Marcadores*, joined by the conjunction *o*, indicates that whatever the noun is, it is used to write, or make marks in color. *Lápices* is the only noun that works in the context. Certainly there can be colored lights, bottles, and spots, but they are not instruments for writing or coloring.

47. (A) The verb you want is *mantener*, in the sense of "to keep." *Regalar* means "to give as a gift," *despertar* means "to awaken," and *suponer* means "to suppose," none of which works here.

48. (B) It helps to know that *ahí* means "there," in an existential sort of time and place. At that point in the instructions, where the advice ends, you are on your own. *Frente* refers to a place in front (of), so (A) is wrong.

49. **(A)** You may not recognize *respaldarte*, but you can figure it out from *espalda*, "back." It means "to fall back." The blank is followed by the word *en*, so *consentirte* makes no sense. *Convertirte* and *tardar* do take *en*, but in the context of the passage, make no sense.

50. **(C)** This question deals with a game: "Who Finds it First," like "I Spy." *Que* does not work, because it is not an interrogative pronoun without the accent mark. *Cuánto*, meaning "how many," doesn't make sense, nor does *cuyo*, meaning "whose."

51. **(B)** Although it seems too obvious, *réplicas* is not a false cognate in this question. While the passage deals with art, it is sculpture, not painting, so *pinturas* does not work. *Obras* does not make sense, because the word would be redundant, "the works of two of his small statues." *Pruebas* does not make sense either; it means "proof" or "evidence."

52. **(C)** *Venta* means "sale," and of all the choices, fits best. *Forma* doesn't make any sense: You may think of *estar en forma*, which means "to be in shape," but statues are inanimate.

53. **(D)** Since all of the answer choices are feminine plural, the adjective must refer to *esculturas*, because that is the closest feminine plural noun in the sentence. Now you can see that the best choice is *exhibidas*, because the statues are being shown for a low price. Do not confuse *dañadas* with *dadas*; *dañar* means "to damage." *Preguntar* does mean "to ask," and is followed by *por*, but in this case, there is no question implied. "To ask for" is *pedir*, but that is not an answer choice. Statues are also sculpted, or carved, *labradas*, from *labrar*, a word you should not confuse with *ladrar*, meaning "to bark."

54. **(A)** When you see *tanto* in the sentence, look to see if a comparison is being made. Such is the case in this sentence. The person who brought in the statues, as well as the store owner, declare that the statues are original. There must be some sort of a fraud going on because the first sentence tells you that the artist is angry. The word *parecer* later in the passage also tells you that some things "seem" to be one way, but are really another. So in the second paragraph, look for the comparison of equality with *tanto ... como*. The other options do not make sense. *Así* does mean "so," but not in this grammatical structure. *Que* does not work in comparisons of equality, just those of inequality (better, worse, etc.).

55. **(A)** When you see a negative indefinite word, see whether you need an adjective, pronoun, or conjunction. In this case you need an adjective. *Ninguno* drops the final *-o* before masculine singular nouns. Remember that "no" is not used as an adjective in Spanish.

56. **(C)** After the auxiliary verb *haber* you need a past participle. In this case, the verb is irregular, so you may not see a past participle with the usual ending *-ado*, or *-ido*. No mater what the subject of the verb, the past participle after *haber* always ends in *-o*.

57. **(A)** The verb you want is "to create." You might think that *se creó* comes from *creer*, but that is wrong. (In fact, the third person singular preterite of *creer* is *creyó*.) *Crear* does mean "to create," but you probably recognize it more easily in the word *creación*. *Se convirtió* does not work, because *en* needs to follow that verb. Really, neither *convertirse* nor *transformarse* works because there is no mention of an antecedent that would undergo a change. The whole situation created something new, a bad feeling between the merchant and the art experts.

58. (C) "Between" is the only logical choice, even though you do not find two separate nouns. *Entre* means "among" as well as "between," which makes it a perfect fit. *Hasta* can mean "even," but that would make an incomplete sentence. *Ante* means "before" in the sense of "being before somebody."

Part C

Questions 59–64

This passage is about what happens when children come home from school. They sit down to watch television, and put off doing their homework until bedtime. Then there is the problem of what to do about the homework, and how parents and children deal with each other.

59. (B) The children relax and talk to their friends while watching television. The passage does not say they talk to their parents while watching television, so (C) is wrong. Nor do they take naps before doing homework, so (D) is out. These wrong answer choices lift words from the text, but use them in a different context.

60. (A) *Animados* is like the English word "animated," meaning that the children are excited about something. They come home in a flurry of motion. They do sit down and watch television for hours, absorbed and attentive, but they are not still because they are bored (*aburridos*) or tired (*cansados*). They are excited about watching television.

61. (B) If you do not know *regañar* in choice (B), you could use the process of elimination. (A) is wrong because they do not all quietly lie down. (C) is wrong because the parents and child do not watch television together. And for (D), in the text the *apuras* ("troubles") begin, but that is quite different from the "el niño *se apura* para hacer su tarea." *Apurarse* means "to hurry up," and the text says quite the opposite: that the children do *not* participate in looking for the book bags and doing the homework. (B) must be the answer.

62. (B) Sleep is most important for good health. The homework is important, but second to health in importance.

63. (C) The last paragraph of the text tells you that the child does not participate in the activity associated with doing homework. He seems to be a spectator.

64. (B) The meaning of the last sentence is not to be taken literally. "Se quiebran la cabeza" means figuratively that they struggle thinking through the homework problems. "Los quebrados" refers to fractions in math problems, though you do not need to know this word to answer the question. *Tarea* tells you that they do the homework. The parents are not happy with the child, but it does not state that they are mad, so (C) is wrong. (D) is wrong as well, because the text does not say they are proud of the child.

Questions 65–66

This ad is deceptive and you need to look at the text. There is a couple dancing, but the words *teja, goteras, clima, instalación,* and *mercado* tell you that the product has to do with something else. Even if you do not know that a *teja* is a roof tile, you could tell that it is something for a house: The product refers to being "a definitive solution," "economical," and something "a single person can install." The photo of the tiles below the couple also relates to the text.

65. (C) The consumer for this product would be someone repairing or building a house. Don't be distracted by the repetition of *pareja* in (D), a word lifted from the ad, nor by the association of *club social* in (A) with the image of the couple dancing.

66. (B) The words *goteras* and *arde* in the ad tell you that the product is waterproof and fireproof. A *gotera* is a leak in a roof, and *arder* menas "to burn." You can deduce the meaning of *gotera* from the phrase *una gota de agua*, meaning "a drop of water."

Questions 67–71

This passage is about a location for sailboarding and how it was discovered. Cabarete is the name of a place. There is a narrator, who is talking to one of two friends who discovered this paradise for playing their sport. In the last paragraph the narrator updates the description. Where before there had been no tourists, phones, or cars, the implication is that all has now changed. The best practitioners of the sport now come to Cabarete to sailboard.

67. (D) The word *carreras* in (D) is another way of saying *competencia* and *campeonato mundial*. The fact that it is far from Hawaii and Florida in (C), and that there are no tourists in (B) is what originally attracted the two friends to Cabarete, but now the competition is what makes it famous.

68. (D) At first the friends took a trip to check out the beaches. A *recorrido* is a "trip" or "a run through."

69. (B) As soon as the two friends had established themselves in Cabarete, they took advantage of the open space on the beach. Don't be fooled by the insertion of *alquilar* in (D), which is a word lifted from the text.

70. (B) *Actualmente* means "presently," so the question asks why people come to Cabarete in the present. (D) is wrong because people do not come to escape telephones. Nor do they come to see other tourists, so (C) is wrong. People come to practice their favorite sport.

71. (A) The narrator seems most interested in the history and discovery of Cabarete. He is probably a reporter.

Questions 72–77

This piece begins with a general statement about life, a philosophical point of departure. What follows is a narration of a specific incident, and then some personal observations about what it all meant.

72. (D) Although the piece details what happened while the writer was driving one day, he tries to put the experience in a larger context. The word *responsabilidad* in the middle of the passage is key: The main topic is about moral responsibility. While these topics are included in the text, the main idea is not about the dangers of driving or the lack of courtesy in society per se, so (B) and (A) are wrong.

73. (D) The writer rounds a curve and almost runs into a tree. *Inesperadamente con un árol en mitad de la carretera* tells you that "the tree is in the middle of the road." He does not hit the woodsmen who have cut down the tree (B), and he does not run off the road (A).

74. (C) The woodsmen do not "make fun" of the writer so (A) is wrong. *No hacerle caso* in (D) is "to not pay attention," but the woodsmen do not ignore him. The word *perplejos* in (C) is "perplexed," which is how they look at him. If you did not readily recognize *perplejos*, remember that the Spanish *j* often replaces the English *x*. *Lujoso* and *ejemplo* are other examples: "luxury" and "example."

75. (C) The men profess innocence for not warning of danger because they had the necessary permit from the Ayuntamiento. The Ayuntamiento did not tell them to post any additional warnings, so they did nothing.

76. (A) The men did nothing not only because they were not required to by law, but also because their point of view was limited. They did not consider the dangers to someone driving along a blind curve. They were unconnected to others with whom they share the road: they lacked imagination.

77. (B) In the end, all of the men, the writer included, come to an understanding. *Brindar* means "to toast," as in "to toast a friendship."

Questions 78–85

This passage is a first person narration of a writer reading his work to some friends. When he says he wanted to "put his feet on the ground" at the end of the first paragraph, it is not to be taken literally. The writer does not know what to expect from the people. He sits in a room under a spotlight. At one point he peered into the darkness and only saw the eyes of the people in the first row. He mentions a silence and tension in the room that caused him to stop reading and peer out beyond the bright lights. From the silence and the looks of rapt attention that he did see, he was happy. He realized then that what he had written was good.

The second paragraph talks about Mercedes, who gives him a big hug at the end. He mentions that she has spent the previous year keeping the household going while he was writing, for which he is very grateful. And he is certain that the book will be a success.

78. (B) There is no indication that the narrator is acting in a play, so (A) is wrong. And since his friends are in the audience, he is not a professor, choice (C). He is quite likely a writer, *un noveliste*.

79. (C) We know that there is a stage (*escenario*), a first row (*la primera fila*) and darkness (*la oscuridad*). The place is too large for a living room (*sala de estar*), so (A) is wrong. (B) is wrong as well, since *cine* is a "movie house." The location is probably a classroom.

80. (D) As the words *leí*, *lectura*, and *libro* are repearted at the end of the passage, (D) is correct. A *lectura* is a "reading."

81. (C) The speaker stopped reading because he was unsure about people's reactions. He stopped to look at their faces.

82. (B) The narrator, not the public, was momentarily terrified, so (A) is wrong. And the text does not specifically state that the public was delighted, so (D) is wrong. *Maravillarse* expresses great wonderment, so (B) is the best answer. Several sentences in the text indicate that the people watched in wonderment.

83. (A) The narrator mentions at the beginning that he is uncertain about the whole event. He does not know if what he writes will be understood by others. In other words, he had self doubt. (B) is wrong because he is very much aware of the people. He does not want to amaze or scare people, so (C) is out as well. (D) is wrong because he is not sorry he gave the reading.

84. (C) Mercedes is happy for him. It is the only choice that fits.

85. (A) *Desahogo* means "relief," so (A) is the right answer. (D) is wrong because he did not feel "rancor" or "ill will." Nor did he feel confused or surprised, so (B) and (C) are wrong.

Practice Test 3

Answer Grid
Practice Test 3

1. (A) (B) (C) (D) (E)
2. (A) (B) (C) (D) (E)
3. (A) (B) (C) (D) (E)
4. (A) (B) (C) (D) (E)
5. (A) (B) (C) (D) (E)
6. (A) (B) (C) (D) (E)
7. (A) (B) (C) (D) (E)
8. (A) (B) (C) (D) (E)
9. (A) (B) (C) (D) (E)
10. (A) (B) (C) (D) (E)
11. (A) (B) (C) (D) (E)
12. (A) (B) (C) (D) (E)
13. (A) (B) (C) (D) (E)
14. (A) (B) (C) (D) (E)
15. (A) (B) (C) (D) (E)
16. (A) (B) (C) (D) (E)
17. (A) (B) (C) (D) (E)
18. (A) (B) (C) (D) (E)
19. (A) (B) (C) (D) (E)
20. (A) (B) (C) (D) (E)
21. (A) (B) (C) (D) (E)
22. (A) (B) (C) (D) (E)
23. (A) (B) (C) (D) (E)
24. (A) (B) (C) (D) (E)
25. (A) (B) (C) (D) (E)
26. (A) (B) (C) (D) (E)
27. (A) (B) (C) (D) (E)
28. (A) (B) (C) (D) (E)
29. (A) (B) (C) (D) (E)

30. (A) (B) (C) (D) (E)
31. (A) (B) (C) (D) (E)
32. (A) (B) (C) (D) (E)
33. (A) (B) (C) (D) (E)
34. (A) (B) (C) (D) (E)
35. (A) (B) (C) (D) (E)
36. (A) (B) (C) (D) (E)
37. (A) (B) (C) (D) (E)
38. (A) (B) (C) (D) (E)
39. (A) (B) (C) (D) (E)
40. (A) (B) (C) (D) (E)
41. (A) (B) (C) (D) (E)
42. (A) (B) (C) (D) (E)
43. (A) (B) (C) (D) (E)
44. (A) (B) (C) (D) (E)
45. (A) (B) (C) (D) (E)
46. (A) (B) (C) (D) (E)
47. (A) (B) (C) (D) (E)
48. (A) (B) (C) (D) (E)
49. (A) (B) (C) (D) (E)
50. (A) (B) (C) (D) (E)
51. (A) (B) (C) (D) (E)
52. (A) (B) (C) (D) (E)
53. (A) (B) (C) (D) (E)
54. (A) (B) (C) (D) (E)
55. (A) (B) (C) (D) (E)
56. (A) (B) (C) (D) (E)
57. (A) (B) (C) (D) (E)
58. (A) (B) (C) (D) (E)

59. (A) (B) (C) (D) (E)
60. (A) (B) (C) (D) (E)
61. (A) (B) (C) (D) (E)
62. (A) (B) (C) (D) (E)
63. (A) (B) (C) (D) (E)
64. (A) (B) (C) (D) (E)
65. (A) (B) (C) (D) (E)
66. (A) (B) (C) (D) (E)
67. (A) (B) (C) (D) (E)
68. (A) (B) (C) (D) (E)
69. (A) (B) (C) (D) (E)
70. (A) (B) (C) (D) (E)
71. (A) (B) (C) (D) (E)
72. (A) (B) (C) (D) (E)
73. (A) (B) (C) (D) (E)
74. (A) (B) (C) (D) (E)
75. (A) (B) (C) (D) (E)
76. (A) (B) (C) (D) (E)
77. (A) (B) (C) (D) (E)
78. (A) (B) (C) (D) (E)
79. (A) (B) (C) (D) (E)
80. (A) (B) (C) (D) (E)
81. (A) (B) (C) (D) (E)
82. (A) (B) (C) (D) (E)
83. (A) (B) (C) (D) (E)
84. (A) (B) (C) (D) (E)
85. (A) (B) (C) (D) (E)

Practice Test 3

Directions: Select the most appropriate word to complete the sentence and fill in the corresponding oval on the answer sheet.

1. No voy porque está ___ y no quiero mojarme.

   (A) llamando
   (B) llegando
   (C) llorando
   (D) lloviendo

2. No me gustan estos aretes, no me ___ bien con el estilo de pelo que llevo.

   (A) caben
   (B) caen
   (C) ruedan
   (D) ponen

3. El futuro será un gran desafío para nuestro país sin nuevas ___ de energía.

   (A) barreras
   (B) botellas
   (C) fuentes
   (D) escaleras

4. En esa clase el profesor dicta ___ sobre la historia española que son muy interesantes.

   (A) términos
   (B) carta
   (C) competencias
   (D) conferencias

5. No me apetecía ___ de los platos que vi en el menú.

   (A) algo
   (B) alguno
   (C) nada
   (D) ninguno

6. Carmen se graduó primera en su clase porque es una estudiante tan ___.

   (A) aplicada
   (B) acertada
   (C) traviesa
   (D) escasa

7. El sastre usó ___ de lana para coserme un abrigo para el invierno próximo.

   (A) fábrica
   (B) tela
   (C) carpa
   (D) tienda

8. En las carreteras los conductores necesitan tener cuidado de los ___ grandes.

   (A) trucos
   (B) camarones
   (C) frenos
   (D) camiones

GO ON TO THE NEXT PAGE

9. Enrique, puedes pasarme su papel y ___ de Susana, también.

   (A) suya
   (B) el
   (C) él
   (D) la

10. ¡Cuánto me gusta que estés ___ la trompeta en la orquesta escolar!

    (A) tomando
    (B) jugando
    (C) plagando
    (D) tocando

11. Algunos estudiantes ___ a sus padres cuando van a la universidad.

    (A) extrañan
    (B) saludan
    (C) peinan
    (D) relacionan

12. No me ___ que no puedes venir; todo el mundo te espera.

    (A) di
    (B) dice
    (C) dices
    (D) digas

13. Mañana tendré ___ mi tema para la clase de inglés.

    (A) imprevisto
    (B) hecho
    (C) dicho
    (D) perdido

14. Por favor, ___ los lazos de los zapatos antes de tropezarte en ellos.

    (A) rompe
    (B) ata
    (C) ahorra
    (D) ahoga

15. La falda de este vestido es demasiada larga; llega a mis ___.

    (A) hombros
    (B) caderas
    (C) tobillos
    (D) manos

16. ¿Dónde ___ la reunión esta noche? Pienso conducir mi propio coche.

    (A) sabrá
    (B) será
    (C) irá
    (D) dirá

17. Anoche llovió ___, causando una inundación que arruinó la cosecha.

    (A) al fin y al cabo
    (B) a cántaros
    (C) sin razón
    (D) de par en par

18. Compraría un cupón de la lotería ___ me diera el dinero.

    (A) con tal que
    (B) aunque
    (C) sino que
    (D) ya que

19. La ___ vez que tenga la oportunidad, voy a volver a España.

    (A) última
    (B) primer
    (C) próxima
    (D) más cerca

20. El ___ en la tienda de la esquina siempre me daba dulces cuando era niño.

    (A) duende
    (B) dependiente
    (C) patriarca
    (D) policía

GO ON TO THE NEXT PAGE

21. Marta, puedes darme el libro mañana cuando ___ veamos en la escuela.

    (A) la
    (B) me
    (C) nos
    (D) se

22. Cuando te digo que vengas, debes hacerlo ___, Juanito.

    (A) en seguida
    (B) sin embargo
    (C) a continuación
    (D) por casualidad

23. ___, durante la caminata en las montañas no vieron a ningunos osos.

    (A) Afortunadamente
    (B) Cautelosamente
    (C) Cotidianamente
    (D) Repentinamente

24. En invierno llevamos ropa ___ porque hace mucho frío.

    (A) ligera
    (B) gruesa
    (C) elegante
    (D) dura

25. Por poco evitamos un accidente con el tren que venía hacia ___ velozmente.

    (A) mi
    (B) los
    (C) nos
    (D) nosotros

26. ___ la gorra rápidamente al salir, nos dijo que regresaría pronto.

    (A) Se pone
    (B) Se pondrá
    (C) Ponerse
    (D) Poniéndose

27. María no ___ acompañar a su hermana al baile anoche porque no conocía a nadie.

    (A) quiso
    (B) quiere
    (C) quiera
    (D) quisiera

28. Los pasajeros estaban cansados de ___ viajar cuando por fin llegaron a la estación.

    (A) así
    (B) como
    (C) tanto
    (D) cuánto

29. Vieron ___ especies de insectos al hacer el viaje por el busque.

    (A) trescientas
    (B) cientos
    (C) miles
    (D) uno

30. Éste es el trabalenguas que me ___ más porque es imposible decirlo rápido.

    (A) gusto
    (B) gusta
    (C) gustan
    (D) gusten

31. Le hemos pedido al camarero que nos ___ unas tazas de café solo.

    (A) trae
    (B) ha traído
    (C) traiga
    (D) haya traído

32. Te agradezco todo el trabajo que ___ en planear las vacaciones.

    (A) hace
    (B) hago
    (C) has hecho
    (D) hubieras hecho

GO ON TO THE NEXT PAGE

Part B

Directions: First read through the entire paragraph. Then, for each numbered blank, choose the completion that is most appropriate given the context of the passage. Fill in the corresponding oval on the answer sheet.

Todas las (33) del día las pasó Laura (34) en el comedor de las reuniones políticas con el periódico (35) sobre la mesa, (36) fijamente la foto de la mujer muy blanca y piel tan fina (37) fuera porcelana. Llegó el crepúsculo y aunque (38) podía ver el retrato, no encendió la (39) . Se sabía ese rostro de (40) . Era el rostro de un rescate moral.

33. (A) veces
    (B) horas
    (C) épocas
    (D) etapas

34. (A) sentando
    (B) sentada
    (C) sentado
    (D) sentó

35. (A) distraído
    (B) colgado
    (C) destacado
    (D) desplegado

36. (A) miraba
    (B) mirar
    (C) mirando
    (D) mirado

37. (A) como si
    (B) tanta
    (C) además
    (D) así que

38. (A) también
    (B) siempre
    (C) no sólo
    (D) ya no

39. (A) televisión
    (B) ducha
    (C) radio
    (D) luz

40. (A) vuelta
    (B) acuerdo
    (C) memoria
    (D) noche

GO ON TO THE NEXT PAGE

Las cosas de Lucas, el anciano del pueblo, (41) reír a las personas mayores. No a (42) , los niños. Porque Lucas era el ser más (43) de la tierra. Mi hermana y yo (44) hacia él una especie de amor, temor, y admiración, que nunca (45) a experimentar. Nos decía que era tan (46) que perdió el último (47) y no lo podía encontrar.

Lucas vivía solo, y él mismo cocinaba sus (48) de carne, cebollas y patatas, de los que (49) nos daba con su cuchara de hueso. Él lavaba su (50) en el río, dándola grandes golpes con una pala.

41. (A) debían
    (B) daban
    (C) hacían
    (D) llevaban

42. (A) me
    (B) él
    (C) ellas
    (D) nosotros

43. (A) desconocido
    (B) extraordinario
    (C) chistoso
    (D) aburrido

44. (A) sentíamos
    (B) corríamos
    (C) llamábamos
    (D) sacábamos

45. (A) volvamos
    (B) volvió
    (C) hemos vuelto
    (D) hayamos vuelto

46. (A) atento
    (B) cuidadoso
    (C) mimado
    (D) viejo

47. (A) concurso
    (B) partido
    (C) año
    (D) juego

48. (A) folletos
    (B) guisos
    (C) guiones
    (D) partos

49. (A) a menudo
    (B) en cuanto
    (C) a causa
    (D) a medida

50. (A) cara
    (B) comida
    (C) ropa
    (D) mano

GO ON TO THE NEXT PAGE

Cuenta la leyenda que el dios Huitzilopochtli abandonó a su hermana, Malinalxochitl ("Flor de Yerba"), debido a sus facultades (51) de hechicería, y (52) que ésta dormía por la noche, (53) del bosque. (54) se despertó, enfurecida por el abandono de su hermano, tomó a su gente y se marchó a otro lugar en (55) finalmente se estableció Malinalco, "Lugar de la flor del zacate."

A (56) hora y media de la ciudad de México, enclavado en un (57) rodeado de montañas y ríos, en una zona de clima semitropical y tierra fértil de donde (58) en abundancia toda clase de frutos, se encuentra Maninalco.

51. (A) secas
    (B) malignas
    (C) benéficas
    (D) cautelosas

52. (A) aprovechando
    (B) terminando
    (C) enviando
    (D) sentando

53. (A) se marchó
    (B) se ha marchado
    (C) marcharse
    (D) marchándose

54. (A) Mientras
    (B) Cuanto
    (C) Donde
    (D) Cuando

55. (A) el que
    (B) quien
    (C) cual
    (D) cuanto

56. (A) más
    (B) sólo
    (C) solo
    (D) menos

57. (A) corral
    (B) valle
    (C) canto
    (D) muro

58. (A) brotan
    (B) parecen
    (C) ruegan
    (D) encantan

GO ON TO THE NEXT PAGE

Part C

Directions: Read the following texts carefully. Then, for each question that follows, select the best answer according to the text. Fill in the corresponding oval on the answer sheet.

El viejo asintió con movimiento de cabeza a las indicaciones del mozo repitiendo que sólo tenían asado de tira, y al recibir la botella de agua fría bebió un largo trago, con los ojos cerrados, con esa satisfacción que sólo pueden demostrar los que han tenido una larga jornada de trabajo.

Se acercó.

—Disculpe, señor. ¿Es usted empleado del ferrocarril?

—Sí y no—cortó el viejo.

La respuesta lo sorprendió de manera incómoda, pero enseguida el viejo sonrió indicándole una silla.

—Sí, en cuanto al ferrocarril. No, en cuanto a lo de empleado. Soy obrero.

—Ah. Entiendo.

—¿Chileno, don?

—Sí.

—¿No quieres comer algo?

Le agradeció indicando que acababa de hacerlo y le preguntó acerca del tren a La Paz. En ese momento llegó la carne. Al viejo le brillaron los ojos y con avidez liberó el cubierto de la servilleta de papel.

59. En el momento de iniciar la conversación ¿qué hacía el viejo?

(A) almorzaba
(B) cocinaba
(C) cantaba
(D) trabajaba

60. El chileno se sentía incómodo porque

(A) el viejo se negó a contestar a su pregunta.
(B) quería molestar al viejo.
(C) no le dio una respuesta amplia.
(D) no quería revelar quién era.

61. ¿Qué le ofreció el viejo al chileno?

(A) Información
(B) Alimento
(C) Solicitud
(D) Boletos

62. ¿Por qué no aceptó el chileno la oferta del viejo?

(A) No tenía dinero para pagar.
(B) No tenía utensilios para tomarlo.
(C) Hacía un ratito que había comido.
(D) Quería escribir en la servilleta.

63. El tono de la conversación es

(A) enigmático.
(B) iracundo.
(C) amistoso.
(D) erudito.

64. Lo que hacía el viejo en los trenes era

(A) servir comida a los viajeros.
(B) ganarse la vida de cualquier modo.
(C) reparar rieles para la empresa.
(D) trabajar de conductor en los trenes.

GO ON TO THE NEXT PAGE

65. ¿Qué tipo de materia contiene este libro?

(A) datos para planear una batalla

(B) una novela de misterios en hoteles pequeños

(C) una guía de lugares en que quedarse

(D) sugerencias para alejarse de la vida tranquila

66. Las personas que beneficiarían más de usar esta materia serían

(A) hombres de negocios.

(B) personas que buscan empleo.

(C) viajeros en busca de algo diferente.

(D) propietarios de hoteles pequeños.

GO ON TO THE NEXT PAGE

Línea   Salí de la carpa. "Estoy bien preparado—pensé
al empezar la carrera—, voy a ganar porque hace
tiempo que he entrenado diariamente." Oí el
sonido que inició la carrera, y pronto cogí la
(5) primera cuesta en cabeza. En cuanto aflojó el
declive, dejé no más que el sol se me calentara
la espalda. No tuve necesidad de mirar muy atrás
para descubrir a Pizarnick del Ferroviario pegado
a mi trasera. Sentí piedad por el muchacho, por
(10) su equipo, por su entrenador que le había dicho
"si toma la delantera, pégate a él hasta donde
aguantes, ¿entiendes?", porque si yo quería
era capaz ahí mismo de ganar sin tener que
esforzarme mucho. Comprendía bien sus
(15) emociones recordando mis propias primeras
carreras.

67. El narrador de esta selección es

   (A) espectador

   (B) ciclista

   (C) entrenador

   (D) árbitro

68. ¿Qué hace el narrador?

   (A) enseña al otro muchacho

   (B) participa en una competencia

   (C) entrena a los atletas

   (D) estudia para una carrera

69. En la situación citada el narrador parece
sentirse

   (A) preocupado.

   (B) enfermo.

   (C) compasivo.

   (D) molestado.

70. Los consejos del entrenador de Pizarnick
eran que éste

   (A) tomara la primera posición.

   (B) siguiera al narrador.

   (C) entrenara mejor la próxima vez.

   (D) mantuviera su distancia.

71. Al final, ¿de qué se da cuenta el narrador?

   (A) pizarnick ganará

   (B) quiere hacerse doctor

   (C) vencerá con facilidad

   (D) seguirá una carrera de derecho

GO ON TO THE NEXT PAGE

Línea   No había ni una nube en el cielo. Sudaba y
al mismo tiempo sentía frío porque había que
ésos eran tiempos de miedo y de pronto, como si
hubiesen escuchado una señal secreta, el eco de
(5) una trompeta de alarma sonando desde siglos en la
perdida intimidad de los cerros, los seres totémicos
apilaron sus mercancías y se esfumó la alegre feria
que ocupara los andenes.

    Al mirar hacia el comienzo. o el fin de las líneas,
(10) hacia la frontera, vio el piquete de soldados bajando
de un camión verde, y avanzando. Respondiendo
a los gestos de un oficial se abrieron en abanico
preparados para repeler una emboscada. Y él estaba
solo, sentado sobre la maleta.

(15) En ese mismo instante se dejó oír el pitazo que
le obligó a volverse hacia el lado opuesto, y vio la
vieja locomotora, como un gran animal verde con
una cicatriz amarilla sobre el vientre.

72. ¿Qué tiempo hacía?

    (A) Hacía calor.

    (B) Hacía mal tiempo.

    (C) Hacía frío.

    (D) Estaba nublado.

73. El hombre estaba sentado en

    (A) un camión en la calle.

    (B) un banco en la estación

    (C) su equipaje en el andén.

    (D) dentro de la estación.

74. ¿Quiénes eran los "seres totémicos" en la
línea 6?

    (A) amigos del hombre

    (B) vendedores campesinos

    (C) obreros del ferrocarril

    (D) soldados que viajaban

75. ¿Qué significa "se esfumó la alegre feria" en la
línea 7?

    (A) La llegada del tren interrumpió la feria.

    (B) El hombre tocó una trompeta avisando
del peligro.

    (C) La gente oyó una señal del peligro.

    (D) Los soldados llegaron en el tren.

76. Parecía que los soldados anticipaban

    (A) la bienvenida de la gente.

    (B) una recepción acogedora.

    (C) alguna acción bélica.

    (D) una manifestación de trabajadores.

77. El ambiente de esta escena es

    (A) festivo.

    (B) desasosegado.

    (C) superado.

    (D) tranquilo.

GO ON TO THE NEXT PAGE

Línea   La mañana de ese día, fue la única del año en
la cual mi padre nos llevó al colegio en su auto. Al
llegar al cruce de dos avenidas, un inconsciente
cruzó con luz roja y arrastró nuestro auto hasta
(5) que lo volcó, desapareciendo luego del lugar.
Mi padre y yo sufrimos graves heridas, no así
mi hermano, Eduardo. Quedé internada en una
clínica en estado de coma profundo. Los médicos
habían intentado todo lo que estaba a su alcance,
(10) sin éxito. Se necesitaba una reacción urgente
por parte mía. Una tía se acordó que yo tenía
a un perrito mezcla. Sin más el doctor ordenó:
"Tráigalo, yo dejaré la orden en recepción."
Cuando el médico se paró al lado de mi cama con
(15) el perro y me preguntó si lo quería, la pregunta
se instaló en mi mente y después del séptimo
día inconsciente respondí que sí. Gracias a él,
hoy estoy aquí, para decirles a aquellos que los
maltratan y abandonan los perros, que deben
(20) pensar antes de hacer cosas horribles. Y a los otros
que dicen, "tan solo es un animal," les digo que
muchas veces son mejores que mucha gente, dan
cariño, compañía y alegría a cambio de una caricia
y un plato de comida.

78.   Cuando sucedió este relato la narradora tendría

    (A) unos tres años.

    (B) unos doce años.

    (C) unos veinte años.

    (D) cincuenta años.

79.   ¿Cómo ocurrió el accidente?

    (A) Alguien los atropelló mientras
        caminaban a la escuela.

    (B) Un hombre ignoró un semáforo y causó
        un accidente.

    (C) Su padre causó un accidente con su coche.

    (D) Ella y su hermano distraían a su padre,
        lo cual causó el accidente.

80.   ¿Qué hizo el "inconsciente" de la línea 3,
    después del accidente?

    (A) Los llevó a la escuela.

    (B) Les indicó la luz roja.

    (C) Salió sin decir nada.

    (D) Los llevó al hospital.

81.   A consecuencia del accidente, la narradora

    (A) sufrió lesiones graves.

    (B) recibió un animal doméstico.

    (C) tuvo unos regalos del doctor.

    (D) salió sin daño de él.

82.   ¿Por qué respondió la narradora a la pregunta
    del doctor?

    (A) Ella prefería hablar con el perro.

    (B) El doctor quería a su perro.

    (C) El perro se comunicó con ella.

    (D) Amaba tanto a su perro.

83.   Al final de la selección la narradora se dirige
    principalmente a los que

    (A) conducen mal.

    (B) no quieren a los perros.

    (C) trabajan en los hospitales.

    (D) aman a sus animales domésticos.

84.   En cuanto a la diferencia entre los perros y
    los hombres, la narradora parece

    (A) creer que los perros no piden tanto
        como los hombres.

    (B) pensar que los perros son más
        inteligentes que los hombres.

    (C) decir que los perros tienen poderes
        sobrenaturales.

    (D) creer que los perros curan mejor que los
        doctores.

GO ON TO THE NEXT PAGE

85. El motivo de esta narradora parece ser

(A) advertir de los peligros de conducir mal.

(B) regañarse a los perros que le han ayudado.

(C) contar algo para entretener al lector.

(D) promocionar más afecto para los perros.

STOP!

**If you finish before time is up,
you may check your work.**

Answer Key
Practice Test 3

Part A	Part B	Part C
1. D	33. B	59. A
2. B	34. B	60. C
3. C	35. D	61. B
4. D	36. C	62. C
5. D	37. A	63. C
6. A	38. D	64. B
7. B	39. D	65. C
8. D	40. C	66. C
9. B	41. C	67. B
10. D	42. D	68. B
11. A	43. B	69. C
12. D	44. A	70. B
13. B	45. C	71. C
14. B	46. D	72. A
15. C	47. C	73. C
16. B	48. B	74. B
17. B	49. A	75. C
18. A	50. C	76. C
19. C	51. B	77. B
20. B	52. A	78. B
21. C	53. A	79. B
22. A	54. D	80. C
23. A	55. A	81. A
24. B	56. B	82. D
25. D	57. B	83. B
26. D	58. A	84. A
27. A		85. D
28. C		
29. A		
30. B		
31. C		
32. C		

ANSWERS AND EXPLANATIONS

Part A

1. (D) The clue here is *mojarme*, which means "to get wet (myself)." The answer, then, is "raining," choice (D).

2. (B) A common expression in Spanish is *caerle bien* or *mal*, meaning "to look good or bad (on someone)." With articles of clothing or jewelry, you might also expect that you could use *ponerse*, but you are not talking about putting something on in this sentence. It is clear that the speaker is concerned about looks and style and how things go together.

3. (C) You might associate choice (A) *barreras*, meaning "obstacles," with the word *desafío*. But the sentence talks about the challenges of finding new sources of energy, so it is not about the obstacles to progress, but rather solutions. So (A) is wrong. (B) is wrong because *botellas* means "bottles." *Escaleras* are stairs, so (D) is also wrong. (C) means "fountains" or "sources."

4. (D) *Dictar* means "to give" in this sense. While it would be easy to try to make a false cognate out of "dictate terms," it would not make sense within the sentence. So (A) can be eliminated. *Dictar* used with *carta* has no meaning, either, so (B) is wrong. *Conferencia* means "lecture."

5. (D) You need the full form of *ninguno*, even though it is masculine singular, because the blank is immediately followed by *de*. *Apetecer* means "to sound good to eat," and you can remember it easily by associating it with *apetito*. Remember to look for double negatives.

6. (A) Think of *aplicada* in the sense of "applying" herself to her studies. *Acertada* means "correct." (C) and (D) make no sense.

7. (B) A *fábrica* is a "factory," a place where something is manufactured. The word for "cloth" is *tela*. Even if you did not know *sastre* (tailor"), you could have guessed the answer from the words *abrigo para el próximo año*. *Lana* means "wool." Other common materials used in making clothing are *algodón* ("cotton"), *seda* ("silk"), and *lienzo* ("linen").

8. (D) *Carreteras* are "highways," *conductores* are "drivers," and *tener cuidado* is "to be careful," so you need the word for trucks. *Camarones* is a word for "shrimp," so (B) is out. *Trucos* are "tricks" (a false cognate!), so (A) is wrong. *Frenos* (C) means "brakes."

9. (B) The word you want here is *el* without an accent. With an accent it is a subject pronoun and a prepositional pronoun. Without it, and with the word *de*, *el* means "the one of," and is used to avoid the repetition of the noun. The article you will use depends on the noun to which it refers.

10. (D) *Tocar* is "to play a musical instrument," while *jugar* is "to play a game."

11. (A) Some students "miss" their parents when they go away to school, so you would need *extrañar*. Another expression for "to miss" is *echar de menos*, so either one would have worked here. You do use (B) and (D) in talking about people, but neither one works in this context. *Peinar* means "to comb," so (C) is wrong.

12. (D) The other verbs in the sentence are second person singular. According to the meaning of the sentence, you need a command form here. Make sure you use the correct form for the negative *tú* command: the second person singular present subjunctive, which is *digas*.

13. (B) The speaker states that he will have the theme done for the next day. You want the past participle of *hacer*, which is irregular. (A) is wrong because while it has to do with "preview," the prefix *im* negates that meaning. *Imprevisto* has to do with not being able to preview.

14. (B) *Atar* means "to tie," which is what you do with shoelaces. *Tropezar* is "to trip over." The form of the verb is an affirmative familiar command. "*Rompe*" means "break," so (A) is wrong. Choice (C) *ahorra*, is "save (money)," and is out as well.

15. (C) The skirt is too long; it comes down to the ankles, *tobillos*. (A) *hombros* are "shoulders," and (B) *caderas* are "hips," so they are clearly wrong.

16. (B) The question is asking where the meeting will be. *Ser* can mean "to take place." Choice (C) *irá*, cannot be used because it would require a preposition at the very beginning of the sentence.

17. (B) You want to describe how hard it rained. *Llover a cántaros* is the Spanish equivalent of "to rain cats and dogs." *Al fin y al cabo* is "in the end," so (A) doesn't fit.

18. (A) The imperfect subjunctive is used in the clause following the blank, so you need a conjunction that requires the subjunctive. The conjunction should express proviso or condition to take the subjunctive. *Con tal que* is the only one that works. *Aunque* doesn't make any sense when used with the conditional tense in the first clause. *Sino que* is not to be confused with *sin que* which does require the subjunctive. *Ya que* does not take the subjunctive here; in fact, it makes no sense. You do not have to translate the whole sentence, just the verbs.

19. (C) Since the event has not happened, you cannot use *última*. *Más cerca* means "closer," but does not make sense here. This question should be easy because the feminine gender of *vez* is provided, thereby helping you eliminate *primer*.

20. (B) The word for "clerk" is *dependiente*. Don't confuse *duende* with *dueño*, which means "owner."

21. (C) You have to use *nos* reflexively in this sentence. The context limits the subject to the two people, Marta and the speaker. You can use *la* to mean "you," but only in the third person singular, and if the object is a female. *Se* cannot be used because the subject is first person plural. *Me* makes no sense, either, because the subject is "we." When the reflexive pronoun is used in this manner it means "when we see each other," indicating a reciprocal action. Remember to look for the reflexive pronoun when it is used to mean "each other."

22. (A) *En seguida* means "immediately," and is the correct answer. *Sin embargo*, means "nevertheless," *por casualidad* means "by chance," and *a continuación* means "below" or "continuing," none of which makes sense.

23. (A) Although you may not know that *osos* are "bears," you do know that the hikers did not see any of them. The adverb needs to communicate an emotion, such as relief. *Afortunadamente* is the best answer. *Cautelosamente* means "cautiously." One would approach bears cautiously, but the sentence does not deal with approaching them *Cotidianamente* means "on a daily basis," works if the hikers had seen bears every day. *Not* seeing bears, however, is a fortunate event.

24. (B) The word for "thick" is *gruesa*. It describes the kind of clothing you would wear to protect yourself from the cold.

25. (D) After a preposition you have to use a prepositional pronoun. *Hacia* is a preposition meaning "toward." *Mi* in choice (A) does not have an accent, so you cannot use it after the preposition. Without the accent, *mi* means "my." *Los* is an article, which would make no sense at all in the sentence, and it is also a direct object pronoun, third person masculine plural. That pronoun is grammatically incorrect in this sentence.

26. (D) At first glance, you may think you need a command form in this sentence, but no answer choice contains a command form. You could use a conjugated verb form, but the choices containing conjugated verbs are all tenses other than the past, which is used in *dijo*. That leaves *poniéndose* as the correct answer.

27. (A) This sentence requires use of the preterite of *querer*, with the meaning of "to refuse." The word *anoche* indicates that you cannot use the present tense of *querer*, since the time sequence would not make sense.

28. (C) The word you want is "so much," and the only word in Spanish is *tanto*. You have learned to use *tanto* in comparisons, but in this case it describes "traveling." Remember that infinitives are used as nouns. No other choice makes sense after *de* and before the infinitive.

29. (A) While *cientos*, choice (B), agrees in number with the noun it precedes, *especies* is feminine. Also, to use *cientos*, you would need *de* before the noun to mean "hundreds of" species of insects. The same would be true for *miles*.

30. (B) *Gustar* has a different subject in Spanish than it does in English. The subject is *trabalenguas*, but the noun is a compound noun, and is singular, in spite of the *-as* ending. The *lo* on *decirlo* is singular. It is not common to use a reflexive pronoun with *gustar*, so (A) can be eliminated. (C) and (D) are wrong, because the subject is singular.

31. (C) You need to use the present subjunctive because of *hemos pedido* in the main clause. With dependent noun clauses after verbs of volition (in other words, requests or orders), you must use the subjunctive. *Haya traído* is not correct because the action has not yet happened, and *ha traído* refers to the immediate past.

32. (C) *Has hecho*, the present perfect, is the answer, because the speaker is referring to something in the immediate past. Choice (A), *hace* is wrong because *te* tells you the speaker is a close friend of the person to whom he is speaking.

Part B

33. (B) The only word that works is *horas*. Don't be misled into thinking that *veces* is correct; even though the word *vez* is very commonly used, don't overlook other words that express time. *Épocas* refer to "eras," or "seasons." *Etapas* are "stages" as units of time.

34. (B) Since Laura is a woman, you have to use the feminine form of the past participle. Do not use the present participle as an adjective, even though it is done in English.

35. (D) You want an adjective describing the newspaper on the desk. *Desplegado* means "spread out." (C) *destacar* means "to stand out," (B) *colgar* means "to hang," and (A) *distraer* means "to distract." A word related to deliveries (newspaper or otherwise) is *repartir*, meaning "to deliver." A *repartidor* is someone who delivers something, such as a *repartidor de pizzas*.

36. (C) After the comma, you might be tempted to use a conjugated verb. But with no conjunction, the present participle is the best choice. If there were a conjugated verb in the second clause, a semicolon could separate the two clauses. Alternatively, a word like *mientras* would introduce the imperfect tense, or *cuando* would introduce the preterite. Even *y* could link the two clauses. (A) makes no sense because the time frame of the action is a specific moment. The preterite in the first clause defines the time of the event, and sets up the narrative of what Laura did. (D) is

wrong because there is no noun that it can modify in the masculine form. (B) won't fit because *fijamente*, meaning "hard," cannot describe an infinitive verb form.

37. (A) The verb following the blank is the imperfect subjective, so *como si* is the answer. It always takes the imperfect subjunctive.

38. (D) *El crepúsculo*, meaning "twilight," is a fairly common word in Spanish. The context is that it is getting dark and Laura can scarcely see the photo in the newspaper, so *ya no*, meaning "no longer," fits. Even if you do not know *crepúsculo*, you perhaps get the idea from the words *podía ver* and *encendió*. *Retrato* means "portrait," usually a portrait painting, but here it refers to the woman in the photo.

39. (D) *Encender* means "to turn on" something. There are several answer choices that you would turn on, though *luz* is the only one suitable in this context. (B) *ducha*, means "shower."

40. (C) *De* could be used in front of any of the four answer choices, but *de memoria*, the expression "by heart," is the only one that makes sense. *De acuerdo* means "to be in agreement" with someone (Remember that *acordarse de* means "to remember"). *De noche* means "night time."

41. (C) You need a verb that will take an infinitive to complete its meaning, or that will act as the object of the conjugated verb. That means you can eliminate (B) and (D). Both of those verbs do take objects, but usually not infinitives functioning as nouns. Also, *reír* is not something that you would give, take, or carry. That leaves (A) and (C); both verbs can take infinitives as objects. *Deber* means "to ought," or "to owe," neither of which makes sense. (C) *hacían* must be the answer. If you were confused about the subject, look back to the plural noun *cosas*, which is the subject, not Lucas.

42. (D) Since *a* is a preposition, you need to find an object of the preposition pronoun. Seeing *los niños* after the blank might make you think you need a third person plural pronoun, but that is not among the answer choices. Later in the text you see the words *mi hermana y yo*, telling you that the first person plural is a possibilty. Since *ellas* is not the right gender to go with *los niños*, (C) is out. (A) *me*, is not an object of the preposition pronoun; in fact, *me* is a distracter, because it looks like the English word "me." You have to use *nosotros*.

43. (B) You need to scan the whole paragraph to understand that the only vocabulary word that fits here is *extraordinario*. (A) is wrong because they seem to know him very well. Similarly, (C) is wrong because he is not *chistoso* to them. He makes the older people laugh, but not the children. He certainly is not boring, *aburrido*, to them, because they are in awe of him.

44. (A) The word *una especia de amor, temor, y admiración* after the blank tells you that you need a word that has to do with feelings. *Experimentar* means "to feel," so it is a false cognate. It is a good word to remember. A synonym for *experimentar* is *sentir*, which is the correct answer.

45. (C) The subject of the verb is *nosotros*, so the third person choices are incorrect. There is also no reason to use the subjunctive. The word *nunca* before the blank gives you a clue about the verbal tense to use. It also helps to remember that *volver a* means "again."

46. (D) This question is related to the next one. Lucas was so "something," that he lost "something" and could not find it. The clue is in the word *perdió*. If he lost something, then he would not be *atento*, "attentive," nor *cuidadoso*, "careful." *Mimado* means "spoiled," which makes no sense. That leaves *viejo*, "old."

47. (C) You know that Lucas was old. What he lost, being so old, was a year. You may associate *concurso*, *partido*, and *juego* with winning and losing. But in this text, Lucas is not involved in a competition, so (A), (B), and (D) are not good answers. He could lose a last game, but it would not be something he could go looking for and find.

48. (B) This vocabulary word has to do with food. He prepares his own food, so the word *guisos* is the correct answer. *Partos* means "birth," so (D) is completely wrong. *Folletos* are "pamphlets," and *guiones* are "scripts," among other meanings, so they are out as well.

49. (A) The expression that fits this context is *a menudo*, meaning "often." *En cuanto* means "as soon as," but is an adverbial conjunction that is not needed here. *A causa* means "because of," a good replacement for *porque*. *A medida* is usually followed by *que* and expresses the idea of something taking place concurrently with another event.

50. (C) *Cara* "face," *comida* "food," and *mano* "hand," are all items you can wash, but the rest of the sentence states that he beat them with a stick to make them clean. The most logical choice is *ropa*, "clothes." The pronoun *la* on the end of the present participle *dando* indicates that the object is feminine singular. Remember that *mano* is a feminine noun, even though it ends in -*o*.

51. (B) The word *hechicería* is a clue here. But if you do not know that it means "witchcraft," you'll have to rely on the context of the passage to tell you that *malignas* is the word you want. The words *abandonó a su hermana* give you the idea that Huitzilopochtli left his sister Malinalxochtli for some reason. *Facultades* means "powers" or "talents" (though in the context of schools, it refers to a school, or a discipline, such as law). If she had good powers, choice (C), that would not be a reason for her brother to leave her. *Cautelosas* means "careful," so (D) is wrong, too.

52. (A) If you know that *aprovechar* means "to take advantage of," then this choice is not hard. *Enviar*, choice (C), means "to send."

53. (A) This blank is the verb in the main clause of the sentence, so you need a conjugated verb. In the text, *ésta* is not a verb, but rather a demonstrative pronoun, referring to Malinalxochtli. Use the preterite to narrate what happened while the sister was sleeping. You may be tempted to use the present perfect, *se ha marchado*, but it is wrong because the time sequence makes no sense.

54. (D) The use of the preterite in the verb following this blank should alert you to using *cuando*. You would normally use the imperfect after *mientras*.

55. (A) This blank calls for a relative pronoun. Both *el que* and *quien* are relative pronouns, but only one is correct because the pronoun refers to a place, *lugar*, instead of to a person. *Cual* can also be a relative pronoun with an article, but there is no article in (C). *Cuanto* means "how much," and does not fit. In this case, *el que* implies a selection of places, "the one where" finally she established Malinalco.

56. (B) In order to use *más* or *menos* before *hora y media*, you would need the preposition *de*. (C) *solo* is an adjective, meaning "lone," or "alone." (B) *sólo* is a short form of *solamente*, an adverb.

57. (B) Look to see what is surrounded by mountains and rivers. You could have a corral (A), but according to the text, the item refers to Malinalco, a town. You may have looked at the adjective, *enclavado*, and thought of *clavos*, meaning "nails," and thought you needed a 'place where you would nail something.' A *muro* is a "wall," but not the kind you find forming rooms in a house, so (D) is wrong. *Canto* is a kind of *song*; do not confuse it with *campo*. The word that fits all the requirements in this passage is *valle*.

58. (A) *Parecen* (B) means "to seem," which does not make sense after *donde* when used in the plural form. You would need *aparecer* in order for the meaning "to appear" to fit the context. *Brotar* means "to spring forth," as in fruits and plants sprouting. It is the correct answer.

Part C
Questions 59–64

This passage is a discussion between two travelers. The crucial point in the passage is the reply the old man gives to the *chileno*. He says he is not an employee of the railroad, though he does work. From his manner and the light-hearted way he speaks, and from the way he hungrily eats and drinks his meals, it is apparent that he works hard. The question is, where? And, for whom? One of the things that makes this passage difficult to interpret is the dialogue. There is little elaboration and you have to note implied meanings, as well as reactions to what has been said.

59. (A) The words *sólo tenían asado de tira*, and at the end, *llegó la carne*, and *libertó el cubierto de la servilleta de papel*, all indicate that he is eating a meal. You might suspect that he is a waiter, but with more clarification from the passage, you realize he is eating some kind of a meal.

60. (C) The old man does not actually refuse to answer the questions, so (A) is wrong. And the *chileno* does *not* want to bother the man, which is the opposite of what (B) says. There is no indication he has something to hide from the old man, so (D) is wrong. The answer is (C), because the old man did not give him a full answer.

61. (B) *Alimento* is another word for *comida*, "food." (Another word for "food" is *comestibles*. Do not get fixated on one word for a vocabulary item. Learn synonyms when possible.)

62. (C) With *acababa de* in the text, we know that the *chileno* has "just" eaten, so he declines the old man's offer. Answer choice (C) means "He has eaten a short while ago," so it is the answer.

63. (C) The tone of the conversation is neither *enigmático* ("mysterious") nor *iracundo* ("angry"). Nor is it "erudite," meaning "scholarly." The tone is rather friendly, choice (C).

64. (B) By now it is apparent that there are several distracters in the text, but that the two men are hobos. When the old man says he "works" the railroad, but not as an employee, you could get the idea. You know he is not a waiter (A), a train conductor (D), or a repairman (C). Rather, he made his living any way that he could.

Question 65

65. (C) *Planear una batalla* ("plan a battle") is completely wrong, as this is a book about hotels. (D) is wrong because *alejarse* is "to go away," but you wouldn't want to "get away" from a tranquil life (you would want just the opposite!) (C) means "a guide of places to stay."

66. (C) All of the answer choices name types of people who would use hotels, but only (C), travelers looking for something different, would want to find tranquil, intimate places to stay. Certainly not business people (A), or people looking for employment (B), or hotel owners (D). The text in the ad says it is for people on vacation who need a guide book.

Questions 67–71

This passage deals with a bicyclist in a race. At the beginning he talks about how he is beginning the race, getting ready for it, coming out of the tent, hearing the starter's pistol, and how he is placed in the pack during the race.

67. (B) There is a first person narrator for this text. When you see the words *Voy a ganar*, you know that the narrator is participating in the race, so *ciclista* is the best choice. An *árbitro* is a referee.

68. (B) *Competencia* in (B) is a competition; you probably picked this answer right away. (D) is wrong, because even though *carrera* can mean "race," the meaning it has in this answer choice is "career." Though he remembers what the trainers say, he is not a trainer himself, so (C) is wrong.

69. (C) The narrator feels invincible when he begins the race. He knows it will be difficult for the other racer to overtake him. He feels somewhat compassionate toward the other racer, indicated by *Sentí piedad por el muchacho, por el equipo, por su entrenador. Piedad* is "pity." The narrator does not feel worried or bothered, so (A) and (D) are wrong.

70. (B) *Seguir* means "to follow." The other boy has instructions to stay with the leader as long as he can, *si toma la delantera, pégate a él hasta donde aguantes*. In this context, *pegar* means "to stick to," not "to hit." Notice the narrator uses the conditional tense in *tendría al muchacho*, meaning that "I would have him." Pizarnick is not to keep his distance (D), but rather to keep up with the narrator as long as he can. *Trasera* means "rear" as in a back seat position. That is where the narrator sees Pizarnick, and that is where the other boy stays. *Delantera* refers to the lead position.

71. (C) The narrator is clearly thinking of defeating his competition. If you were looking for the word *ganar* in (A), be careful. In (A), the subject is wrong. *Vencerá* also works. If you did not notice the verb, you should have noticed *con facilidad*, meaning "with ease." (D) refers to a "career in law," which is completely off the topic.

Questions 72–77

This passage is about a narrator who finds himself at a train station in the midst of a gathering of people, when suddenly, some soldiers appear. When the soldiers appear and fan out as if expecting an ambush, the people seem to evaporate into thin air. Almost simultaneously, a train comes into sight, described as if it were a large green animal with a yellow scar across its belly.

72. (A) You may not recognize *sudar* ("to sweat") in the first paragraph, but the text does say *sentía frío*. The reason the narrator felt cold, though, is that those were "times of fear." The man was sweating, even though he was fearful, which means it was a hot day. The soldiers arriving as they did also underscores the man's correct assessment of his situation. The fact that there was not a cloud in the sky, choice (D), does not help decide whether it was hot or cold. (B) indicates just that the weather was bad, not what the weather was, as the question asks.

73. (C) The clue word is *maleta*. The text does not say that the narrator is seated on the train platform, just that he is on his suitcase. But he can clearly see the whole scene. He is probably just outside a station.

74. (B) The *seres totémicos* are people selling things, *vendedores*. The words *apilaron sus mercancías* give you that information. The narrator does not appear to have any friends there, so (A) is out. There is no reference to railroad workers, so (C) is wrong as well.

75. (C) *Esfumarse* means "to vanish." In that same sentece in the text, *ocupara* is in the past subjunctive, so that relates things that may not have happened. The word *alegre* seems out of place in this passage. When you see the subjunctive, you can imagine that the happy festival did not take place, then, because the sound of that "secret signal" warned people that the soldiers were coming, and they left. They were dispersed by the time the soldiers arrived because they had been warned.

76. (C) The word *bélica* in choice (C) means "war-like." The soldiers expected hostile action, so they fanned out in a defensive formation. (B) is wrong because a *recepción acogedora* is a "welcoming reception."

77. (B) The atmosphere in the scene is *desasosegado*, "uneasy." (A) *festivo* is wrong because the festival disappeared before it ever got started. You also couldn't call the scene "tranquil," so (D) is wrong. (C) *superado* means "overcome," as in rising above obstacles, so that doesn't fit the context.

Questions 78–85

This passage deals with an event that happened to a young girl. She was going to school one day with her brother and father, when another driver ran a red light and hit their car. She wound up in the hospital in a coma. The main point of the story is that when they brought her pet dog to her bedside, she regained consciousness. As a result, she attributes her recovery to her dog as well as to medicine. She is a proponent for the humane treatment of animals, especially dogs, as a result of her experience.

78. (B) When this situation occured, the narrator must have been around 12. She was not able to drive herself, so (C) and (D) can be eliminated. And three years of age, choice (A), sounds too young. *Suceder* is a frequently used verb meaning "to happen," as are *pasar* and *ocurrir*.

79. (B) The accident did not occur while they were walking to school, so (A) is out. Nothing says she and her brother distracted her father, so (D) is wrong. A *semáforo* is a traffic light, so (B) means "A man did not pay attention to the traffic light and caused the accident."

80. (C) After the accident, the man left without saying anything, indicated by the words *desapareciendo luego del lugar*. Don't be misled by words you recognize from the text in the other answer choices; they are used incorrectly.

81. (A) As a consequence of the accident, the narrator suffered serious injuries. She already had a dog, so (B) is wrong, as is (C), since she received no gifts from the doctor. (D) means she left with no damage, so that is wrong as well.

82. (D) The narrator had such a strong bond with her dog, that she was able to respond when the mention of him came up. The doctor did not want her dog, so (B) is wrong. And the dog could not communicate with her, so (C) is wrong. In effect, her love for her dog "willed" her to speak.

83. (B) This narrator clearly wants to communicate that dogs deserve more respect than they get. She has no kind words for people who say that dogs are only animals.

84. (A) At the end of the passage, the narrator draws a comparison between people and dogs. Dogs ask little in return for their affection. Certainly she does not claim that dogs have supernatural powers, so (C) is clearly out. Nor does she claim that dogs can cure ills better than doctors, so (D) is wrong as well.

85. (D) There is no attempt to entertain, so (C) is wrong. *Regañarse* means "to scold" the dogs, which is the opposite of what she does, so (B) is clearly wrong. The narrator wants to urge people to treat dogs with more affection, choice (D).

Practice Test 4

Answer Grid
Practice Test 4

1. Ⓐ Ⓑ Ⓒ Ⓓ Ⓔ
2. Ⓐ Ⓑ Ⓒ Ⓓ Ⓔ
3. Ⓐ Ⓑ Ⓒ Ⓓ Ⓔ
4. Ⓐ Ⓑ Ⓒ Ⓓ Ⓔ
5. Ⓐ Ⓑ Ⓒ Ⓓ Ⓔ
6. Ⓐ Ⓑ Ⓒ Ⓓ Ⓔ
7. Ⓐ Ⓑ Ⓒ Ⓓ Ⓔ
8. Ⓐ Ⓑ Ⓒ Ⓓ Ⓔ
9. Ⓐ Ⓑ Ⓒ Ⓓ Ⓔ
10. Ⓐ Ⓑ Ⓒ Ⓓ Ⓔ
11. Ⓐ Ⓑ Ⓒ Ⓓ Ⓔ
12. Ⓐ Ⓑ Ⓒ Ⓓ Ⓔ
13. Ⓐ Ⓑ Ⓒ Ⓓ Ⓔ
14. Ⓐ Ⓑ Ⓒ Ⓓ Ⓔ
15. Ⓐ Ⓑ Ⓒ Ⓓ Ⓔ
16. Ⓐ Ⓑ Ⓒ Ⓓ Ⓔ
17. Ⓐ Ⓑ Ⓒ Ⓓ Ⓔ
18. Ⓐ Ⓑ Ⓒ Ⓓ Ⓔ
19. Ⓐ Ⓑ Ⓒ Ⓓ Ⓔ
20. Ⓐ Ⓑ Ⓒ Ⓓ Ⓔ
21. Ⓐ Ⓑ Ⓒ Ⓓ Ⓔ
22. Ⓐ Ⓑ Ⓒ Ⓓ Ⓔ
23. Ⓐ Ⓑ Ⓒ Ⓓ Ⓔ
24. Ⓐ Ⓑ Ⓒ Ⓓ Ⓔ
25. Ⓐ Ⓑ Ⓒ Ⓓ Ⓔ
26. Ⓐ Ⓑ Ⓒ Ⓓ Ⓔ
27. Ⓐ Ⓑ Ⓒ Ⓓ Ⓔ
28. Ⓐ Ⓑ Ⓒ Ⓓ Ⓔ
29. Ⓐ Ⓑ Ⓒ Ⓓ Ⓔ

30. Ⓐ Ⓑ Ⓒ Ⓓ Ⓔ
31. Ⓐ Ⓑ Ⓒ Ⓓ Ⓔ
32. Ⓐ Ⓑ Ⓒ Ⓓ Ⓔ
33. Ⓐ Ⓑ Ⓒ Ⓓ Ⓔ
34. Ⓐ Ⓑ Ⓒ Ⓓ Ⓔ
35. Ⓐ Ⓑ Ⓒ Ⓓ Ⓔ
36. Ⓐ Ⓑ Ⓒ Ⓓ Ⓔ
37. Ⓐ Ⓑ Ⓒ Ⓓ Ⓔ
38. Ⓐ Ⓑ Ⓒ Ⓓ Ⓔ
39. Ⓐ Ⓑ Ⓒ Ⓓ Ⓔ
40. Ⓐ Ⓑ Ⓒ Ⓓ Ⓔ
41. Ⓐ Ⓑ Ⓒ Ⓓ Ⓔ
42. Ⓐ Ⓑ Ⓒ Ⓓ Ⓔ
43. Ⓐ Ⓑ Ⓒ Ⓓ Ⓔ
44. Ⓐ Ⓑ Ⓒ Ⓓ Ⓔ
45. Ⓐ Ⓑ Ⓒ Ⓓ Ⓔ
46. Ⓐ Ⓑ Ⓒ Ⓓ Ⓔ
47. Ⓐ Ⓑ Ⓒ Ⓓ Ⓔ
48. Ⓐ Ⓑ Ⓒ Ⓓ Ⓔ
49. Ⓐ Ⓑ Ⓒ Ⓓ Ⓔ
50. Ⓐ Ⓑ Ⓒ Ⓓ Ⓔ
51. Ⓐ Ⓑ Ⓒ Ⓓ Ⓔ
52. Ⓐ Ⓑ Ⓒ Ⓓ Ⓔ
53. Ⓐ Ⓑ Ⓒ Ⓓ Ⓔ
54. Ⓐ Ⓑ Ⓒ Ⓓ Ⓔ
55. Ⓐ Ⓑ Ⓒ Ⓓ Ⓔ
56. Ⓐ Ⓑ Ⓒ Ⓓ Ⓔ
57. Ⓐ Ⓑ Ⓒ Ⓓ Ⓔ
58. Ⓐ Ⓑ Ⓒ Ⓓ Ⓔ

59. Ⓐ Ⓑ Ⓒ Ⓓ Ⓔ
60. Ⓐ Ⓑ Ⓒ Ⓓ Ⓔ
61. Ⓐ Ⓑ Ⓒ Ⓓ Ⓔ
62. Ⓐ Ⓑ Ⓒ Ⓓ Ⓔ
63. Ⓐ Ⓑ Ⓒ Ⓓ Ⓔ
64. Ⓐ Ⓑ Ⓒ Ⓓ Ⓔ
65. Ⓐ Ⓑ Ⓒ Ⓓ Ⓔ
66. Ⓐ Ⓑ Ⓒ Ⓓ Ⓔ
67. Ⓐ Ⓑ Ⓒ Ⓓ Ⓔ
68. Ⓐ Ⓑ Ⓒ Ⓓ Ⓔ
69. Ⓐ Ⓑ Ⓒ Ⓓ Ⓔ
70. Ⓐ Ⓑ Ⓒ Ⓓ Ⓔ
71. Ⓐ Ⓑ Ⓒ Ⓓ Ⓔ
72. Ⓐ Ⓑ Ⓒ Ⓓ Ⓔ
73. Ⓐ Ⓑ Ⓒ Ⓓ Ⓔ
74. Ⓐ Ⓑ Ⓒ Ⓓ Ⓔ
75. Ⓐ Ⓑ Ⓒ Ⓓ Ⓔ
76. Ⓐ Ⓑ Ⓒ Ⓓ Ⓔ
77. Ⓐ Ⓑ Ⓒ Ⓓ Ⓔ
78. Ⓐ Ⓑ Ⓒ Ⓓ Ⓔ
79. Ⓐ Ⓑ Ⓒ Ⓓ Ⓔ
80. Ⓐ Ⓑ Ⓒ Ⓓ Ⓔ
81. Ⓐ Ⓑ Ⓒ Ⓓ Ⓔ
82. Ⓐ Ⓑ Ⓒ Ⓓ Ⓔ
83. Ⓐ Ⓑ Ⓒ Ⓓ Ⓔ
84. Ⓐ Ⓑ Ⓒ Ⓓ Ⓔ
85. Ⓐ Ⓑ Ⓒ Ⓓ Ⓔ

Practice Test 4

Part A

Directions: Select the most appropriate word to complete the sentence and fill in the corresponding oval on the answer sheet.

1. Señora Ramírez, ¿podría Rosa salir para ___ conmigo en el parque?

    (A) tocar
    (B) llevar
    (C) jugar
    (D) tomar

2. Si ___ frío puedo prestarte un suéter.

    (A) haces
    (B) estás
    (C) tienes
    (D) eres

3. Las pocas ___ que oí me parecían muy débiles.

    (A) épocas
    (B) voces
    (C) mesas
    (D) veces

4. Es difícil calcular cuánto tiempo toma volar ___ hay muchos cambios de zonas.

    (A) sino que
    (B) auque
    (C) porque
    (D) pero

5. ___ de mis mapas me indica la ruta más directa a la ciudad.

    (A) Nada
    (B) Ningún
    (C) Ninguna
    (D) Ninguno

6. Se puede cruzar ese rió fácilmente porque no es muy ___.

    (A) denso
    (B) hondo
    (C) suave
    (D) flojo

7. Busco una ___ barata para un vuelo entre Miami y Santiago de Chile.

    (A) copa
    (B) rata
    (C) tarifa
    (D) tasa

8. ¡Qué linda fue la boda el año pasado en ___ medieval de Valencia!

    (A) la inglesa
    (B) el catedrático
    (C) la iglesia
    (D) el siglo

9. Parece que en estos días todo el mundo sólo se preocupa de ___.

    (A) la suya
    (B) lo suyo
    (C) cuyo
    (D) suyo

GO ON TO THE NEXT PAGE

10. Le ___ diez dólares al hombre por la entrada al club.

    (A) cobró
    (B) ahogó
    (C) regateó
    (D) repartió

11. El pobre deportista sufría porque los zapatos no le ___ bien.

    (A) caían
    (B) cabían
    (C) lucían
    (D) parecían

12. Vds. ___ más tarde cómo salieron en el examen de ayer.

    (A) sabían
    (B) han sabido
    (C) supieron
    (D) sabrán

13. A lo lejos la cumbre de la montaña pareció completamente ___ de nieve.

    (A) descrita
    (B) girada
    (C) cubierta
    (D) vuelta

14. Los niños van a ___ al ver los payasos cómicos del circo.

    (A) reír
    (B) llorar
    (C) estudiar
    (D) dormir

15. Si el servicio del café es bueno, vale dejar ___ en la mesa para el camarero.

    (A) un piropo
    (B) un propuesto
    (C) una propina
    (D) una promesa

16. Qué raro fue ___ por el bosque de noche con todos los ruidos espantosos.

    (A) viaja
    (B) viajar
    (C) viajado
    (D) viajando

17. Cuando llegues, necesitas llamarme ___, para que no me preocupe de ti demasiado.

    (A) sin querer
    (B) sin falta
    (C) apenas
    (D) no obstante

18. ___ no he recibido una carta de mi hermana que salió la semana pasada.

    (A) Más
    (B) Nunca
    (C) Pronto
    (D) Todavía

19. Necesito comprar una ___ nueva para cubrir el suelo en la sala de estar.

    (A) alfombra
    (B) almohada
    (C) pluma
    (D) tapa

20. Me gustó mucho la ___ postal con la foto de las montañas.

    (A) pintura
    (B) tarjeta
    (C) letra
    (D) casa

21. Prefiero unos calcetines de algodón si ___ tiene Vd.

    (A) el
    (B) lo
    (C) los
    (D) ellos

GO ON TO THE NEXT PAGE

22. Recibió cien por cien en el examen, ___ salió primero.

    (A) a propósito
    (B) mediante
    (C) por eso
    (D) sin embargo

23. El gato persiguió el pájaro ___ , pero el sonido de la campana en el cuello lo denunció.

    (A) sigilosamente
    (B) sumamente
    (C) inmediatamente
    (D) secamente

24. Este jarro ya no sirve para agua porque está ___ .

    (A) completo
    (B) lleno
    (C) vacío
    (D) roto

25. Compare Vd. sus gastos de teléfono con ___ de nuestra compañía.

    (A) el
    (B) él
    (C) ellos
    (D) los

26. Miguel, ___ a tu dormitorio hasta que te llame otra vez.

    (A) te hayas ido
    (B) te vayas
    (C) vete
    (D) va

27. ___ el chile un alimento básico, ha llegado a ser alimento popular por todas partes.

    (A) Sea
    (B) Ser
    (C) Sido
    (D) Siendo

28. Cuando llegué, no vi a ninguo de mis amigo ___ no habían llegado todavía.

    (A) apenas
    (B) sin embargo
    (C) también
    (D) puesto que

29. Tienes que pagar el alquiler el ___ del mes.

    (A) primer
    (B) primero
    (C) permiso
    (D) premio

30. ___ decir que no todo salió como lo habíamos planeado.

    (A) Basta
    (B) Hasta
    (C) Hacia
    (D) Tiene

31. Haremos este viaje otra vez si ___ la oportunidad.

    (A) tenemos
    (B) tengamos
    (C) tuviéramos
    (D) hemos tenido

32. Superando sus debilidades ___ el nivel de jugar un deporte.

    (A) mejorarse
    (B) se mejora
    (C) se mejoren
    (D) mejorándose

GO ON TO THE NEXT PAGE

Part B

Directions: First read through the entire paragraph. Then, for each numbered blank, choose the completion that is most appropriate given the context of the passage. Fill in the corresponding oval on the answer sheet.

Mi madre asegura que en las (33) ciudades se vive de una manera (34) con la plenitud de una sabiduría que (35) conoceremos. Ella reprueba la (36) de la provincia en que habitamos y (37) a aprender los dialectos con los que se entienden los pueblos (38) que nos rodean. Pero yo sé que ella conoce la mayoría de esos dialectos. Mi madre afirma que su tristeza y la mía son (39) por el monótono sopor de la provincia y que estamos tan (40) de su naturaleza como el esclavo a la piedra.

33. (A) gran
    (B) grande
    (C) grandes
    (D) grandísimos

34. (A) chistosa
    (B) culta
    (C) empobrecida
    (D) simple

35. (A) jamás
    (B) ningún
    (C) según
    (D) hasta

36. (A) inteligencia
    (B) nobleza
    (C) tienda
    (D) sencillez

37. (A) se niega
    (B) trata
    (C) pierde
    (D) se alegra

38. (A) alertos
    (B) oprimidos
    (C) estrechos
    (D) sacudidos

39. (A) producido
    (B) producidas
    (C) productos
    (D) produciendo

40. (A) felices
    (B) adivinadas
    (C) subrayadas
    (D) cautivas

GO ON TO THE NEXT PAGE

Cuando yo llegaba del colegio por la tarde, iba directamente a la planta baja, y (41) mi bicicleta nueva (42) vuelta tras vuelta por el estrecho jardín del fondo de la casa, (43) en torno al árbol y al par de bancos de hierro. Detrás de la tapia, los nogales de la otra casa comenzaban a mostrar un leve bozo primaveral, (44) yo no hacía caso de las (45) y sus regalos porque tenía cosas (46) graves en que pensar. Y (47) sabía que nadie bajaba al jardín hasta que el (48) de pleno verano lo (49) urgente, era el mejor (50) para meditar sobre lo que en casa sucedía.

41. (A) pintando
    (B) montando
    (C) describiendo
    (D) regando

42. (A) ponía
    (B) volaba
    (C) daba
    (D) mecía

43. (A) centrado
    (B) extrañado
    (C) rodeado
    (D) podido

44. (A) sino
    (B) sino que
    (C) también
    (D) pero

45. (A) estaciones
    (B) cortinas
    (C) paredes
    (D) casas

46. (A) demasiada
    (B) demasiados
    (C) demasiadas
    (D) demasiado

47. (A) ya no
    (B) tanto
    (C) más
    (D) como

48. (A) socorro
    (B) ahogo
    (C) humor
    (D) apoyo

49. (A) hace
    (B) haga
    (C) hizo
    (D) hiciera

50. (A) aliento
    (B) cuarto
    (C) sitio
    (D) caso

GO ON TO THE NEXT PAGE

Amores imposibles han sido los (51) ingredientes que (52) décadas han mantenido grandes audiencias (53) a los televisores. Estas telenovelas son los programas más criticados (54) también los más vistos. Esto motivó a (55) grupo a crear la primera telenovela en (56) los personajes son caricaturas: blanca y pura.

Después de dos años de trabajo, (57) el programa popular, veintiséis capítulos que demuestran que el secreto del éxito consiste en saber cómo (58) la historia.

56. (A) que
    (B) quien
    (C) cuya
    (D) cual

57. (A) se realizó
    (B) se escondió
    (C) se dio cuenta
    (D) se estrechó

58. (A) borrar
    (B) enterrar
    (C) contar
    (D) impedir

51. (A) pequeños
    (B) eruditos
    (C) inagotables
    (D) insoportables

52. (A) hace
    (B) hacen
    (C) han hecho
    (D) hacían

53. (A) detrás
    (B) frente
    (C) sobre
    (D) lejos

54. (A) según
    (B) sino que
    (C) tampoco
    (D) pero

55. (A) uno
    (B) cierto
    (C) propio
    (D) alguno

GO ON TO THE NEXT PAGE

Part C

Directions: Read the following texts carefully. Then, for each question that follows, select the best answer according to the text. Fill in the corresponding oval on the answer sheet.

Línea   —¿Señora Pérez?
       —Diga, señor.
       —Soy un amigo de su hijo Pedro, señora. Él me pidió si podía venir a verla.
(5)   —¿De Pedrito? Gracias a Dios. No sabe la alegría que me da, señor. Adelante, pase, pase, no vaya a tomar frío, señor, qué bueno, que linda sorpresa. ¿Y cómo está Pedrito? Porque le voy a decir que no me escribe a menudo. Es un
(10) hijo excelente. No es que me lamente. Me llega regularmente plata que él me manda desde Kansas. ¿Usted también viene de Kansas?
       —Sí, señora. Trabajamos juntos.
       —¿Y cómo está Pedro? ¿Cómo lo dejó?
(15) —Justamente, señora, a eso vengo. Traigo buenas noticias. Pedro va a casarse.
       —¿Se va a casar? ¿Pedrito? Tan repentino, Madre Purísima. Pero ¿de qué me estoy quejando? Casarse. Qué linda noticia, señor. Perdone, pero la
(20) verdad es que me quedé sin aliento con la noticia. Ud. sabe, una piensa que los hijos son como si recién nacidos, se los imagina indefensos. Ya era hora, pero .... ¿Y para cuándo es la boda, si es que hay fecha?
(25) —Justamente, señora, para eso tenía que venir a verla. Su hijo le manda dinero para comprarse un pasaje.

59. ¿Con quién habla la señora Pérez?

   (A) un pariente
   (B) el cartero
   (C) un mensajero
   (D) un noticiero

60. ¿Qué noticias trae el señor?

   (A) recuerdos de un antiguo amigo
   (B) detalles de su trabajo en Kansas
   (C) un acontecimiento que sucederá
   (D) un reportaje de la vida en el extranjero

61. Al principio de la conversación, parece que la Señora Pérez

   (A) está enojada.
   (B) está agradecida.
   (C) lamenta la visita.
   (D) está confundida.

62. ¿A qué se refiere "plata" en la línea 11?

   (A) dinero
   (B) tesoro
   (C) comida
   (D) joyas

63. Parece que la relación entre madre e hijo es

   (A) muy buena, como era cuando era niño.
   (B) constante a pesar de la distancia.
   (C) tenue debido a la distancia entre ellos.
   (D) estrecha porque así debe ser.

64. Al final, el dinero mencionado en la línea 26, es para pagar por

   (A) la comida para la mamá.
   (B) un boleto para la mamá.
   (C) el viaje del amigo de Pedrito.
   (D) el hospedaje del amigo en casa de la mamá.

GO ON TO THE NEXT PAGE

65. Según este anuncio ¿cuál es una de las ventajas de un teléfono portátil?

   (A) Puedes ignorar las llamadas deseadas.
   (B) Siempre estarás al alcance de alguien con buenas noticias.
   (C) Nunca sabrás si ganaste un millón a menos que estés en casa.
   (D) La llamada millonaria siempre se hace por teléfono portátil.

GO ON TO THE NEXT PAGE

Línea Decir San Fermín es invocar Pamplona, tanto
como decir encierro o pensar en la fiesta en que
se celebran las fiestas y las carreras en su honor.
Lo que no sabe el forastero es que San Fermín
(5) tampoco es (ni nunca fue) patrono de Pamplona.
Antiguamente, los toros caminaban hasta el
corral de la plaza por medio de una singular
carrera a través de las calles de la ciudad. Los
pastores iban detrás y algunos vecinos de
(10) Pamplona castigaban a los animales cuando
pasaban junto a las cercas. Con el tiempo, se pasó
de correr detrás a correr delante.
En la actualidad, dos cohetes anuncian
el principio de las carreras por un tramo
(15) urbano, siguen unos pocos minutos en que los
pamploneses siguen con el aliento contenido,
frente a la radio o pegados a la televisión, en la
esperanza de que la emoción sea mucha y los
percances escasos. Aunque se ha mejorado el
(20) firme y se han suavizado algunos obstáculos del
camino, el estado de los corredores no siempre
es el óptimo. Por último, la autoridad ve a los
corredores para que únicamente corran aquellas
personas que estén en condiciones de hacerlo.

66. Lo que se celebran en las fiestas de San
    Fermín es

    (A) lo rápido que corren los toros.
    (B) lo valiente que son los forasteros.
    (C) la relación entre el santo y la ciudad.
    (D) la importancia del turismo en Pamplona.

67. ¿Por dónde pasan los toros en las carreras?

    (A) la plaza
    (B) el corral
    (C) las calles
    (D) los encierros

68. Según la selección, antiguamente los
    pamploneses

    (A) se jubilaban cuando los toros pasaban
        junto a las cercas.
    (B) permitán que corrieran los toros muchas
        veces por las calles.
    (C) gritaban para hacer que los toros
        corrieran más rápido.
    (D) dejaban a los pastores correr detrás de
        los animales.

69. Actualmente, las carreras empiezan cuando

    (A) suena el ruido de fuegos artificiales.
    (B) los corredores entran en las calles,
    (C) los pamploneses encienden sus
        televisores.
    (D) se abre la puerta del corral de la plaza.

70. A medida que corren los toros, ¿qué hacen
    los pamploneses hoy en día?

    (A) Esperan ver algún percance.
    (B) Suavizan los obstáculos del camino.
    (C) Se emocionan escuchando las noticias.
    (D) No prestan ninguna atención al suceso.

71. La autoridad municipal aconseja a los
    corredores que

    (A) la eviten si es posible.
    (B) se entrenen para estar en forma.
    (C) busquen tantos percances que puedan.
    (D) estudien la ruta de las carreras.

GO ON TO THE NEXT PAGE

Línea   A las tres de la tarde un grupo de jóvenes
sin camiseta camina por una de las polvorosas
calles de una zona de Cali, en donde es bien
conocido el problema de falta de oportunidades
(5) entre los habitantes. Se acercan y saludan a dos
líderes que hace cinco años se unieron para
crear la corporación para los jóvenes. Todos van
a reunirse con los funcionarios de la Alcaldía,
que semanalmente los visitan para escucharlos
(10) y adelantar un programa de educación y
capacitación que busca mejorar la calidad de vida
de más de ciento cincuenta jóvenes vinculados a
la corporación. "No queremos que se repitan los
errores del pasado."
(15)   Esta vez la administración ha dejado en manos
de los jóvenes el desarrollo de proyectos de
capacitación empresarial. No se trata de regalar
empleo, sino abrir espacios de trabajo. Dice un
joven, "Por primera vez, sentimos que confían en
(20) nosotros y nos dan la oportunidad de demostrar
nuestras capacidades." De la administración
reciben un auxilio de transporte para movilizarse,
un representante para contratar con la Alcaldía
por su parte, y reconocimiento por su buen
(25) trabajo y contribución al mantenimiento del
espacio público en la ciudad.

72. La selección enfoca en un grupo de jóvenes
que viven en

(A) un barrio próspero.
(B) un barrio desventajado.
(C) una región fecunda.
(D) un vecindario cómodo.

73. Los jóvenes y sus líderes van a encontrarse con

(A) sus padres.
(B) sus profesores.
(C) un grupo de clientes.
(D) unos delegados municipales.

74. ¿Por qué viene la Alcaldía a visitar a los
jóvenes?

(A) Les aconseja estar contentos como son.
(B) Quiere venderles una corporación.
(C) Está tratando de mejorar su vida.
(D) Quiere repetir la historia pasada.

75. ¿Qué significan las palabras de la línea 18,
"sino abrir espacios de trabajo?"

(A) Los adultos van a tomar todas las
decisiones.
(B) Los adultos van a regalarles trabajo para
que lo tengan.
(C) Los jóvenes van a poder encargarse de su
trabajo.
(D) Los jóvenes van a trabajar en el campo
fuera de la ciudad.

76. ¿Por qué siente el joven tanta confianza?

(A) La Alcaldía toma todas las decisiones.
(B) La Alcaldía decide por él cuáles son los
talentos para desarrollar.
(C) El joven recibe el apoyo necesaria para
realizar sus posibilidades.
(D) No le dice al joven nada que tiene que
ver con su trabajo.

GO ON TO THE NEXT PAGE

Línea   Salíamos siempre por la puerta de atrás. Nos
pegábamos al muro de la casa, hasta desaparecer
del campo visual de la abuela, que nos creía
dando clase. Desde la ventana de su gabinete, ella
(5) escudriñaba su fila de casitas blancas, cuadradas,
donde vivían los colonos. Aquellas casitas, al
atardecer, se encendían con luces amarillentas,
y eran como peones de un mundo de juguete, y
muñecos sus habitantes. Sentada en la mecedora
(10) o en el sillón de cuero negro con clavos dorados,
la abuela enfilaba sus gemelos de raso amarillento
con falsos zafiros, y jugaba a mirar. Entre los
troncos oscuros de los almendros y las hojas de
los olivos, se extendía el declive, hacia las rocas de
(15) la costa.
    La barca de Borja se llamaba Leontina. Por
unos escalones tallados en la roca se bajaba al
pequeño embarcadero. Nosotros dos, solamente,
íbamos allí. En la Leontina bordeábamos la
(20) costa rocosa, hasta la pequeña cala de Santa
Catalina. No había otra en varios kilómetros, y la
llamábamos el cementerio de las barcas, pues en
ella los del Port abandonaban las suyas inservibles.

77. La casa de la abuela está situada

    (A) en un bosque.

    (B) cerca del mar.

    (C) en un pueblo.

    (D) en una montaña.

78. ¿Cómo salen los dos de la casa?

    (A) torpemente

    (B) ruidosamente

    (C) plenamente

    (D) furtivamente

79. La abuela creía que los dos

    (A) estaban en la cocina.

    (B) siguen sus lecciones en casa.

    (C) se pasean en una barca.

    (D) iban a visitar un teatro.

80. ¿Qué miraba la abuela?

    (A) unos juguetes de los nietos

    (B) una obra teatral

    (C) un pueblo a lo lejos

    (D) unos muchachos que jugaban

81. La actitud de la abuela al mirar por la ventana
era

    (A) entretenida.

    (B) preocupada.

    (C) ansiosa.

    (D) desdeñosa.

82. La narradora dice que al pie de unos
escalones había

    (A) un lugar para poner barcas.

    (B) unas barcas sumergidas.

    (C) muchas personas en sus casas.

    (D) unos hombres trabajando en el huerto.

83. ¿Qué era Santa Catalina?

    (A) un pueblo

    (B) una isla

    (C) una barca

    (D) una bahía pequeña

84. Ellos querían ir a Santa Catalina porque

    (A) estaba aislado de todo.

    (B) les gustaba visitar el cementerio.

    (C) sus amigos del Port los esperaban allí.

    (D) tenía un embarcadero para muchos
barcos.

85. Parece que la familia gozaba de unas relaciones

    (A) fuertes.

    (B) tirantes.

    (C) afectuosas.

    (D) estrechas.

STOP!

**If you finish before time is up,
you may check your work.**

Answer Key
Practice Test 4

Part A	Part B	Part C
1. C	33. C	59. C
2. C	34. B	60. C
3. B	35. A	61. B
4. C	36. D	62. A
5. D	37. A	63. C
6. B	38. B	64. B
7. C	39. B	65. B
8. C	40. D	66. C
9. B	41. B	67. C
10. A	42. C	68. D
11. B	43. A	69. A
12. D	44. D	70. C
13. C	45. A	71. B
14. A	46. D	72. B
15. C	47. D	73. D
16. B	48. B	74. C
17. B	49. D	75. C
18. D	50. C	76. C
19. A	51. C	77. B
20. B	52. A	78. D
21. C	53. B	79. B
22. C	54. D	80. C
23. A	55. B	81. D
24. D	56. A	82. A
25. D	57. A	83. D
26. C	58. C	84. A
27. D		85. B
28. D		
29. B		
30. A		
31. A		
32. B		

ANSWERS AND EXPLANATIONS

Part A

1. (C) The word for "to play games" is *jugar*.

2. (C) Just the person and number of the verb tell you that you have to use *tener*. You would not use *hacer* or *estar,* normally, in anything but the third person. When commenting that a person is cold using *estar*, it usually means that the body lacks vital signs; in other words, is dead. When someone feels chilly, it is *tener frío*.

3. (B) You need to use *voces*, meaning "voices." Just because *pocas* comes before the noun does not mean you automatically use *veces*. The *z* from the singular form changes to a *c* before adding the *-es*.

4. (C) *Porque* is the only possibility here, because the second clause explains the first one.

5. (D) *Mapas* is a masculine noun, and since "none" is followed by the preposition *de*, you have to use the full form of the indefinite adjective, *ninguno*. Notice that the verb in the sentence is singular, because "none" is always singular.

6. (B) "Deep" is *hondo*. Remember this word by remembering the name of a Central American country, Honduras, which means "depths." Since the sentence talks about crossing a river easily, *denso* ("dense,") *suave* ("gentle" or "smooth,") and *flojo* ("loose") are clearly wrong.

7. (C) *Tarifa* is a common word meaning "fare," as in "airfare," "fare for a hotel," etc. A *copa* is a number of things, from "treetops" to a "glass" for brandy, a "snowflake" to a a "goblet."

8. (C) A *boda* is a wedding, so it would take place in a church. You might be tempted by the word *catedráctico*, but that means a "distinguished professor at a university." Do not confuse the word for *inglesa* with *iglesia*. *Inglesa* means "Englishwoman." Remember that to make adjectives of nationality feminine, many times an *-a* is added. If there is an accent on the masculine singular form, it is dropped when the adjective is feminine, so *inglés* becomes *inglesa*.

9. (B) There is no noun to which this possessive pronoun refers, so you have to use the neuter article. This is a special use of this article and it is difficult to translate literally. Probably the best way would be "what is his own," with "his" referring to "everyone." *Todo el mundo* is the Spanish way of saying "everybody." *Cuyo*, meaning "whose" does not mean anything in the context of the sentence, so (C) is wrong.

10. (A) This is a favorite word in Spanish: *cobrar*. It means "to charge," as in charging a fee for a service. *Regatear* in (C) means "to bargain."

11. (B) Several of these answer choices take an indirect pronoun. You have already seen the verb *caerle* with *bien* or *mal*, for "to look good (bad) on someone," especially used with an article of clothing. This sentence does mention *zapatos*, but with the verb *sufría*, the verb *caer* does not work. *Parecer* an also take an indirect object pronoun, but it does not make sense here with the verb *sufría*. That means (A) and (D) are wrong. *Lucir* would be like *caerle bien*, but after *porque*, it doesn't fit, either. The only verb left is *caber, meaning "to fit."*

12. (D) The simple future tense is needed here because of *más tarde*. Do not be distracted by the preterite in *salieron*; that verb refers to the test that was taken the day before. The preterite is a distracter, especially if you were not paying attention to "later." As a point of grammar, the simple present tense can sometimes be used for the future, but in this case the future is indefinite. The present would refer to sometime soon in the future.

13. (C) *Cubierta* means "covered," an obvious choice. *Descrita* is the irregular past participle of *describir*, which is like *escribir*. *Vuelta*, the irregular past participle of *volver* ("to return"), does not work in the context of the sentence.

14. (A) The reflexive form *reírse de*, which means "to laugh" or "to laugh at," is somewhat like *burlarse de*, meaning "to make fun of."

15. (C) What you leave in a restaurant is a "tip," *una propina*. A *piropo* is "a compliment," and waiters generally would rather have the money. And you do not leave a *piropo* on a table. A *propuesto* is a "budget," so (B) is out. That noun comes from *proponer*, meaning "to propose" a plan of action.

16. (B) You cannot use a conjugated verb form after *ser* unless there is a change of subject, or a present participle, so (A) and (D) are wrong. That leaves (B) and (C). For (B), use the infinitive as a noun. *Espantosos* means "scary."

17. (B) You need an expression of obligation here: *sin falta*, "without fail." *Sin querer* is "without wanting." *Apenas* means "scarcely," which might make sense, except for the part of the sentence after *para que*.

18. (D) You can reject (B) because you wouldn't use *no* before the verb if you used *nunca*. *Pronto* doesn't make sense, either: "Soon I have not received," so (C) is wrong. The word order is strange in that phrase. *Más* means "more," so it doesn't make sense. That leaves *todavía*, meaning "still."

19. (A) An *alfombra* goes on the floor. No other choice makes sense, given the word *suelo* ("floor"). The *almohada* goes on a bed.

20. (B) A *postal* is a generic word for a card: a credit card, a birthday card, etc. A *tarjeta postal* is a "postcard."

21. (C) This pronoun is a direct object pronoun, referring to *calcetines*. *De algodón* is a prepositional phrase describing the *calcetines*, so you have to look carefully to see which noun goes with the pronoun. Although *ellos* can mean "them" when it is a prepositional pronoun, it does not have that function in the sentence. If it came in front of the verb, it would be the subject, and the ending of the verb would be third person plural. *Lo* can be a neuter pronoun, but would not work here because you want the pronoun that refers to *calcetines*.

22. (C) This phrase connects two ideas: scoring 100, and coming out first in the class. Neither *mediante* ("nevertheless") nor *sin embargo* ("however") makes sense. The speaker came out first in the class as a result of scoring 100.

23. (A) You're looking for a word that means "quietly." Only *sigilosamente* ("secretly") fits.

24. (D) Even if you do not recognize the word *jarro*, you can get the idea from the words *no sirve para agua*, that a *jarro* is a container for water. You want a word to show that there is something wrong with the *jarro*. If something is *completo*, there would be nothing wrong with it. *Lleno* means "full," so (B) is wrong. Being "empty" has nothing to do with the condition described, so (C) *vacío* is wrong. *Roto* is the irregular past participle of *romper*, "to break," and it is the correct answer.

25. (D) *Los*, meaning "those of," refers to *gastos*, which is what you are being asked to compare in this sentence. Prepositional phrases are not usually the items of comparison. When in doubt, think of what you would replace if you used a noun instead of the pronoun. In this case, it would be the expenditures for telephone service.

26. (C) Look for the proper command form for the verb *ir*, irregular in the command forms. The familiar *tú* command even looks like it is a form of the verb *ver*, but is not. A *dormitorio* is a bedroom, and the little child is being told to go to his room. You cannot use the present perfect subjunctive for a command form, so (A) is wrong. (B) has the pronoun in front of the verb, which is wrong because the pronoun is always attached to the end of an affirmative command. (D), the third person singular, is wrong, because the subject is second person singular.

27. (D) The subjunctive makes no sense here if you read the whole sentence, so (A) is wrong. The infinitive (B) cannot be used, because it would function as a noun in the sentence, and there is already a noun. (C), the past participle, could be used as an adjective, but makes no sense since "been" is not normally used as an adjective. That leaves the present participle as the correct answer. It is used here to describe how the chile has come to be so popular in so many different places. Remember, you can use a present participle as an adverb.

28. (D) *También* makes no sense. The speaker has just arrived, so she would not say that her friends "have also not arrived yet." *Sin embargo* ("nevertheless") and *casi* ("almost") also do not make sense in this context. That only leaves *puesto que*, which means "given that" or "since."

29. (B) In giving the date for the first of the month, always use *el primero*. But if you say, "on the first day," that would be *el primer día*. It is also worth remembering that you need to use *el* for "on" when talking about when something takes place. "On Wednesday..." is *el miércoles* for example.

30. (A) These choices may look similar, but in fact they're quite distinct. *Hasta* can be either an adverb, or a preposition, so it could come in front of a conjugated verb as an adverb, but not as a preposition. As a preposition, it can introduce an infinitive, but makes no sense here. *Hacia* is also a preposition, so it could come in front of an infinitive, also. *Tiene* (D) is wrong, because you would have to use *que* between it and the infinitive in the expression *tener que*. *Bastar* means "to suffice," or "to be enough," so in this sentence it means "suffice it to say..." This word can also be used by itself: *¡Basta!* can get attention quickly, since it means "Enough, already!"

31. (A) For all practical purposes, you do not use the present subjunctive after *si*. There are some cases where it is used, but the grammar is ambiguous, and on this test, there cannot be any room for other possible answers. You cannot use the present perfect because the action communicated in the verb has not yet happened: *Haremos* is the future of *hacer*.

32. (B) Note the impersonal "you" in the expression. The present participle *superando* ("overcoming") is a clue to the answer. *Deblidades* are "weaknesses," as you will recognize from the similarity to *débil*. You need the singular form because the verb and subject are singular. If there were two objects as in *se mejoran el talento y la facilidad de jugar* you would use the third person plural. You can eliminate (A) and (D) because you need a conjugated verb in the sentence.

Part B

33. (C) *Grandes* is always shortened before singular nouns of either gender, but not plural nouns. *Grandísimas* means "very great," but does not fit here because it is a masculine form.

34. (B) The narrator talks about how his mother thinks the cities are wonderful and the provinces are backwards. You must read the entire passage to get the full meaning. The full sentence speaks about the way of life in the cities, so (C) and (D) can be ruled out: When you think of the countryside, you usually think of stereotypes like "poor" and "simple." *Culta* means "cultured," which is how the narrator's mother thinks of the city.

35. (A) The only word that makes any sense is *jamás*, meaning "never." *Ningún* would have to have an antecedent, so (B) is out. In any case, if *ningún* were a possibility, it would have to be the full form, not the shortened one. *Según* ("according to") doesn't make sense, so (C) is out. And *hasta* would be followed by an infinitive, or *que* plus a conjugated verb, so (D) is wrong.

36. (D) The phrase *de la provincia* after the blank here tells you that this noun should be something that describes the province. *Sencillez*, "simplicity," best does that.

37. (A) *Negarse a* in choice (A) means "to refuse." Although you see later on that the mother does understand some provincial dialects, the phrase *Pero yo sé que ella conoce la mayoría de esos dialectos*, tells you that she didn't want anyone to know that she understood them. *Tratar* means "to treat," so (B) can be ruled out (*tratar de* means "to try," but the blank here is followed by *a*). *Alegrarse* means "to be happy," but it too is followed by *de*, not *a*, so (D) can be eliminated as well. *Perder* in (C) means "to lose," and makes no sense.

38. (B) Only *oprimidos*, meaning "oppressed," makes sense, because the other adjectives would not describe a country village. *Estrechos* means "close" or "narrow." *Sacudir* is "to shake," as in shaking anything except a hand ("to shake hands" is *darle la mano*).

39. (B) Here you must identify what the adjective modifies. Look at the sentence and you will see *su tristeza y la mía*. The conjunction *y* makes this a plural antecedent, and it is feminine. The correct answer is *producidas*. If you were just looking at a word to go after *son*, you might think that *productos* would work, but it doesn't fit with *por el monótono sopor de la provincia*. Remember that after the verb *ser* you can use an infinitive or a past participle, but not a present participle.

40. (D) If you don't know the answer, try process of elimination. After *estamos...como*, which introduces a simile, you see the words *esclavo a la* piedra, "a slave to a rock." That same relationship is being set up for something and *naturaleza*. *Adivinadas* means "guessed," so (B) doesn't work. (A), "happy," doesn't really fit either. (D) *cautivas*, means "captive," and it is the correct answer. This is a difficult passage, especially if you missed the contrast between the city and the country, *provincia*.

41. (B) This passage is about a boy on his bicycle in the small garden at his house. "to get on a bicycle" is to *montar* a bicycle. *Regar* means "to water" and *pintar* means "to paint."

42. (C) *Dar vueltas* means "to take turns around," which is what the narrator does on his bicycle. *Mecer* is "to rock" as in a rocking chair and *volar* is "to fly," neither of which makes sense. *Poner* also makes no sense with *vueltas*.

43. (A) With *en torno* ("around") after the blank, (C) can be eliminated because it means "surrounded around." But "centered around" does make sense, especially with the rest of the sentence. *Bancos de hierro* are "iron benches." *Podido* is from *poder*, so this past participle has no meaning here; it is not used as an adjective.

44. (D) *Comenzaba* and *primaveral* are the clues here: They indicate that spring is about to arrive. The phrase *yo no hacía caso* tells you that *pero* is the only conjunction that makes sense. No contrast to the season is implied, so (A) and (B) can be eliminated. The meaning of *hacer caso de* following the blank is "not paying attention to"; the narrator is stating that he didn't see the signs of spring.

45. (A) The narrator is not paying attention to the season. *Estación* can mean "season," "station," or "parking" if used as *estacionamiento*. You might be confused by *regalos* linked with *y*, but the narrator uses fairly fanciful language to describe the signs, indicating that he would probably have enjoyed spring had he not been worried about other things, *cosas ... graves en que pensar* and later *para meditar sobre lo que en la casa sucedía*.

46. (D) *Demasiado* is used as an adverb here, so it has to end in *-o*. Only when it is used as an adjective (right in front of a noun) can it agree in gender and number with the noun, as in *demasiadas veces*. If you have difficulty telling when *demasiado* is an adverb, think of an adverb like *muy*. Remembering that *muy* is invariable in front of an adjective may help you remember that *demasiado* doesn't change either (in front of an adjective).

47. (D) The word in the blank should mean "as." This is a long sentence about the garden and why the narrator likes it. The first part tells why he likes it, so *como* is the only choice that fits.

48. (B) ___ *de pleno verano* tells you that you want a word that goes with "height of the summer" when it is very hot. That word is (B) *ahogo*, which means suffocation from the heat and humidity. *Socorro* means "help," as in what someone in trouble yells. *Apoyo* is "support" (Remember, *soportar* means "to tolerate"). *Humor* is a cognate. It does not fit in this context because there is nothing humorous about the hot summer or the narrator's situation.

49. (D) You have to use the subjunctive. Even though the time of the passage is past, the summer had not yet arrived. So the heat had not arrived, and he was merely anticipating what it would be like.

50. (C) *Aliento*, "breath," does not fit here. You want a word that describes what the garden is: *sitio*, "site." (B) and (D) are wrong because the garden is neither a "room" nor a "case."

51. (C) This passage deals with the most popular topic of soap operas on television: impossible love stories. You need an adjective to describe what makes them so popular. "Small" ingredients wouldn't work, so (A) is wrong. (D) is wrong because *insoportables* means "intolerable." If the topic were intolerable, the shows would not be popular. By process of elimination you could guess *inagotable*, even if you don't know its meaning, however, look in the middle of the word for *gota*, meaning "drop" of water. The combined meaning of the prefix *ina-* and the adjective ending *-bles* could help you get the idea of an unending stream (drops of water) of ingredients that have made soap operas popular.

52. (A) Do not be fooled into thinking you have to use the present perfect here because you see other present perfect forms in the sentence. You should recognize the grammatical structure as an expression of time. *Décadas* is not a common unit of time, but it is one, and its structure is *hace* + an expression of time. In this case the relative *que* comes before the blank. All the components are there, if you look for them.

53. (B) Audiences sit in front of their television sets, so *frente* is the only choice here.

54. (D) You cannot use *sino* or *sino que* because there is no contrast stated. *Pero* is the only possible choice because the phrase following the conjunction elaborates on the statement that the shows are highly criticized: They are the most watched, also.

55. (B) There are some adjectives whose meanings change depending on where they are placed. *Cierto* is one of them. When it comes in front of the noun, it means a "particular" group, which is what is needed here.

56. (A) All you need here is *que*, a simple relative pronoun. The pronoun refers to the noun *telenovela*. If you were translating directly from English, you might have been tempted to use *cual*, "which," but it doesn't work: It would need the article *el*. You cannot use *quien* to refer to anything other than people, so (B) is wrong.

57. (A) *Realizarse* choice (A) means "to fulfill" or "to become a reality" and is a false cognate. Do not confuse it with *darse cuenta* which also means "to realize," but in the sense of becoming aware of something. *Esconderse* is "to hide," so (B) is out.

58. (C) *Historia* means a "story" here, not a "history" as we know it in English. You may think that *contar* means only "to count," but it also means "to relate," as in "to tell a story." The word *cuento*, meaning a "short story," comes from this verb. *Borrar* means "to erase," *enterrar* means "to bury," and *impedir* means "to impede," so (A), (B), and (D) are wrong.

Part C

Questions 59–64

This passage is a conversation between two people who have just met. A young man has come to visit his friend's mother. The woman's son is living in Kansas. There seems not to be much substantial communication between the mother and son, even though she says he sends her money regularly. He evidently does not tell her much about what he is doing. The young man brings news that the son is going to be married, but it's a little odd that the son is not telling her himself.

59. (C) A *mensaje* is a "message." The young man brings money and news, so he would be a messenger. He is not a relative, *pariente*, nor is he a mailman, *un cartero*, so (A) and (B) are wrong. And although he brings *noticias*, he is not a *noticiero*, a "newscaster" or "journalist," so (D) is out as well.

60. (C) The question asks what news the man brought. He does not provide details about Kansas, so (B) is wrong. (C) means "an event that will take place." (A) is wrong because he does not bring regards from an old friend.

61. (B) At the beginning of the conversation, the woman is grateful to the man for coming. *Agradecer* means "to be thankful."

62. (A) The literal translation of *plata* is "silver," but it is commonly used to mean money. It is clear in this context that she gets money from him, not a treasure, food, or jewels.

63. (C) If the relationship with the mother were a close one, the son would be telling her directly that he was getting married. It is neither good nor constant, (A) and (B) are wrong. In fact, the main reason he left was to find work, not because they did not get along.

64. (B) *Pasaje* is "passage," as in a ticket to travel. Her son wants her to come to his wedding, so he has sent her money to buy a ticket. The money is not to pay for the friend's trip, so (C) is wrong.

Question 65

65. (B) This ad states, "Are you prepared for the 'million dollar' call?" In other words, as long as you have a cell phone, you'll always be able to receive good news—anytime, anywhere. The advantage to having the cell phone is explained in choice (B): *alcanzar* means "to reach," so it says, "You'll always be at the reach of someone with good news." Choice (C) says, "You'll never know if you won a million unless you are at home," and is too literal and narrow: The real advantage to the cell phone is that it allows you receive any type of good news.

Question 66–71

This passage discusses the running of the bulls in Pamplona. Be sure that you don't read things into the passage that you may have heard about the event but are not stated here. The passage recounts how people in Pamplona view the event, and how it differs from the events of the past.

66. (C) While it is true that the bulls run fast and tourism is important in Pamplona, the first paragraph of this passage focuses on the relationship between the town and San Fermín, so (A) and (D) are incorrect. At the end of the passage, it is clear that the good judgment of the foreigners who run with the bulls is suspect, so (B) is incorrect, also.

67. (C) The words that indicate this correct answer are *un tramo urbano*. Even though you may not know *tramo*, you get the idea that the bulls run through the streets. The other choices are nouns of location lifted from the text, but are either in the wrong place or are not big enough to allow a running of the bulls.

68. (D) *Se jubilaban* is a false cognate, meaning "to retire" from a job. A close reading of the second paragraph reveals that at the beginning the bulls passed through the streets only once, so (B) is wrong. The correct answer is indicated by the words *se pasó a correr detrás a correr delante*.

69. (A) *Fuegos artificiales* is a synonym for *cohetes*. Even if you did not know the synonym, you should recognize *ruido*. (D) might appear to be a logical choice, except that *hasta el corral* means "until the corral," or "up to the corral," so it would be the end, not the beginning of the running.

70. (C) Nowadays, *hoy en día*, the citizens of Pamplona still eagerly watch the running of the bulls, although hoping not to see any mishaps. This answer is found in lines 15–20. Be wary of words and phrases lifted from the passage.

71. (B) In the last paragraph the passage states that the authorities have noted that not all the runners are in the best physical condition. Training for the event will certainly make it safer than it is for those who do not prepare, which is what (B) says. (D) would seem logical, but the passage does not say that the authorities recommend studying the route, so it is incorrect.

Questions 72–76

This passage is about a new program for young people in a poor neighborhood of Cali. The passage starts out with a group of boys on their way down a dusty street to meet with two leaders of a program in which the city helps young people better their lives through education and work.

The government wants to help create opportunities and not repeat the mistakes of similar programs in the past. The new program is different in that it empowers young people to develop their own skills in establishing a corporation. They manage it themselves, instead of being told simply how it should be run.

72. (B) The boys live in a poor neighborhood, indicated by the words *calles polvorosas*, and *el problema de la falta de oportnidades Desventajada* means "disadvantaged."

73. (D) The group is going to meet with some delegates from the city. You should associate *municipales* with city government. Since the passage talks about clients (C), they would not be going to discuss education and organization.

74. (C) The government group wants to better the lives of the young people. *Calidad de vida* at the end of paragraph one means "quality of life."(A) is out because the government group is not counseling the youths to be content as they are—that is the opposite of what the program intends. And (D) is wrong because the government group clearly does not want to repeat the mistakes of the past.

75. (C) The words *sino abrir espacios de trabajo* literally mean "but rather to open spaces for work." The conjunction *sino* ("but rather") indicates that "opening spaces for work" is the object of the program, as opposed to what is stated in (A) and (B), meaning they can be eliminated. (C) means the youths will be in charge.

76. (C) The young man feels confident because he has received the support (*apoyo*) that he needs. He doesn't feel strong because the government group makes the decisions, so (A) is wrong. Nor does the government group decide for him which talents he should develop, so (B) is out as well.

Questions 77—85

In this passage, the narrator is one of two children who lived with their grandmother. The narrator recounts what they did, especially when they were out of their grandmother's sight. She talks about going down to the water and taking a boat someplace. She also describes the view from the grandmother's *gabinete*.

77. (B) The grandmother's house is situated near the ocean, (B). You know this from the words *el declive, la costa,* and *el embarcadero*. The field of sight extends down a slope to the rocky coast, where a few steps lead down to a pier.

78. (D) The question asks about how the two children left the house. *Furtivamente* means "stealthily" or "secretly." The words *nos pegábamos al muro de la casa, hasta desaparecer del campo visual de la abuela* tell you they tried to sneak out of the house. They would not be making a lot of noise, so (B) is wrong. (A) is out because *torpemente* means "clumsily," and even though the children are sneaky, they're not dull or befuddled.

79. (B) The grandmother though that the children were doing their lessons in the house.

80. (C) The grandmother looked at a village in the distance. It looked like a miniature village to her. Nowhere in the passage do you get the idea that she is watching a play or watching children play, so (B) and (D) are out.

81. (D) The grandmother's attitude while looking through the window was not "entertained," so (A) is out. At the end of paragraph one, *jugaba a mirar* does not mean that she played anything. Rather it means that she "played at" something, not really doing what it looked like she was doing. She "played at" watching what went on in the village. She was not worried or anxious, so (B) and (C) can be eliminated. But you could say she was *desdeñosa*, "disdainful," because of the way she sat inside watching all the other people going about their lives. She felt "above them all."

82. (A) The *embarcadero* is a place to put boats. The sunken boats were at Santa Catalina, not at the bottom of the stairs. The words "*bordeábamos hasta*" tell you that Santa Catalina was a different place. The trees were closer to the house, and the people in their houses were off to the side, not at the foot of the *declive*.

83. (D) You know that Santa Catalina is a place where there are sunken boats from the port. And you know that it's the only place around of its kind. Therefore, you can reason that it is not an island, a boat, or a village. It must be a small bay or harbor.

84. (A) In the second paragraph, the narrator says that she liked to go to Santa Catalina because they went alone. (B) is completely wrong, since it refers to a cemetary. And though there are sunken boats in Santa Catalina, that's not what they went to see, so (D) is wrong. They went to be alone, away from the grandmother and her house.

85. (B) *Estrechas* means "close," something you would not call this family, so (D) is out. The relations with the grandmother appear strained, *tirantes*, not affectionate or strong, as one would expect.

Practice Test 5:
Spanish with Listening Test

The Spanish with Listening Test is a bit different. Remember that you'll have to bring a CD player to the test center. There are two sections as follows:

Section I

Listening: 20 minutes long

Questions: 1–33

Part A: Pictures

Part B: Spoken selections

Part C: Spoken selections

Section II

Reading: 40 minutes

Questions: 34–85

Part A: Sentences with vocabulary and structures

Part B: Vocabulary and structures in context

Part C: Reading comprehension

Answer Grid
Practice Test 5

1. Ⓐ Ⓑ Ⓒ Ⓓ Ⓔ
2. Ⓐ Ⓑ Ⓒ Ⓓ Ⓔ
3. Ⓐ Ⓑ Ⓒ Ⓓ Ⓔ
4. Ⓐ Ⓑ Ⓒ Ⓓ Ⓔ
5. Ⓐ Ⓑ Ⓒ Ⓓ Ⓔ
6. Ⓐ Ⓑ Ⓒ Ⓓ Ⓔ
7. Ⓐ Ⓑ Ⓒ Ⓓ Ⓔ
8. Ⓐ Ⓑ Ⓒ Ⓓ Ⓔ
9. Ⓐ Ⓑ Ⓒ Ⓓ Ⓔ
10. Ⓐ Ⓑ Ⓒ Ⓓ Ⓔ
11. Ⓐ Ⓑ Ⓒ Ⓓ Ⓔ
12. Ⓐ Ⓑ Ⓒ Ⓓ Ⓔ
13. Ⓐ Ⓑ Ⓒ Ⓓ Ⓔ
14. Ⓐ Ⓑ Ⓒ Ⓓ Ⓔ
15. Ⓐ Ⓑ Ⓒ Ⓓ Ⓔ
16. Ⓐ Ⓑ Ⓒ Ⓓ Ⓔ
17. Ⓐ Ⓑ Ⓒ Ⓓ Ⓔ
18. Ⓐ Ⓑ Ⓒ Ⓓ Ⓔ
19. Ⓐ Ⓑ Ⓒ Ⓓ Ⓔ
20. Ⓐ Ⓑ Ⓒ Ⓓ Ⓔ
21. Ⓐ Ⓑ Ⓒ Ⓓ Ⓔ
22. Ⓐ Ⓑ Ⓒ Ⓓ Ⓔ
23. Ⓐ Ⓑ Ⓒ Ⓓ Ⓔ
24. Ⓐ Ⓑ Ⓒ Ⓓ Ⓔ
25. Ⓐ Ⓑ Ⓒ Ⓓ Ⓔ
26. Ⓐ Ⓑ Ⓒ Ⓓ Ⓔ
27. Ⓐ Ⓑ Ⓒ Ⓓ Ⓔ
28. Ⓐ Ⓑ Ⓒ Ⓓ Ⓔ
29. Ⓐ Ⓑ Ⓒ Ⓓ Ⓔ

30. Ⓐ Ⓑ Ⓒ Ⓓ Ⓔ
31. Ⓐ Ⓑ Ⓒ Ⓓ Ⓔ
32. Ⓐ Ⓑ Ⓒ Ⓓ Ⓔ
33. Ⓐ Ⓑ Ⓒ Ⓓ Ⓔ
34. Ⓐ Ⓑ Ⓒ Ⓓ Ⓔ
35. Ⓐ Ⓑ Ⓒ Ⓓ Ⓔ
36. Ⓐ Ⓑ Ⓒ Ⓓ Ⓔ
37. Ⓐ Ⓑ Ⓒ Ⓓ Ⓔ
38. Ⓐ Ⓑ Ⓒ Ⓓ Ⓔ
39. Ⓐ Ⓑ Ⓒ Ⓓ Ⓔ
40. Ⓐ Ⓑ Ⓒ Ⓓ Ⓔ
41. Ⓐ Ⓑ Ⓒ Ⓓ Ⓔ
42. Ⓐ Ⓑ Ⓒ Ⓓ Ⓔ
43. Ⓐ Ⓑ Ⓒ Ⓓ Ⓔ
44. Ⓐ Ⓑ Ⓒ Ⓓ Ⓔ
45. Ⓐ Ⓑ Ⓒ Ⓓ Ⓔ
46. Ⓐ Ⓑ Ⓒ Ⓓ Ⓔ
47. Ⓐ Ⓑ Ⓒ Ⓓ Ⓔ
48. Ⓐ Ⓑ Ⓒ Ⓓ Ⓔ
49. Ⓐ Ⓑ Ⓒ Ⓓ Ⓔ
50. Ⓐ Ⓑ Ⓒ Ⓓ Ⓔ
51. Ⓐ Ⓑ Ⓒ Ⓓ Ⓔ
52. Ⓐ Ⓑ Ⓒ Ⓓ Ⓔ
53. Ⓐ Ⓑ Ⓒ Ⓓ Ⓔ
54. Ⓐ Ⓑ Ⓒ Ⓓ Ⓔ
55. Ⓐ Ⓑ Ⓒ Ⓓ Ⓔ
56. Ⓐ Ⓑ Ⓒ Ⓓ Ⓔ
57. Ⓐ Ⓑ Ⓒ Ⓓ Ⓔ
58. Ⓐ Ⓑ Ⓒ Ⓓ Ⓔ

59. Ⓐ Ⓑ Ⓒ Ⓓ Ⓔ
60. Ⓐ Ⓑ Ⓒ Ⓓ Ⓔ
61. Ⓐ Ⓑ Ⓒ Ⓓ Ⓔ
62. Ⓐ Ⓑ Ⓒ Ⓓ Ⓔ
63. Ⓐ Ⓑ Ⓒ Ⓓ Ⓔ
64. Ⓐ Ⓑ Ⓒ Ⓓ Ⓔ
65. Ⓐ Ⓑ Ⓒ Ⓓ Ⓔ
66. Ⓐ Ⓑ Ⓒ Ⓓ Ⓔ
67. Ⓐ Ⓑ Ⓒ Ⓓ Ⓔ
68. Ⓐ Ⓑ Ⓒ Ⓓ Ⓔ
69. Ⓐ Ⓑ Ⓒ Ⓓ Ⓔ
70. Ⓐ Ⓑ Ⓒ Ⓓ Ⓔ
71. Ⓐ Ⓑ Ⓒ Ⓓ Ⓔ
72. Ⓐ Ⓑ Ⓒ Ⓓ Ⓔ
73. Ⓐ Ⓑ Ⓒ Ⓓ Ⓔ
74. Ⓐ Ⓑ Ⓒ Ⓓ Ⓔ
75. Ⓐ Ⓑ Ⓒ Ⓓ Ⓔ
76. Ⓐ Ⓑ Ⓒ Ⓓ Ⓔ
77. Ⓐ Ⓑ Ⓒ Ⓓ Ⓔ
78. Ⓐ Ⓑ Ⓒ Ⓓ Ⓔ
79. Ⓐ Ⓑ Ⓒ Ⓓ Ⓔ
80. Ⓐ Ⓑ Ⓒ Ⓓ Ⓔ
81. Ⓐ Ⓑ Ⓒ Ⓓ Ⓔ
82. Ⓐ Ⓑ Ⓒ Ⓓ Ⓔ
83. Ⓐ Ⓑ Ⓒ Ⓓ Ⓔ
84. Ⓐ Ⓑ Ⓒ Ⓓ Ⓔ
85. Ⓐ Ⓑ Ⓒ Ⓓ Ⓔ

The calculations for the score on the Spanish with Listening Test are a bit more complicated. Please turn to page 358 for step-by-step instructions.

Practice Test 5: Spanish with Listening Test

SECTION I

LISTENING

Approximate Time–20 minutes

Questions 1–33

Part A

Directions: You will hear four sentences, seen as A,B, C, and D on your answer sheet. They are not printed in your test booklet. As you listen to the sentences, look at the picture in your test booklet and select the sentence that best reflects what you see in the picture or what someone in the picture might be saying. Mark your answer in the corresponding oval on your answer sheet. Each sentence will be spoken only once. Look at the following example.

You will see:

You will hear:

    (A) Espero que perdamos el partido.

    (B) Será estupendo si marco un gol.

    (C) Ojalá que el otro jugador me pegue.

    (D) No toques la pelota, Juan.

The best answer is (B), so you would mark (B) on your answer sheet.

GO ON TO THE NEXT PAGE

Look at the following pictures, then answer the question for each.

1.

You will hear:

1. (A) Esta ciudad está situada en un valle.
   (B) El pueblo está en un desierto.
   (C) Muchos barcos vienen a este puerto.
   (D) Hay muchos edificios altos en la montaña.

2.

You will hear:

2. (A) No tengo mucho apetito hoy.
   (B) La pata es buena para comer.
   (C) ¿Cuál prefiere Vd. para el almuerzo?
   (D) El pan es muy barato hoy.

GO ON TO THE NEXT PAGE

3.

You will hear:

3. (A) Vamos a bañarnos con jabón en el mar.

   (B) ¡Qué placer jugar un deporte en la playa!

   (C) Nos gusta construir castillos de arena.

   (D) Durmamos un poco y más tarde nadaremos.

4.

You will hear:

4. (A) Es un placer pasar un día descansando en el campo.

   (B) ¡Cuánto me gustan los caballos de este lugar!

   (C) Estos burros no bailan muy bien.

   (D) ¡Uf! Esto es más difícil de lo que había pensado.

GO ON TO THE NEXT PAGE

5.

You will hear:

5. (A) El muchacho toca una pieza musical.

(B) Le gusta al chico practicar un deporte.

(C) El muchacho baila música clásica.

(D) Es buena idea jugar con el violoncelo.

6.

You will hear:

6. (A) ¡Qué raro ver el gato debajo de la rama!

(B) ¡Pocas veces se ve un gato sobre una rama!

(C) El gato está en frente de una rama.

(D) ¿Quién vio el gato delante de una rama?

GO ON TO THE NEXT PAGE

7.

You will hear:

7. (A) Se gana mucho dinero limpiando la calle.
   (B) Los turistas llevan la última moda.
   (C) ¡Los romanos han invadido la ciudad!
   (D) Los disfraces entretienen mucho al público.

8.

You will hear:

8. (A) ¿A cuánto están las piñas hoy?
   (B) ¿Por qué no tienen Vds. bananas hoy?
   (C) ¿Tiene Vd. planos en venta hoy?
   (D) ¿Son buenas las sandalias hoy?

GO ON TO THE NEXT PAGE

9.

You will hear:

9. (A) Nadie me invitó a la boda en la iglesia.

   (B) Siempre me visto de manera formal para la cena.

   (C) Vamos al concierto de música popular.

   (D) Estoy lista para la ceremonia nupcial.

10.

You will hear:

10. (A) El negocio emplea a peatones para anunciar su negocio.

    (B) Unas personas buscan muñecas en los balcones.

    (C) Nadie en la calle presta atención a las figuras.

    (D) Todo el mundo mira a unos hombres que lavan ventanas.

GO ON TO THE NEXT PAGE

Part B

Directions: You will hear several short conversations, followed by four spoken answer choices. After you hear the four choices, (A), (B), (C), and (D), select the one that most logically continues or completes the conversation, and mark it in your answer sheet.

Note: Neither the conversations nor the answer choices will be printed in your test booklet. Read the text only once; do not go back to read it twice. You will have several seconds to make your selection.

Conversation 1

(Speaker 1) —Marta, ¿quieres ir conmigo a la casa de Emilia el viernes?
(Speaker 2) —¡Ay! Me gustaría, pero mi prima que vive en Los Ángeles estará de visita este fin de semana. Pero gracias por invitarme.

(Speaker 1)
11. (A) Te llamo antes de pasar por tu casa para llevarla conmigo.
    (B) Su hermana está en casa con ella ahora.
    (C) ¡Qué bueno que puedes acompañarme!
    (D) Lo siento mucho. Entonces otra vez, quizás.

Conversation 2

(Speaker 1) —Dispense Vd., señor. ¿Cuánto cuesta esta pintura? Me gustaría regalarla a mi esposa para su cumpleaños.
(Speaker 2) —Mil quinientos dólares. Es de un artista muy famoso.
(Speaker 1) —¡Tan alto! ¡Qué lástima que no pueda comprársela!

(Speaker 2)
12. (A) Sería mejor no comprarle nada para su cumpleaños.
    (B) Estoy seguro que su esposa se sorprenderá al verla.
    (C) Tal vez haya otra que le guste. Tenemos otras más económicas.
    (D) Las pinturas de los artistas famosos siempre cuestan poco.

Conversation 3

(Speaker 1) —¡Las mismas noticias de siempre! Ahora sube el precio del petróleo otra vez. Pronto gastaremos tanto por el combustible como por la comida.
(Speaker 2) —Tienes razón. Pero no hay remedio, tenemos que conducir para poder llegar al trabajo.
(Speaker 1)—Sí, lo sé, pero de todos modos, no me gusta.

(Speaker 2)
13. (A) Te aconsejo que escuches las noticias otra vez.
    (B) Ten paciencia, querida, lo que sube siempre baja.
    (C) Sí, no tenemos que conducir tanto al trabajo.
    (D) Pues, el combustible es buena comida.

GO ON TO THE NEXT PAGE

Conversation 4

(Speaker 1) —Señor, mi coche dejó de funcionar. ¿Puede Vd. venir pronto?

(Speaker 2) —¿Qué dice Vd? Con todo el ruido no puedo oírlo bien.

(Speaker 1) —Necesito que me ayude, señor. Mi coche no funciona y tengo que ir al aeropuerto ahorita.

(Speaker 2)

14. (A) No quiero ayudarlo en este momento, señor.

    (B) Ah sí, tiene Vd. problemas con el coche. ¿Dónde está Vd?

    (C) Vd. puede usar su coche para llegar al aeropuerto a tiempo.

    (D) No tenga tanta prisa, señor. El avión no saldrá sin Vd.

Conversation 5

(Speaker 1) —Raquel, ¿has visto la nueva película de Lucinda Estrella? Se estrenó en el cine Multiplex.

(Speaker 2) —Sí, me encantó. Me imagino que ella ganará algún premio por esa representación. Ahora ella es más famosa que nunca. Esa película es la mejor de todas que ha hecho.

(Speaker 1)

15. (A) Ya sé que Lucinda Estrella no es muy famosa.

    (B) Qué lástima que no pudiste verla en el cine Multiplex.

    (C) Sí, y ella ha hecho otras muy buenas también.

    (D) Estoy de acuerdo que ha hecho otras peores.

Conversation 6

(Speaker 1) —Miguel, ¿tienes mucha tarea esta noche?

(Speaker 2) —No, gracias a Dios. Dos de mis profesores estaban ausentes hoy.

(Speaker 1) —Bueno, a menudo cuando estos dos están ausentes no dejan mucho trabajo.

(Speaker 2)

16. (A) Pues, afortunadamente, hoy te dejaron poco trabajo.

    (B) Bueno, si trabajas duro puedes terminar la tarea pronto.

    (C) ¡Qué suerte! Todos los profesores estaban en clase hoy!

    (D) Sí, estos dos son muy exigentes, si están presentes o no.

Conversation 7

(Speaker 1) —María, Miguel me invitó al baile este fin de semana, pero no tengo ningún vestido para llevar. No sé qué voy a hacer.

(Speaker 2) —Cálmate, Raquel. No hay problema. Podemos ir de compras juntas, o puedo prestarte uno de los míos.

(Speaker 1) —¿De veras? Estoy pensando en algo elegante, pero a la vez apropiado.

(Speaker 2)

17. (A) Creo que no tengo nada que puedes llevar.

    (B) ¿Recuerdas el azul que tengo? Si quieres, puedo prestártelo.

    (C) Tengo un par de pantalones vaquero y un suéter perfectos para ti.

    (D) Te sugiero que no vayas al baile con Miguel si no tienes vestido.

GO ON TO THE NEXT PAGE

Conversation 8

(Speaker 1) —Perdón, señor. ¿Dónde se encuentra el andén número cinco? El tren sale pronto y no conozco bien esta estación.

(Speaker 2) —Bueno, pase Vd. por esa puerta, y doble a la izquierda. Está al fondo de la estación a la izquierda. Creo que el tren está para salir ahora.

(Speaker 1)

18. (A) Le agradezco mucho.

    (B) No importa, señor.

    (C) Lo siento mucho, señor.

    (D) El tren no está en el andén.

Conversation 9

(Speaker 1) —¡Qué buen tiempo hoy! Debemos ir a la playa para gozar del sol hoy.

(Speaker 2) —Buena idea. Por lo general está nublado durante este mes. No nos quedan muchos días tan brillantes para relajar en la playa.

(Speaker 1) —Ana me dijo que iría si tuviera la oportunidad también. Déjame hablar con ella, y entonces vamos.

(Speaker 2)

19. (A) No tengo tiempo para ir a la playa.

    (B) Nunca hace mal tiempo en este mes.

    (C) Nos divertiremos mucho si ella viene también.

    (D) Nos falta la oportunidad para quedarnos en casa.

Conversation 10

(Speaker 1) —Ramón, ¿qué te pasó?

(Speaker 2) —Desafortunadamente, durante el partido anoche, me caí y me rompió la mano.

(Speaker 1) —Lo siento mucho. Estoy seguro que te hace difícil escribir en las clases. ¿Verdad? ¿Quieres que tomemos apuntes para dártelas?

(Speaker 2)

20. (A) Pues, no sé por qué nadie quiere ayudarme.

    (B) Bueno, saldré bien con tal que mis amigos me ayuden.

    (C) Oye, quiero que me ayuden a suspender las clases.

    (D) Mira, recomiendo que me presten una mano rota.

GO ON TO THE NEXT PAGE

Part C

Directions: You will hear a series of extended selections. For each selection, a question or questions and four answer choices will appear in your test booklet. They will not be spoken. Select the best answer and fill it in on the answer sheet.

Note: You will have 12 seconds to answer each question. When you take the real test, scan the upcoming questions if you have time between questions. Only the questions and answer choices will appear in your test booklet, not the selections.

Selection 1

—Señores y señoras pasajeros. Por favor, les pedimos su atención a las advertencias de seguridad antes de empezar nuestro vuelo. Antes de poder salir de la puerta se necesita poner todos los asientos y las mesas en su posición vertical. También la ley federal prohíbe fumar a bordo. También requiere que todos los teléfonos portátiles, juguetes con control remoto, transmisores de radio, o cualquier otro dispositivo que no se haya mencionado antes, esté desconectado mientras están dentro del avión.

—Ahora, estamos listos para salir. Por favor, siéntense y abróchense los cinturones de seguridad para que podamos salir de la puerto.

21. ¿Quién habla en esta selección?

   (A) una recepcionista
   (B) una niñera
   (C) una telefonista
   (D) una azafata

22. ¿Dónde están todas estas personas?

   (A) en una cabina de avión
   (B) en un café en un aeropuerto
   (C) en la sala de espera en un aeropuerto
   (D) en la sala de estar de una casa

Selection 2

Hoy en día el mercado nos ofrece ropa que nos van a servir para todo el tiempo y a un precio entre el más alto y el más bajo. Por ejemplo, vemos a Alfredo, todo arreglado para una excursión de pesca en las montañas. Lleva calcetines, pantalón de malla y camiseta de manga larga, abrigo de forro polar y un gorro. Ahora está tan concentrado en la pesca, que no presta atención al tiempo. Empezó a nevar fuertemente, pero Alfredo podía concentrarse en la maravilla de las cañas modernas en vez de la baja precipitada de temperatura, gracias a la selección de ropa. Para Alfredo todo lo que gastó en la ropa, y fue mucho, le liberó de preocupaciones ajenas en su excursión.

23. ¿Para qué estación se viste uno como Alfredo en esta selección?

   (A) primavera
   (B) invierno
   (C) verano
   (D) otoño

24. Según esta selección, ¿Cuál es el beneficio de tener esa ropa?

   (A) Es de la última moda.
   (B) Tiene un precio muy alto.
   (C) Pescará más pescado llevándola.
   (D) Podrá concentrar en pescar.

GO ON TO THE NEXT PAGE

Selection 3

—Buenas tardes, señoras. ¿Cuántas hay?

—Somos tres, por favor. ¿Tiene una mesa cerca de la ventana, en la sección de no fumar?

—A ver. Tenemos una mesa preparada ahora y otra que estará lista en unos minutos.

—¿Dónde está la vacante?

—Al fondo, cerca de la cocina.

—Preferimos no sentarnos allí.

—Bueno, el grupo en la otra mesa está para salir. Aquí tienen Vds. el menú si quieren mirarlo mientras esperan.

—Gracias. De lo que hemos oído, vale esperar. Se dice que la comida aquí es estupenda, y la presentación no falta nada.

—Bueno, eso es nuestra esperanza.

25. ¿Por qué no pueden las señoras sentarse inmediatamente?

    (A) Necesitan esperar hasta que vengan otras personas.
    (B) El hombre les pide mirar el menú antes de sentarse.
    (C) El señor necesita hablar con el grupo primero.
    (D) Prefieren no sentarse cerca de la cocina.

26. ¿Cuál es la esperanza del restaurante?

    (A) que los clientes tengan que esperar
    (B) que la comida no valga nada
    (C) que los clientes coman rápido
    (D) que la espera valga la pena

Selection 4

Hasta años recientes, algunas manifestaciones teatrales principalmente de la frontera con los Estados Unidos han trascendido su carácter espontáneo y han logrado articular un lenguaje artístico complejo. Esto es un hecho muy interesante respecto de la resistencia cultural del país. Este teatro regional ha contribuido con su característica vitalidad a mostrar los múltiples rostros de una nación. Un rostro, sin embargo, permanece invisible. Hoy día, cuando el reconocimiento de las culturas indias es uno de los puntos centrales en la agenda política, es curioso que haya sólo una región donde se ve y se oye ese rostro del rostro más antiguamente mexicano.

27. Según este autor, ¿qué debe reflejar el teatro nacional?

    (A) un rostro unido del país
    (B) rostros de las culturas actuales
    (C) sólo los rostros indios
    (D) el rostro del español peninsular

GO ON TO THE NEXT PAGE

Selection 5

Hace cinco años quienes llevaban un arete en la cara eran personas que querían diferenciarse de los demás. Pero poco a poco ha ido convirtiéndose en una moda nueva para todos los jóvenes. En MTV se realizan unas 20 perforaciones diarias en jóvenes cuyas edades oscilan entre 12 y 23 años. Los sitios más reconocidos exigen un permiso de los padres a menores de edad pero este requerimiento no existe para puestos en la calle. La perforación dura unos cuantos minutos y mucho dinero. El precio depende del lugar del cuerpo en donde se vaya a perforar y de la joya escogida.

28. ¿Qué moda comenta esta selección?

    (A) la ropa que llevan en MTV
    (B) la exploración en busca de petróleo
    (C) la moda en adornos corporales
    (D) el encuentro con amigos en las calles

29. ¿Entre quiénes es popular la nueva moda?

    (A) los adolescentes
    (B) los padres de los jóvenes
    (C) los mayores de 23 años de edad
    (D) los menores de 12 años de edad

30. ¿De qué depende el precio?

    (A) del permiso de los padres
    (B) del taller donde se realiza el procedimiento
    (C) el tamaño del cuerpo del joven
    (D) el sitio y la piedra preciosa que se seleccionan

Selection 6

—Hola, María. ¿Qué tal fue el verano?
—Ay, Miguel, estaba muy ocupada.
—Ya lo creo. No te vi por ninguna parte.
—Tuve una oportunidad imprescindible para mi carrera futura.
—¿De veras? Rápido, ¿qué hacías?
—Trabajaba en un laboratorio en el hospital este verano. Pero un fin de semana fui con mi papá a una conferencia. Conoció a un doctor a quien no había visto hace años. Al enterarse él de que yo estudiaba quechua además de biología y química, me invitó a trabajar en su laboratorio en Ecuador el verano que viene. Me gustaría hacerme médica allí.
—¡Ni modo! ¡Qué oportunidad será!

31. ¿Dónde estaba María el verano pasado?

    (A) En Ecuador.
    (B) En una conferencia.
    (C) En un hospital.
    (D) En la universidad.

32. ¿En qué carrera piensa María para el futuro?

    (A) Maestría para enseñar quechua.
    (B) Química para conseguir trabajo en un laboratorio.
    (C) Medicina para trabajar en Ecuador.
    (D) Antropología para usar las ciencias naturales.

GO ON TO THE NEXT PAGE

Selection 7

—Querido, ¿adónde vamos de vacaciones este verano? ¿Tienes algunas ideas?

—Bueno, podemos ir adónde quieras. El año pasado escogí el lugar.

—Pero quiero que los dos nos divirtamos. Sé que a ti te gustan las actividades del campo, montar en bicicleta de montaña, acampar, todo eso.

—No importa. Ya te toca a ti seleccionar. Prefieres un balneario que brinde sol, brisas frescas, playas calurosas, quizás unas tiendas para comprar algunas cositas.

—Ya veo que me conoces muy bien. Voy a buscar un buen hotel en la playa al pie de unas montañas. ¿Existe tal lugar?

33. ¿En qué están de acuerdo los dos?

(A) Van a la playa de vacaciones.

(B) Van a las montañas de vacaciones.

(C) Uno no estará contento ese verano.

(D) Uno va a esperar su turno.

STOP!

**If you finish before time is up,
you may check your work.**

SECTION II

READING

Approximate Time—40 minutes

Questions 34–85

Part A

Directions: Select the most appropriate word to complete the sentence and fill in the corresponding oval on the answer sheet.

34. Después de jugar en el sol todo el día, quiero ___ un vaso grande de limonada.

    (A) vivir
    (B) tomar
    (C) deber
    (D) saludar

35. Ese profesor tiene fama de dar ___ muy altas en todos sus cursos.

    (A) notas
    (B) firmas
    (C) lecturas
    (D) temas

36. Si tienes ___, ¿por qué no duermes una siesta?

    (A) razón
    (B) sueño
    (C) hambre
    (D) suerte

37. Para los jóvenes, sería buena idea ___ para su educación universitaria.

    (A) apoyar
    (B) salvar
    (C) desarrollar
    (D) ahorrar

38. Debes ___ una camisa con mangas largas para proteger los brazos del sol.

    (A) llevar
    (B) llegar
    (C) vender
    (D) seguir

39. ¿___ vieron Vds. en la fiesta anoche?

    (A) Quiénes
    (B) Cómo
    (C) A quién
    (D) Dónde

40. La clase ___ lunes pasado a las ocho fue difícil.

    (A) del
    (B) los
    (C) de las
    (D) de los

41. Espero aprobar todas mis asignaturas este semestre sin suspender ___.

    (A) ninguno
    (B) alguno
    (C) ninguna
    (D) alguien

GO ON TO THE NEXT PAGE

42. ___ de poco tiempo puedes ir al parque, Juanito.

    (A) Hasta
    (B) Dentro
    (C) Ante
    (D) Alrededor

43. Tenía ___ muy largas y negras que le caían hasta la cintura.

    (A) trenes
    (B) hilas
    (C) cebollas
    (D) trenzas

44. Porque el agua bajaba de los glaciares helados, no se entraba en ___ para nadar.

    (A) sí
    (B) el
    (C) él
    (D) ella

45. Parece que va a ___ buen tiempo mañana y podemos ir a la playa.

    (A) tener
    (B) hacer
    (C) estar
    (D) ser

46. Este parque no es uno de los más grandes, ___ me gusta de todos modos.

    (A) como
    (B) pero
    (C) sino
    (D) tampoco

47. Si ___ tiempo, puedes empezar la tarea para mañana.

    (A) tienes
    (B) tendías
    (C) tengas
    (D) has tenido

48. La voz se le quedó completamente ___ de tanto gritar en el partido.

    (A) salida
    (B) ronca
    (C) sorda
    (D) dulce

49. Es importante que los padres se lleven ___ bien como los hijos.

    (A) tan
    (B) tanto
    (C) tal
    (D) tales

50. Parece increíble que las mariposas ___ a México, pero lo hacen cada año.

    (A) viajan
    (B) viajen
    (C) han viajado
    (D) habían viajado

GO ON TO THE NEXT PAGE

Part B

Directions: First read through the entire paragraph. Then, for each numbered blank, choose the completion that is most appropriate given the context of the passage. Fill in the corresponding oval on the answer sheet.

Ahora todos buscan algo. Siempre (51) igual, dice mamá, pero como tú eres muy joven no lo sabes.

Yo pienso y digo que ahora es de otra forma: (52) locos buscando. También nosotros. Mamá y yo hemos pasado de hospital en hospital tratando de hallar un especialista para hacerle ver mi (53) derecho que no podía apoyar bien en el suelo. (54) que un señor que guardaba las manos en los bolsillos de su delantal blanco dijo que lo (55) gratis. Me hizo sacar el calcetín (56) de una puerta en el hospital, a la entrada del comedor, donde las enfermeras se sientan a tomar (57) de pollo con letras de pasta que (58) en el agua.

51. (A) sea
    (B) han sido
    (C) haya sido
    (D) ha sido

52. (A) se vuelven
    (B) se hacen
    (C) se convierten
    (D) se transforman

53. (A) cabeza
    (B) pie
    (C) rodilla
    (D) mano

54. (A) Aún
    (B) Hasta
    (C) Pero
    (D) Hacia

55. (A) hace
    (B) haría
    (C) haya hecho
    (D) hubiera hecho

56. (A) detrás
    (B) encima
    (C) sobre
    (D) bajo

57. (A) cartas
    (B) vaso
    (C) jabón
    (D) sopa

58. (A) soplan
    (B) brincan
    (C) flotan
    (D) picotean

GO ON TO THE NEXT PAGE

Una noche estábamos todos despidiéndonos al pie de la escalera antes de irnos a dormir. Tío Gustavo ya había __(59)__ todas las luces, menos __(60)__ la escalera. Tía Matilde, que __(61)__ a tío Armando que abriera la __(62)__ de su cuarto para que __(63)__ un poco de aire, de pronto __(64)__, dejando sus despedidas inconclusas, y los movimientos de todos nosotros, que comenzábamos a subir, __(65)__.

—¿Qué __(66)__? —preguntó mi padre bajando un escalón.

—Suban —murmuró tía Matilde, dándose la vuelta para mirar la __(67)__ del vestíbulo.

__(68)__ no subimos.

59. (A) agarrado
    (B) encendido
    (C) tornado
    (D) apagado

60. (A) ella de
    (B) la de
    (C) la que
    (D) lo de

61. (A) veía
    (B) creía
    (C) pensaba
    (D) recomendaba

62. (A) luz
    (B) cubierta
    (C) ventana
    (D) tapia

63. (A) entra
    (B) entraba
    (C) entrara
    (D) hubiera entrada

64. (A) vociferó
    (B) enmudeció
    (C) entregó
    (D) abrazó

65. (A) lentos
    (B) pasados
    (C) rápidos
    (D) detenidos

66. (A) pasa
    (B) pasara
    (C) pase
    (D) haya pasado

67. (A) penumbra
    (B) fantasma
    (C) mapa
    (D) pantalla

68. (A) Cuando
    (B) Sino
    (C) Mas
    (D) Mientras

GO ON TO THE NEXT PAGE

Part C

Directions: Read the following texts carefully. Then, for each question that follows, select the best answer according to the text. Fill in the corresponding oval on the answer sheet.

Línea   El lunes pasado, los metropolitanos olvidaron citas, trabajos y negocios importantes—muchas personas ni siquiera abrieron sus tiendas—para ir al encuentro de la nieve. Las gentes que iban
(5) en camión a sus habituales ocupaciones al ver nuestras montañas cubiertas de nieve, pidieron "esquina" antes de llegar al centro. Contagió a todos. La carretera de Cuernavaca estaba llena de coches y, a su vez, los coches repletos de niños
(10) y papás que recordaban aquellos tiempos en que esquiaban en el Canadá. Los niños venían preparados para revolcarse en la nieve, construir un inmenso muñeco, jugar a la guerra y tirarse por primera vez una bola de nieve a la cara.
(15) Saludaban con gritos de alegría a los coches que regresaban de Cuernavaca—ya sea porque habían pasado el fin de semana allá o porque habían salido más temprano, antes de que los policías prohibieran el paso.

69. Según lo que dice en la selección, la nieve en Cuernavaca es un acontecimiento

(A) frecuente
(B) insigne
(C) desprovisto
(D) insólito

70. El efecto de la nieve era

(A) facilitar la pereza.
(B) unir a toda la comunidad.
(C) mejorar la circulación de coches.
(D) promocionar viajes al Canadá.

71. ¿Qué anticipaban los niños?

(A) divertirse
(B) esquiar
(C) lavarse la cara
(D) trabajar

72. ¿Qué solía hacer la policía?

(A) Jugar con los niños en la nieve.
(B) Pasar la semana en Cuernavaca.
(C) Cerrar los caminos a Cuernavaca.
(D) Regocijarse de la nieve con los adultos.

GO ON TO THE NEXT PAGE

Línea   Antonio subía mercancías de Palomar cada
semana. Además de posaderos, tenían el único
comercio de la aldea. Su casa, ancha y grande,
rodeada por el huerto, estaba a la entrada del
(5)   pueblo. Vivían con desahogo, y en el pueblo
Antonio tenía fama de rico. "Fama de rico,"
pensaba Mariana, inquieta. "Y si no lo fuera, ¿me
habría casado con él, acaso?" No. No era difícil
comprender por qué se había casado con aquel
(10)   hombre brutal, que tenía catorce años más que
ella. Un hombre hosco y temido, solitario. Ella
era guapa. Sí; todo el pueblo lo sabía y decía que
era guapa. También Constantino, que estaba
enamorado de ella. Pero Constantino era un
(15)   simple aparcero, como ella. Y ella estaba harta
del hambre, y trabajos, y tristezas. Sí; estaba harta.
Por eso se casó con Antonio.

73. ¿Por qué se casó Mariana con Antonio?

(A) Ella quería un esposo próspero.

(B) Antonio la adoraba porque era rica.

(C) Ella quería alguien tan rico como ella.

(D) Él era mayor que ella y la trataba bien.

74. ¿Quién era Constantino?

(A) un comerciante

(B) un cliente de Antonio

(C) un amigo de Antonio

(D) un antiguo novio de Mariana

75. En la línea 6, "fama de rico" significa que
Antonio era

(A) más rico que otros de Palomar.

(B) más rico comparado a otros de su aldea.

(C) tan pobre como otros del pueblo.

(D) pobre en realidad.

76. Antonio se casó con Mariana porque

(A) ella era hermosa.

(B) ella tenía dinero de su familia.

(C) Constantino le aconsejó casarse con ella.

(D) quería una esposa más joven que él.

77. En esta selección parece que Mariana se sentía

(A) ansiosa.

(B) tranquila.

(C) satisfecha.

(D) celosa.

GO ON TO THE NEXT PAGE

78. Según el anuncio, el romance consiste en

    (A) el alcance de lo inasequible.

    (B) el conocimiento de una lengua extranjera.

    (C) expressiones facilitadas por Visa.

    (D) palabras sentimentales sin acciones que corresponden.

79. ¿Cómo sería más romántica un mundo que usa Visa?

    (A) Todo cuesta menos comprando con ella.

    (B) Es más fácil disfrutar de la vida buena.

    (C) Es necesario tener más dinero en efectivo.

    (D) Nunca se tiene que pagar las cuentas.

GO ON TO THE NEXT PAGE

Línea   Pablo asegura que el sistema de enseñanza en
la universidad no era práctico pues no se tenía en
cuenta que él y sus compañeros ya habían tenido
una agotadora jornada en sus colegios. Cuando
(5) se retiró sintió un alivio y una gran aversión por
la música clásica—que sólo años después pudo
superar. Piensa que fue un gran desperdicio
porque aunque no aspiraba a ser gran músico sí le
hubiera gustado tocar bien el piano.
(10)   Para remediar el problema de estudiantes como
Pablo, muchos profesores hoy dicen que se debe
hacer el aprendizaje de una manera agradable,
en medio de juegos y actividades divertidas.
De hecho, en muchos idiomas (como inglés y
(15) francés), se utiliza la misma palabra para decir
tocar y jugar. Lo más importante hoy es que exista
una integración entre lo que se oye, lo que se
toca y los códigos de este lenguaje, lo cual pica el
interés del estudiante a medida que practica.

80. El problema para Pablo al estudiar música
era que

(A) el programa era demasiado fácil.

(B) había sólo un de tipo de música que
estudiaba.

(C) no tocaba bastante bien para ser
profesional.

(D) no comprendía lo que trataban de
enseñarle.

81. A causa de su experiencia como estudiante de
música, al retirarse del programa, sentía

(A) orgullo de su talento.

(B) amargura por no haber tenido éxito.

(C) alegría de saber tocar bien.

(D) melancolía por haber perdido una
oportunidad.

82. Según Pablo, la meta de la enseñanza musical
puede ser que

(A) todo el mundo pueda tocar bien.

(B) cada cual pueda ser profesional.

(C) cada uno alcance su nivel más alto.

(D) se aprenda sin tener que practicar.

83. Según los profesores modernos, los niños
aprenden mejor

(A) en un programa riguroso.

(B) cuando no tienen que practicar.

(C) de una manera más intuitiva.

(D) hablando de lo que hacen.

84. Según esta selección los dos verbos, tocar y
jugar, se asocian por la idea de que

(A) la práctica puede ser un placer.

(B) se aprende hablando de lo que quiere
aprender.

(C) no se tiene que trabajar para aprender.

(D) aprender es una actividad física.

85. ¿Qué resultado tiene la nueva metodología de
enseñar la música?

(A) Todo el mundo aprende a tocar como
profesional.

(B) Se mezclan la teoría con la música al
tocarla.

(C) Los estudiantes hablan mejor.

(D) Los niños no se interesan en practicar.

STOP!

**If you finish before time is up,
you may check your work.**

Answer Key
Practice Test 5

Section I

Part A

1. C
2. C
3. D
4. D
5. A
6. B
7. D
8. A
9. D
10. C

Part B

11. D
12. C
13. B
14. B
15. C
16. A
17. B
18. A
19. C
20. B

Part C

21. D
22. A
23. B
24. D
25. D
26. D
27. B
28. C
29. A
30. D
31. C
32. C
33. D

Section II

Part A

34. B
35. A
36. B
37. D
38. A
39. C
40. A
41. C
42. B
43. D
44. B
45. B
46. B
47. A
48. B
49. A
50. B

Part B

51. D
52. A
53. B
54. B
55. B
56. A
57. D
58. C
59. D
60. B
61. D
62. C

63. C
64. B
65. D
66. A
67. A
68. C

Part C

69. D
70. B
71. A
72. C
73. A
74. D
75. B
76. A
77. A
78. C
79. B
80. B
81. D
82. C
83. C
84. A
85. B

ANSWERS AND EXPLANATIONS

Section I

Part A

1. (C) This picture is of a port, so many boats come here.

2. (C) This man would likely be asking what you would like for lunch. A *pata* is the foot of an animal, but it is not eaten as you would a sandwich, which is held in the man's other hand. There is bread (D) in the sandwich, but the price of bread is not the point of the picture.

3. (D) *Arena* in (C) does mean "sand," but the men are not building sandcastles. They are on the beach, but they are reclining in the sun. (D) says "Let's sleep a little, and later we'll swim," which is likely what these men would say. *Bañarnos* in (A) means "to bathe," but they would not be bathing with soap in the sea.

4. (D) These animals are not donkeys, *burros*, so (C) is wrong. The animals are *bueyes*, not *burros*, but the word *bailan* should tell you that this is not the answer. And the young man is not relaxing in the country, so (A) is out as well. The work is harder than the boy had thought it would be, choice (D).

5. (A) *Tocar* is "to play a musical instrument," so (A is correct. The man is obviously not practicing a sport, and he is not dancing to classical music, so (B) and (C) are wrong.

6. (B) In this photo, a cat is perched on a branch in a tree. *En frente de* and *delante de* both mean "in front of," so (C) and (D) are wrong. *Debajo* is "beneath," so (A) is out as well. *Sobre* means "on top of," and it is the correct answer.

7. (D) Two mimes are entertaining people on the Ramblas, a broad pedestrian walkway in the city of Barcelona. These men are not earning money by cleaning the street, so (A) is out. Nor have the romans invaded the city, so (C) is out. Though they look like statues, they are actually mimes. And although you may not have recognized that they are mimes, you could have used the process of elimination.

8. (A) A woman is asking how much the pineapples cost today. (A) is the correct choice. She would not be asking why there aren't any bananas, since you see plenty on the stand. That means (B) is wrong. Don't confuse *planos* in (C) with *plátanos*, another word for *bananas* in some countries, or *sandalias* ("sandals") in (D) with *sandías*, watermelons.

9. (D) *Boda* and *ceremonia nupcial* both mean "wedding," but (A) can't be right, because it states that "nobody invited me to the wedding in the church." (D) is the better choice, since it says "I am ready for the wedding," which is quite likely what the lady in the photo would say. The words *manera formal* in (B) are distracters; the sentence does not refer to going to dinner.

10. (C) The people on the street do not appear to be paying attention to the figures on the balcony. The figures are not washing windows, so (D) is wrong. *Buscar* in (B) means "to look for," which does not work in this situation: The people aren't looking for the figures on the balcony. *Peatones* are "pedestrians," but the store owner does not employ them to advertise his business, so (A) is wrong. Do not choose an answer choice just because it contains a word for something you see in the picture.

Part B

11. (D) In the conversation Marta has other plans, so (D) is the only correct answer. (A) and (C) present the idea that she can go, and (B) is not something the first speaker would say.

12. (C) The salesperson quickly offered the client another picture, since the one he wanted was too expensive. He would certainly try to make a sale, which makes (A) incorrect. (B) assumes that the client is going to buy the expensive picture. (D) doesn't work because the salesperson has made the connection between famous painters and expensive paintings.

13. (B) The lady is complaining about the high price of gasoline, but the second speaker tries to be reassuring. It does not make sense to listen to the news again if all it does is make you mad, so (A) is incorrect. (C) is wrong, because in the conversation the second speaker states that they need to drive to get to work. (D) makes no sense at all. Don't pick an answer just because it may have some words from the conversation.

14. (B) After not hearing clearly the first time, the second speaker finally gets the idea that the caller want help quickly so he can get to the airport on time. He might say that he was too busy to help, but he would not say that he does not want to help the caller, so (A) is not a good choice. Clearly, if the caller's car is not working, he can't use it to get to the airport, so (C) is wrong. The second speaker has no way of knowing whether the plane will leave without the caller, or even if the caller is trying to catch a flight, so (D) is wrong.

15. (C) The girls are talking about a famous movie star and how many good films she has made, making (C) the only possible right answer.

16. (A) The words *gracias a Dios* tell you that the second speaker is quite happy not to have too much homework that night, so (B) and (D) and wrong. (C) is not true.

17. (B) María wants to lend Raquel a dress to wear, so (A) is wrong. Jeans and a sweater are not what María wants to wear; it is a more formal type of dance, indicated by the words *elegante* and *apropiado*, making (C) incorrect. (D) is wrong because since María has offered to help find a dress, she would not be advising her not to go to the dance.

18. (A) *Agradecer* means "to thank." The other choices are nonsensical.

19. (C) Both speakers clearly want to go to the beach, making (A) incorrect. (B) is not true, according to the second speaker. Since they are talking about going to the beach, (D) makes no sense. *Divertirse*, meaning "to have fun," is a good word to remember.

20. (B) The first speaker wants to help his friend, so he offers to help, making (A), (D), and (C) wrong.

Part C

21. (D) This selection features a cabin attendant getting ready to depart from the gate at an airport. The person giving the instructions is a cabin attendant, *una azafata*. A *niñiera* is a babysitter, so (B) is wrong.

22. (A) The people are inside an airplane cabin, waiting to depart. A *sala de espera* is a "waiting room," and a *sala de estar* is a "living room," so (C) and (D) are wrong.

23. (B) You can tell Alfredi is dressed for cold weather with his long sleeved undershirt, jacket and a cap for his head. The passage also mentions snow, so the correct answer is (B), winter.

24. (D) The advantage of this clothing is that it protects from the cold. Fashion is not mentioned, so (A) is wrong. And the text says the price is between a high and a low price, which isn't quite the same as ((B), so that is out as well. Once he is warm, Alfredo will be able to concentrate more on fishing, (D).

25. (D) Three women are waiting for a table in a restaurant. Though there is one free table, it is near the kitchen, so the women chose to wait for another.

26. (D) The restaurant hopes that the women will think the wait is "worth it."

27. (B) The author feels that theater should reflect all aspects of a people, even though he is most interested in the underrepresentation of native Indian people in theater.

28. (C) "Piercing" is the newest fashion among some teenagers who watch MTV. The word comes from *perforacíon* ("perforation"). *Adornos corporales* in (C) is "body adornment."

29. (A) This new wave of fashion is popular among adolescents (those between 12–23). *Mayores* in (C) means "older," and *menores* in (D) means "younger."

30. (D) The price of the piercing varies according to what part of the body will be pierced, as well as what stone is chose. The price has nothing to do with adolescents getting their parents' permission, so (A) is wrong. The size of the person's body has nothing to do with the price either, so (C) is out, too.

31. (C) María worked in a hospital during the summer. She was not in Ecuador, she only met a doctor who had a lab there, so (A) is wrong. She says nothing about a university, so (D) is out as well.

32. (C) You can assume Maria is interested in a career in medicine, since she speaks of the doctor she met, as well the fact that she is studying biology and chemistry. She displays excitement at the prospect of one day working in Ecuador.

33. (D) The couple has decided to take turns on choosing vacations, since they each like to do different things. He likes the mountains, she likes the beach. *Balneario* in paragraph four is a resort.

Section II
Part A

34. (B) *Tomar* means "to drink." If a waiter asks *¿Qué desea Vd. tomar?*, he is asking you what you'd like to drink. No other choice makes any sense.

35. (A) *Notas* means "grades" almost everywhere in the Spanish speaking world. The other word that is common for "grades" is *calificaciones*. "Notes," as in what you take in a lecture class, is *apuntes*. Remember that words like *tema* are almost all cognates, because *th* does not exist in Spanish.

36. (B) *Dormir la siesta* indicates that you need the expression *tener sueño*.

37. (D) *Salvar* (B) is to save something or someone, but when you save money, use *ahorrar*. This use is required here.

38. (A) *Llevar* can mean "to wear," as well as "to take" or "to carry." It is also used in expressions that are harder to translate: *Llevo tres años aquí*, for example, means "I have been here three years." *Seguir* means "to follow."

39. (C) In Spanish, when you want to ask "whom" did you see last night, you have to use a personal *a* in front of the interrogative pronoun. Then there is no uncertainty as to when "who" is appropriate and when "whom" is appropriate. The personal *a* tells you that *quién* is the object of the verb, "whom" in English, so (C) is the only correct choice. (B) and (D) do not work because they do not refer to people or things that are seen.

40. (A) The word that eliminates all answers except *del* is *pasado*. You cannot tell from *lunes* if the word is used as a singular or a plural noun. The adjective will tell you, though. To make *lunes* plural, you use a plural article, *los*. Also, remember that *el lunes* means "on Monday."

41. (C) The indefinite negative pronoun refers to *asignatura*, so you have to use the full feminine form. *Sin* in front of the verb makes the negative possible. *Alguno* cannot be used because it is masculine. *Suspender* means "to fail" a course, etc.

42. (B) With the preposition *de* following the blank, you cannot use *hasta* or *ante*. Grammatically, *alrededor*, meaning "around," does take *de* after it, but it does not make sense in this context. *Dentro de* means "within."

43. (D) This vocabulary question is best done by the process of elimination. *Caer al cinturón* is "to fall to the waist," and it is long and black. You want a word for hair, but you do not see *pelo* or *cabello*. Do not mistake *cebollas*, meaning "onions," for *cabello*. You know *tren* is a train, but perhaps you don't recognize *hilas* or *trenzas*. If you're really stuck, see if you can reduce the number of answer choices to two, and then guess. The word for "tresses," meaning "locks of hair," is *trenzas*. *Hilas* are "threads," both literally and figuratively.

44. (D) Be careful with this question. *Agua* is feminine: The masculine article *el* is used in the singular form only because *agua* begins with a stressed *a*. And after a preposition, you have to use a prepositional pronoun. *Ella* is the only possible answer.

45. (B) *Hacer buen tiempo* means "to be nice weather," which is what is necessary to go to the beach. Always look in the rest of the sentence when you see a verb that can mean "to be," in order to see the context.

46. (B) *De todos modos* on the end of the sentence tells you that this is a simple sentence, not a comparison, so *como* and *sino* do not fit. *Tampoco* doesn't make sense because the speaker is not agreeing with anything, or corroborating an opinion. Only *pero* makes sense.

47. (A) This grammar question is easy if you remember that you should not use the present subjunctive after *si*. Notice that the other verb in the sentence says "you can begin," meaning that the action has not happened. That means the imperfect and the present perfect wouldn't make sense, because the time frame is present. "If you have the time, you can begin the homework for tomorrow."

48. (B) This vocabulary has some words you may not recognize. You may associate *dulce* with a tone of voice, but the context states that the person has been yelling at a game. The word you are looking for is probably "gone." Regarding (A), *salir* is "to leave," but as a past participle ("gone") it is usually used with *haber* in a compound tense. That leaves (B) and (C). *Sorda* means "deaf." *Ronca* means "hoarse," and is the answer.

49. (A) Remember that before an adverb you need to use *tan*. *Tantos* is used before nouns, or adjectives used as nouns. *Tal* means "such" and makes no sense in this sentence. Neither does *tales* for the same reason.

50. (B) First scan the sentence to see what kind of clause is used. It is in a noun clause, because *parece* is the verb in the main clause, followed by *que* and a new subject. This is also an impersonal expression, because there is an indefinite subject for *parece*. It means "it seems." You now know you have to use the subjunctive, and you haven't even translated the sentence.

Part B

51. (D) This is a grammar question about verbs, so look for possible subjects. The only clue you have is that *igual* is singular, so (B) with a third person plural form is wrong. There is also no reason to use the subjunctive, so (A) and (C) can be eliminated. That leaves the present perfect as the correct answer.

52. (A) Several of these answer choices mean "to become" or "to get." You also see that the word following the blank is *locos. Volverse loco* is the expression for "to go crazy." *Hacerse* means "to become" in the sense of "making something of yourself." *Convertirse* usually suggests a physical change, as in a chemical transformation. *Transformarse* makes no sense in this sentence.

53. (B) The words in the passage telling you what part of the body is involved: *No podía apoyar bien en el suelo*, and *Me hizo sacar el calcetín*. You wear *calcetines* on your feet.

54. (B) The context tells you the speaker and his mother had gone from hospital to hospital looking for a doctor that would do it for free. *Hasta* is the only word. *Aún*, with an accent means "still" or "yet," which is the same meaning as *todavía*.

55. (B) This is a grammar question, so look to see where in the sentence the verb comes. The main clause says *dijo que*, a structure that could require the subjunctive if *decir* were meant as an order. When you look at the rest of the sentence, though, you can tell that this is a statement of fact, so you'll need the indicative. That means (C) and (D) can be eliminated. The passage starts out in the present, so you might think choice (A) was correct. If you are paying attention, though, you'll see that you need the conditional, meaning "he would do" it for free.

56. (A) You want an adverb that places the narrator someplace around a door. The only one that works is *detrás*. "Beneath," "over," and "above" do not describe where he would be to take off a sock.

57. (D) *Sopa* means "soup." The reference to *cartas* is a distractor based on the reference to *letras de masa*. Actually, the nurses, *enfermeras*, are eating alphabet chicken soup. You could talk about "having a glass" of some beverage, but the rest of the sentence makes (B) incorrect. Make sure you understand all the distinctions between *enfermeras* "nurses," *enfermos* "sick people," *enfermedad* "an illness," *enfermizo* "sickly," and *enfermarse* "to get sick."

58. (C) This word is obvious; *flotan* is a cognate. *Brincar* means "to jump" or "to hop," like *saltar. Soplar* describes wind; it means "to blow."

59. (D) Both *encender* and *apagar* are included in the answer choices, so read carefully to see which one you need. The phrase *irnos a dormir* indicates that the people were getting ready to go upstairs to bed. One turns out the lights to go to bed; use *apagar*.

60. (B) The phrase you want to use is "except the one" by the stairs. For this pronoun, you need to find what "one" refers to: the previous noun *luz. La de* tells which noun, *la luz*, and where it is located, *de*. (C) is wrong in this context because the noun after *la que* would make the phrase meaningless.

61. (D) In the clause that follows this verb, the verb takes the subjunctive form. That means there must be something in the main clause that requires the subjunctive in the dependent clause. The blank is followed by a personal *a*, so whatever the word is, it will be something that tía Matilde says or does to tío Armando. *Recomendaba* would work. For *creía* or *pensaba* to fit, you would have to use *que* after the blank.

62. (C) The only thing that can be opened in a room from this set is a window.

63. (C) After *para que* you need the subjunctive. Since all of the other verbs in the passage are in the past tense, you'll need to use *entrara*, the past subjunctive of *entrar*.

64. (B) The phrase *dejando sus despedidas inconclusas* indicates that the narrator and the older men did not say anything. *Despedidas* are "goodbyes," and *inconclusas* means "unfinished." The word you want in the blank, then, is something about speech. You may wonder where the subject of the verb

is, also. At the end of the sentence, the narrator says, *los movimientos de todos nosotros*, meaning that tía Matilde is the one who suddenly stopped talking. *Vociferó* won't work, because there would not be anything left unsaid. *Mudo*, in *enmudeció*, means "mute."

65. (D) The word required to complete the meaning of the sentence is an adjective that goes with the words *despedidas inconclusas* and *dejando*. No other choice fits.

66. (A) This verb form occurs in a quotation. In Spanish, the dash is used to indicate a quotation mark; it indicates dialogue. This form will be in the present tense. Think of the common phrase *¿Qué pasa?*, meaning, "What's happening?" as opposed to *¿Qué pasó?*, which means "What happened?."

67. (A) *Penumbra* means "darkness." Go back to the beginning of the piece and remember that tió Gustavo already turned out the lights, so the foyer is dark. No other choice works here.

68. (C) The only word that works here is *mas* without an accent (meaning "but"), because the narrator is saying that they did not do what she had said. *Cuando* would introduce a subordinate clause, needing another clause to complete the thought. And *mientras* would indicate duration of an action, which is not the case here.

Part C

Questions 69–72

69. (D) This passage recounts a day when it snowed in Cuernavaca. Everyone was excited, and all came prepared to play in the snow. From the general reaction of people, you can guess that the snow is not a common sight. What else would make them forget normal schedules except a rare event. (A) can be ruled out. *Desprovisto* means "lacking," and *insigne* means "distinguished." *Acontemimiento* is a long word, but a good one to know. It means "event." That leaves *insólito*, which means "unusual," or "unaccustomed." It is a good word to remember.

70. (B) *Pereza* is "sloth;" it goes with the adjective *perezoso*. That was clearly not the effect of the snow, so (A) is wrong. (C) refers to improving the flow of traffic. That was the opposite of what happened, so that is wrong as well. The snow brought together the community, choice (B).

71. (A) *Divertirse* means "to have fun."

72. (C) The words *antes de que los policías prohibieran el paso* in the text indicate that the police were ready to close the road if it got too dangerous.

Questions 73–77

This passage is about a woman, Mariana, who speaks about the man she married. She married Antonio because he was wealthy, though cruel. Fed up with her impoverished situation, she decided to marry Antonio and not Constantino, a boyfriend who also had little money.

73. (A) Mariana married Antonio because she was tired of being poor: Antonio was rich, though much older than she. The passage does not say that Antonio adored her, nor that he even loved her. He was *un hombre brutal*.

74. (D) Constantino was an old boyfriend that Maria didn't marry because he was poor. When *antiguo* comes in front of a noun, it can mean "former."

75. (B) *Fama de rico* is in quotation marks to indicate that Antonio has the reputation of being rich, but his wealth is relative. That is, even though he is wealthy, he does not have an easy life. Antonio has an inn, the only business in the village, just on the edge of town. Compared to others in the town, he is wealthy.

76. (A) The text clearly states Mariana is pretty: [*Ella*] *era guapa*.

77. (A) Mariana certainly is not satisfied, so (C) won't work. *Celosa*, "jealous," does not fit the situation, either, so (D) is wrong. *Ansiosa* means "anxious," which best describes her emotional state.

Questions 78–79

78. (C) According to this ad, romance is possible if you can purchase those things that communicate love and romance. The word *lengua* in (B) is a distractor: The text does not indicate that the language of love is a foreign language. Romance is not necessarily the attainment of impossible things (choice A), just ordinary things like flowers. But the text does not say that any of these things necessarily have to be so expensive that they are impossible. The card facilitates romance by making it possible to give gifts of love with a Visa card.

79. (B) It is easier to enjoy life with a credit card. *Dinero en efectivo* is "cash," but you don't have to carry more cash if you have a credit card, so (C) is out. Things definitely do not cost less, so (A) is out.

Questions 80–85

According to this passage, music that is taught in a traditional manner kills interest. It begins with the case of Pablo, who had a bad experience learning to play the piano. The first paragraph describes how Pablo took an intensive music course in high school, but still had to study classical music at the university level. The second paragraph talks of changing the way students are taught music to be more fun and engaging. It points out that in many languages, the word play is one word, whereas in Spanish it is two words, *tocar* and *jugar*.

80. (B) The passage does not say that Pablo thought the program easy, but rather very hard, so (A) is wrong. The focus was on classical music only, to such an extent that Pablo could not stand it by the time he quit taking music lessons. His problem was not that he couldn't do the work, just that it wasn't of interest to him, so (D) is wrong.

81. (D) Because of his experience, Pablo is sorry over the loss of an opportunity. He is not bitter for not having succeeded, so (B) is wrong. Nor does the text say anything about his being proud of his musical talent, so (A) is not appropriate.

82. (C) According to Pablo, the goal of teaching music should be that each person reaches (*alcance*) his highest level. He does not expect students will not have to practice, so (D) is wrong. Nor does he expect each student to reach a professional level, so (B) is wrong.

83. (C) Teachers today claim that if children study music using games, they'll learn in a more intuitive way.

84. (A) The passage points to the fact that in Spanish, there are two words for "to play," while in other languages there's only one. *Tocar* is an activity associated with hours of practice in the traditional methodology. But *jugar* implies fun, the opposite of the practice implied by *tocar*. Using one word to express the same activity reflects an attitude toward the way one learns to play music: One can have fun learning to play well.

85. (B) When theory is integrated into playing the music, it becomes less of a chore to learn. Practice can become more like a game, and a student's interest is aroused so that he learns more readily. (D) is wrong because it states that students lose interest in practicing. And (C) is wrong because the passage has nothing to do with talking better.

Chapter 10: **Scoring Your Practice Tests**

For each correct answer on both tests, you receive one point. For each incorrect answer you lose one-third of a point. Unanswered questions are not counted. That means if you leave a question blank, or if you accidentally mark two answers on the same line, nothing is counted.

Your answer sheet will be scanned by a machine that will record your answers, and a computer will produce your raw score. The raw score is converted into a score on a scale from 200–800. This scaled score is the one reported to the colleges you select. The Spanish with Listening Test also reports subscores in listening and reading, on a 20–80 scale.

Below is the worksheet for finding your raw score. Use your raw score from the Diagnostic Test to gauge how well you improve on the subsequent practice tests.

SCORING THE SPANISH TEST

Step 1: Check your answers with the answer key. Remember that items you leave blank or misgrid will not be counted.

Step 2: Add up the number of correct answers.   _____

Step 3: Add up the number of incorrect answers.   _____

Step 4: Multiply the number of incorrect answers by .333.   _____

Step 5: Subtract the result in step 4 from the number in step 2.   _____

Step 6: Round up to the nearest whole number.   _____

The number you get in Step 6 is your raw score. Your raw score is converted to a scaled score by computer, which is why we don't have a real-score-to-scaled-score conversion chart in this book. Scaled scores take into account the fact that some test editions are harder (or easier) than other test editions. So if you take the Spanish Test one year and get a 500, and then take it again another year and again get a 500, those two scores indicate the same level of achievement. In general, if you get about 50 percent of the answers correct, your score should be somewhere around 550. That's 43 out of 85 items. With conscientious preparation, you can do much better than average. A 600 (about 50 out of 85) or above is a good score.

After you take the Diagnostic Test and work through this book, take the remaining practice tests at different intervals to see if your scores are improving. If you find that you are not improving even after studying the answer explanations, you probably need to memorize more vocabulary and clarify key points of grammar.

SCORING THE SPANISH WITH LISTENING TEST

For this test, score each section individually.

Section I: Listening

Step 1:   Check your answers with the answer key. Remember that items left blank or misgrid will not be counted.

Step 2:   Add up the number of correct answers for questions 1–33.   _____

Step 3:   Add up the number of incorrect answers for questions 1–33.   _____

Step 4:   Multiply the number of incorrect answers by .333.   _____

Step 5:   Subtract the result in step 4 from the number in step 2.   _____

Step 6:   Round up to the nearest whole number. This is your raw subscore for Listening. _____

Section II: Reading

Step 7:   Add up the number of correct answers for questions 34–85.   _____

Step 8:   Add up the number of incorrect answers for questions 34–85.   _____

Step 9:   Multiply the number of incorrect answers by .333.   _____

Step 10: Subtract the result in step 9 from the number in step 7.   _____

Step 11: Round up to the nearest whole number: This is your raw subscore for Reading. _____

To find Your Raw Composite Score:

Step 12: Fill in the unrounded number from step 10: Multiply this by 1.120.   _____

Step 13: Fill in the unrounded number from step 5: Multiply this by .8810*.   _____

Step 16: Add the results of steps 12 and 13.   _____

Step 17: Round up to the nearest whole number. This is your raw composite score.   _____

The maximum raw score you can receive is 85. But remember that when the scores are converted, 50 percent of the answers correct (43 out of 85) is about average.

---

*The reason the sections are not multiplied by the same number is that you spend twice as much time on section II as you do on section I.

Spanish-Language Resources

Part Four

Spanish-Language Resources

SPANISH-LANGUAGE RESOURCES

These resources focus on Spanish vocabulary and are divided into three sections.

Appendix A focuses on verbs that may appear to be interchangeable because their meanings are similar, or are usually translated into the same English verb. They are included in a separate section because it is very important for you to keep them straight.

Appendix B has words grouped together by theme, because it can be easier to remember words in a group. They are presented in tables with instructions on how to study them to learn a basic vocabulary.

Appendix C is a standard Spanish to English dictionary type of list. Words are listed alphabetically. This listing is extensive though not complete, so you may still need a dictionary.

Appendix A:
Confusing Verbs

Several groups of verbs have similar meanings, but are not interchangeable. You need to be able to distinguish nuances of meaning in these cases.

Pedir, *Preguntar*, and *Hacer Una Pregunta*

Pedir means "to ask for" or "to request." It is used a lot. It is important to know that the English word *for* is not translated; its meaning is contained in the infinitive. Three kinds of words follow *pedir*.

- Another verb, in the infinitive form, and often with an indirect object pronoun in front of *pedir*.
- The relative *que*, in which case the next verb is in the subjunctive mood.
- A noun, the direct object of *pedir*. It will tell what someone wants or requests.

   Me pide acompañarlo.
   He asks me to go with him.

   Pide que lo acompañe.
   He asks me to go with him. (He asks that I go with him.)

   Me pide dinero
   He asks me for money.

Preguntar means "to question," which for most English speaking people means "to ask." When you mean to ask in the sense of "asking for someone," then use *preguntar por*.

   Me pregunta cuándo voy.
   He asks me when I am going.

   Pregunta por la enfermera.
   He asks for the doctor.

Hacer una pregunta means "to ask a question (that you want answered)." Several types of expressions use *hacer*, so learn them well. Moreover, the way in which *hacer* is used is foreign to most English speakers.

> ¿Puedo hacerle una pregunta?.
> Can I ask you a question?

Decir and Hablar

Decir means "to say" or "to tell." You see this verb most often in references to spoken dialogue. **Hablar** means "to talk" or "to speak." This meaning is quite literal. It is sometimes followed by a preposition, indicating *about* in the sense "to talk about." You might see *sobre, acerca de* or just *de.*

> The line dash represents *quotation marks* in Spanish.

> —No puedo creerlo,— dijo el estudiante.
> "I can't believe it," said the student.

> Le dijo que vendría.
> He told her that he would come.

> La mujer habló sobre la importancia de preparar bien.
> The woman talked about the importance of preparing well.

Tocar and Jugar

Tocar means "to play" a musical instrument, a tape, or CD—whatever produces music or sound. It has other meanings too, such as "to touch." **Jugar** means "to play" a game. One way to remember this verb is to think of the word for *toy*, which is "juguete."

> Su hijo tocó la trompeta.
> His son played the trumpet.

> Ayer jugué al fútbol en el parque con mis amigos.
> Yesterday I played soccer in the park with my friends.

Asistir a and Atender

Asistir means "to attend" a school, classes, or an event. It is followed by the preposition *a*. On the other hand, *atender* means "to attend" in the sense of "attending *to*" something. If that "something" is a person, then this verb is followed by a personal *a*.

> El año que viene asistiré a la universidad.
> Next year, I will attend the university.

> Anoche asistí a un concierto.
> Last night I attended a concert.

> El doctor atendió al paciente.
> The doctor attended to the patient.

Buscar, Mirar, and Ver

Buscar is "to look for," in the sense of "to search." The English preposition *for* is not translated, as its meaning is included in *buscar*. Use a personal *a* after it if the object is a person. **Mirar** is "to look at," or "to watch." Remember the personal *a*, when it is necessary. **Ver** means "to see."

> Busqué mis libros para estudiar un poco.
> I looked for my books to study a little.

> El chico miró a los jugadores.
> The boy watched the players.

> Anoche vi una película muy interesante.
> Last night I saw a very interesting movie.

Escuchar and Oír

Escuchar means "to listen to." *Escuchar* is the act of giving someone your attention. The English word *to* is not translated into Spanish. When this verb is followed by *a*, it means that the object is a person. **Oír** is "to hear." *Escuchar* and *oír* have the same differences in Spanish that they have in English.

> Escucharon un ruido terrible.
> They heard a terrible noise.

> Los estudiantes escucharon al profesor.
> The students listened to the professor.

> ¿Oíste las noticias? ¡Recibí una beca para la universidad!
> Did you hear the news? I got a scholarship to the university!

Dejar and Salir

Dejar is "to leave behind" in the sense that something is physically or figuratively left remaining. **Salir** is "to leave" in the sense of going away from a location.

> Dejé mis libros en casa esta mañana.
> I left my books at home this morning.

> Dejamos ese asunto para otro día.
> We left that topic for another day.

> Salió sin despedirse.
> She left without saying good-bye.

> No sabemos cuándo saldremos.
> We do not know when we will leave.

Saber and Conocer

Saber means "to know" in the sense that you know information. You know facts about something, some place, or someone. *Conocer* refers to knowing people, or being familiar with people, places, or things. When the object is a person, you have to use the personal *a*.

> **Saben todo lo que necesitan para el examen.**
> They know everything they need to know for the test.

> **Sabe quién es ese señor misterioso.**
> He knows who that mysterious man is.
> (The object of the verb *saber* is *quién*, meaning that the subject knows something *about* the man. It does not refer to knowing him in the sense of having his acquaintance.)

> **Conocemos a los estudiante de la otra clase de español.**
> We know the students from the other Spanish class.

> **Conocen bien la ciudad de Barcelona.**
> They know the city of Barcelona well.

Verbs That Mean "To Be"

Ser, *estar*, *tener* (in certain expressions), *haber*, and *hacer* can all be defined as "to be," though they have slightly different meanings. You will have to decide which one is appropriate based on the context..

Ser is one of the two most common verbs to mean "to be." It is used as a linking verb to communicate definitive characteristics, or characteristics that we generally associate with people or things, such as what something is made of and where it is from.

> **Muchos anillos son de oro.**
> Many rings are (made) of gold.

> **Pamela es de México.**
> Pamela es from Mexico.

> **Juan es muy alto y delgado.**
> John is very tall and slender.

> **¿Cómo es el nuevo profesor?**
> What is the new teacher like? (his personality)

In addition, *ser* is used to tell time. In the expression, *¿Qué hora es?* ("What time is it?"), the verb is used in the third person singular for asking the time, and for telling time when it is one o'clock. Use *ser* for expressions of time, even time in general. All you have to do is recognize the correct forms of *ser*.

> *Ser* implies a more "definitive" condition than *estar*. *Estar* communicates how someone or something appears, whether it is location, state of mind, etc.

Estar, the other common verb meaning "to be," communicates a mental, emotional, or physical state of being. When you talk about how someone is feeling or where something is located, you use *estar*. While you might think of *estar* in terms of a "temporary" condition, be careful. "Temporary" is not always a reliable indicator. A "changeable" condition might be another way to think of it.

¿Dónde está mi mochila?
Where is my book bag?

María está muy contenta.
Mary is very happy.

Santiago está en Chile.
Santiago is in Chile.

Look at the following sentences. You'll see that for the same sentence, the use of *ser* or *estar* makes a big difference.

Gazpacho es una sopa fría.	La sopa está fría.
Gazpacho is a cold soup. (By definition, it is served cold.)	The soup is cold. (cold to the touch)
El pobre niño es enfermizo.	El niño está enfermo.
The poor boy is a sick boy. (with serious health problems)	The boy is sick. (not feeling well)

Tener means "to be" only in certain expressions. Be careful though: The verb *tener* is followed by a noun in these expressions. So when you want to say "very," use *mucho*, not *muy*. *Tengo mucha suerte* means "I am very lucky." The literal translation means "I *have* a lot of luck."

tener sueño	to be sleepy
tener cuidado	to be careful
tener ganas de	to feel like doing something
tener razón	to be right
tener sed	to be thirsty
tener hambre	to be hungry
tener miedo	to be afraid
tener prisa	to be in a hurry
tener verguenza	to be ashamed
tener suerte	to be lucky
tener calor	to be hot (a person feels hot, warm)
tener frío	to be cold (a person feels chilly)
tener la culpa	to be guilty (for something)
tener éxito	to be successful (notice the word for "success")

Haber is usually used in the third person singular. First, it is used in expressions having to do with weather—mostly visual aspects of weather. Second, it is used in neutral expressions meaning "there is (*there are*, etc.)."

Hay sol.	It is sunny.
Hay luna.	It is moonlit.
Hay mucha gente.	There are a lot of people.
Había muchas personas.	There were a lot of people.
Habrá mucho que hacer.	There will be a lot to do.
Habrá que venir temprano.	It will be necessary to come early.

Haber can also be used with the preposition *de* to mean "to have to." This phrase expresses mild personal obligation.

He de estudiar un poco.	I have to study a little.

Hacer is used to describe the weather.

Hace buen tiempo.	The weather is nice. (It is good weather.)
Hace mal tiempo.	The weather is bad. (It is bad weather.)
Hace viento.	It is windy.
Hace sol.	It is sunny.
Hace calor.	It is hot, warm. (The weather is warm.)
Hace frío.	It is cold. (The weather is cold.)

Verbs That Mean "To Become"

Several words mean "to become," though each is distinct. The main verbs in this category are: ***ponerse, hacerse, llegar a ser, volverse,*** and ***convertirse.***

Ponerse means "to become" in the sense of changing one's appearance, or one's physical or emotional state. It applies to people or things and is used with adjectives. Often in English, we use verbs other than "to become."

La niña se puso roja.
The girl blushed.

Se puso blanco al ver el fantasma.
He turned white when he saw the ghost.

Hacerse means "to become" in the sense of a voluntary change or natural transition.

Mi antiguo compañero de cuarto se hizo rico.
My former roommate became rich. (He worked to make himself rich.)

Quiero hacerme doctor un día.
I want to become a doctor some day.

Llegar a ser is "to become" over a length of time. It implies a gradual process. ***Volverse*** implies a sudden, unexpected change.

> Many verbs can also convey the idea of "becoming" something by adding a reflexive pronoun. *Se enriquecieron trabajando duro* means "They got (became) rich by working hard."

El señor Pérez llegó a ser presidente del banco.
Mr. Perez became president of the bank.

Al ganar la lotería, se volvió millonario.
Upon winning the lottery, she became a millionaire.

Se volvió loca de todo el ruido.
She went crazy from all the noise.

Convertirse indicates a change in physical composition. That is, a change from one state of being to another.

Todo se convirtió en ceniza en el fuego.
Everything turned to ashes in the fire.

Desafortunadamente, las piedras no se convierten en oro fácilmente.
Unfortunately, rocks are not easily changed into gold.

Appendix B:
Grouped Vocabulary

The words in this section are listed in table format, organized by topic area. It is often easier to memorize words in topic areas, by associating them with words you already know. On the SAT Subject Test: Spanish you will not have to translate words from English to Spanish, you will simply have to be able to recognize the Spanish words.

To use the tables on the following pages, cover with paper the English words to see which words you know. Circle any word you cannot recall within three seconds. When you have gone through all the words in a group, go back and review the ones you have circled.

- As you go down the list, say each word out loud to help imprint it in your memory.
- Create your own personal study sheet using selected words in sentences.
- Make up rhymes or tongue twisters using the words.

Resist the temptation to peek at the English translations. The whole point of the exercise is assess what you do not know.

Las Profesiones y el Trabajo

el abogado	lawyer	el arquitecto	architect
el antropólogo	anthropologist	el artista	artist
el astronauto	astronaut	la azafata	stewardess
el carnicero	butcher	el sastre	tailor
el banquero	banker	el contable	accountant
el psiquiatra	psychiatrist	el doctor	doctor
el médico	doctor	la enfermera	nurse
el comerciante	businessman	el hombre de negocios	businessman
el marinero	sailor	el profesor	teacher
el maestro	teacher	el cocinero	cook
el interlocutor	interviewer	el periodista	reporter
el músico	musician	el decano	dean of a college
el vaquero	cowboy	el entrenador	trainer, coach
el cirujano	surgeon	el policía	policeman
el programador	programer	el plomero	plumber
el bombero	fireman	el padre, sacerdote	priest
el guardaespaldas	bodyguard	el salvavidas	lifeguard
el cajero	teller, cashier	el cartero	mailman
el criado	servant	la niñera	babbysitter, nanny
el ingeniero	engineer	el noticiero	newscaster, newscast
el guía turístico	tourist guide	el fotógrafo	photographer
el soldado	soldier	el repartidor	deliveryman
el pescador	fisherman	el pintor	painter
el carpintero	carpenter	el escultor	sculptor
el panadero	baker	el psicólogo	psychologist

El Transporte

el avión	airplane	el piloto	pilot
el aeromozo	steward	el boleto (billete)	round trip ticket
la azafata	stewardess	de ida y vuelta	
el equipaje	luggage	la pista	runway
la línea aérea	airline	hacer las maletas	to pack the suitcases
la maleta	suitcase	la visa	visa
la seguridad	security	el aduana	customs
el pasaporte	passport	el cinturón de seguridad	seatbelt
el aduana	customs	aterrizar	to land
el agente de viajes	travel agent	tarjeta de embarque	boarding pass
despegar	to take off	el barco	boat, ship
reclamar el equipaje	claim luggage	embarcar	to board
el asiento	seat	el andén	train platform
el crucero	cruise	el coche-comedor	dining car
el tren	train	la tarifa	the fare
el coche-cama	sleeping car	la carretera	highway
el horario	schedule		
el coche/el carro	car		

la calle	street	la avenida	avenue
montar en bicicleta	to ride a bicycle	el camión	truck
el semáforo	traffic light	alto	stop sign
la bocacalle/	intersection	la esquina	street corner
la encrucijada		la habitación sencilla	single room
doblar la esquina	to turn a corner	a la izquierda	to the left
a la derecha	to the right	sigue recto	go straight
el estacionamiento	parking	en embotellamiento	traffic jam
la bocina	horn	el parabrisas	windshield
volar	to fly	manejar/conducir	to drive
la motocicleta	motorcycle	el parachoques	bumper
la acera	sidewalk	el barril	highway lane
la estación	train station	el viajero	traveler
del ferrocarril		el tren expreso	express train
el pasajero	passenger	hacer las reservaciones	make reservation
el itinerario	itinerary	la puerta	the gate
facturar el equipaje	to check luggage	el vuelo	flight
la sala de espera	waiting room	viajar	to travel
perder el vuelo	to miss a flight	la ventanilla	window of a plane
abordar el avión	board a plane	pasar por la inmigración	go through immigration
revisar el equipaje	inspect the luggage	tardar en	to be late in
demorar	to delay	el autobús	bus
pagar los derechos	to pay customs duties	hacer escala	to stop over on a flight
hacer una parada	to make a stop	marcharse	to leave
partir	to leave	la habitación	hotel room
la congestión	congestion	la recepción	lobby
el botones	bellboy	la habitación doble	double room
el gerente	manager	subir el equipaje	to bring up the luggage
la planta baja	first floor	pagar la cuenta	pay the bill

Las Partes del Cuerpo y la Salud

el cuerpo	body	el hueso	bone
el pie	foot	la pierna	leg
la rodilla	knee	las caderas	hips
la cintura	waist	el estómago	stomach
el pecho	chest	el cuello	neck
el brazo	arm	el codo	elbow
la muñeca	wrist	la mano	hand
la cabeza	head	el cerebro	brain
la barba	beard	el hombro	shoulder
el dedo	finger, toe	la frente	forehead
la garganta	throat	el rostro/la cara	face
la nuca	nape of the neck	la uña	fingernail
la mejilla	cheek	las cejas	eyebrows
el pelo	hair	las orejas	ears
el cabello		los oídos	

la boca	mouth	los labios	lips
la nariz	nose	los dientes	teeth
la lengua	tongue	los ojos	eyes
la salud	health	la enfermedad	illness, disease
la dieta	diet	el resfriado	cold
estar constipado	to have a cold	tener hora con	to have an appointment
el consultorio	doctor's office	la sangre	blood
la receta	prescription	la pastilla/las píldoras	pills
las muletas	crutches	la vacuna	vaccine
poner una inyección	to give a shot	la aguja	needle
la venda	bandage	la herida	wound
dolerle (a uno)	to hurt	herir	to wound
lesiones	cuts	la cicatriz	scar
la silla de ruedas	wheel chair	la radiografía	X-Rays
la presión sanguínea	blood pressure	sacar la lengua	to stick out the tongue
el aliento	breath	el antibiótico	antibiotics
la espalda	back	la columna vertebral	spine
la medicina	medicine	el remedio	remedy
el tratamiento	treatment	respirar	to breathe
toser	to cough	hacer ejercicio	to exercise
sentirse	to feel	sufrir	to suffer
enfermarse	to get sick	mejorarse	to get better
estornudar	to sneeze	guardar cama	to stay in bed

Las Familias y Relaciones Familiares

los padres	parents	los parientes	relatives
los tíos	aunts and uncles	los abuelos	grandparents
los nietos	grandchildren	los sobrinos	nephews and nieces
los primos	cousins	los suegros	mothers-in-law fathers-in-law
la nuera	daughter-in-law	el yerno	son-in-law
los cuñados	brothers-in-law sisters-in-law	la madrastra	stepmother
el padrastro	stepfather	los hijastros	stepchildren
los bisabuelos	great grandparents	los hermanos	brothers and sisters
los hijos	sons and daughter	los niños	children
llevarse bien	to get along	llevarse mal	to not get along
relaciones estrechas	close relationships	amar, querer	to love
cariñoso	loving, affectionate	odiar	to hate
afectuoso	affectionate	celoso	jealous
envidia	envy	el novio	boyfriend
la novia	girlfriend	el noviazgo	courtship
la boda	wedding	el compromiso	engagement
el viudo	widow	el divorcio	divorce
casarse	to get married	los gemelos	twins

el esposo	husband	el marido	husband
la esposa	wife	el anillo	ring
el matrimonio	the marriage	el casamiento	marriage
el soltero	bachelor	soportar	to tolerate
enfadarse	to get mad	confiar	to trust
aislar, enajenar	to isolate	amistoso, amigable	friendly
contar con	to count on	envidiar	to envy

La Escuela

el aula	classroom	la sala de clase	classroom
la pizarra	blackboard	el borrador	eraser
la pared	wall	la materia	course subject
la tarea	homework	el reloj	clock
el edificio	building	el gimnasio	gymnasium
el papel	paper	el lápiz	pencil
el bolígrafo	ball point pen	la pluma	fountain pen
el cuaderno	notebook	el director	principal, headmaster
el estudiante	student	el profesor	teacher. high school
el alumno		el maestro	teacher, elementary
la primaria	elementary school	la secundaria	high school
el colegio	preparatory school	la asignatura	course
solicitar una beca	to apply for a scholarship	matricular	to enroll
escribir	to write	aprender (a)	to learn
dictar una conferencia	to give a lecture	tomar apuntes	to take notes
las notas	grades	la prueba/el examen	test
las calificaciones		suspender	to fail a class
aprobar	to pass	las ciencias naturales	natural sciences
aprender de memoria	to memorize	la historia	history
las matemáticas	math	graduarse	to graduate
las lenguas extranjeras	foreign languages	la matrícula	registration
asistir a la clase	to attend class	la lectura	reading
el requisito	requirement	llenar los impresos (formularios)	to fill out forms
el título	diploma		

Los Deportes

el equipo	team, equipment	el partido	game
el entrenador	trainer, coach	el jugador	player
marcar un gol	score a goal	jugar	to play a game
la competencia	match, game, race, competition	vencer	to beat
		perder	to lose
ganar	to win	el trofeo	trophy
el campeonato	championship	la liga	league
torneo	tournament	el baloncesto	basketball
el árbitro	referee	nadar	to swim
el corredor	runner	la piscina	pool

la natación	swimming	el béisbol	baseball
la pista	track	el fútbol americano	football
el fútbol	soccer	estar en forma	to be in shape
reclutar	to recruit	hacer ejercicio	to exercise
la lucha libre	wrestling	la multa	penalty
el golf	golf	el balón	ball (large)
la pelota	ball	la cancha	court
el tenis	tennis	patinar	to skate
el campo	field	el esquí acuático	water ski
esquiar	to ski	alzar pesa	to lift weights
el alpinismo	mountain climbing	el ciclismo	cycling
Juegos Olímpicos	Olympic Games	el paracaidismo	sky diving
las carreras	races	dar un paseo	take a walk
montar a caballo	horseback riding	bucear	to dive, snorkel
dar una caminata	hiking	defender	to defend
el volibol	volleyball	lanzar	to throw
tirar	to throw		

La Ciudad y Las Tiendas

el centro	downtown	la calle	street
la avenida	avenue	el paseo	boulevard
las afueras	outskirts	el barrio/la colonia	neighborhood
las tiendas	stores	el almacén	department store
la tienda departamental	department store	la panadería	bakery
lechería	milk store	la zapatería	shoe store
confitería	candy store	la lavandería	laundromat
el mercado	market	la carnicería	butcher shop
el ayuntamiento	city government	el gobierno	government
el alcalde	the mayor	los diputados	delegate
la policía	police force	los ciudadanos	citizens
la aldea	town	la casa de correo	post office
el banco	bank	la elección	election
votar	to vote	la iglesia	church
la ferretería	hardware store	el taller	shop
la gasolinera	gas station	la manzana	city block
		la cuadra	
el supermercado	supermarket	el restaurante	restaurant
el estadio	stadium	el ferrocarril	railroad
localizar	to be located	la plaza	plaza
el parque	park	gobernar	to govern
el dependiente	clerk	la empresa	business
el puesto	stand, position	el rascacielos	skyscraper
la fuente	fountain	el monumento	monument
el metro/el subterráneo	subway	el comercio	commerce

La Casa

el vestíbulo	foyer	la entrada	entry way
la puerta	door	la cocina	kitchen
el garaje	garage	el dormitorio/la alcoba	bedroom
la sala de estar	living room	cuarto de baño	bathroom
el despacho	den, office	el desván	attic
el sótano	basement	la lámpara	lamp
la alfombra	rug, carpet	el suelo	floor
el techo, la teja	roof	el patio	patio
el jardín	garden	las paredes	walls (of a room)
la cama	bed	los muebles	furniture
la silla	chair	el sillón/la butaca	large chair
el sofá	sofa	la mesa	table
la mecedora	rocking chair	la almohada	pillow
el estante	bookcase	limpiar	to clean
lavar	to wash	fregar	to scrub
los platos	plates	el tenedor	fork
la cuchara	spoon	el cuchillo	knife
el mantel	table cloth	el cubierto	place setting
la servilleta	napkin	la aspiradora	vacuum cleaner
el lavaplatos	dishwasher	la lavadora	washing machine
la secadora	dryer	la nevera	freezer, refrigerator
la estufa	stove	la refrigeradora	refrigerator
el delantal	apron	el horno	oven
las persianas	blinds	las cortinas	curtains
el cuadro	picture	la pintura	painting
la hierba	grass	el cortacésped	lawn mower
comer	to eat	la flor	flower
poner la mesa	to set the table	cocinar	to cook
confeccionar	to cook up, to make	la parrilla	grill
batir	to beat, to mix	la receta	recipe
		mezclar	to mix
despertarse	to wake up	levantarse	to get up
sentarse	to sit down	desayunar	to eat breakfast
el desayuno	breakfast	almuerzo	to eat lunch
el almuerzo	lunch	merendar	to snack (in the late afternoon)
la merienda	afternoon snack	cenar	to dine, to eat dinner
la cena	supper	lavarse	to wash up
bañarse	to bathe	ducharse	to shower
la toalla	towel	afeitarse	to shave
la ropera	clothes closet	las herramientas	tools
el martillo	hammer	el destornillador	screwdriver
el serrucho	saw	las tijeras	scissors

las escaleras	stairs	el balcón	balcony
el hogar	hearth, home	la chimenea	chimney
el teléfono	telephone	la televisión	television
el televisor	television set	la radio	radio
el radio	radio set	el tocadiscos	record player
la grabadora	tape recorder	la videocasetera	VCR
la olla	pot	el sartén	frying pan
la plancha	iron	planchar	to iron
coser	to sew	arreglar	to arrange
desordenado	messy	deshecho	broken down
la limpieza	cleanliness	el gabinete	study (room)

La Ropa

el traje	dress, suit	los pantalones	pants
el vestido	dress	el saco	suit jacket
la chaqueta	jacket	el sombrero	hat
la gorra	baseball cap	la bufanda	scarf
el gorro	cap, tam	la camisa	shirt
los guantes	gloves	la manga	sleeve
la camisa con cuello	shirt with a collar	los zapatos	shoes
la corbata	necktie	la bata	bathrobe
las pantuflas	slippers	el impermeable	raincoat
el abrigo	overcoat	la blusa	blouse
la falda	skirt	la pulsera	bracelet
tacones	heels	el pendiente	necklace
el collar	necklace	el brillante	diamond ring
los aretes	earrings	el anillo	ring
la sortija	ring	el cinturón	belt
la joya	jewel	ponerse	to put on
vestirse	to get dress, to dress	el bastón	walking stick
quitarse	to take off	el báculo	cane
llevar/usar	to wear	los calcetines	socks
el traje de baño	bathing suit	las sandalias	sandals
los huaraches	sandals	las botas	boots
ropa interior	underwear	las medias	stockings
el pijama	pyjamas	descalzo	shoeless
el pañuelo	handkerchief	el bolsillo	pocket
los lazos/ los cordones	shoe laces	las prendas de ropa	garments

Los Colores

rojo	red	amarillo	yellow
negro	black	blanco	white
verde	green	azul	blue
gris	gray	violeta	violet
carmesí	crimson	anaranjado	orange
pardo/castáño	brown	purpúreo	purple
marrón/café			
castaño			
marrón			
café			

El Tiempo

el tiempo	weather	hacer buen tiempo	to be good weather
llover	to rain	hacer mal tiempo	to be bad weather
la lluvia	rain	nevar	to snow
el granizo	hail	la nieve	to snow
hacer sol	to be sunny	las nubes	clouds
estar escampado/	to be clear	estar nublado	to be cloudy
estar despejado		la tormenta/	storm
el relámpago	lightning	la tempestad	
el rayo	bolt of lightning	el trueno	thunder
el viento	wind	tronar	to thunder
el aguacero	rain storm	hacer viento	to be windy
el pronóstico	weather forecaster	la escarcha	frost
		el mapa	map

Los Números

uno	one	dos	two
tres	three	cuatro	four
cinco	five	seis	six
siete	seven	ocho	eight
nueve	nine	diez	ten
once	eleven	doce	twelve
trece	thirteen	catorce	fourteen
quince	fifteen	diez y seis/dieciséis	sixteen
diez y siete	seventeen	diez y ocho/dieciocho	eighteen
diecisiete			
diez y nueve	nineteen	veinte	twenty
treinta	thirty	cuarenta	forty
cincuenta	fifty	sesenta	sixty
setenta	seventy	ochenta	eighty
noventa	ninety	doscientos	two hundred
ciento	one hundred	cuatrocientos	four hundred
trescientos	three hundred	seiscientos	six hundred
quinientos	five hundred	ochocientos	eight hundred

setecientos	seven hundred	millón	million
novecientos	nine hundred		
mil	thousand		

La Comida

las bebidas	drinks	los refrescos	refreshments
el agua	water	el café	coffee
el agua mineral	bottled water	el café con leche	coffee with cream
el agua con/sin gas	carbonated water	el café solo	black coffee
la carne	meat	el café con azúcar	coffee with sugar
el pollo	chicken	la chuleta	chop (pork, veal)
el pescado	fish	carne asada	roasted meat
los vegetales	vegetables	la ensalada	salad
el postre	dessert	la fruta	fruit
las fresas	strawberries	el aperitivo/el antojito	appetizers
los melocotones/	peaches	los piños	pineapples
los duraznos		el melón	melon, any kind
la naranja	orange	la manzana	apple
la cereza	cherry	la pera	pear
las espinacas	spinach	las verduras	greens
los judías verdes	green beans	frijoles	beans
las habichuelas	beans	el maíz	corn
el arroz	rice	la harina	flour
la masa	dough	el aceite	oil
los olivos	olives	el queso	cheese
la nata	cream	el pastel	pie
la torta	cake	el pan	bread
la manteca	butter	la jalea	jelly
la mantequilla		la mermelada	marmalade
la zanahoria	carrot	el pepino	cucumber
el chile	chilli pepper	la lechuga	lettuce
las patatas	potatoes	el huevo	egg
la salsa	sauce	el plátano	plantain, banana (it depends on country)
la ternera	veal	carne de cordero	lamb, mutton
la entrada	entrée, main course	la sopa	soup
guisar	to cook, to stew	freír	to fry
preparar	to fix a meal	la lista de platos la carta el menú	the menu
la galleta	biscuit, cracker, cookie	el helado	Ice cream
el pavo	turkey	el pato	duck
el cerdo	pork	carne de res carne de vaca	beef
el atún	tuna	la trucha	trout
la tortilla	tortilla omelet (in Spain)	el flan	flan, custard

Los Meses del Año

enero	January	febrero	February
marzo	March	abril	April
mayo	May	junio	June
julio	July	agosto	August
septiembre	September	octubre	October
noviembre	November	diciembre	December

Los Días de la Semana

lunes	Monday	martes	Tuesday
miércoles	Wednesday	jueves	Thursday
viernes	Friday	sábado	Saturday
domingo	Sunday		

La Tierra

la tierra	earth, world	las montañas	mountains
el lago	lake	la cordillera	mountain range
el valle	valley	el cerro/ la colina/la loma	hill
el desierto	desert	el arroyo	stream, river, brook
el declive	slope	la altura	height
la yerba/la hierba	grass	el árbol	tree
el bosque	forest	la selva	jungle
el bosque nublado	rain forest	el medio ambiente	environment
la llanura	plains	la lluvia	rain
la tormenta/ la tempestad	storm	el granizo	hail
		la nieve	snow
la llovizna	drizzle	el aguacero	downpour
la borrasca	squall	la peña	rock
el viento	wind	el mar	sea
el lago	lake	la cala	cove
la bahía	bay	helar	to freeze
el hielo	ice	el relámpago	lightening
el trueno	thunder	el remolina	whirlwind
la nube	cloud	el rayo	bolt of lightning
la escarcha	frost	gotear	to drip
la estrella	star	la brisa	breeze
el arco iris	rainbow	despejado	cloudless, clear
la playa	beach	la franja	strip of land, edge
la arena	sand	la ola	wave (water)
soleado	sunny		

Para Describir a Personas

perezoso	lazy	pequeño	small
lento	slow	pálido	pale
alegre	happy	hermoso	beautiful
cortés	courteous	bonito/lindo	pretty
sabio	wise	simpático/amable	nice
rubio	blond, fair	travieso	mischievous
moreno	brunette, dark	manso	gentle
pesado	heavy, tiresome	respetuoso	respectful
robusto	healthy	indolente	indolent
guapo	handsome	enfermo	sickly
gordo	fat	generoso	generous
fuerte	strong	valiente	valiant
aplicado	hard working	elegante	elegant
inteligente	intelligent	analfabeto	illiterate
joven	young	delgado	thin
listo	clever	esbelto	slender
loco	crazy	distraído	absent-minded
mentiroso/embustero	liar	feo	ugly
culto	refined, cultured	débil	weak
ciego	blind	celoso	jealous
cuerdo	sane	envidioso	envious
cojo	lame	triste	sad
compasivo	compassionate	sensible	sensitive
descortés	rude	sensato	sensible

Appendix C:
Listed Vocabulary

The following vocabulary list contains most of the words you have seen in this book. Be aware that some of these words have other meanings, too. Unless the gender of the nouns is noted with *m.* for masculine or *f.* for feminine, the gender follows regular rules.

A

abandonar	to abandon	agarrar	to grasp
abanico	fan	agotador	exhausting
abogado	lawyer	agua	f. water
abrir	to open	aguacero	downpour, hard rain
abierto	opened	aguantar	to stand, to put up with
abuelo	grandfather	águila	eagle
abundancia	abundance	ahí	there
aburrir	to bore	ahogar	to drown
acá	here	ahogo	breathing trouble, breathlessness
acabar (de)	to have just		
acantilado	cliff	ahora	now
acariciar	to caress, to pat	ahorrar	to save (money)
acaso	perhaps	ajeno	foreign, distant
acelerado	accelerated, faster	alarmar	to alarm
aclarar	to clarify	alcanzar	to reach
acontecimiento	event, happening	alcoba	bedroom
acera	sidewalk	aldea	village
acercarse	to get closer, to draw near	alegrarse	to be happy
acertado	correct, right	alemán	German
acomodar	to accommodate	alfombra	carpet, rug
aconsejar	to advise	algo	something
acontecer	to happen	alguien	someone
acordarse de	to remember	alguno	some
actitud	f. attitude	alimentar	to feed
actual	present, now	alivio	relief
actualmente	presently, at the moment	alma	soul
acudir	to come to, to attend	almendros	almond trees
adecuado	adequate	almuerzo	lunch
adelante	forward	almohada, almohadón	pillow, large pillow
adelgazar	to get thin, to diet	almorzar (ue)	to eat lunch
además	in addition	alto	tall, stop (sign)
adivinanzas	riddles	alojamiento	lodging
adorar	adore	alojarse	to lodge, to spend the night
adornos	adornments, jewelry	allá	there
advertir	to advise, to warm	allí	there
advertencia	warning	amargo	bitter
aerolínea	airline	amigo	friend
aeronave	f. airplane	amplio	wide, ample
afectuoso	affectionate	ancho	wide
afilado	sharpened	andar	to walk
afortunadamente	fortunately	andén	train platform
agradecer	to thank	anfiteatro	amphitheater

anhelar	*to long for*	arriba	*above*
anhelo	*longing*	arriesgar	*to risk*
animar	*to animate, to make lively*	asado	*roasted*
anoche	*last night*	asignatura	*course (subject in school)*
ansioso	*anxious, nervous*	asistir a	*to attend (school, classes)*
ante	*prep. before*	asomar	*to appear (at a window, doorway)*
anterior	*previous, before*		
antes	*adv. before*	asombrar	*to amaze*
antibiótico	*antibiotic*	aspirar	*to aspire, to hope to become*
anuncio	*ad, announcement*		
año	*year*	aspirina	*aspirin*
apaciguar	*to pacify*	asunto	*astute, smart, sharp*
apagar	*to turn off, to turn out (lights)*	asustar	*to frighten*
		atacar	*to attack*
aparcero	*sharecropper, farmer who rents land*	atar	*to tie*
		atravesar	*to cross*
apenas	*scarcely*	atemorizar	*to frighten*
apilar	*to pile up*	aterrizar	*to land (a plane)*
aprender a	*to learn*	aterrorizar	*to frighten*
aprendizaje	*apprenticeship, training*	atraer	*attract*
aprobar	*to pass (a course)*	atropellar	*to run over, to run into*
aproximar	*to get close to*	aun	*even*
apuraciones	*troubles*	aún	*still*
apurarse	*to hurry*	aunque	*although*
aquel	*dem. adj. that*	autoestima	*self esteem*
aquí	*here*	autor	*author*
árbol	*tree*	ave	*m. bird*
arcón	*large chest, box*	avergonzar	*to be ashamed*
arduas	*difficult*	averiguar	*to find out, to verify*
argumento	*plot of a story*	aversión	*aversion, dislike*
arma	*pistol, side arm*	avión	*airplane*
artesanía	*crafts (arts and crafts)*	avisar	*to advise*
artículo	*article*	ayudar	*to help*
arremetida	*assault, attack*	ayuntamiento	*city government*

B

bahía	bay	boca	mouth
bañarse	to bathe	bocacalle	intersection of streets
baño	bath	bocinas	horns (of a car)
bailar	to dance	boda	wedding
balneario	resort, spa	boleto	ticket
balón	ball	bolsillo	pocket
baloncesto	basketball (Spain)	bonito	pretty
banco	bank, bench	bordear	to border on
bandera	flag	bosque	m. forest
banquero	banker	borracho	drunk
barca	little boat	botella	bottle
barco	boat, ship	botones	bellhop, bell boy
barrio	neighborhood	brasero	brazier, grill on a hearth
barro	clay	brazo	arm
batir	to beat	bribón	rascal
beber	to drink	brincar	to jump, to hop
bebida	drink, refreshment	brindar	to toast, to offer an
béisbol	baseball		opportunity
besar	to kiss	bronceador	tanning lotion
bicicleta	bicycle	buey	m. ox
bien	adv. well	bufanda	scarf
bienes	property	burharda	attic
bienes raíces	real estate	burlarse de	to make fun of
bienvenido	welcome	burro	donkey
bigote	m. beard	buscar	to look for
billete	m. ticket, bill (money)	bucear	to snorkel, to dive

C

caballo	horse	cambio	change
cabello	hair	en cambio	on the other hand
caber	to fit	caminata	hike
cabeza	head	camino	road
cacahuates	peanuts	camiones	trucks
cada	adv. each	campo	countryside, country, field
caderas	hips	canción	song
cala	cove	cancha	tennis court
calidad	quality	canasta	basket
caliente	hot	cansar	to tire
calor	heat	cansado	tired
caluroso	warm	cantante	singer
calle	street	cantar	to sing
cama	bed	cantidad	quantity
camarones	shrimp	caña	rod (fishing), reed

capaz	*capable*	cinco	*five*
cara	*face*	cincuenta	*fifty*
característico	*characteristic*	cinturón	*belt*
cardumen	*school of fish*	circo	*circus*
cariño	*warmth, love*	circunstancia	*circumstance*
carnaval	*carnival*	cisne	*m. swan*
carne	*f. meat*	cuello de cisne	*turtleneck sweater*
carnicería	*butcher shop*	cita	*appointment*
carnicero	*butcher*	ciudad	*city*
caro	*expensive*	clavos	*nails*
carpa	*tent*	clientes	*clients, patrons*
carta	*letter*	clima	*m. climate*
cartera	*wallet*	cobarde	*coward*
cartero	*mailman*	cobrar	*to charge a fee, to collect*
carreras	*races, careers*		*money for*
carretera	*highway*	cocido	*cooked*
casamiento	*marriage*	coche	*m. car, auto*
casarse	*to get married*	codicioso	*jealous*
caso	*case*	codo	*elbow*
castigar	*to punish, to spank*	coexistir	*to coexist*
catador	*inspector, careful looker*	coger	*to catch*
catedrático	*professor at a university*	cohete	*m. rockets, fireworks*
catorce	*fourteen*	cola	*f. tail*
causar	*to cause*	hacer cola	*to form a line*
cauteloso	*careful*	colchón	*mattress*
cautivo	*captive*	colegio	*preparatory school*
cazar	*to hunt*	colgar	*to hang, to hang up*
cejas	*eyebrows*	comedor	*dining room*
celofán	*cellophane*	comensal	*fellow diners*
celos	*jealousy*	comer	*to eat*
celoso	*jealous*	comercio	*commerce, trade*
cenar	*to eat dinner*	comida	*food, meal*
centrado	*centered around*	comienzo	*m. beginning*
cepillarse los dientes	*to brush your teeth*	como	*avd. as, like*
ceremonia	*ceremony*	compañero	*companion*
cesta	*basket*	compartir	*to share*
cerca	*near*	competencia	*competition, contest,*
cerrar	*to close*		*match*
cerro	*hill*	complacer	*to please*
cicatriz	*f. scar*	complejo	*complex*
ciclismo	*cycling*	comportamiento	*behavior*
ciclista	*biker*	comprar	*to buy*
ciento	*hundred*	comprender	*to understand*
cierto	*certain, sure*		

comprensivo	compassionate, understanding	cotidiano	daily
con	with	cuadra	city block
concentrado	concentrated, focused	crecer	to grow, to raise
concierto	concert	creencia	belief
concluir	to conclude	creer	to believe
concursos	contests	crepúsculo	twilight, dusk, dark
conducir	to drive	criada	maid, servant
conductores	drivers	criar	to raise
conferencia	lecture	criatura	creature
confiar	to trust	cruce	crossing
confitería	candy shop	cruz	cross
confuso	confused	cruzar	to cross
conjunto	group	cuadro	picture
conmigo	with me	cual	which
conseguir	to get, to obtain	cualquier	whichever
conservación	preservation, conservation	cuando	when
consigo	with himself, herself, etc.	cuanto	how much
construir	to build	cuánto	how much?
consumidores	consumers	cuarenta	forty
contagiar	to spread sickness, to spread	cuarto	room, fourth
contar	to count, to tell	cuatro	four
contemplar	to contemplate, to think about	cubrir	to cover
		cubierta	f. covering
contigo	with you	cubierto	m. place setting at a table
contra	against	cuchara	spoon
contrario	against, opposite	cucharita	teaspoon
contraseña	password	cuchillo	knife
contrato	contract	cuello	neck, collar
convertirse en	to change into, to convert	cuenta	f. bill, tab of money owed
convivencia	coexistence	tomar en cuenta	to take into account
corazón	m. heart	cuento	m. story
cortar	to cut	cuento corto	short story
corte	m. court of law	cuerda	f. chord dar cuerda to wind a clock
corte	f. palace court	cueva	cave
cortacésped	lawn mower	cuidado	f. care
correo	mail	tener cuidado	to be careful
correr	to run	cuidarse de	to care for
corresponder	to correspond	cumbre	f. peak, mountain top
corriente	current	cumpleaños,	m. birthday
cosa	thing	cupón	m. coupon
coser	to sew	cura	m. priest cura f. cure
costal	m. sack, bag, burlap bag	curandero	healer, chaman
costar	to cost	cuyo	whose

CH

chaqueta	*jacket*	chisme	*gossip*
chico	*boy*	chiste	*m. joke*
chino	*Chinese*	chistoso	*m. funny*
chiquillos	*little boys, little children*	chuleta	*chop (of meat)*

D

dañar	*to hurt*	desorientar	*to confuse, disorient*
dar	*to give*	destacado	*outstanding*
dar un paseo	*to take a walk*	desterrar	*to exile*
datos	*data*	desván	*attic or loft*
debajo	*beneath*	desviar	*to detour, to get off track*
decir	*to say, to tell*	deterioro	*deterioration*
declarar	*to declare*	devolver	*to return (something)*
dejar	*to leave*	devoradora	*devouring*
delgado	*thin, slender*	día	*m. day*
demostrar	*to show*	diariamente	*daily*
dentado	*toothed*	dichos	*sayings*
dentro	*within*	dictar una conferencia	*to give a lecture*
deporte	*m. sport*	difícil	*difficult*
deportista	*player*	dificultad	*difficulty*
derramar	*to spill*	dinero	*money*
derretir	*to melt*	disculpar	*to excuse*
desahogo	*relief*	diseño	*design*
desaparecer	*to disappear*	disfrazar	*costume, disguise*
desconocido	*unknown*	disfrutar	*to enjoy*
desde	*adv. from*	disponible	*available, disposable*
desear	*to want*	dispuestos	*inclined to (do something)*
deseo	*wish*	diversa	*diverse*
desfile	*parade*	divertirse	*to have fun*
despacio	*slow*	doler	*to hurt*
despegar	*to take off (a plane)*	dolor	*m. pain, ache*
despertarse	*to awaken*	dormir	*to sleep*
despertarse	*to wake up*	dormitorio	*bedroom*
despedir	*to fire*	dudar	*to doubt*
despedirse	*to say good-bye*	dueño	*owner*
despiadada	*pitiless, merciless*	dulce	*sweet*
desplegar	*to spread out*	duro	*hard*
después	*after*		

E

edad	*f. age*	envasado	*bottled*
el	*m. it*	envase	*m. can, canning*
él	*he*	enviar	*to send*
elegir	*to elect, to select*	envolver	*to wrap up*
ello	*it*	época	*era, time, season*
embarcadero	*dock*	equilibrio	*balance*
embarcar	*to embark, to get on board*	equipo	*team*
embarque	*embark, aboard*	equivocarse	*to be mistaken*
emboscada	*ambush*	erguido	*erect, straight up*
embotellamiento	*bottleneck, traffic jam*	erudito	*wise, learned*
empacar	*to pack*	escalón	*step*
empezar	*to begin*	escaleras	*stairs*
emplear	*to employ, to use*	escaparate	*m. store window*
en	*in, at*	escasez	*f. scarcity*
en cuanto a	*with respect to*	escolar	*scholastic*
en realidad	*really*	escoger	*to pick, to choose*
en seguida	*immediately*	escuchar	*to listen to*
en torno	*around*	escudilla	*bowl*
encaminar	*to put on the right road*	escuela	*school*
encantar	*to charm, to enchant*	escultura	*sculpture*
encender	*to light, to turn on*	esforzar	*to force*
encerrar	*to enclose*	esforzarse a	*to try hard*
encierro	*enclosure*	espacio	*space*
encontrar	*to find*	espantar	*to frighten, to scare*
encontrarse con	*to meet*	especial	*special*
enfadarse	*to get mad, to get angry*	espectáculo	*spectacle, show*
enfurecer	*infuriate*	esperanza	*hope*
enojarse	*to get mad, to get angry*	esperar	*to hope to wait*
ensalada	*salad*	esquiar	*to ski*
ensayar	*to rehearse*	esquí acuático	*water ski*
ensayo	*essay, rehearsal*	esquina	*corner*
escenario	*setting, scene*	esta	*dem. adj. f. this*
enseñanza	*teaching*	ésta	*dem. pro. f. this*
enseñar	*to teach*	estancia	*stay, estate*
entender	*(ie) to understand*	estar	*to be*
entendimiento	*understanding*	este	*dem. adj. m. this*
entrada	*entry, ticket to a concert*	estación	*season, station*
entre	*prep. between*	estacionamiento	*parking*
entregar	*to hand in, to hand over*	estatua	*statue*
enterarse de	*to find out about*	estatura	*stature, height*
enterrar	*to bury*	estipendio	*allowance (money)*
entrevistar	*to interview*	esto	*dem. pro. n. this*
entubados	*packaged in tubes*	estos	*dem. adj. m. these*

estrecho	*narrow, close*	éxito	*success*
estrechar	*to get closer*	experimentar	*to feel*
estrella	*star*	extrañar	*to miss*
estudiantes	*students*	extranjero	*foreign*
etapas	*stages*		

F

fábrica	*factory*	fracaso	*failure*
fallas	*festival in Spain*	frecuente	*frequently*
falta	*lacking*	frenar	*to brake*
faltar	*to lack*	fresas	*strawberries*
fama	*reputation, fame*	fresco	*fresh*
familia	*family*	frontera	*border, frontier*
fecha	*date*	frotar	*to rub*
feria	*fair*	fuego	*fire*
ferrocarril	*m. railroad*	fuente	*fountain*
fijar	*to fix, to fasten*	fuera	*outside*
fijarse en	*to notice*	fuerte	*strong*
firma	*signature*	fumar	*to smoke*
firmar	*to sign*	funcionar	*to operate, (a machine)*
flotar	*to float*	furtivamente	*furtively, stealthily*
fortaleza	*fort*	fúsil	*gun*
fracasar	*to fail*	futuro	*future*

G

gabinete	*m. study (room)*	grande	*large*
gallina	*hen*	granizo	*hail (frozen rain)*
gallo	*rooster*	grueso	*heavy, thick (clothing)*
gastar	*to spend (money)*	guardar	*to keep*
gato	*cat*	guardar cama	*to stay in bed*
gemelos	*twins, opera glasses (Spain)*	guayabera	*type of shirt*
gente	*f. people*	guapo	*handsome*
gesto	*gesture*	guía	*guide*
gitano	*gypsy*	guisar	*to cook, to stew*
gordo	*fat*	gusto	*pleasure, liking*
gota	*drop*	gustar	*to be pleasing to*
gozar de	*to enjoy*		

H

haber	to have (helping verb only)	hielo	ice
hábil	talented	helar	to freeze
habilidades	talents	hermano	brother
hablar	to talk, to speak	hierro	iron (metal)
hacer	to do, to make	hijastro	step child
hacer calor	to be hot	hijo	son
hacer frío	to be cold	hermandad	brotherhood
hacer la maleta	to pack	hermoso	beautiful
hambre	f. hunger	herramientas	tools
harta	fed up with	hombre	m. man
estar harta	to be fed up	hombro	shoulder
hechicería	witchcraft	huerto	orchard
herir	to injure		

I

idioma	m. language	interlocutor	interviewer
iglesia	church	invierno	winter
imprevisto	unforeseen	ir	to go
inglés	English	iracundo	irate
insólito	unusual, rare		

J

jamás	never, ever	juego	game, sport
jardín	garden	jugar	to play a game
jarro	jug	juguete	toy
jaula	cage	junto	adv. together with
jabón	m. soap	junto	adj. together
joven	youth, young		

L

lavar	to wash	levantar	to raise
lavarse	to wash oneself	levantarse	to get up
lástima	pity	libras	pounds (weight)
lastimar	to hurt	libres	free
lectura	reading	ligero	light (weight)
leer	to read	lindo	pretty
lentamente	slowly	lisonjero	flattering
lento	slow	listo	clever, ready
letra	letter (of the alphabet)	lugar	m. place

LL

llamar	to call	llenar	to fill
llamarse	to be called	llevar	to carry, to wear
llama	flame	llegar	to arrive
llano	flat	llover	to rain
llaves	keys	lluvia	rain
lleno	full	llovizna	drizzle

M

mal	adv. badly	mercado	market
maleta	suitcase	mercancías	merchandise
maligno	evil	mezclar	to mix
malo	bad, evil	mientras	while
maltratar	to mistreat	mirar	to look at
mandar	to order, to send	mismo	same
manifestación	demonstration, rally	mitad	middle
mantener	to maintain	modalidad	manner, way
marcharse	to go away	moneda	money, coin
más	more	montaña	mountain
mas	cinj. but	montar	to ride
mayor	greater, older	mojado	wet
maravillarse	to wonder, to marvel at	mojar	to wet
mecedora	rocking chair	mojarse	to get wet
mecer	to rock	momento	moment
medias	stockings	mosca	fly
médico,	medic, doctor	mostrador	counter (store)
medio	middle	motivo	motive, reason
mejor	better	mozo	waiter
mejorarse	to get better	mucho	adj. much, a lot
menor	younger	mundo	world
menos	less	mutuo	mutual
mente	f. mind	muy	adv. very

N

nada	nothing	nombre	name
nadar	to swim	noticia	news
nadie	no one	noticiero	newscast
natación	swimming	noventa	ninety
negarse a	to refuse	nubes	f. cloud
ninguno	none, no	nublado	cloudy
niño	child	nueve	nine
nivel	level	nuevo	new
nogal	walnut tree	nunca	never

O

o	*or*
obligar	*to make, to oblige*
obrero	*worker*
obstáculos	*obstacles*
octavo	*eighth*
ochenta	*eighty*
ocho	*eight*
oídos	*ears*
oír	*to hear*
ojos	*eyes*

oponer	*to oppose*
opuesto	*opposite*
oprimir	*to depress*
orden	*f. order, command*
orgulloso	*proud*
orejas	*ears*
oscilar	*to waver, to vary*
otoño	*autumn*
otro	*adj. other, another*

P

país	*m. country*
paisaje	*m. countryside*
pájaro	*bird*
pantalla	*screen*
par	*m. pair*
de par en par	*wide open*
para	*prep. for*
paraguas	*umbrella*
parecer	*to seem*
participante	*participant*
pasaje	*passage*
pasajero	*passenger*
patriarca	*m. patriarch*
payaso	*clown*
paz	*peace*
pedazo	*piece*
pedir	*to ask for*
peligro	*danger*
pensar	*to think*
penumbra	*darkness*
peón	*farmer*
pequeño	*small*
percance	*misfortune*
perder	*to lose*
perderse	*to get lost*
preferir	*to prefer*
perforación	*well, piercing (nouns)*
perfumado	*perfumed*
periódico	*newspaper*
periodista	*reporter*
permanecer	*to remain*

pero	*conj. but*
perro	*dog*
perplejos	*perplexed*
pescado	*fish (out of water)*
pescar	*to fish*
pez	*m. fish (in water)*
picotear	*to peck at*
pie	*m. foot*
pieza	*piece*
piropo	*flattering comment*
pista	*track, runway*
placer	*pleasure*
plata,	*silver, money*
planchar	*to iron*
playa	*beach*
plenitud	*plenty*
pluma	*feather, fountain pen*
poco	*little*
poco a poco	*little by little*
por poco	*scarcely*
poder	*to be able*
poner	*to put, to place*
ponerse	*to put on*
por	*by, through*
por casualidad	*by chance*
por eso	*for that reason, therefore*
porque	*because*
¿por qué?	*inter. pro. why?*
por supuesto	*of course*
postre	*m. desert*
práctica	*practice*
preguntar	*to ask, to question*

premio	*prize*	pronosticar	*to forecast*
prestar	*to lend*	pronto	*soon*
prestar atención	*to pay attention*	propaganda	*commericals, ads*
primavera	*spring*	propina	*tip (money)*
primero	*first*	propuesto	*budget, proposal*
primo	*cousin*	proponer	*to propose (something)*
principio	*beginning*	próximo	*next*
prisa	*haste*	prueba	*test*
probar	*to prove, to test*	público	*audience*
problema	*m. problem*	pueblo	*town*
procedimiento	*procedure*	puente	*m. bridge*
profundo	*deep, profound*	puerta	*door*
programa	*m. program*	puerto	*port*
promesa	*promise*	pulmones	*lungs*
prometer	*to promise*		

Q

querer	*to wish, to want, to love*	quejarse	*to complain*
quebrar	*to break*	quien	*who, whom*
quedarse	*to stay. to remain*	quitarse	*to take off*

R

		requerir	*to require*
rato	*while*	rescate	*m. rescue*
rápido	*fast, rapid*	resolver	*to solve*
raro	*strange*	respirar	*to breathe*
razón	*f. reason*	responder	*to reply*
reclamar	*to claim*	respuesta	*answer*
recomendar	*to recommend*	resultado	*result*
reconocer	*to recognize*	retirarse de	*to withdraw from*
recorrer	*to tour*	retrato	*portrait*
recurso	*resource*	reunión	*meeting*
referirse a	*to refer to*	revista	*magazine*
regar	*to water*	revolver	*to spin around*
regocijo	*happiness*	rico	*rich*
regresar	*to return*	riguroso	*rigorous, hard*
reírse de	*to laugh at*	rodar	*to film*
relacionar	*to relate*	rodear	*to surround*
remedio	*remedy, cure*	rodilla	*knee*
rencor	*bitterness*	ronca	*hoarse*
reparar	*to repair*	ropa	*clothes*
repentinamente	*suddenly*	rostro	*face*
reprobar	*to condemn*	ruido	*noise*

S

saber	to know
sabiduría	wisdom
sabor	m. taste
sacar	to take off, to take out
sacudir	to shake
sala	room
salir	to leave, to go out
salir bien	to do well
salir mal	to do poorly
saludar	to greet
satisfacer	to satisfy
secar	to dry
seco	dry
seguir	to follow, to keep on
según	according
segundo	second
seguridad	safety
seguro	sure, safe
semáforo	traffic light
semana	week
sencillez	f. simplicity
sencillo	simple
sentar	(ie) to seat
sentarse	to sit down
sentimiento	feeling
sentir	to regret, to feel,
sentirse	to feel
señal	f. signal
ser	to be
siempre	always
sigilosamente	quietly
siglo	century
sin	prep. without
sin embargo	nevertheless
sin falta	without fail

sino	conj. but, rather
sitio	site, place
sobre	m. envelope
sobre	prep. over, above, on
sobrenatural	supernatural
sobreponer	suppose
sobrevivir	to survive
socorro	help
soldado	soldier
soler	to be accustomed to
solicitar	to apply (for something)
solicitud	helpfulness, care
solo	alone
sólo	only
soltar	to lose
someter	to subdue
someter	to subdue
sonar	to sound
soñar	to dream
sonido	sound
sonreír	to smile
soplar	to blow
sordo	deaf
sorprender	to surprise
suave	smooth, gentle
suavizar	to smooth out
suceder	to happen
sudar	to sweat
sucumbir	to give way to, to succumb
suelo	floor
sueño	dream, sleep
sumamente	supremely, exceedingly
superar	to overcome, to surmount
suspender	to fail (a course)

T

tacón	m. heel (of a shoe)
tal	such
tallados	carved
también	also
tan	so

tanto	so many, so much
tapa	lid, cap (of a container)
tapia	covering
tarifa	fare, rate
tarjeta	card
tarjeta postal	post card

taza	*cup*	tocar	*to play an instrument*
techo	*roof*	todavía	*still*
tejas	*roof tiles*	todo	*all, every*
tela	*cloth*	tomar	*to take*
tema	*m. theme*	torpemente	*dully*
temblor	*m. shaking*	trabajar	*to work*
temer	*to fear*	traer	*to bring*
tenedor	*fork*	trago	*swallow, gulp*
tener	*to have*	tratar	*to treat*
tercero	*third*	tratar de	*to try*
tesoro	*treasure*	travieso	*daring*
tiempo	*time*	transeúnte	*pedestrian*
tienda	*store*	trasladar	*to move (to another place)*
tierra	*earth*	tratamiento	*treatment*
tintorería	*dry cleaner*	trenzas	*locks of hair, tresses*
tío	*uncle*	triste	*sad*
tipo	*type*	tristeza	*sadness*
tobillo	*ankle*	trompeta	*trumpet*

U

último	*last*	urgente	*urgent, pressing*
único	*only*	utilizar	*to use*
únicamente	*only, solely*		

V

vaso	*glass*	viajero	*traveler*
vecindario	*neighborhood*	vida	*life*
vecino	*neighbor*	viejo	*old*
veloz	*fast*	vientre	*belly*
venir	*to come*	vista	*sight, vista*
ventanas	*windows*	visitar	*to visit*
ver	*to see*	volibol	*volleyball*
verano	*summer*	volver	*to return*
verdad	*truth*	volverse loco	*to go crazy*
verde	*green*	voz	*f. voice*
vez	*f. time*	en voz alta	*in a loud voice*
viajar	*to travel*		

Y

y	*and*		
ya	*already*		
ya no	*no longer*		

Z

zapatos	*shoes*

NOTE FOR INTERNATIONAL STUDENTS

If you are an international student considering attending an American university, you are not alone. Over 586,323 international students pursued academic degrees at the undergraduate, graduate, or professional school level at U.S. universities during the 2002–2003 academic year, according to the Institute of International Education's *Open Doors* report. Almost half of these students were studying for a bachelor's or first university degree. This number of international students pursuing higher education in the United States is expected to continue to grow. Business, management, engineering, and the physical and life sciences are particularly popular majors for students coming to the United States from other countries.

If you are not a U.S. citizen and you are interested in attending college or university in the United States, here is what you'll need to get started.

- If English is not your first language, you'll probably need to take the TOEFL® (Test of English as a Foreign Language) or provide some other evidence that you are proficient in English in order to complete an academic degree program. Colleges and universities in the United States will differ on what they consider to be an acceptable TOEFL score. Because American undergraduate programs require all students to take a certain number of general education courses, all students—even math and computer science students—need to be able to communicate well in spoken and written English.
- You may also need to take the SAT® or the ACT®. Many undergraduate institutions in the United States require both the SAT and TOEFL of international students.
- There are over 3,400 accredited colleges and universities in the United States, so selecting the correct undergraduate school can be a confusing task for anyone. You will need to get help from a good advisor or at least a good college guide that gives you detailed information on the different schools available. Since admission to many undergraduate programs is quite competitive, you may want to select three or four colleges and complete applications for each school.
- You should begin the application process at least one year in advance. An increasing number of schools accept applications throughout the year. In any case, learn the application deadlines and plan accordingly. Although September (the fall semester) is the traditional time to begin university study in the United States, you can begin your studies at many schools in January (the spring semester).

In addition, you will need to obtain an I-20 Certificate of Eligibility from the school you plan to attend if you intend to apply for an F-1 Student Visa to study in the United States.

KAPLAN ENGLISH PROGRAMS

If you need more help with the complex process of university admissions, assistance preparing for the SAT, ACT, or TOEFL, or help building your English language skills in general, you may be interested in Kaplan's programs for international students.

Kaplan English Programs were designed to help students and professionals from outside the United States meet their educational and career goals. At locations throughout the United States, international students take advantage of Kaplan's programs to help them improve their academic and conversational English skills, raise their scores on the TOEFL, SAT, ACT, and other standardized exams, and gain admission to the schools of their choice. Our staff and instructors give international students the individualized attention they need to succeed. Here is a brief description of some of Kaplan's programs for international students:

General Intensive English

Kaplan's General Intensive English classes are designed to help you improve your skills in all areas of English and to increase your fluency in spoken and written English. Classes are available for beginning to advanced students, and the average class size is 12 students.

General English Self-Study

For students needing a flexible schedule, this course helps improve general fluency skills. Kaplan's General English Self-Study course employs the communicative approach and focuses on vocabulary building, reading and writing. You will receive books, audio and video materials as well as three hours of instructor contact per week.

TOEFL and Academic English

Kaplan has updated its world-famous TOEFL course to prepare students for the new TOEFL iBT. Designed for high-intermediate to advanced-level English speakers, our new course focuses on the academic English skills you will need to succeed on the new test. The course includes TOEFL-focused reading, writing, listening and speaking instruction, and hundreds of practice items similar to those on the exam. Kaplan's expert instructors help you prepare for the four sections of the TOEFL iBT, including the new Speaking Section. Our new simulated online TOEFL tests help you monitor your progress and provide you with feedback on areas where you require improvement. We will teach you how to get a higher score!

SAT Test Preparation Course

The SAT is an important admission criterion for U.S. colleges and universities. A high score can help you stand out from other applicants. This course includes the skills you need to succeed on each section of the SAT, as well as access to Kaplan's exclusive practice materials.

Other Kaplan Programs

Since 1938, more than 3 million students have come to Kaplan to advance their studies, prepare for entry to American universities, and further their careers. In addition to the above programs, Kaplan offers courses to prepare for the ACT, GMAT, GRE, MCAT, DAT, USMLE, NCLEX-RN® exam, and other standardized exams at locations throughout the United States.

Applying to Kaplan International Programs

To get more information, or to apply for admission to any of Kaplan's programs for international students and professionals, contact us at:

Kaplan International Programs
700 South Flower, Suite 2900
Los Angeles, CA 90017, USA
Phone (if calling from within the United States): 800-818-9128
Phone (if calling from outside the United States): 213-452-5800
Fax: 213-892-1364
Email: world@kaplan.com
Web: www.kaplanenglish.com

FREE Services for International Students

Kaplan now offers international students many services online—*free of charge*!
Students may assess their TOEFL skills and gain valuable feedback on their English
language proficiency in just a few hours with Kaplan's TOEFL Skills Assessment.
Log onto www.kaplanenglish.com today.

Kaplan is authorized under federal law to enroll nonimmigrant alien students. Kaplan is accredited by ACCET (Accrediting Council for Continuing Education and Training).

Test names are registered trademarks of their respective owners.

Notes

Notes

Notes

Notes